ANXIETY IN RELATIONSHIPS UNVEILED

REMOVE THE FILTER THAT CLOUDS YOUR VISION OF ROMANTIC LOVE.

OVERCOME INSECURITY, NEGATIVE THINKING AND JEALOUSY, FIGHT YOUR FEAR OF ABANDONMENT, AND AVOID CONFLICTS.

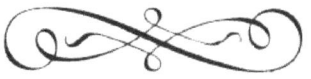

KYLEIGH WYATT

Author's Note:

Do you know what makes anxiousness so challenging to manage in relationships? Many people do not understand what anxiety is, rendering the simple act of recognizing it a difficult one.

If anxiety is not recognized and left untreated, it will persist, potentially derailing the anxious individual's familial and romantic relationships and preventing them from forming new, enduring ones. This book aims to help the anxious person's partner become more supportive, which may be so crucial for that person that it can change the course of their life.

Anxiety can be beaten, but it will take effort, and reading this book will be the first step in your accomplishment of this important work.

In this guide, you will find out:

Part 1 – **Anxiety in Relationship**

- How Anxiety and Insecurity Start in Relationships
- How Anxiety Take Over Your Relationship

Part 2 – **Couples Therapy for Relationship**

- Dialog in Relationship
- Working to Improve your Relationship

Part 3 – **Communication in Relationship**

- Determining What is Important to You
- Improve Your Communication and Social Skills

Part 4 – **Mindfulness Meditation for Anxiety**

- Basic and Benefits of Mindfulness Meditation
- How to Manage Anxiety, Stress, and Panic Attacks with Meditation

Kyleigh Wyatt

Table of Content

MINDFULNESS MEDITATION FOR ANXIETY

Part 1

ANXIETY IN RELATIONSHIP

1. Introduction

As you should know, communication is particularly important when it comes to romantic relationships. Discussing all issues freely, making plans, and setting future goals is vital for a successful relationship. Otherwise, how could two partners handle their responsibilities, challenges, and expectations?

However, what happens if one of you is suffering from anxiety? We learned about any disorders that could severely pact your ability to maintain a healthy way of communicating in your relationship. Of course, it depends on how severe the anxiety is. However, no matter its level of development, a personal connection will be in some way affected. You or your partner might encounter difficulties in reacting in a healthy way when either of you expresses an opinion or an emotion. For instance, it is common to misread someone's intent or misinterpret the meaning of individual conversations. Anxiety works in many ways as a filter. When it clouds your vision, you might act in a rude manner that will eventually damage your relationship. Any joke, comment, or harmless critique can lead to an overreaction that will put a strain on any couple, even more than the anxiety itself.

Your partner may be suffering from a form of anxiety, and they are overwhelmed by the strain. On the extra side, if you are the one with this problem, you need to acknowledge what is wrong and express it. If not, your partner will think you are cruel or aggressive for no reason or that they are the problem.

Relationship Communication Anxiety

Anxiety has a severe emotional effect on people. The partner is affected somehow due to seeing his or her significant other suffering and going through the whole life-crippling experience. And many cases in which the one suffering from anxiety will suppress any emotion or feeling. Emotions carry a great deal of power, and some people find it too challenging to face them. Those who are afraid to express themselves emotionally have likely lived in a household where the behavior was discouraged.

The act of suppressing emotions is a sign that the person is trying to hold onto a semblance of control. If you find yourself behaving this way, it might be because you are scared at the thought of losing that control and allowing the locked-up feelings to overwhelm you. Naturally, the biggest issue here is when it comes to negative emotions as they have such a substantial impact on a person's life. You might think that if you let it all out, you will change your partner's feelings. And whatever good opinions and thoughts he or she has about you will be gone, damage the relationship. However, while you may think of this as a solution, it leads to even more problems. Acting this way will increase the amount of anxiety you experience. You will find less and less peace of mind until one day when it will all come out in a wild burst. It is difficult to suppress those feelings forever, and when they do come to the surface, the emotion will cloud all judgment.

Communication anxiety can also oppositely manifest itself without involving any emotion suppression. For instance, let us say your partner unloads only her most powerful feelings and emotions regularly. Some people cannot hold back on certain beliefs, so they lash out. As a result, both of you end up feeling overwhelmed and confused, leading to another problem. Experiencing these outbursts often enough, you can start feeling that it is your job to find a solution to your partner's issues. It is not enough to notice the anxiety and the

> The act of suppressing emotions is a sign that the person is trying to hold onto a semblance of control.

strain it is putting on your relationship. You get the feeling you are the sole savior of this partnership. Unfortunately, this usually makes things worse as your partner could start developing resentment towards you for their behavior.

Another communication problem is when you consider expressing yourself as a risky affair. Maybe you are wondering what will happen if you reveal what you honestly think. It is enough to trigger your anxiety as you are afraid of the uncertainty of the outcome. Frequently, this symptom stems from not having confidence in yourself.

You are worried about an adverse reaction from your partner. In this case, you might be taking a great deal of time to rehearse what you will say and complicate things further by imagining all the possible scenarios.

Also, anxiety can have even worse repercussions if you or your partner refuse to admit that you are suffering from it. Not acknowledging that there is a problem, especially one as grave as anxiety, will only lead to anger and irritable behavior that pushes the other person away. Running away from this problem often feels like it is a more straightforward solution, especially by thinking that doing so will shelter the other person. Many people then act based on instinct and do not notice they are avoiding the problem or derailing the discussion by acting irritated. This defensive reaction is almost always caused by anxiety. They do not feel comfortable during the conversation, so they react without even thinking about their behavior, commonly leading to frustration and resentment for both parties.

Social Situations

Being in certain social situations is difficult for many people who do not even suffer from anxiety. However, those with anxiety will encounter other problems that would not cross other people's minds. It is typical behavior to deny meal invitations from coworkers or friends, ignore unnecessary phone calls, and even avoid small family gatherings. While social situations are more specific and do not occur every day, there are also daily occurrences that can cause extreme anxiety levels. For instance, some have issues performing any task or responsibility if another human is in their presence, looking over their shoulder. We will focus on the broader social situation, referring to any environment in which other people are around.

Isolating yourself from any social situation usually leads to more than just personal social isolation. In some cases, this behavior can turn into a never-ending cycle of avoidance. The social aspects of life causing you anxiety can, in turn, create even more tension in new situations. Release reduces your ability to cope, and you will be dealing with even more fear during a social gathering. This self-perpetuating cycle often leads to relationship problems, especially breakups, immensely if one party does not suffer from anxiety.

With that in mind, you should take note that a disorder does not necessarily cause anxiety in social situations.

This problem is not limited only to those who fit that case. Either type of stress can manifest itself in a social setting and determine how you behave when forced to interact with other people, including your partner. For example, your home behavior may seem familiar because you are in a safe space, but you may seem unrecognizable to your partner in a social event. Your behavior changes as soon as you are around others, especially strangers. Some common signs are stuttering, prolonged silence, or pretending you are busy to avoid conversations, talking a lot more than what you may consider "normal," and relying on your partner to carry any conversations. There are also some physical signs that we mentioned earlier when discussing various disorders, such as excessive sweating, nail-biting, playing with an innate object or hair, and avoiding direct eye contact. Some people feel so uncomfortable during social engagements that they suddenly leave the conversation or leave the room altogether.

Once away, the post-anxiety process of overanalyzing everything that happened begins. The person will most often obsess over their behavior, if they were likable, talked too much, or if others might have seen them as unintelligent or rude. This kind of behavior can place an incredible amount of pressure on any relationship as it affects not only your social interaction as a couple but your partner's ability to establish connections and meet new people. In such an example, you might even find yourself blaming your partner for your stress and anxiety because he or she placed you in that situation in the first place. It may lead to nothing but resentment and less and less interaction between the two of you.

The reason why social events are so stressful for anyone suffering from anxiety disorder or phobia is too many new elements in which you have no control over. At home, you and your partner have full control over everything that is happening; therefore, there is very little reason to feel anxious. However, at a concert surrounded by thousands of people, you are just one of many, and anything can happen, meaning you have nearly no control. As a result, the relaxing activities for you to participate in together with your significant other are limited.

How It Affects Your Relationship?

Social interactions are more crucial than ever, and if you (or your partner) are suffering from social anxiety, your career and relationships may suffer as a result. Participating in social gatherings and popular events is essential to developing healthy relationships. Building friendships and expanding your career opportunities can almost exclusively be achieved only in a social setting, whether it is an office Christmas party or someone's birthday.

If you are suffering from anxiety and it makes it impossible for you to socialize with anyone other than your partner, you will unknowingly isolate yourself and feel left out. Besides, your partner will start resenting you for all the pressure you place on him or her whenever you must avoid a social event. Your partner must always come up with an excuse regarding your absence and feel out of place. Keep in mind that after a while, some of those people will no longer send invitations to your partner as they can feel that something is wrong or that they will only receive an excuse instead of attending. Your partner will also feel even worse about the entire situation as he or she listens to you, blaming yourself and judging yourself over something you have little control over. At the same time, if your anxiety does cause a rude overreaction during a social event, your partner will feel torn between siding with her hosts or with you. In either case, unnecessary damage is done to your relationship.

> Social interactions are more crucial than ever, and if you are suffering from social anxiety, your career and relationships may suffer as a result.

Do not forget that anxiety does not always manifest itself in obvious ways. Even if you are the one in the relationship with it, you might not be aware of how it manipulates some of the decisions you make. For instance, let us say your partner asks you to go to a concert or a party. You do not start talking about your anxiety, as you may not even be aware of it at this point. You may refuse the idea because you are just not in the right mood that day or that you want to spend time at home watching a movie.

This scenario will likely repeat itself, slowly increasing the level of frustration building up inside your partner.

Why are you acting like this? You may be feeling shameful or guilty because you do not want to disappoint your partner by admitting a problem. Hence, you make up an excuse for not wanting to go out.

2. How Do Anxiety And Insecurity Start In Relationships

When you begin a relationship, the initial stage can get you worried and tense with different questions in your head, begging for answers. You begin to think: "Does he/she like me?" "Will this work out?" "How serious will this get?"

It is sad to know that these worries do not diminish in the advanced stages of the relationship when you're plagued with anxiety. The closer and more intimate you get in a relationship, the higher the intensity of the pressure displayed in such a relationship can be.

Worry, stress, and anxiety about your relationships can leave you feeling lonely and discouraged. You may unknowingly create a distance between yourself and your loved one. Another grave consequence of stress is its ability to make us give up on love altogether. That is rather devastating because love is a beautiful thing.

Falling in love puts a demand on you in countless ways - more ways than you can imagine. The more you cherish a person, the more you stand to lose. How ironic is that? This intense feeling of love and the powerful emotions that come with it consciously and unconsciously create the fear of being hurt and the fear of the unknown in you.

Oddly enough, this fear comes from being treated exactly how you want to be treated in your relationship. When you begin to experience love, as it should be, or when you are treated in a tender and caring way, which is unfamiliar to you, anxiety might set in.

More often than not, it is not only the events between you and your partner that lead to anxiety. It is the things you tell yourself and feed your mind regarding those events that ultimately lead to stress. Your most prominent critic, which is also the "mean coach" you have in your head, can criticize you and feed you with bad advice, ultimately fueling your fear of intimacy.

It is this mean critic that suggests to you that:

"You are not smart. He/she would soon get bored with you."

"You will never meet anyone who will love you, so why try?"

"Don't trust him. He's probably searching for a better person."

"She doesn't love you. Get out before you get hurt."

This mean coach in your head manipulates you and turns you against yourself and the people you love. It encourages hostility, and you soon discover that you are paranoid. You begin to suspect every move your partner makes, which reduces your self-esteem and drives unhealthy levels of distrust, defensiveness, jealousy, anxiety, and stress.

This mean coach in your head continually feeds you with thoughts that jeopardize your happiness and make you worry about your relationship rather than allowing you just to enjoy it. When you begin to focus so much on these unhealthy thoughts, you become distracted from the real relationship, which involves healthy communication and love with your partner.

You soon discover that you are reacting to unnecessary issues and uttering nasty and destructive remarks. You may also become childish or parental towards your partner.

Sitting alone after some time, your inner critic goes on a rampage and asks, "How can he refuse my food? What has he eaten all day? Who has been bringing food to him at work? Can I believe him?" These thoughts can continually grow in your mind until you are insecure, furious, and temperamental until the following morning. You may begin to act cold or angry, and this can put your partner off, making them frustrated and defensive. They won't know what's been going on in your head, so your behavior will seem like it comes out of nowhere.

In just a few hours, you have successfully shifted the dynamics of your relationship. Instead of savoring the time you are spending together, you may waste an entire day feeling troubled and drawn apart from each other. What you have just done is initiate and enthrone the distance you feared so much. The responsible factor for this turn of events is not the situation itself - it is that critical inner voice that clouded your thoughts, distorted your perceptions, suggested wrong opinions to you, and, as a result, led you to a disastrous path.

When it comes to the issues you worry about so much in your relationship, what you don't know—and what your inner critic doesn't tell you - is that you are stronger and more resilient than you think. The reality is that you can handle the hurts, rejections, and disappointments that you are so afraid of. We are made so that it is possible to absorb negative situations, heal from them, and deal with them. You are capable of experiencing pain and ultimately healing and coming out stronger. However, in your head, the mean coach, that inner critical voice, more often than not, puts you under pressure and makes reality look like a tragedy. It creates scenarios in your head that are non-existent and brings out threats that are not tangible. Even when, in fact, there are real issues and unhealthy situations, that inner voice in your head will magnify such cases and tear you apart in ways you do not deserve. It will completely misrepresent the reality of the situation and dampen your resilience and determination. It will always give you unpleasant opinions and advice.

These critical voices you hear in your head are formed due to your unique experiences and what you've adapted to overtime. When you feel anxious or insecure, there tends to become overly attached and desperate in our actions. Possessiveness and control towards your partner set in. On the other hand, you may feel an intrusion in your relationship. You may begin to retreat from your partner and detach from your emotional desires. You may start to act unforthcoming or withdrawn.

These patterns of responding to issues may stem out from your early attachment styles. These style patterns influence how you react to your needs and how you go about getting them met.

Signs Of Insecure Attachment

There are a few practices that are brought about by attachments as a result of insecurity. An assortment of undesirable ways can show in early adolescence as a result of unreliable connections.

Too Demanding

For instance, you don't want your partner to get things done without you. Your longing is to burn through the majority of your and their extra time together. You request their time and consideration, to the detriment of other friendships and relationships.

Doubt Or Jealousy

For instance, you are suspicious of your partner or companion's conduct and the general population they work with. You question their work connections and whom they communicate within the work environment.

You are suspicious of anybody that you feel they are getting too close to, as you dread that they may leave you for another person.

Absence Of Emotional Intimacy

For example, your buddy or accomplice feels that they earnestly can't gravitate toward you. They depict you as someone who "sets up dividers" or state that you are usually testing to gravitate toward to internally.

Enthusiastic Dependency

You rely upon your companion or partner for your enthusiastic prosperity. You desire that your joy originates from your relationship.

You trust your accomplice or friend isn't fulfilling you on the off chance that you are disturbed.

Frightful

You desire closeness in your connections. It makes you have a blend of feelings.

You draw your accomplice close, and this way drives them away when it turns out to be "to an extreme." Your fear of getting unnecessarily close, since you would incline toward not to be harmed, makes your relationship endure.

Nonattendance Of Trust

You don't confide in your companion out of fear that they may undermine you or leave you. You're afraid that you may tell them something or reveal a part of yourself that they won't like and prompt them to end the relationship.

Anger Issues

Getting angry unnecessarily is also a sign of insecure attachment in a relationship.

When you pick a fight over an issue that could be solved amicably, it shows that you are not ready to tolerate your partner or you are fed up with their excesses. This behavior, if not addressed, can affect the relationship adversely

Let me conclude by saying that you begin to push your partner away from you when you act out your insecurities, thus creating a self-fulfilling prophecy. By self-fulfilling prophecy, I mean validating and giving life to those negative thoughts, which come to your mind, also known as your inner voice. It begins to look like that voice was right after all. But no, it wasn't right. The struggle is internal and goes on regardless of the circumstances. When you live with anxiety, your life could, in reality, be like a fairy tale, but that inner voice will still have something negative to point out. It is vital to deal with your insecurities without dragging your partner into them. You can do this by taking two steps:

Uncover the roots of your insecurities and find out what led to them.

Challenge the inner critical voice and mean coach that obstruct the free flow of love in your relationship.

3. How Can Anxiety Take Over Your Relationship

Love is undoubtedly the most potent possible emotion. If you begin to feel guilty about this love, it is not unusual for it to significantly affect your relationship and life quality. Relationship anxiety is confusing and means different things for different people. Still, you can do little to stop it once you have it.

Relationship Anxiety Types And Tips

So many factors can trigger anxiety in relationships, and sometimes the concern varies according to the outcome. Abusive relationships induce stress for reasons entirely different than those who experience anxiety due to children's issues. Some people are first afraid that their connection will leak in another way.

When We Talk About Anxiety About Relationships, We Can Talk About:

My Husband Or Boyfriend Provides Me Anxiety (Or Girlfriend)

Both women and men are troubled about their significant others' behavior. Some of these conducts include:

- Mean language.
- They are hiding things (like texting in secret or staying out late and being vague).
- Physical intimidation.

These potentially problematic issues need to be addressed in a relationship to work and all potential anxiety causes.

Successfully appraising the quality of the relationship is serious for determining how to eliminate anxiety.

I'm Perplexed Or Frightened Of An Affiliation

Some relationship uneasiness has little to do with the accomplice and more to do with the dread of being seeing someone the primary spot. Known as a "dread of duty," it is pervasive for those that:

- I have never been in a relationship.

- I have been in awful connections.

- Have worries that on the off chance that they submit, they may pass up something different.

A few people have a dream of being seeing someone who can't be handily clarified. This kind of nervousness is a test due to uneasiness and because it might hurt conceivably great connections.

My Partner Has Anxiety, And I Struggle With What To Do

Nervousness doesn't simply pressure the individual that is battling. It can cause trouble in the relationship overall too. Dating somebody with suspicion or a wedding with uneasiness can be befuddling, and it isn't phenomenal to learn approaches to beat it.

Relationship Itself Causes Anxiety

Notwithstanding, the issue can be set on the quality and encounters in the relationship itself. It isn't really about the solitary conduct of an accomplice or an expansive dread of duty. Again, tension emerges after some time as the relationship advances because of a wide range of variables.

Beneath, we are zeroing in on here, as it is basic seeing someone, everything being equal, styles, and lengths. It can emerge in happy relationships, and it can arise in despondent momentary dating. It is consistently a smart thought to assess it to figure out what the accompanying advances perhaps

Tension Manifestations

These are just the crucial reasons that nervousness seeing someone is normal, not by any means the only ones, yet you can see where it turns into a significant issue.

Those that have relationship uneasiness frequently begin to have similar manifestations of nervousness issues, for instance:

- Shaking

- Insomnia

- Muscle pressure

- Feelings of sorrow

- Sweating

This fear also frequently bleeds into other realms of the person's life, but in some respects, it no longer constitutes relationship fear. It may be an anxiety condition caused by a disrupted relationship.

A Supportive Partner Can Alleviate Symptoms Of Anxiety

It can be frustrating to have a partner that has anxiety or an anxiety disorder.

"Partners can take roles like a compromise, protectors, or comforts that they don't want," said Kate Thieda, MS, LPCA, NCC, a therapist.

You might have to tolerate the brunt of additional responsibility and avoid those locations or events that cause your partner's anxiety, she said. For couples and their marriages, this can be stressful.

"Partners of loved ones with anxiety can find their dreams about what the relationship will be restricted by anxieties angry, upset, sad, or disappointed."

Here Are Ways To Do This, As Well As What To Do If Your Partner Refuses Treatment.

Educate Yourself About Anxiety.

It is essential to acquire as much anxiety as possible, like the various forms of stress and its treatment. It makes you understand what your partner is doing.

Please be mindful that your partner does not suit any of these categories. As Thieda says, "Indeed, it does not matter if the anxiety of your partner is 'diagnosable.'

Whether it affects your relationship, or diminishes the quality of life of your partner or your quality of life, improvements are worth making."

Avoid Accommodating Your Partner's Anxiety.

"Partners are also able to tolerate the anxiety of their partner, because they are willing [for instance] to play the hero, or just to make things simpler because their partner is nervous about the drive

They make all the orders," said Thiede, who also created Psych Central's famous "Partners in Wellness" blog.

However, lodging further exacerbates the distress of your partner. For one thing, she said, it provides the partner with none to conquer their fear. Secondly, it sends out the message that anything can be expected that just fuel their anxiety.

Set Boundaries.

Thieda said that your partner would continue to ask for accommodation, such as traveling anywhere or staying with them daily. "You also have the accurate to have a life, which could mean telling your partner at times, and with respect, that you can do what you want and need to do."

For example: instead of saying, "You worry so much about what other people think of you," you might say, "I'm worried that your worries of what other people think of you keep you at work."

Instead of saying, "Don't call me too much at work," you might suggest, "It is good that you use some of the strategies you have learned to relax before calling me into the office."

"Always think about whether a solution is feasible, but also understand that you have the right to do things independently,"

Relax Together.

There are several advances that you can use to relieve anxiety together. According to Thieda, "The body scan is a perfect technique for couples who can direct others through the process."

It encourages knowledge between the two partners.

The partner who gives orders must be careful about timing and precise directions, she said. And the partner receiving the instructions must pay attention to every part of the body and relieve its stress.

It's Physical.

Anxiety is a natural physical reaction to an over-protective brain. It's not mad and not psychotic. A primitive portion of the brain is oriented towards sensing risks. It's all movement and not much thought, and it's in us all. Some people fire up much faster and with much less justification than others. When it does, the body floods with cortisol (stress hormone) and adrenaline to brace the body for or fight for its life. This is the battle or the flight, and this is in everyone. It's just that the 'move' button is a little more sensitive in some people (people with anxiety).

You'll Need Them As Element Of Your Tribe. (Seriously. They're Pretty Great To Have Around.)

Their desire to stay healthy and prepare against the following time fear comes up. People dealing with anxiety will generally have a strategy – and they will have worked hard to make sure that it does not only for themselves but also for everyone involved. They will ensure that everything is planned to keep everyone safe, happy, timely, and trouble-free. They're trying to make sure everybody has what they need, and if anything hasn't been thought about, it probably won't be worth worrying about. Note the positive stuff they're doing – there's a lot.

Anxiety Has Not Anything To Execute With Courage Or Character. Nothing At All.

Courage senses the edge and moves beyond it. We all have our limits, so those that are nervous know more about them. But they are continually challenged by the things that force their boundaries. It is bravery, and worried people have it in lorries. Retell them that you see who they are and often have little to do with the fear. Anxious people are influential – you must live with something like that. They are adaptive – they will be as adaptive to you and to the atmosphere you need. That makes them pretty cool. They should be optimistic – nervous people will go the extra step to ensure that there's a strategy to manage the possibility of everything that causes an attack and that everyone is safe, secure, and have all they need. They're smart — thinkers (which often gets in their way).

You can be funny, kind, courageous, and inspired. So I think it's that way – they're no different than anyone else. Like everybody else, the thing that often brings them up (their anxieties) is also what pushes them over the crowd.

Ways To Survive With Anxiety In A Relationship

In that respect, managing your anxiety regarding your relationship is more connected to you than to you, and you do not expect them to contribute. The following are the main strategies to ensure that your relationship will heal:

Exercise and Other Anxiety Reduction Techniques – Anxiety is still anxiety first and foremost, and this ensures that acceptable anxiety reduction methods will help regulate your feelings. Training is the best way to incorporate right now into your life. There is a lot of evidence that exercise is as powerful as other anxiety drugs to manage anxiety symptoms.

Starting over – If the confidence has expired, speak to your partner about starting up and dating as if you were never together. Trust is about establishing a base and must be built from the ground up. Yet you have to stick with it. If things get better after a few weeks, it's still too early to say that faith is back. You don't need to slip back into old traditions.

Exchange of needs-speak with your partner about the needs of each other. Write them down to ensure that both of you know what they are. Then do your best to do everything your partner wants, given your morality is not harmed. Don't wait for them to make all of your lists – just give them what they have requested and be their best partner. You will also note that they are inspired to better themselves. If they aren't after about a month, they probably don't want to.

Staying mentally busy-It can be difficult to be interested in connections, but something proven to improve the mood is to remain mentally engaged. You can also find that your mind in relationships is your adversary, as you imagine competing with your partner. Keep your mind away from your relationship by doing outdoor things, watching TV, dates, etc. It reduces the walking in negative feelings in your mind.

Be physically affectionate-even if you are mad about another human. Touching and holding is very soothing.

It is one of the motives why happy couples always hug after a long and stressful day. Try to be emotionally fond for a bit, even though you are angry about them because it reminds you and your partner not to go something.

4. Self-Evaluation Of Anxiety In A Relationship And How To Changing Yourself

How are you present to know that you are suffering from relationship anxiety? Are there any definite signs that can determine the various kinds of negative emotions regarding your relationship? How can pressure affect your relationship? All such questions can be quickly answered when you opt for what is known as self-evaluation of relationship anxiety. The aim of this is to properly evaluate the issue for putting a complete end to it.

Anxiety can reap up at any time in relationships. The truth is that every one of us is vulnerable to this necessary kind of problem. You will find that the tendency to get anxious in a healthy relationship will increase as the bond grows stronger. So, everyone needs to opt for self-evaluation. Are you in the habit of spending most of your time worrying about all those things that could go bad in your relationship? A definite sign of relationship anxiety is when you keep worrying as an outcome of all the questions that run in your mind. For the perfect self-evaluation of this substantial problem, you will first learn about the signs that will depict whether you are anxious or not. You will also require to assess the effects and causes of the problem you think persists in your relationship. As already mentioned before, the evaluation is to learn about the issues before they can develop.

How To Find Out You Are Suffering From Anxiety In Your Relationship?

You might be submerged in the deep sea of relationship anxiety without having any idea of it. In this part, you will find the symptoms of the problems related to you.

- When you are jealous of your romantic partner: Take a good look at your everyday behavior.

  Do you feel like breaking someone's face when your partner gets close to someone else of the opposite sex? Are you scared of any of your partner's friends who you think might rob your partner from you? You are suffering from jealousy if that is the case. It is one of the signs that you are suffering from relationship anxiety. At times, you might also feel like testing the love and commitment of your partner towards you. All of this is a clear indication of relationship anxiety sparked by jealousy.

- When your self-esteem level tends to low: Do you always try to be cautious regarding how you behave in front of your partner? You might manage to do this because you are not sure how your partner will react. You are scared to express your true self in front of your partner because you fear rejection. It is an unambiguous indication of low self-esteem, which is also a sign of relationship anxiety.

- Trust issues: When you are in a healthy relationship, your partner should be the person whom you can trust the most. If you confirm what your partner says right before you can believe them, it indicates your relationship's trust issues. Most of the time, lack of trust results from past betrayal. But you should never let your betrayals from the past negatively impact your relationship. You will need to understand that no one is perfect in this world. Once your partner assures you that specific incidences will not happen again, try to believe them. A relationship will never work if you cannot blindly trust your partner.

- Emotional imbalance: You feel angry today, frustrated tomorrow, and happy the next day. It is known as dynamic instability. You might not have any clear idea about the same. However, continuous mood swings are also an indication of emotional imbalance. They are not going to help the matter in any way. They will be worsening it only. No matter what problems or tensions you are going through, try to talk about them with your romantic partner. When both partners try to solve a problem, the chances are high that the issue will get resolved very quickly. When you find out that you cannot stabilize your mood, it signifies relationship anxiety.

- Reduced sex drive and lack of sleep: The immediate result of constant worry is insomnia. You will be unable to have a proper sleep. As you cannot sleep, you are most likely to feel stressed, resulting in decreased libido. All of these can also be regarded as a symptom of relationship anxiety.

In case you are experiencing any or all of these symptoms, you will need to determine its cause. Dealing with the causes of relationship anxiety is very important. Let's have a look at some of the causes of all these problems.

Probable Causes Of Relationship Anxiety

The majority of the time, relationship anxiety might turn out to be the manifestation of a rooted deep problem. Some of the most common causes are:

- Relationship complication: When the relationship is not defined clearly, or you are not sure about the same, it is classified as being complicated. It can be regarded as all those people who are in the dating stage. For example, a woman might not be clear about a man's motive – whether they are in the relationship just for fun or want to take it to marriage. Even long-distance relationships can lead to relationship anxiety. If this is the case, then both partners are required to trust each other.

- Continuous fights: When you just keep on fighting or quarreling with your partner, you will not be able to put an end to your worries. You will always feel tensed or worried as you are unsure when the resulting fight will crop up. It is a major cause of relationship anxiety. The reason behind this is that your intention of avoiding disputes will not let you spend some quality time with your romantic partner.

- Always comparing: Comparison of the current relationship with the past ones needs to be avoided. It is not at all a healthy practice. You might breed in feelings of intense regret if you find out that the last relationship was far better regarding communication, intimacy, finance, and various aspects. To keep yourself away from such feelings, never compare your relationship or even marriage regarding others or the ones from your past.

- Less understanding: Partners who do not want to invest time to understand one another is bound to suffer from difficulties. As already mentioned above, continuous fights will lead to relationship anxiety. Can you notice the anxiety symptoms along with miscommunications? When understanding is lacking between two partners, relationship anxiety will crop up. Try to invest some time to get to know your partner in a better way. Also, encourage your partner to do the same.

- Miscellaneous issues: Tough experiences from your past relationships can lead to other serious problems. Also, neglect or abuse in the past and lack of affection are definite reasons you might suffer from relationship anxiety.

After you have successfully figured out the prime cause of the issues related to your relationship, getting purge of that cause will be the following significant step. The following are the steps for dealing with the issues' cause.

How To Get Rid Of The Root Cause?

Couples/partners are bound to face various types of challenges which they need to address as they progress. Your capability to manage the issues as they crop up in the relationship will help determine the relationship growth. In case a challenge or problem is not addressed correctly, you might find your healthy relationship in a phase of the crisis. You might also need to take some serious steps to find your way out of the issue. Some of the most conjoint challenges faced by people in their relationships are relationship needs, communication, developing jointly as a couple, equal rights, contentedness, habit, routine, loyalty, sexuality, fights, stress, value differences, conflicts, illness, distance, and this list will keep going on.

How careful are you and your partner in the relationship? Being considerate and cautious can help in avoiding most of the frustrations in your relationship. Are you able to enjoy the moment? Living in the present sounds much more comfortable than doing the same. It might not be now, but sometimes our thoughts from the past or the future will try to slide in. There are certainly other questions that you will need to ask yourself. How much are you enjoying the present moment? Can you make your partner understand what you want to say? Do you both spend a lot of time together doing everyday things? Can you feel tenderness, sexual satisfaction, and security with your partner?

Do you find support and peace in the relationship? Can you discuss anything openly with your partner? Do you feel healthy with your partner?

As you answer all of these questions, you will guide yourself properly in the road of self-evaluation of various issues that you are facing in the relationship. In most cases, men, in particular, do not like to get indulged in relationship talks. Regardless of that, it is crucial to exchange your wishes and needs with your partner regularly. Communication strategies play a vital role, especially in resolving conflicts. First, you will need to distinguish between general communication as partners and communication resulting from conflict resolution.

Communicating about each other's wishes, hopes, plans, and ideas forms a critical foundation block of a relationship. Those couples who are happy for a long time in their relationships can communicate with each other about their feelings. They do not see the connection or themselves being threatened by all their expressions. It won't even matter if both are negative about their feelings without having an idea. They can develop their gestures, facial expressions, and subtle language throughout their relationship. Fights and quarrels are very regular in a healthy relationship. All that matters are the 'how.' Clashes tend to arise whenever you or the other person feels strained by various external stresses. For example, conflicts in the family, problems in raising children, problems in the job, and many others. The partner who feels stressed will communicate with the other person in a more violent or irritated tone.

It is always in your most significant interest to be inventive and proactive concerning how you communicate with all those closest to you. Creating, nurturing, and maintaining relationships with family, friends, and coworkers, not just our partners, is vital for our well-being. Instead of just waiting for others to bring in changes in the relationships, the best and the most accessible place for starting is with yourself.

5. Getting Over Relationship Insecurity And Obstacles In Your Relationship

There are moments when the relationship feels uncomfortable. You may feel frustrated. You not only have to control your partnership; you do have to handle external stressors as well. Both associations surpass peaks and lows. What is essential in your association is that you can take the lows. Know relationships are moving through stages. When you get past one hump, there's bound to be a chance you're going to run up against another. You should fix issues in the partnership without breaking up.

Passion requires effort is a pretty general belief. Yet 80 percent of Americans under 30 believe in a soulmate, only waiting to be discovered, thinking that there is a better human out there. Just the word "fallen in love" makes us feel like life is out of our hands — that it only happens to us. It typically isn't easy to find long-lasting love, except though we encounter the right guy. It's also not an excessively laborious job, though, but sucks up more complicated than it gives of enjoyment. And how do we decide when to give up on friendship, and how do we choose when to struggle for the partnership?

We will then perceive that associations are always delivered complex, even though they can be generally exquisite and agreeable all by themselves. For any two individuals with two different heads, two separate fields, and two different gear sets meet up. What's to come isn't probably going to be only one smooth sail into the dusk. The most pleasant inclination in an individual's life can be becoming hopelessly enamored, yet we keep ignoring the measure of fear, uneasiness, distress, and even fury it can raise.

Through a perverse twist, the closest we come to someone else, those worries continue to grow ever higher. We still have defenses in us without realizing it, centered on hurtful past encounters that even work to drive the love out.

And when it comes to knowing whether to call it quits on a partnership that we once cherished, the first question that we have to ask ourselves is how well my defenses are at work? What am I taking closeness to the table that might be sabotaging?

It is necessary to follow the mentality that the only one you will influence is yourself while considering the steps you will take when you agree to split up. You control 100 percent of the dynamics in your part. Despite your friendship, you are not a victim; you will both opt to pass on in the end. Playing the role of guilt will leave you feeling helpless and walking around in circles. And if you finally agree that it is not worth maintaining the friendship as long as you're in it, you can practice being the best individual you can be. You will build your capacity to love, be transparent, and be vulnerable — skills that can profoundly help you in life and relationships to come. To help you heal your friendship, you have to acquire and exercise specific skills in order. Before we say goodbye to the company, here are five items to do with that in mind. The positive thing is being able to benefit from the errors. This is what they term lectures. Now let's think about the techniques and suggestions that will help you overcome partnership problems.

Talk It Out

If you start having issues, it's convenient not to think about them. I should have one partner as a speaker when I see a couple and one as a listener. It is essential that you not only speak about your issues but that you listen. This ensures you have no interruptions, and you have no mobile phone. It is how you feel that your partner is attentive. These let us realize that you worry about your partner and that you've got your partner back. Begin the talk about what's happening in the partnership now. Instead, tell your partner what your partner appreciates. That has to be real. This is the position where the smallest stuff creates a huge difference. Being truthful, too, is relevant. That does not mean that you've had to damage the emotions of your partner. Nevertheless, having your partner know how you feel and what you need in the partnership is vital.

Let Go Of Your Expectations

You may hope to see stuff moving in some direction. When it's the case, it will push you off. Note, even because the relationship has improved, so has it? If you have aspirations, so anticipate things to shift.

That needn't be evil. Let go of exactly what's right. There's no best direction the mate should be, or the partnership should be. That implies letting go of block "should." When people who dictate to you how your collaboration will function in your life, it might be time to let go of them. It works for one partnership, for another, cannot fit.

Stop The Comparison Game

It may sound as if everyone else has a better relationship right now. Yet maybe this is not the case. Most citizens are not concerned about their issues with the partnerships. That indicates you are unable to assess a journal by its cover. When you look at social networking, this occurs. Most people show the best side of their relationship and respect their life, which results in your relationship feelings of loneliness. Note, there is the stuff that you would like in a partnership. Other people don't. So, that's Good. It's your partnership, which is significant. Let go about what other people say. That just makes things worse.

Make Sure You Both Compromise

A balance in the partnership is something you still feel comfortable about. I gain we fail / we lose situation because you disagree, then you build the. This would produce a wedge in the connection as time goes by. This is also defined as the start to end. It is where you will, indeed, attempt. When you're not coming to a consensus right away, that's perfect. You should still decide to start up the topic after the date. Be alert not to let that run over the emotions. Be sure you have enough time until you continue to work for a solution. That's not as horrible as it does seem. When you think about your partner, in the end, all of you will feel fine.

Make Sure You Both Feel Safe

It is vital that both of you feel safe emotionally. When you can't communicate your emotions, otherwise the relationship isn't safe. It's essential to learn your partner appreciates your feelings. For specific individuals, this may be extremely challenging. You could not have grown up in a home where voicing your feelings was free. Or maybe everybody only held their feelings inside. That will leave you feeling trapped when you do this. This can also build a safety net for the partnership as all parties can healthily communicate their emotions.

There is still pair counseling when everything that fails. Even if you believe these suggestions support, you may want to see a pair of therapists. Getting a third party facilitates. This is someone who can listen and help lead you through this phase without taking sides. Couple counseling can further enhance connectivity, which can help with the relationship's friendship and intimacy. Often, couple counseling is a position where you can tell, 'I don't know what to do.' Make sure you choose a couple of therapists with whom you will be comfortable and that you can interact.

Reflect On What Drew You Together

We don't necessarily pick partners for the right reasons. We choose people often who question us, who drive us to develop and broaden our universes. On most occasions, we pick individuals whose protections and derogatory attributes match with ours. E.g., if we prefer to be passive or indecisive, we may select someone pushy and assertive. Such characteristics that pull us in the first time can become why we end up dropping out. Sadly, the sparkly attraction we sense is not always a positive indication at the outset. This could draw on our history — a divisive pattern from our experience that we are subconsciously seeking to reinforce. E.g., suppose we were invisible in our homes. In that case, we could be waiting for a common situation with a spouse who is not displaying any initial concern, who doesn't consider us a priority or express their affections. When we have a parent that wished to "improve us," we may have partners to "support us," but we then come after to hate them for treating us still as the issue that needs to be solved or mastered.

Although our partners' range will often be wrong, it is not necessarily to blame for a partnership's demise. If the appeal and anticipation we feel initially start to disappear, it doesn't automatically imply we have selected the wrong person. This is why awareness of our early feelings in the partnership is so critical. When, at one point, we were genuinely in love with somebody, we will recover those feelings. We should consider what attracted us to our companion and the years of mutual experience in which we experienced interaction, love, and intimacy. Instead, we will search at the real causes of why things have taken a turn for the worse and create a transition that can lead us closer to those original emotions and have a positive effect.

Try Breaking Your Routine

One of the key reasons a partnership falls is that the pair have formed a "Fantasy Bond." A Fantasy Bond is a word used at some stage in their collaboration to explain an impression of attachment that couples experience. A Fantasy Relationship varies from true love. Heartfelt gestures of compassion are substituted by ritual, and type in comparison is preferred over the material. Couples join this situation without really knowing it, as a way of experiencing a false sense of comfort, an impression of fusion or "oneness." A Fantasy Bond has a "deadening" impact on a partnership. Two spouses tend to dominate one another and restrict one another's perceptions. They are a "we," although they lack a sense of each of their origins as two different individuals. Apparent interaction is reduced; only intimate interactions give and take. Partners take each other for granted and lack each other's passion. We stop supporting the specific interests and traits of personality that illuminate the other individual and make them who they are. In effect, that generates a staled partnership atmosphere in which all sides experience frustration and loss of interest for each other.

Several aspects of a Fantasy Bond are worth investigating but note that this relationship is not a black or white state. There remains a Fantasy Relationship within a line. Many people, having formed an association of different degrees, consider themselves somewhere in the continuum. We will start breaking free of imagination by adjusting the way we connect in our partnership. You will follow this approach by deciding to take more responsibility in your collaboration, rather than passively with whatever your spouse wants. You should do this on your own, without your partner doing it.

6. Conflicts In Relationships: What Are The Reasons For Conflict Between Couples?

The problem belongs to all relations. In an intimate relationship, where the risks are top and sensations run deep, the problem is unavoidable. Nonetheless, the problem can wear at the fabric of a relationship if it is regular or crowds out love, love, and support.

The best study on the dispute in couples was done by John Gottman, the master pairs' study. In one research study, Gottman took an example of high conflict pairs and separated them right into two therapy groups. One team discovered problem resolution skills, and the other group focused on enhancing what he calls the "marital friendship." Pairs in this 2nd group worked on structure trust, goodwill, and also compassion in their relationships. Gottman found that couples who reinforced their relationship reduced the problem to a much better degree than those who discovered dispute resolution skills.

In a new collection of researches, Gottman intended to learn if there was a direct relationship between problem and also marriage distress. He wished to know, "do happier pairs fight less than unhappy ones?" The solution he discovered was not necessarily. He located that some happy couples battled higher than miserable ones. So, what made these satisfied couples pleased? The number of clear communications these delighted pairs had was much higher than their dissatisfied equivalents.

Gottman located that happy couples had a 5:1 proportion of favorable to unfavorable communications. Good communications are ones that reveal pleasure, wit, love, validation, and support. Hostile interactions were ones who express anger, aggressiveness, or defensiveness. As compared with the happy pairs' positive to adverse communications, unhappy couples had a ratio. The bottom line is one positive for each one unfavorable discussion isn't neutral. It causes marriage distress. Likewise, even pairs who do not have many problems might be unhappy if they also don't have much happiness in their life, support, and love.

So, what is the message from these two sets of researches? If you want to reduce disputes in your relationship, focus on increasing the favorable instead of lowering the negative. Look for opportunities to improve your relationship with your partner. Look for methods to reveal affection and support. Search for chances to produce goodwill and also depend on it. Be kind. Be empathic.

As anybody who has been in a romantic relationship understands, differences and battles are unpreventable. When two individuals spend a great deal of time together, they are bound to disagree every so often with their lives intertwined. These disagreements can be big or tiny, ranging from what to consume for dinner or stop working on finishing a job to debate whether the couple needs to move for one companion's profession or choose youngsters' spiritual training.

The mere truth that you combat with your partner isn't a sign; there is a genuine problem in your relation. When handled appropriately, battling can enhance your relationship. If you never deal with and also never talk about your issues, you will never fix them. By taking care of problems constructively, you can better understand your companion and come to an option that helps both of you. On the other hand, it is likewise feasible for problems to escalate and create hostility without fixing anything. How can you boost the odds of a successful resolution to the disputes in your relation? Here are ten research-backed suggestions:

1. Be Straight.

Sporadically people don't just come out and obviously state what is disturbing them and instead select more aberrant methods for communicating their annoyance. One buddy may condescendingly converse with the different other and demonstrates hidden antagonism. On various occasions, accomplices may sulk and even grimace without truly managing an issue. Moreover, sidekicks may just forestall examining an issue by quickly exchanging over themes when the subject turns up or by being unfathomably tricky. Such roundabout methods of communicating temper are not helpful since they don't give the person who is the objective of the practices absolutely how to respond. They comprehend their friend is disturbed; however, the nonappearance of certainty leaves them without exhortation regarding what they can do to tackle the issue.

2. Discuss Exactly How You Feel Without Blaming Your Partner.

Declarations that straight assault your companion's character can be incredibly destructive to a relationship.3 If a guy frustrated by his sweetheart's envy claims, "You're unreasonable!" he is inviting her to become protective, and also, this can close down the new conversation. An even more constructive method is to use "I declarations" and couple them with "behavior descriptions." statements focus on how you feel, without condemning your partner. Even habits summaries concentrate on your partner's specific action instead of a character flaw. For example, this male might say, "I obtain aggravated when you declare I'm flirting with somebody during an innocent discussion." These techniques are direct yet do not impugn your partner's character.

Nonetheless, it must be noted that these direct negative techniques can be constructive-- in some circumstances. The study has revealed that for pairs with reasonably small troubles, criticizing and turning down one's companion during a problem discussion was related to lower relationship fulfillment in time and also often tended to make issues worse. For couples with significant problems, a different picture arose: Blaming and also declining habits caused much less fulfillment right away, complying with the dispute conversation, but over the long-term, the troubles boosted, and this brought about increases concerning satisfaction.

3. Never Say Never (Or "Always").

When you're dealing with a problem, you must stay clear of making generalizations about your partner. Statements like "You never assist around your house" or "You're constantly staring at your mobile phone" are likely to make your partner defensive. As opposed to promoting a discussion regarding how your companion could be more useful or mindful, this method is most likely to lead your companion to start producing counterexamples of all the times they were valuable or alert. Again, you don't want to place your companion on the defensive.

4. Choose Your Fights.

If you wish to have a constructive discussion, you need to stay with one problem each time. Unhappy pairs are likely to drag several topics right into one study, a routine distinguished conflict scientist John Gottman calls "kitchen-sinking."

When you wish to address personal issues, this is probably not the strategy you take with yourself. Envision that you wanted to consider just how to integrate even more physical exercise into your daily regimen. You would probably not choose that this would also be an excellent time to think about just how to conserve more money for retirement, arrange your storage room, and also find out just how to handle an awkward situation at work. You would try to fix these troubles individually. This seems noticeable. However, in the warm of the minute, a fight concerning one subject can turn into a whining session, with both companions trading gripes. The more grievances you raise, the much less likely it is that any kind of will get informed entirely and fixed.

5. Listen To Your Partner.

It can be very discouraging to seem like your partner is not taking note of you. When you disrupt your partner or think that you understand what they're believing, you're not giving them a chance to share themselves. Even if you are positive that you recognize where your partner is coming from or know what they're going to claim, you could still be wrong. Your partner will again feel like you're not listening.

You can uncover to your accomplice that you're tuning in by using vigorous focusing methods.7 When your accomplice talks, rework what they state- - that is, reword it in your own words. This can keep away from misguided judgments before they start. You can use discernment check likewise by guaranteeing that you're deciphering your friend's responses fittingly. For instance, "You appear to be aroused by that remark - Am I right?" These systems both forestall mistaken assumptions and uncover to your partner that you're considering them and regarding what they're asserting.

6. Don't Automatically Object To Your Partner's Complaints.

At the point when you're condemned, it's troublesome not to get guarded. However, preventiveness doesn't address inconveniences. Imagine a couple contending since the other half needs her hubby to perform more responsibilities around the house. At the point when she suggests that he do a brisk tidy up after he sets yourself up to leave in the early morning, he asserts, "Truly, that would help, yet I don't have time in the first part of the day." When she recommends that he put aside time toward the end of the week, he guarantees, "Truly, that could be a strategy to plan it in.

In any case, we, as a rule, have expected on ends of the week, just as I have something important to make up for lost time with, to ensure that won't work." This "yes-butting" propensity proposes that her ideas and sees are not useful. Another violent, defensive conduct is "cross-grumbling," when you answer to your accomplice's concern with among your special. For example, reacting to "You don't clean up adequate around your home" with "You're a cool enthusiast." It is essential to listen to your accomplice and consider what they're expressing.

7. Take Various Viewpoints.

In addition to listening to your companion, you need to take their viewpoint and attempt to comprehend where they're originating from. Those who can gain their companion's perspective are less likely to become angry throughout a dispute conversation.

Various other research study has revealed that taking a more unbiased point of view can additionally be valuable.

8. Do Not Show Contempt For Your Partner.

Of all of the negative things you can do and claim throughout a problem, the worst might be ridiculed. Gottman has located that it is the leading predictor of separation.3 Contemptuous statements are those that belittle your partner. This can involve mockery as well as name-calling. It can additionally include nonverbal actions like rolling your eyes or smirking. Such habits are incredibly rude and indicate that you're revolted with your partner.

7. Jealousy In Relationship And Marriage

Ending jealousy is like altering every mental or behavioral response. It begins with consciousness. Awareness lets you see that the predicted stories are not real in your head. If you are so straightforward, you no longer respond to the possibilities your imagination might imagine. Jealousy and anger are emotional results that are not true in believing situations in your head. You should change what you think affects what your imagination projects and remove these harmful emotional reactions. Even if the response is warranted, envy and rage are not good ways to cope with the situation and get what we want—trying to change anxiety or resentment when you feel like controlling a car skidding on ice. Your capacity to deal with the situation will significantly improve if you can clear the risk before we get there. This means addressing the beliefs that cause jealousy rather than trying to control your emotions.

Dissolving relationships permanently means changing the underlying beliefs of fear and unconscious expectations of what the partner is doing.

The Steps To End Jealous Reactions Permanently Are:

1. Recover personal power so that you can control your emotions and stop reactive behavior.

2. Change your point of view so you can step back from your plot.

3. Be mindful that your convictions are not valid; this is distinct from scientifically "knowing" that the claims are not real.

4. Gain power over your focus so that you can actively select your mind's story and emotions.

Several factors establish the envy dynamic. Practical solutions will tackle multiple elements of values, experiences, feelings, and strength of personal will. You will leave the doors open to those negative emotions and behaviors if you lack one or more of these components.

You can step back from the story by practicing some simple exercises and refrain from the emotional reaction. If you want to change your feelings and actions, you can do it. It only takes the readiness to acquire sufficient skills.

Principle Triggers Of Jealousy Are Convictions That Create Insecurity Feelings.

Low self-esteem is based on convictions of who we are. We do not have to change our confidence in the false self-image to eradicate fear and low self-esteem. While some people believe this may be difficult, it's only tricky because most people haven't learned the skills needed to change their faith. When you practice your skills, it takes minimal effort to change a belief. You just stop thinking about the story. It takes more energy than it does to believe something.

Self-Judgment May Intensify The Feeling Of Insecurity

It is not enough to "learn" the emotion intellectually. Only in this way will the Inner Judge abuse us with criticism of what we do. The Interior Judge could use this knowledge to push us into more vulnerability by an emotional downward spiral. You have to develop skills to dissolve beliefs and falsified self-images and control your mind projects. The practices and capabilities of the audio sessions are available. The first and second sessions are free and should give us an idea of how the mind works to create emotions. Sessions 1 and 2 also give you great exercises to regain some personal power and adjust your feelings.

One of the steps to changing behavior is to see how we create the emotion of wrath or jealousy from our minds. This very step will allow us to take responsibility and puts us in a position to change our feelings.

We don't take responsibility if we're in a relationship with a jealous partner. We might want to change your behavior to avoid envy. Saying things like, "When you wouldn't, then I wouldn't react like this." This kind of language flags a powerless attitude and attempts to control your behavior by dealing with it.

How The Mind Produces The Emotions Of Anger And Jealousy?

I described in the description below the mechanism of jealousy and anger. When you try to overcome envy, you probably already know the complexities I explain. This explanation can help to fill the holes in how the mind turns knowledge into self-judgment and increases low self-esteem and insecurity. This theoretical understanding will contribute to the development of consciousness to see these complexities when you do so. But you necessary a different set of skills to make significant changes. You don't have enough details about how you build your emotional reactions. Just like realizing you have a flat tire, you didn't know how to patch it because you stumbled over the screw.

I will use a guy as a jealous companion for the example. I am talking about different pictures in mind, and you can refer to the chart below or see the Relationship Matrix for a more detailed description of these images.

It starts with a man who feels nervous. Insecurity stems from his "not perfect" False Hidden Image. The man creates self-rejection in his mind because he believes that this false image is who he is rather than a picture. The mental consequence of self-rejection is a feeling of indignity, vulnerability, apprehension, and unhappiness.

Compensating For Fear

To overcome the emotion created from the hidden false image, he concentrates on his perceived positive qualities to counteract the feeling created by his secret model. From these attributes, the man will make a false impression of himself. I call this the Projected Picture because he needs to be seen like this. The mental consequence of a positive self-image is not self-rejection or indignity. There is greater acceptance, and he generates more love and happiness. Notice that he has not changed; depending on the moment, he only has a different image in his mind.

The hidden image belief causes unhappiness, while the projected image causes more pleasant emotions. It must be remembered that both pictures are fake. Both photos are in the mind of the man, and nobody is him. He is the one who creates and reacts in his imagination to the images. In his vision, he's not an image.

The mind of the man blends the projected image with the qualities attracted by women. The characteristics are often considered positive because women are attracted to them. When a man receives attention from a woman, he links himself to the projected image instead of the image "Not Good Enough." The increased trust in the projected image leads to more social acceptance, love, and happiness.

The man's mind also makes the idea "she makes him happy" or "needs" it to be glad. It only appears this way because he notices the relationship between the woman and her emotional state. The man often does not know that his mind is only a sensitive tool to express love. He may not have developed other opportunities to communicate his acceptance and love, so he relies on a woman for a catalyst. If the man realized that she is only a trigger and that his role in expressing acceptance and love changed his emotional state, the man did not "need" his partner to be happy.

8. Fear Of Abandonment

Many individuals grow up with estrangement with concerns. These feelings of trepidation plague some for the duration of their lives decently and reliably. We dread that guardians, companions, universities, organizations, or whole social gatherings will overlook them.

Numerous individuals do not comprehend these feelings of dread until they arrive at a close connection. Things will go smoothly, and out of nowhere, they feel immersed with weakness and fear that their partner will separate, disregard, or leave them. Everybody is encountering that dread at different levels. A considerable lot of us can add to elevated nervousness about dismissal sentiments. From a reserved first date to a long-lasting partner that appears to be occupied and inaccessible, we might be set off by anything.

In outrageous cases, individuals may battle with "auto phobia," a mind-boggling apprehension of being separated from everyone else or confined. They see themselves to be overlooked or neglected in any event when they are with someone else. They may likewise encounter a dread of fear of relinquishment, which is portrayed by excessive reliance on others and is generally observed among individuals determined to have disarrangements of borderline personality.

How much an individual faces this dread can shape how they live their lives and experience associations. There are, be that as it may, powerful ways for people to create more critical security inside themselves and beat their dread of surrender. They can start by understanding where that dread begins from. How can it develop, and why? How does that influence me in my life today? What are the methodologies to address the tension that surfaces? How might I grow greater strength around connections and feel less dread?

Where Does Fear Of Abandonment Come From?

As children, individuals may encounter genuine misfortunes, dismissals, or injuries that cause them to feel the world's uncertainty and doubt.

Like a friend or family member's passing, disregard, or emotional and physical maltreatment, those misfortunes and injuries can be biased. In any case, they can frequently exist at a considerably more inconspicuous level in the day-by-day collaborations among guardians and youngsters. Children need to have a sense of security, seen and alleviated when they're disturbed to have a sense of safety. It has been said that even the best guardians are just around 30% of the time wholly tuned to their youngsters. Investigating their initial examples of connection may offer understanding to people into their interests of misfortune and dismissal. Seeing how their folks reacted to them and how they had a steady responsibility or a temperamental duty will explain how they see connections in the present.

On the off chance that guardians are consistently present and tuned to a newborn child's requirements, stable connections create. Breaks in these early connections, however, will lead children to develop shaky relationships. From the most initial stages, individuals figure out how to carry on in manners. Their folks or parental figures will best address their issues.

At one phase, a parent may be available and address the kid's issues, yet at some other point, be completely missing and denying or, at the far edge, troublesome and "genuinely ravenous" may make the kid build up an undecided/restless example of connection.

Children encountering this sort of connection will, in general, feel unreliable. They could stick to the parent trying to address their issues. They may likewise be battling to feel relieved by the parent, however. Youngsters are here and there apprehensive and unsure about the grown-up, who is flighty in conduct, frequently willing and mindful, and regularly denying or troublesome in manners that disappoint the young one.

How Early Attachment Patterns And Fears Of Abandonment Affect Us In Adulthood?

An individual's early history goes about as an inward working model for how connections are required. Therefore, individuals will bear frailties and presumptions of their young people of how others should act in their grown-up relationships.

Kids who experience an irresolute example of an attachment may grow up as grown-ups with a stressed example of passion, where they keep on feeling unreliable in their connections.

They "frequently feel urgent and assume the follower role in a relationship," said Joyce Catlett, Compassionate Child Rearing's co-creator. "They have a solid dependence on their partner to approve their self-esteem. Since they have become shaky in light of their parental figures' incomprehensible accessibility, they are "dismissal touchy." They foresee dismissal or surrender and search for signs that their partner is losing interest."

Adults who have a dread of deserting can battle with a concerned style of attachment. Frequently they envision their partner's dismissal and search for indications of lack of engagement. They may feel activated by even unobtrusive or envisioned expressions of their partner's discharge dependent on the real bursts they encountered during their youth. They can carry on possessive, predominant, desirous, or tenacious towards their partner subsequently. Frequently, they may search for consolation or show doubt.

"Yet, their unfortunate dependence, requests, and possessiveness appear to reverse discharge and accelerate the very distance they fear," Catlett said. She clarifies how specific individuals who dread dismissal react in correctional, angry, and disappointed manners when their life partner doesn't give them the friendship and consolation they think they have to have a sense of safety. "We likewise feel it is inconceivable that the other individual will respond to them, except if we exhibit their dread and dissatisfaction significantly," Catlett said. Numerous people with unreliable connections, however, are increasingly "ready to communicate their irate sentiments toward a partner inspired by a paranoid fear of conceivable dissatisfaction or excusal," which may lead them to disregard their feelings, which can permit them to develop, and eventually spill out in profound, passionate upheavals. These people are being activated in the present dependent on occasions from quite a while ago, regardless of whether they curb or pass on their forceful feelings. Settling these emotions is additionally fundamental to getting better and having stable connections between themselves.

The early attachment style of an individual may likewise impact the choice of their mate. Individuals also pick partners from their history to suit designs. For instance, they can incline toward an egotistical or far-off partner on the off chance that they feel dismissed as babies.

Individuals are once in a while mindful of this procedure. However, an individual who helps them to remember somebody from their past may feel an additional fascination.

What's more, they may discover approaches to re-create their youth's passionate condition. Individuals who dread dismissal may just pick partners that are less qualified; however, they can frequently misconstrue their partners, accepting they are more rebuffing than they are. At long last, they, in some cases, even incite the other individual to pull back and make more separation, in manners that impact their partner—getting on those examples that doctors call "determination, contortion, and incitement." Robert and Lisa Firestone can help individuals who fear deserting settle on better decisions to make greater security.

How Will This Fear Impact My Relationships?

One may believe that this dread would break down within sight of a serious relationship, yet that usually is not the situation. Those worries will show in manners that the individual genuinely accepts that their partner will relinquish them and that it is just a matter of when not if. In this way, they consistently live agonizing over being submitted and not having the option to give their relationship all to themselves. They blame their partners for cheating or endeavoring to leave. They feel as though they cannot confide in their partner's expression, as in the past, others have broken their trust.

However, this does construct a partition among them and their companion, which will self-satisfy the prescience. They end the relationship by living like their relationship is finishing. For the most part, they don't perceive how they prompted the destruction of their association. They just accept that they are "damned" seeing someone, they are "unlovable," and are left without clarification by everybody in their lives. Along these lines, the current issues won't be corrected without understanding, and they will proceed onward to the following relationship, and the battles will proceed.

Can This Affect Other Relationships?

Answer: Yes. Many people who are fearful of being rejected have that fear, not just about a love partner. With parents, friends, and children, it can also manifest. Such anxieties typically grow through a child's infancy.

A parent can be away from home or leaving home suddenly and without warning. When this happens, then the kid believes his parent has abandoned them. However, when this adult often comes and goes in the child's life, they won't think their adult will stick around.

Quick forward into teenage years, and you have someone who can be a very cuddly friend. They're always going to want to be with their friends and be upset if their friend finds a new friend out of fear of being left behind. Once their friend knows their family's history, their clinginess may be respected, but it can also get annoying. If that's the case, the relationship will then stop. It will then represent a disappointment, which will only intensify their youth issues. By having the insight on how they contributed to the loss, the loop will continue.

They are in and out of relationships because of their fears of rejection until they reach maturity. They get involved with a person they have trouble trusting and who they think would betray them. They are afraid of touch and passion. The companion leaves without reciprocating feelings. They continue to take responsibility for the deterioration of yet another friend, and the process continues. Sadly, this can continue in all partnerships in an individual's existence before realizing how they can contribute to a cycle of "everything" leaving them. Perhaps, they weren't able to regulate their mom's actions, but it's important to remember that this was when those emotions began, and they don't have to end. Once it is known, the reconstruction will begin, and they will enjoy a healthy and secure life with a life-long companion.

How Can I Have A Lasting Relationship?

The first step in sharing your life with others is to curb the fear they leave you behind. Far better than done, it is said. However, it needs to be done. You have to restore your trust, both in yourself and in your ties. You have to understand that you are lovable and worthy of love, indeed.

By improving your self-esteem, you'll learn to understand that you deserve love, and you need to find someone worthy of your pet. And doing that would make you feel like you're going to be in a serious relationship. Perhaps this isn't something you should do on your own.

With help, you can reach certified therapists who offer online therapy on this very subject.

Virtual counseling is entirely confidential and private, which offers full treatment services from the privacy of your own home.

The following step is challenging. You ought to be able to get the confidence. This is an enormous challenge for certain people, significantly if their past moral trust has been compromised. However, any new human being in our lives is worth another effort. We cannot blame them for the errors committed by anyone else. Instead of life waiting for them to leave you every day, make every effort to keep them alive.

9. Creating A Sense Of Security In Your Relationship

To sustain your relationship healthy and happy, you and your partner will continuously nurture your relationship. You'll focus on what helps strengthen your relationship and work out any issues along the way, including when your anxiety comes back to haunt you again. This is especially true when building trust and overcoming fear in your relationship. You must realize now, and this work isn't something that you'll only do in the beginning—it's an ongoing process that keeps the foundations of the commitment between two people healthy.

The Secrets Of A Happy, Long-Lasting, Anxiety-Controlled Relationship

There are many secrets to building a happy, long-lasting relationship that's anxiety-controlled. What this means is that you're never directly free of your anxiety. It will still jump out at you during specific situations. No relationship is ever completely free of pressure, but you can learn to manage stress, so you have a healthy relationship for the rest of your life. It's important to note that the secrets I discuss here often come up with my clients in therapy. There are many others that you'll find more personal to you that I don't mention. The key is to follow the secrets that work for you and your partner.

Honesty is unique to the essential factors in a relationship. Even when it hurts, you still want to be honest with your partner and yourself. If somewhat is bothering you, speak up and talk to your partner. Don't let it build up until you burst, tell them that everything is fine when they ask what's wrong, or avoid a topic because you don't want to hurt your partner. Even if you feel that your relationship is more peaceful when you don't bring up specific issues, you're going backward instead of forward—being honest means that you need to take time to reflect on your relationship now. Think about how you feel, what you like, and what you wouldn't mind changing. Chitchat to your partner about this and ask them to answer the same questions.

You always want to ask your partner questions. You don't want to assume, and you aren't a mind reader, even if you've been with them for a long time. For example, you're talking to your partner about how they want to change their job. You know they have a good-paying job with great benefits, but they want to change direction completely. Their potential new career would mean less money and no services. As your partner is talking, you can't understand why they want to change. You want to know how long they've been thinking about this change. Don't keep the questions to yourself—ask them. The more you fathom what your partner is feeling and where they're coming from, the easier it'll be to support your partner without strings attached, such as hidden negative emotions.

Another secret is emotional attunement. When you don't just listen to the words your partner says, you also feel them. You become attuned to their emotions and show empathy. For example, you're listening to your partner talks about their current job, and you can see that they are stressed, so you start feeling this stress. You also think that they are genuinely unhappy when they're talking about their job; it's like they don't have any energy for it anymore, so they're just going through the motions. You then listen to them as they talk about a new potential job and feel their happiness and excitement as their eyes light up. You can notice your partner's emotions by noticing their body language, tone of voice, and what they're not saying. Emotional attunement will become more comfortable as time goes on, and your relationship starts to strengthen.

You need to make sure you set aside time to check in with each other. It's vital to ensure that you're still on the same page regarding long-term goals, commitment, and values. You can talk about your relationship, what you feel is going well, and what you can improve on. Setting aside time once a week will become a habit, and you'll start focusing on it throughout the week. However, it's also essential to build sure that this isn't the only time you communicate or talk about any problems.

During your weekly talk, you can continue enforcing the relationship barriers that make both of you feel respected, taken care of, and honored. For example, you can check in to make sure that you're giving your partner the privacy they trust you will and that you feel comfortable and confident in your relationship. This is also an excellent time to discuss all of the boundaries you and your partner agreed to.

It's always good to devour a refresher now and then as it'll help keep everyone on track and increase happiness, respect, and trust in your relationship.

You need to work on improving your relationship every day. As you know, relationships are a lot of work. You must put forth the effort to make sure that you're communicating, listening, compromising, and completing your roles. Yes, there are days where you're just so mentally exhausted or an emergency comes up, and your relationship takes a step back, but this doesn't mean that you continue the trend. If your relationship goes on the back burner today, you need to put it back on the front burner tomorrow. Remember to communicate with your partner about how you're feeling and that you need a little downtime.

It's essential to have a spiritual component in your relationship. This doesn't necessarily refer to religion. It can mean that you talk about what love means to both of you, and you find a connection in your answers. You gaze at how you can give back to the community or talk about your faith. For example, if you both believe in a higher power, you need to ensure this is part of your relationship.

Do your greatest not to fall into "the blame game" trap. It always takes two people to tango, and this means that both of you are at fault. It's relaxed to point fingers and blame someone else when something isn't right, or a mistake was made. When you need to put your finger away and discuss what happened without focusing on who is to blame, it's at this topic. You'll talk to your partner about what you can both do to make the situation better subsequent time, and then you can talk about something positive or what went right within the problem to help the conversation end on a fair and robust note. Then, you need to let it go.

No difficulty how strong your relationship is; you can't avoid every argument. You can't ignore the feelings of anger over something that's happened, or someone did. However, you can choose to take a break and calm down before you discuss the topic. You also want to focus on solving the problem together. Research shows that 70% of couples say this is a significant factor when conflict arises (Harrar & DeMaria, n.d.). The first step you can talk about is to follow this pattern is not to criticize each other. Realize that conflict is part of a healthy relationship, and you can use it as a tool to make your relationship stronger by acting calmly and rationally. If you do feel that your anger is about to boil over, let your partner know that you need time to relax alone before discussing the topic.

It might help to talk about a plan of action when you say you need time alone before a conflict arises, so your partner understands that this is part of the process, and they should take a step back and focus on relaxing their mind as well.

There is a difference between hearing and listening. When you hear someone, you know what they're saying, but you don't comprehend their words. You don't notice their emotions, and you quickly forget what they said. When you listen to someone, you know exactly what they're saying and seeing how they're feeling. You are considering what they're saying and working it into your part of the conversation. You must be listening to what they're saying and not just hearing them every time you communicate. This also means that you'll want to turn off the television, put down your phone, and put away any other distractions that you can.

Another tip is to go back to when you realized you loved your partner. Discuss the reasons why you fell in love with them and why you still feel the same way. You can even talk about some of their annoying habits that you think are a little cute at the same time (you know there is at least one). It's also important to touch your partners, such as when you pass each other in the kitchen or the hallway. All you need to do is gently graze their arm or hold their hand for a second. Physical touch makes you feel special and that you're loved.

10. Cultivating New And Healthy Relationships And Keeping Your Relationship Flourishing

The best part of enjoying such a supportive bond is that you feel secure in yourself and your relationship. According to research, a healthy and successful relationship is based on a sense of security. The more confident you feel, the stronger your relationship will become. You can feel even more assured when you find a partner who is emotionally available and provides a supportive role in your life. In such a relationship, both of you will appreciate each other, share your thoughts and feelings, communicate successfully, and trust one another. You both have to be factual to yourselves to be able to trust each other. Even in worst-case scenarios, you will try to coordinate with each other to maintain a successful relationship. You'll discover the best approaches to understanding and working on the differences between you and your partner. Remember to avoid trying to change your partner according to your requirements. Try using mentalization to understand them instead.

Discovering Yourself

You will gradually discover many things about your new relationship, the more you get to know your partner. The level of appreciative and compatibility with your significant other will indicate how strong your relationship is. For example, if one of you shares something persona and the other reacts with compassion, understanding, and also discloses something personal. Sharing personal information can help create a strong bond of affection and trust in a relationship. As you fill more and more time together, you likewise build up a feeling of compassion and trust in one another's company.

Being in a relationship based on give-and-take or mutual sharing might become troublesome if you have an insecure attachment style. Your anxious need for closeness could cause you to feel powerless if you share your secrets.

As a result, you may remain distant and become unavailable most of the time. In both scenarios, you are risking your relationship with your partner. Primarily, your main focus is to understand how your partner will help you or hurt you. This particular thing will keep on interfering between you and your partner because misunderstandings are based solely on misperceptions.

In case your way of disclosing your thoughts and feelings to your partner has caused damage to your relationship in the past, it might be time to go about it differently. Start by thinking about your motivations for opening up to or withholding information from your partner. Self-awareness is crucial for this. Start thinking critically about how and when you disclose certain information. This will help you in analyzing the situation more accurately.

If you're pushing yourself closer to your partner only to get away from your loneliness, then think again and evaluate your actions. Try to spend time with your old or new friends. To occupy yourself, you can also find an activity that can keep you busy and make you feel happy, safe, and validated. You can also devote your energy and time to charity or volunteer work.

Instead of looking only toward your partner for comfort, try to find new ways to overcome your problems. Remember that many strings are holding you up—don't neglect them. In this manner, you can build a sense of connection, both with your partner and with other people in your life, all the while establishing a sense of trust and harmony.

Relying On Each Other

It's simply not possible to develop a relationship in which you and your partner don't rely on each other to a certain extent. This is one of the cornerstones of any healthy relationship. You should feel free to depend on one another for love and comfort as both of you navigate through your lives.

To trust your partner and let them depend on you, you should measure their requirements for autonomy and closeness, as well as your own. When both of you feel that these requirements are not being met—and this will inevitably happen at some point in your relationship—you should try to fix issues together before making any rash decisions. Allowing yourself to be vulnerable and communicating in such situations will make it easier for you to understand each other honestly.

This sense of understanding will help you to resolve the issues in your relationship more effectively.

Keeping an open mind to your and your partner's viewpoints will also eliminate any negative thoughts. Whenever a problem arises in a relationship, it's not uncommon for people to start thinking bad things about their partners. If this goes on unaddressed, it can drive a potentially fatal wedge into your relationship.

As we've mentioned before, never blame yourself when things go wrong in the relationship. Remember to practice self-compassion, first and foremost. Resolve your issues alongside your partner rather than carrying the weight of them alone. The two of you are a team, and you both need each other's love, compassion, comfort, and reassurance to build intimacy.

Increase Intimacy

Speaking of intimacy, there are many different ways to cultivate it in your relationship. Dancing or exercising together is a great way to grow closer to your partner. Essentially, any activity that you both enjoy doing will guide you in the right direction of maintaining a healthy relationship.

Once you overcome the initial shyness in your relationship, you can become more open and vulnerable with your partner, increasing intimacy.

Remember that there no specific formula for a balanced amount of independence and closeness between two people. Different people tend to have different needs and desires, and these requirements are continually changing. Your relationship will be successful when you both acknowledge, adapt, and accept each other's conditions. Flexibility between two people also brings positivity and closeness in relationships.

Explore Your Anxious Attachment

In the event when you're strongly compelled always to feel that you're overly attached to them, assume the role of devil's advocate for a moment. Imagine doing all the things you enjoy doing, but imagine it without your partner. This can be anything that brings joy and happiness to your life.

For example, taking a class, starting a garden, or spending the weekends with your friends. Just imagine how enjoyable and freeing it might be to do these things, even if your significant other isn't with you.

If this exercise causes you too much anxiety, you don't have to think about it right now. You're in no way indebted to do anything you don't want to do.

To overcome this anxiety, you can try communicating your feelings to the people who love and support you. Think about discussing with your partner as well when you feel ready to do so.

Try To Maintain A Close Connection

After the honeymoon phase has passed, your relationship will start being affected by you and your partner's personal and professional hardships. Because of this, it can feel like you're losing the sense of closeness with your partner. People living with attachment-related anxiety can be significantly affected by this.

You have to preserve in mind that this is a standard step for any relationship. But just because your relationship is settling down and your lives are returning to normal, it doesn't mean that your bond will break. On the contrary, this is when real closeness and intimacy begin to appear.

Keep Yourself Engaged With Your Partner

Interacting daily with your partner can help you in overcoming the communication gap. Make a routine of talking with your partner every day. Ask them about their day, what made them happy, and their plans for the following day. This conversation will help you both in staying synchronized and give a chance to support one another through both exciting and challenging times. It doesn't matter if you talk for an hour or ten minutes. Talking regularly and getting an update from your partner is what's important.

This conversation will be more fruitful if you and your partner have similar interests and hobbies. This way, you can pursue your interests by following your partner's interests. This activity will bring a positive impact on your relationship.

Share Experiences With Your Partner

Sharing your victories and struggles with your partner is one of the main things that will bring you closer together. If two people in a relationship don't share their life experiences, their distance will only increase.

Sharing will also help you in identifying your compatibilities. So, try to make plans each week to spend quality time together to understand each other better. Go on walks, to the movies, for dinner, or just spend some alone time together.

Other activities you can do together include hiking, bicycling, swimming, going on a picnic, playing tennis, dancing, and traveling to new places.

Work On A Project Together

This is a fantastic way to increase harmony and love between you and your partner. Starting a project together like redecorating your home, volunteering, taking a class, or learning a language is one of the fittest and most fun activities that couples can engage in.

Try To Make Visible Actions Of Love

If you and your partner sense comfortable with visible displays of affection, try to make your partner feel special by kissing, hugging, or giving them gifts and compliments. These small actions of love can help you in growing closer to your partner.

Express Your Feelings Of Love

Your partner should always know how important they are to you. This is something that often falls by the wayside when you've been with someone for a long time. But everyone needs to hear how much they matter to their significant other once in a while.

You can express your feelings through actions or words. Whichever option you choose depends on the situation. The key is always to make an effort to express your love to your partner and make them feel special.

Compliment Your Partner

Most people love compliments. Especially when they come from our significant other. In a relationship, compliments and small gifts play a vital role in bringing people closer together. Whenever you find the moment or occasion, try to compliment your partner. It will bring energy and love to your relationship.

Find New Ways To Show Love

If you feel your relationship is in a rut, try expressing your love in fresh new ways. You can give your partner a gift you made yourself, make them a playlist of songs that mean approximately to both of you or surprise them with a weekend away.

Know When To Yield

Acts of kindness and love in a relationship can be a tremendous help when solving your problems. There are times when your relationship will face hardships, and both you and your partner can become inflexible on an issue. Think critically about the situation. Sometimes, a conflict just isn't worth the amount of energy that you're both giving it or the sadness it brings. This is the time to make yourself flexible and accommodating of the situation. By doing this, you are saving the love between you and your partner and keeping your relationship.

11. Commons Errors in Love Affairs

Relationships are lovely things, yet they can now and again be muddled. Figuring out how to manufacture a stable association, one that makes us cheerful and, the more significant part of all, develops on an establishment of certainty and trust isn't at all simple.

Inevitable, normal slip-ups individuals make seeing someone are essential for what shields us from having that.

It's typical for connections to have their difficult stretches, yet traversing them (accepting that is the thing that you need and that it's conceivable) adds to development.

During periods of turmoil, people in relationships sometimes have irrational thoughts or ideas that don't help the relationship, partner, or themselves. Some of these notions include:

You Need A Partner To Be Happy

Some singles are desperately looking for a partner because they think - or, as in most cases, have heard - that it is essential to have someone by their side to be happy. If you do not have that, life is much less fun, and you feel alone and somehow worthless.

Of course, such a statement is not universal, if only because every person is different, and thus their version of "happiness" will be different. However, the fact is that you can feel good even without a permanent partner - and whoever radiates this outwardly will immediately be more attractive to potential new love.

A Child Can Save A Relationship

It is not a good idea to think that a child will improve your relationship. Children are lovely, but they put a relationship under new challenges and stress.

If a relationship is already fraught with conflict, then you should think very carefully about the desire to have a baby or wait a little longer so that you have fewer conflicts with your partner. Children are only enriching when their parents know that they will have less time for each other, themselves, and more financial responsibility.

Dependencies Do Not Make You Happy

Do not commit the mistake and put all positive experiences and feelings into the relationship with your partner. Retain in mind at the beginning of the relationship, and further in that, you have to make yourself happy. Please do not give your partner the responsibility, and do not make yourself dependent on them to be satisfied.

Preserve the ability to be responsible for yourself and your happiness. In this way, your relationship will grow more comfortable and be more stable, and you both will be happier, knowing one isn't relying on the other.

Relationship And Sex Don't Necessarily Belong Together

The importance of having sex in a partnership varies from person to person. Some couples live their sex life very passionately and often, while others are rarely intimate but still romantic.

It is crucial that both sides are happy with the level of intimacy and acknowledge each other's needs. If you have glitches in this regard, you should not shy away from an open conversation. Just remember that if you're both happy with the way things are, but the influences of the media and society tell you it should be different, listen to your heart. Only the two of you know what's right for your relationship.

12. Consult With A Professional

If You Love A Person With Stress And Anxiety!!!

1. The Very Best Thing You Can Do Is Pay Attention.

You do not need to have the responses. It cannot be repaired even though you wish to improve it. Just pay attention. Let them recognize that you exist. Let them have room if they require it, or if they need a hug, please delight."

2. Acknowledge Our Stress And Anxiety Rather Than Sweeping It Under The Carpet.

"Do not treat it as if it is a passing point or that it does not exist. Recognize if your partner could make it go away, they would."

3. Your Support Indicates The Globe To Us.

"I have stayed with my boyfriend for a year. I recognize I am not constantly the simplest to like. I will hop on his nerves and occasionally make him wonder why I act the means I do. But when I am overthinking as well as doubting myself, it implies the globe that he's still by my side-- accepting our distinctions and still caring me when I often find it hard to enjoy myself."

4. Please Do Not Tell Us To Simply 'Relax' Or That We Are Unreasonable.

"' Cooldown' is about as useful as trying to baptize a feline. We are frequently 1000 percent aware whatever we fear concerning is unreasonable. Informing ourselves that does not amazingly turn our brains off."

5. Do Not Take It Personally When We Are Having A Negative Day.

"Know that our anxiousness is not concerning you, even if you believe you triggered it. We are feeling extremely overwhelmed. Deal us something that might assist distract or decrease the strength. Part of our worry is in the brain and cannot be aided.

Other externals elements can be. Offer a getaway or anything you recognize could help in reducing our signs."

6. Remember: Not All Anxiety Coincides.

7. Not All Symptoms Of Our Stress And Anxiety Misbehave.

"Stress and anxiety are not constantly poor. Some days, liking an individual with anxiousness implies they will think deeply and passionately concerning caring for you. Worried power is still power. Hardly ever does my anxiousness enable me to make decisions without deep and thorough thought. You will be considered as well as took care of like you never have in the past."

8. We Are Deeply Grateful For Your Perseverance.

"Persistence is a virtue. You might not constantly recognize our stress and anxiety, yet if you show love and compassion for our pain, that is one of the most important points. My sweetheart will usually simply check-in if we go to a party, inconspicuously asking if I am OKAY. Just a basic way to reveal he cares."

9. Do Some Study Regarding Our Condition-- It Could Assist You To Comprehend Us.

"Be educated about our illness. Understand the sensations and truth of what your companion is facing and be there similarly, you would certainly for an individual who has a physical health problem. Learn our triggers."

10. No, You Cannot "Take Care Of" Us, Which's Okay.

"My husband needed to find out that often what's wrong does not require dealing with-- simply a minute for me to procedure."

11. Take Our Sensations Seriously.

"When my anxiety condition was undiagnosed and neglected, I had panic attacks that I believed were cardiovascular disease or blot embolisms. My fiancé drove me to the health center both times and took it extremely seriously. It implied that somebody believed me that something was wrong, even if it was not as lethal as we assumed. Anxiety can be debilitating, and it just helps sometimes for somebody not to lessen it or clean it off."

12. Motivate Us To Look After Ourselves.

"Join recovery activities with me or encourage me to remain active in things like yoga, dance as well as walking. Encouraging me additionally suggests enabling me time to do these activities by taking the youngsters for a bit."

13. Advise Us That There Is No Shame In Seeking Expert Assistance.

"Urge your companion to see a therapist. Obtaining treatment for anxiety can conserve your partner's life, raise their total well-being as well as boost your relationship."

14. Simply Be There For Us On The Dark Days.

" I have an extremely recognizing guy that not just 'obtains' my demand to being in the closet sometimes, however, purchased me a blanket for when I am being in the storage room and will certainly join me in there when my anxiousness is excessive for me to leave my safe place."

Understand The Anxieties Of The Partner

Living with anxiety can be tricky-- your thoughts might race, you may fear tasks others locate straightforward (like driving to function), as well as your fears, might feel unavoidable. However, caring for a person with stress and anxiety can be challenging too. You might feel helpless to assist or bewildered by how your companion's feelings affect your life. If so, you are not the solitary one: Several studies have revealed that anxiety problems may add to marriage discontentment. " We often find that our patients' ... partners are in some way linked in their anxiety," claims Sandy Capaldi, an associate supervisor at the Facility for the Treatment and Study of Anxiousness at the College of Pennsylvania.

Stress and anxiety are experienced at several levels and in various kinds-- from moderate to disabling, from generalized anxiety to fears, and even its influences can vary. But psychoanalysts and specialists state there are methods to help your companion navigate challenges while you also deal with yourself.

Start By Dealing With Signs.

Because a stress and anxiety problem can be consuming, it can be best to begin by chatting with your companion concerning the ways stress and anxiety impacts daily life, like sleep loss, claims Jeffrey Borenstein, the president as well as Chief Executive Officer of the Mind & Actions Research Structure in New York City. Something as straightforward as utilizing the words "tension" instead of medical tags can assist too. "Frequently, people might feel a little comfier speaking about anxiety as opposed to ... stress and anxiety [disorders]," Borenstein states.

Do Not Minimize Feelings.

Aid your partner, look for therapy-- and participate when you can.

If your partner is overwhelmed by anxiety, urge your companion to seek therapy. You can also recommend the names of therapists or offices; however, do not call the therapist as well as established the appointment yourself, Borenstein says. You desire the individual to have a degree of the company over treatment.

Capaldi claims she often generates an individual's partner to participate in treatment and strengthen the patient's support group in your home. "The 3 of us-- person, companion, specialist-- are a group, which team is opposed to the anxiousness problem," she states.

Yet do not speak with your companion at home the method a specialist might. As an example, do not recommend your partner attempt medication or means of modifying behavior. "Let the referrals about therapy originated from the professional" even if you on your remain in the mental health care area, Borenstein says. "I directly am a specialist, and I wouldn't to a liked one."

Likewise, it can be valuable to do some research study on whatever form of stress and anxiety your companion could be coping with, Capaldi claims (The National Relationship on Mental disease' guide to stress and anxiety conditions is a great base). "Many times, people with anxiousness feel as if they are misunderstood," she states. "If the companion takes the time to research it a little bit, that can go a long way."

For pointers on just how to aid your companion to choose the right sort of therapy, have a look at this guide from the Anxiety and Clinical Depression Association of America.

Motivate-- Do Not Push.

When your partner deals with crippling anxiousness as well as you do not, your companion's behavior can be frustrating, states Cory Newman, a teacher at the University of Pennsylvania's Perelman School of Medicine. Yet you need never to buy or decrease your companion's concerns. Comments such as "Why cannot you do this? What's your issue?" will most likely be ineffective.

Instead, attempt to encourage your companion to get rid of the anxiety. "Channel your motivation in a favorable direction," Newman states. "Say something like 'Below's how it will certainly profit you if you can encounter discomfort.' "

Daitch points out the instance of someone with an immense concern of flying: "Start claiming, 'I recognize exactly how terrified you are of flying. It makes good sense you'd be frightened. You cannot get off the airplane if you have a panic attack, scared you may shame on your own … or it seems like you run out control when there's turbulence.' See things from their perspective." After that, you can attempt to push your companion to get over those fears carefully.

Cultivate A Life Outside Your Companion's Anxiousness.

To keep your psychological wellness, it is necessary to cultivate habits and relations for you alone, such as a regular workout regimen or weekly hangouts with pals. Have your very own assistance network, like a best friend or a therapist, for when your companion's anxiousness bewilders you.

Companions certainly need the assistance of their own, Capaldi claims, "whether that implies their restorative relation or simply pals, household other passions or tasks that set them besides the globe of stress and anxiety they could be residing in."

And do not let your companion's anxiety run your family's life. For example, a person with an obsessive-compulsive problem, which is carefully connected to stress and anxiety conditions, could want a family member to maintain whatever spick-and-span or organized in approximate methods. Newman claims it is essential to restrict just how much you will manage your household around your companion's stress and anxiety-- and not indulge every request or required.

"Attempt to be respectful, however additionally established limitations," he claims. Assist your partner in remembering that the objective is to take care of anxiousness and not remove it.

"A lot of people with anxiousness problems not surprisingly see anxiety as the opponent," Newman claims. "It is not. The actual opponent is avoidance. Anxiousness triggers to prevent things-- like putting on schools, flying to a cousin's wedding-- an enriched life. ... Which causes anxiety."

It can also decrease the number of life experiences you and even your partner share. "You can have a distressed life, but if you make points-- you are doing that job interview, you are saying yes to social invites, you are entering that car as well as driving to the sea even though ... you do not wish to drive 10 miles-- you are doing those things still," Newman claims. "OK, you might require or therapy, yet you are still living life."

13. Love And Relationship: Advice For Couples

All of us desire a long and happy relationship. However, we do not get lessons at school on how to be in and maintain a lasting relationship. There are so many interferences in the world that keep us from achieving perfect and happiest relationships. You have the power to design your relationship and how you feel about it. First, you must be open to a constructive relationship. Secondly, you must commit daily to avoid all distractions that do not serve any purpose in your relationship. Thirdly, do not give up too first.

Every relationship is different, and the person you love might not be the choice of another. A happy relationship will feel positive, additive, profound, equal, and acceptable and has room for vulnerability. From the introductory, you have to make choices and have the clear intention of heading somewhere. How can one cultivate a long and happy relationship?

A. Be Clear From The Beginning

While some people take time to get into a relationship, others hit it off on the first date. Regardless of whether you decide to be in a relationship on the first date or after years of friendship, you have to be open to each other about what you want. Talk about your true self as soon as the relationship starts. What do you want from the relationship? What can you do to ensure that you meet the desired goals?

Staging your needs clearly from the beginning ensures that you understand whether you and your partner are compatible. It also aids you to know if there are things you will have to compromise on. Do you desire to get married and have kids in the succeeding two years? Say it as it is. Do you want to be in a long term relationship or a contract kind of relationship? Tell your partner.

B. Share Your Most Deep Secrets And Dreams

Sharing creates room for intimacy. It also invites the other person to open up. It is okay to talk about your childish desires like building a tiny house on the edge of a cliff and spending the rest of your life there.

Again, this sharing helps you to determine if you are compatible. If you realize early enough that the relationship will not work because of incompatibility, you will spare yourself many heartaches.

C. Have A Wide-Open Communication Channel.

Communication determines if you will be happy or sad in your relationship—every rule of a happy relationship links to proper communication. If you want a happy relationship, make sure that you communicate openly, even when the topic is uncomfortable. Pay compliments when deserved, and ask questions if need be.

None of you should be afraid of what will happen if they bring a particular subject up. Address issues calmly and use compassion and empathy in your communications.

D. Embrace Your Self

There is nothing wrong with loving yourself. Your life has different facets, and you must embrace them all. Embracing yourself is the first step to understanding yourself and knowing what needs to be changed or otherwise.

E. Support Each Other

Everyone has dreams and ambitions they would like to achieve. A good relationship should allow both parties to offer to each other. If you provide support to your partner and he/she reciprocates, that relationship will last.

F. Explore Growth Together.

Life is about change, and there are things every couple wants to change in each other. Everybody wants to live their best life. It is essential to expose every opportunity of growth together, Support one another through the changes.

G. Work Towards Being Better Partners.

We are work in progress and learners. Remember that no one teaches us how to be in a relationship; therefore, we have to learn on the go. Probably, there are things you wish you had done differently in your past relationships. Maybe you need to use more love language or how to open up to your partner. Everyone should attempt to be a better partner.

H. Dream Together

A relationship is about two people. The future belongs to both of you. Therefore, it is vital that you sit and talk about tomorrow, a month from now, a year, and even forever. What would you like to achieve together? Talk about everything, for instance, kids, a home, finances, vacations, etcetera. Realize that the more you talk with a person, the easier it is to determine if they are a good fit.

I. Be Present

Sometimes we are overwhelmed by other things that we forget how to connect with our loved ones. For instance, you might have gotten home after a long day at work, and all you want to do is shut people prohibited and rest. On the other hand, your partner might have a hard stricter day and is looking forward to sharing with you. Relationships require sacrifice, and that means putting the needs of your partner at heart. So, be present for your partner.

14. How Your Bond Pattern Controls Your Relationship

The connection type influences everything from accomplices' determination to how far our relationships advance and, tragically, how they finish. That is why perceiving our connection design in a relationship can help us understand our qualities and weaknesses. Connection design creates in youth connections, which fills in as a working model for grown-up relations. This relationship worldview influences how everyone responds to our requirements and how we satisfy them. When there is a safe connection design, an individual is guaranteed and reserved and can associate effectively with others, fulfilling the requirements of both themselves as well as other people. Nonetheless, when there is a restless or maintaining a strategic distance from connection design, and an individual chooses an accomplice that fits that evil versatile example, they will, in all probability, choose somebody who isn't the ideal decision to fulfill them.

E.g., the individual with an on-edge/distracted relationship working model thinks you should be with your accomplice all an opportunity to get consolation since you need to be near somebody and get your requirements met. They pick somebody detached and difficult to associate with to help that impression of the real world. The person with a pretentious/avoidant relationship working model has all the earmarks of being confined, so their model is that how your needs are met is to carry on as you don't have any. The individual in question at that point chooses somebody who is more possessive or unreasonably requesting consideration. We set ourselves up, and it might be said, by discovering accomplices to affirm our models. Assume we have grown up with a shaky connection design. We might be anticipating or endeavoring to copy close connections as grown-ups, regardless of whether these examples hurt us and are not to our most significant advantage.

Secure Attachment

Securely linked adults appear to find their relationships more fulfilled. Children with a secure attachment perceive their parents as a secure base from which to venture out and independently explore the world. A confident adult has a positive relationship with their intimate one, feeling safe and linked while encouraging them to travel openly with their one.

On the off chance that your buddy is discouraged, stable grown-ups help. At the point when they feel grieved, they likewise go to their accomplice for comfort. Their relationship has all the earmarks of being honest, open, and reasonable, with the two people feeling sure yet thinking about each past. Safely included couples don't generally take part in what my dad, the clinician Robert Firestone, depicts as a "Dream Bond," an association hallucination that gives an incorrect feeling that all is well with the world. A couple overlooks genuine demonstrations of adoration for a more ordinary, sincerely cut-off sort of relationship in a dream relationship.

Anxious Preoccupied Attachment

In contrast to solidly associated accomplices, restlessly joined people have all the urgent earmarks to shape a dream bond. They frequently feel the passionate craving, as opposed to feeling genuine love or trust towards their accomplice. They generally look to their ally to spare or full them. While they seek a feeling of assurance by adhering to their accomplice, they take acts that drive away their accomplice.

Also, if individuals who are restlessly joined to carry on naturally or uncertainly, their activities, as a rule, intensify their feelings of dread. They frequently become tenacious, requesting, or possessive towards their accomplices when they feel uncertain of their emotions and danger in their relationship. They may likewise decipher their accomplice's autonomous activities as insisting on their tensions. On the off chance that your accomplice begins mingling more with companions, for instance, they may think, "See? He doesn't adore me. This implies he's leaving me. I simply didn't confide in him."

Dismissive Avoidant Attachment

People with a dismissive, evasive attachment tend to distance themselves emotionally from their partner.

They may be seeking isolation and feeling "pseudo-independent," taking on the parenting role themselves. They habitually come off as focused on themselves, and their creature comforts may be overly attended. Pseudo-independence is an illusion since every human being needs a connection.

Be that as it may, individuals with a cavalier equivocal relationship will, in general, lead all the more inner lives, keeping the significance of getting friends and family and productively disengaging themselves from them. They are likewise protected intellectually and can close down genuinely. They can stop their feelings and not react, even in warmed or passionate circumstances. On the off chance that their accomplice is upset, for instance, and takes steps to leave them, they would react by saying, "I couldn't care less."

Fearful Avoidant Attachment

A person with a fearful, avoiding attachment lives in an ambivalent state of fear of being either too near or too far away from others. They try to hold their emotions at bay but fail; they cannot quickly stop their fear or run away from their feelings. Instead, their feelings overtake them and sometimes undergo intense storms. In their moods, they appear to be messed up or unpredictable. From the working paradigm, people see your relationships where you need to reach out to them to fulfill your needs, but people will harm you once you get attached to others. That is to add, the one they want to run to for help is the same one they are scared to get close to. As a result, they do not have an organized strategy for getting others to meet their needs.

As youths, these individuals appear to be in unpleasant or turbulent connections, with many highs and lows. They frequently have fears of being deserted yet additionally battle to be private. When they feel dismissed, they can stick to their accomplice and afterward feel stuck when they are together. Ordinarily, the separating among them and their accomplice have all the earmarks of being incorrect. In an abusive relationship, an individual with a frightful, dodging connection may even twist up.

The good news is, creating a stable connection rarely is too late. The attachment style you established as a child-centered on your relationship with a parent or early caregiver does not have to define how you relate in your adult life to those you love.

When you learn to know the type of connection, you will discover areas in which you protect yourself against becoming stronger and emotionally linked and work towards building a "successful stable relationship."

One profound way of doing this is by making the story meaningful. Attachment analysis suggests that "the greatest measure of a child's attachment stability is not what happened to his parents as infants, but how his parents make sense of those memories of adolescence." The trick to making sense of your life experiences is to compose a cohesive story that makes you appreciate how your childhood experiences often impact you in your life today. You rewire your brain when you create a coherent narrative to cultivate more security within yourself and relationships.

By indicating a partner with a secure attachment style, you can also challenge your defenses and develop yourself in that relationship. Therapy can also be of assistance in changing patterns of maladaptive attachment. By becoming aware of your attachment type, both you and your partner will question the insecurities and prejudices that your age-old working models endorse and create new forms of attachment to maintain a rewarding, intimate relationship.

15. Communication Is Fundamental To A Happy Relationship

Communication is hard work. That's why it's the secret to a stable relationship. When you want to connect well in a relationship, so not only do you have to learn how to bring out your thoughts, but you have to be able to listen to your friend genuinely. If you want to discover how to connect virtually in a relationship, follow these steps.

Making an Argument

Learn to know what you're talking about. We've seen jokes about the purpose and actual dialogue — when she says "this," she means — or, "what she's trying to tell you is..." Such jokes are amusing because of how much they're valid. Often, we want our spouse to grasp our hidden intentions. Still, it's not realistic or efficient to trust or rely on—instead, precisely layout your feelings.

When you make your point, provide clear explanations of what you say and make your comments more critical. Don't merely say, "I feel like you haven't done your share of the house..." Then, say, "I've had to do the dishes every night for the last two weeks..." Talk softly enough to enable your spouse to hear from you. Don't just confuse all your hurt thoughts, or he or she won't be able to understand your argument.

Note, there's no bonus for chatting for as long as you can. Reach all the essential notes you want to reach, but don't just speak and talk until your partner is exhausted.

Directly setting forward your feelings removes anger and doubt over your motivations. Instead of proposing solutions to your boyfriend's plans to introduce you to dance, tell him the truth: you simply don't want to see all those people after a rough week at work, followed by, "I'm sorry to say I'm just not in a party mood tonight." Use "I" or "you" phrases. Don't launch a fight by accusing your friend of making a mistake.

Having a conversation based on your emotions can help your husband feel less like he's being humiliated and more like he's part of a constructive discussion.

Just stating, "Lately, I've been feeling a little overlooked" feels more conciliatory than "You've been neglecting me." While you're trying to mean the same thing by "I" remarks, this soft-blow presentation may render your partner less aggressive and more able to interact freely.

Hold it as cool as you can. While you may not be as smooth as a cucumber when you and your partner are in the middle of a twitchy conversation, the calmer you are, the easier it is for you to express your feelings. If you get frustrated in the middle of a debate, or even livid until you address the topic, take a breath before feeling relaxed enough to continue a constructive discussion.

- Talk in a soft tone to express your thoughts.

- Don't speak to your friend about it. It is only working to make you more furious.

- Take a deep breath. Don't get hysteric in the middle of the debate.

Keep a supportive body language in place. Getting supportive body language will help to set a constructive tone for the conversation. Look at your friend in the head and turn your body around. You should use your arms to make a gesture, but don't push them so quickly that you're going to get out of hand. Don't fold your arms over your eyes, or your partner will believe like you're too oblivious to what he has to say.

Don't fidget with the things around you because that lets you get the nervous tension out of the way.

Produce ideas with confidence. That doesn't mean you're going to have to head through the conversation like you're off to a company conference. Try not to walk into the house, shake your partner's hand, and put forth a defense for yourself. Instead, bolster the venture by being as sure as possible with the circumstance. Grin now and then, talk delicately and don't stop, pose such a large number of inquiries, or sound befuddled of what you need to state. At the point when your companion has questions regarding your devotion to your feelings, he won't pay attention to you.

The more relaxed you are, the less likely you are to be afraid or dismayed. It is going to help you articulate your thoughts.

Have a game plan before you get going. Don't just step into the fight when you least foresee it and start showing your partner the 15 things he or she did wrong. Also, suppose you're frustrated or hurt for several reasons. In that case, it's crucial to concentrate on the fundamental argument that you want to make and to care about the result of the interaction that you want to achieve; if your whole aim is to make your friend feel guilty for what he or she has finished, then you can talk more about that before you continue.

Part of the approach will be when to resolve the matter. Bringing up a logical statement at an untimely moment, such as at a family barbecue or during a big sports event on television, will make the entire case null and void.

Thought of the particular reasons you're going to use to explain your argument. Let's just assume that you want your partner to be a better listener. Do you think about two or three times when he didn't care and hurt you? Don't bombard him or her with harsh feedback but use persuasive facts to get the support you deserve.

Consider what your aim is —ask your partner that you have been upset, bring about a big confrontation, find a solution that can make you all happier, or explore ways to cope with tension as a family. Holding your target in the back of your mind is going to help keep you on track.

Listening To Your Spouse

Put yourself in the role of your spouse. Use the power of imagination to grasp better what your partner's viewpoint could be in a given situation. Be mindful that there may be variables you don't know about. As he or she talks, putting yourself in his shoes may make you understand that your actions or the situation at hand can be upsetting for him. When you're mad or frustrated, it's hard to see past your side of the conflict. Still, this strategy will potentially help you achieve a quicker resolution.

Empathy will generally help you overcome a dilemma in your relationship. Emphasizing that you're trying to communicate by saying, "I know you need to be irritated because ..." or, "I know you've had a rough week at work ..." will make your spouse see that you're listening to their point of view as a context.

Putting yourself in your partner's position will help you justify your emotions and let him know that you understand his problems and respect his feelings.

Enable your partner the ability to work through internal conflict. While it's nice to be able to hash out all of your anger, sometimes your partner is always sorting out his emotions and feelings, and he wants more time to figure out his feelings for himself. Giving him time and space to think will keep him from rushing into the debate and doing something he regrets. There is a fine line between facilitating dialogue and pressuring your friend until he can speak and share.

Only saying, "I'm here anytime you need to talk," will make your spouse feel like you're taking care of him.

Give him or her all your energy. Know the signs that your partner needs to speak to — and that this is urgent. If he or she needs to chat, you need to shut off the television, switch off your work, cover your phone, and do whatever you can to give your friend your full attention. If you're multi-tasking or irritated, he or she is likely to get even more frustrated. If you're still in the middle of something, wonder if you should only tie things up for a few minutes, and you're less distracted when the time comes.

Instead of looking around at other items that could capture your attention, holding eye contact will also make your companion feel like you're listening.

Allow him or her to end, then nod your head or say, "I understand how you feel," to remain linked from time to time.

Let him end that. While he could suggest something ridiculous or something you feel that you just ought to fix, don't step in and disturb him while expressing his thoughts and feelings. Make a mental note on every issue that you believe you need to discuss after but let your spouse say everything that he has to say. When it's over, it's going to be your turn, so you can dive through these points one by one or opt to tackle them afterward, at a different moment.

This can sound nearly daunting because you feel like you just have to hop in and out and make a counter-argument, but your partner may feel much happier after he has it all off his chest.

Hold in mind the distance. If you listen to your friend, you will know that you don't have to acknowledge or appreciate everything that he has to say. No matter how compatible you are, how similar you are, and how consistent your priorities are, there will be instants when you don't see a scenario eye to eye, no matter how hard you all try to express your emotions. That's all right. – Being mindful of the difference between your perception of the situation and that of your husband will make you more open to what he has to say.

Being mindful of this disparity can make you feel less upset when you're not talking to each other.

Creating A Solid Base

Maintain anonymity. That doesn't mean you're going to jump into bed with your wife every chance you get to make up after fighting. This means that you can be as comfortable as you can, whether that means cuddling, caressing each other and smiling over nothing, or merely sharing time on the sofa with your hands and enjoying your favorite television shows. Allow time for affection at least a couple of days a week, no matter how busy you are — this can support you when the time comes to chat about the rough stuff.

Feeling relational has a more essential significance than being physical. It's about seeing someone else and wanting to create a space in your mind for your partner's words, body language, or acts.

16. Effects Of Anxiety On Relationships And How To Stop It

Anxiety is described as the act of having persistent and excessive worry. However, the issue with pressure goes far beyond a single concern. If an individual were only dealing with one fear, it probably would not seem like a big deal. Unfortunately, people who have anxiety disorders, more specifically generalized anxiety disorder, tend to be swarmed by one worry that leads to another concern, then another, and so on. This explains why anxiety is a cycle.

Worries are also what keeps that cycle going around and around. Even though a person might be experiencing a concern that could be solved, the matter continues for multiple reasons. The first reason for why is that some of a person's worries can fall under the category of biased thinking. This could mean an individual is giving too much weight to the likelihood that a negative outcome will occur. Narrow thinking can also tell a person is exaggerating how bad the negative result will end up being.

Some types of worries are strengthened by the negative thoughts that a person has about themselves, like the person cannot cope with any unfavorable outcome.

The second reason people might find their worries continuing to take up most of their thoughts is that some concerns persist because of how certain information in an environment goes about being processed. Someone who suffers from generalized anxiety disorder will sometimes selectively choose to look into the data that will support their worries while ignoring any information that refutes their worrying thoughts.

Memories can also be selective, just like a person's worries. In some instances, people who have anxiety issues have difficulty remembering any data that portrays a contradiction to the particular concern they are currently dealing with.

The third possible reason why an individual's worries might be persistent is how they respond to those worries.

Someone who has an untreated anxiety disorder might react to their fears by trying one of three things. They might attempt to suppress their concerns, seek reassurance that nothing negative will happen, or they could end up avoiding a situation the triggers their fear.

The greatest downfall to choosing any of those responses is that any of those strategies will make a person feel horrible, which will lead to their worries being reinforced. This all ends up making the person's anxiety cycle extremely difficult to break shortly down the line.

However, with the right mindset and some helpful changes in a person's thoughts and behaviors, someone can break their anxiety cycle. A simple example of a negative review can help prepare people to begin breaking the cycle of anxiety.

Even though that thought may be expected for a person to have, someone who suffers from extreme anxiety would give that thought too much weight and meaning. This leads to the person mulling over all of the possible reasons why their opinion could become real. The person will try to lessen their anxiety in the short-term. Unfortunately, when a person tries to reduce their stress in the short-term, this only makes that same anxiety stronger in the long-term.

In this case, the belief is that a person's boyfriend will break up with them- becomes that much more significant and is experienced a lot more regularly. The opinion will also be much more intense than it would be for someone who does not have an anxiety problem.

The above points are some of the significant reasons why a person should overcome their anxiety by breaking its cycle. The first strategy to doing so is for the person to accept that not each thought a person had warranted an actual reason to become worried. Not every thought that a person has is going to be true.

Rather than battle with one's negative beliefs, they should start focusing on acceptance-based techniques that involve identifying the negative thought they are having and putting a label on it. The title might be that the review is a worry or a judgment. The person should also be trying to show mindfulness when the belief first comes out and at the particular moment when the idea begins to fade from the person's awareness.

The after that strategy for breaking the cycle of anxiety is to begin raising the right questions.

The way a person goes about doing so is to sever the link between their biases created from their thoughts and gathered information. The person's process is called cognitive restructuring, which is the foundation for the treatment approach known as cognitive-behavioral therapy.

The cognitive restructuring allows an individual to evaluate any possible distorted thought they might be having critically. The cognitive restructuring comes into play when the individual begins asking themselves a series of questions about the belief that will result in a more balanced view of all of the relevant facts a person needs to make their thoughts more rational.

The cognitive restructuring process will take a bit of time, but the results will be worth it in the end. The first step to restructuring one's thoughts is to learn how to notice when one is having their distorted reflections. However, it is best to only focus on one type of cognitive distortion at a time. A few examples of distorted thoughts include mindreading, personalizing, underestimated coping abilities, catastrophizing, and entitlement beliefs.

The second step to cognitive restructuring is for an individual to begin keeping track of how accurate their thoughts are. For instance, a person could think about how thinking about their problem will help them find a problem.

When the week's finale comes around, the person should determine what percentage of time their overthinking led to them conducting some useful problem-solving moments.

A person could also choose to record the estimated number of minutes they spent overthinking when they noticed when it occurred. This approach can allow a person to see how many minutes of overthinking they did in succession with their useful problem-solving moments.

The third step for cognitive restructuring is for a person to find out a way to test their thoughts behaviorally. During the second week, the individual is asked to take a five-minute break every hour. They are also invited to do the same rating at the end of each day that week. At the end of the second week, the person will look at the ratings for both weeks one and two and compare their productivity ratings.

The afterward step in the cognitive restructuring process is for an individual to evaluate all evidence that strengthens and weakens a particular thought.

Like tracking the accuracy of one's thoughts, the person can write down their objective evidence, which supports the view that they cannot get something right in one column and put the factual evidence that supports the idea that their thought is not right in the second column.

Once the individual has done this, they would then want to write out a few balanced thoughts that accurately reflect their evidence. It is okay for a person to not wholly believe in their new idea that proves their original negative idea to be wrong. It is merely essential to start experimenting with trying out thoughts that poke holes in their negative thinking.

Mindfulness meditation is the following step to cognitive restructuring. During this process, a person picks a focus of attention, for example, their breathing. Then, for a certain number of minutes, the person will have to put all of their attention on the sensations they are experiencing while they are breathing, rather than merely thinking about the fact that they are living.

Whenever the person finds that they have any other thoughts other than the sensations that go along with their breathing, they are asked to gently- and without any self-judgment- return their focus to their feelings while breathing.

While mindfulness meditation is not explicitly a tool used for cognitive restructuring, it is a great tool to train a person to become mindful and aware of when they become too wrapped up in their thoughts. When someone can reach conscious awareness about their ideas, it becomes an essential starting point in the cognitive restructuring process.

The final step to the cognitive restructuring process is for a person to learn how to utilize self-compassion. When a person has self-compassion, that means they can talk to themselves in a kind manner, even when they find that they are going through some form of suffering at that moment.

Like mindfulness meditation, self-compassion is not particular distinctly used in cognitive restructuring; however, that does not mean that self-compassion is not highly effective for cognitive restructuring.

This means the person is still acknowledging that they made a mistake and embarrassed by that mistake. Still, the event was also part of the typical human experience.

As a result, the person will find that since they replace their self-judgment in exchange for the self-compassion approach, their thoughts will also begin to change over time. A person may even notice that their thoughts regarding other people become more empathetic and accepting along the way too.

The last tip for overcoming the cycle of anxiety is to expose oneself to the part of life that causes their pressure to come out. With exposure, a person can learn how to break away from the anxious thoughts once they can eliminate their reliance on futile anxiety reduction strategies.

The exposure process centers around an individual's ability to lean into their anxiety when they confront the root of their fear rather than attempting to avoid what makes them anxious. This is important because when individuals choose to ignore their anxiety-provoking instances, they cannot see what facing their fears can show them. When a person encounters an anxiety-provoking situation head-on, they will likely conclude that nothing wrong will happen, or the lousy outcome that does occur is much more manageable than they initially thought. There may even be cases where the work leads to an upside.

17. Believing In Your Partner

When somebody does something you don't like or doesn't meet your expectations, you're very likely to forgive them. If they repeat the mistake or do something similar, then your understanding and hope begin to head from the window. After that, your partner is frequently reminded of the inability to keep their word, and they're judged according to what happened. The relationship changes and the guilty partner might find him/herself reluctant to invest in it, as the outcomes aren't always positive.

When you stop allowing your partner to redeem themselves, then you've undoubtedly also stopped believing in him/her. Whatever they may tell you, a little voice in your head will start reminding you that you should not trust them. Then, before you realize what happened, there will be frustration, discord, and pain in your relationship.

That's the point where you start to become suspicious, and your ideas can negatively influence your activities. Sometimes you might believe that your partner did something, even if you've got zero proof to back up your thesis; many of the things they say seem to be a lie.

If they don't act how you expect, you may believe they are intentionally dishonest. You'll continuously end up checking for anything out of the ordinary.

Jealousy stems from a lack of confidence and fear, and it induces insecurity and nervousness in the relationship. Whenever you're jealous, insecure, and nervous, you're permanently on the watch for unproven lies or inconsistencies out of your partner. You patiently wait for them to slide up, proving that your concerns were set. Your feelings are rooted in fear, and even though you attempt to find proof to back up your ideas, you do it with your heart continuously racing because of hope.

You wish to understand "the facts," yet you're reluctant to do so. So why are you fearful? Jealous individuals fear more than merely losing their partner. They fear to lose their self-respect along with others' esteem.

They're scared of being laughed at by their peers. They might also be fearful of appearing naïve and absurd.

First and foremost, they might fear they will eventually wind up entirely alone. This mostly happens where cheating has occurred before.

However, unconfounded jealousy is harmful to an existing relationship, and it'll continue to irritate you unless you treat it today.

Strategies For Trusting On Your Partner

What we mentioned until now is an excellent way to start putting your relationship on the ideal path. The truth is that both parties of a couple have trust issues.

What both of you have to do is to find out how to trust each other. One of the best ways to start doing it is to believe on your own. In reality, trusting yourself is the first thing that anyone must consider when seeking to address any trust issues, and that makes sense since if you do not trust yourself, you're never likely to trust someone else.

Another thing to consider is what precisely does trust mean. Frequently trust problems are made because we have a different idea about what confidence means. Not only this, but you also have unique relationships. Since it's never the same, you have to speak openly and understand with your partner so that you may find together what precisely confidence means in your relationship.

If it comes to trust your loved one, you will have to have a critical look at yourself, and no, we aren't talking about believing in yourself. All you have to know when it comes to trust problems is that they often turn into an issue because you're struggling with some type of questions. For example, if you're concerned about your partner cheating on you, it might be associated with you having ideas about cheating them.

If you genuinely wish to build confidence with your partner, you will have an open relationship. By genuine, we are talking about being honest with each other, no more hiding things. Speak to one another about what's happening. The greater your communication, the better chance you've got at saving your relationship.

And remember that you need to give to get. Trust isn't just a one-sided thing; if you reveal a lack of confidence towards your partner, he/she will demonstrate a lack of confidence in you as well. By believing each other, you're likely to see your confidence problems fading away rapidly.

Trust-Building Exercises

As simple as trusting your partner may sound, it is not that simple, especially if some problems have started to irritate your complete relationship. After the trust has been broken, it can be too complicated to reconstruct it, but not impossible.

Trust-building exercises may help to build it back again, but they may also be used to earn a fantastic and healthier relationship. If you're all set to focus on fixing these problems, below are a few very efficient exercises you should try.

Fall Back

Probably this is the most known one, as everyone has heard about it, but also the most difficult one to execute, even if you fully trust your partner. This exercise requires that you stand facing your spouse and just let yourself fall back, expecting them to grab you.

If you're successful, do it again but with a further distance between the two of you; if it's possible to accomplish that, your relationship is worth saving.

Walking Blindfolded

During the time you're blindfolded, have your companion take you for a stroll around an area that's filled with different obstacles. They can direct you through the room with a small touch or verbal instructions. As a variation, you can try this exercise outside. To complete this practice, you'll need to have complete trust in your partner, and, same as for the first example, achieving to complete this will help you build even more confidence in your relationship, or build one if you lost yours.

Filling In The Blanks

This exercise is not only attractive but also quite entertaining. You're going to need two sheets of paper; on the first one, you want to write down a couple of sentences on how you feel about your partner. On the second piece of paper, write down the same penalties, and remove adjectives, verbs, and feelings. Then, have your girlfriend/boyfriend fill in the blanks.

This practice is of different utilities for couples: it permits you to find out exactly what your partner feels about you, but besides, it lets you openly express your feelings on him/her; it's an excellent way to assist in improving communication between you and your loved one, as you're able to say things which you may not otherwise express to your other half. Remember that these exercises are not only about positive annotations, as you're likely to encounter some negative ones also. The meaning of this practice is to help you and your partner fix and improve your relationship.

Eye Contact

Many individuals don't see the importance of eye contact; it's fundamental for building trust in a relationship. It helps communication between you and your wife/husband, but many couples do not understand how to get it done. Here's an excellent way to do it: begin with standing face to face with your partner, about a foot away from one another.

Look into each other's eyes without smiling or making any sort of faces for like 60 seconds. If you can accomplish this, move closer. Now repeat it. Once you start feeling how strong your bond with your partner is, step back till you're about two feet away from one another and repeat the process once more. Notice how the bond now is not as powerful as before at this distance; the feelings of trust will also be lower.

When Your Partner Doesn't Trust You

These exercises are great for helping to establish trust in a relationship. But what can you do if your partner doesn't trust you? You may indicate that you participate in these exercises, even though it's very likely you won't end up with the solution to the problem.

Maybe you did something that broke your partner's confidence towards you; perhaps you didn't do anything in any way. Whatever the situation, you have to have the ability to build confidence back. Below are a few suggestions which should help your partner to trust you again and improve your connection.

Apologize

In case you did something wrong, ensure you being the recovery procedure with a sincere apology.

Take accountability for your actions and give any explanations that whatsoever justify what you'd done wrong. By apologizing, your goal isn't to decrease the seriousness of the matter. Instead, it's to be sure your partner sees that you are genuinely sorry and ready to make the proper actions to increase your relationship.

Patience

Don't expect your partner to get up, accept your apology, and move ahead instantly. It will take time to return to normal, and also for your partner to trust you again. Don't push your loved one for a quick resolution. This might backfire on you, trying your partner farther away instead of getting him/her closer; it could be seen as disrespectful. In no way will this help your attempts.

Empathize

Put yourself in your partner's shoes and think of how you'd respond to a similar scenario that affected trust. Would you blame your partner for getting that response? You have to be comprehensive, to show your partner that you admit the pain you could have given them, and you would be happy to do what's needed to move past the pain and rebuild the relationship.

18. Cultivating Self Awareness

A) Know Your Buttons

Emotions don't just happen. Happiness, joy, sadness, anger, love, or hate are all things we feel react to something else. Learn to identify the things that push your buttons, giving you a better insight into your emotions.

For instance, if you have abandonment issues from childhood, always examine your emotions to make sure that what you are feeling is related to your current relationship and not an extension of emotional baggage from your past.

Many people who have had poor relationships in the past carry these scars into their subsequent relationships. It is common to find that someone cheated on in the past has trouble trusting their partner. This happens because our experiences tend to shape our beliefs, and they become the triggers that set us up to revert to familiar patterns of behavior.

When you do not know what triggers your negative emotions, you will be in a constant anxiety state. Stop taking your feelings at face value and question your beliefs. Why do I think this way? Why am I so angry, is my jealousy justified? This kind of self-reflection will help you get to the root of your emotions and understand what triggers you.

Journaling is a great way to cultivate self-awareness. Writing things down will not only help work through your feelings, but it will also give you a record that allows you to get an idea of how you feel when certain things happen. Keeping a journal will prompt you to explore your emotions at a deeper level.

Personality tests can also help you understand your innate tendencies and emotions better. Once you know where your feelings are coming from, you can achieve better emotional balance, and your relationship will benefit greatly from this.

B) Switch Off The Auto Pilot

Do you find yourself listening to someone and not being able to recall anything they said five minutes after?

Life can be busy, and we often get caught up in the hustle and bustle of keeping all the balls rolling. When you are operating on autopilot, you are absent-minded and rarely present in the moment.

You may be preoccupied with your phone, the children, or work. When this happens, most of your relationship starts happening without you paying attention. Then one day, you wake up, and you have no idea how things got so bad. The danger of being preoccupied is that you do not even realize when things start to go wrong until it is too late.

Making your relationship a priority and setting time aside to spend with your partner will keep you in touch with each other. When you cultivate a sense of mindfulness, it allows you to be fully present in the moment. You can effectively switch off your worry about the future or the past and simply enjoy the moment by practicing mindfulness.

Many people miss great moments in their lives because they do not merely smell the roses. It is so easy to get caught up in worrying about tomorrow and miss the present moment. When you cannot unplug from life and make time for your relationship, you risk creating emotional distance between you and your partner.

Switch off the phone, get off your laptop, and turn off the emotional roller coaster in your mind long enough to spend some quality time with your partner. Healthy relationships take two people who are actively engaging with each other and paying attention to their relationship. Set aside time to be with your partner, free from distractions and other people. This way, you will always have a connection to each other regardless of what is going on in your lives.

C) Seek Feedback

It may be uncomfortable to see yourself through other people's eyes, but seeking feedback may help you uncover things you may not be aware of yourself. Close friends and family have seen us at our worst and our best, and they know some of the traits that make us who we are. Seeking feedback from the close to you will help you build up your level of self-awareness.

Ask your partner what he thinks are your best qualities and what he thinks your triggers are. Not only will you get to know each other better in the process, but you will get an insight into how your partner sees you.

Getting feedback is not always comfortable, but sometimes it's the only way to get an objective insight into your behavior. To make it easier, talk to people who you trust and have a close relationship with. They are more likely to be honest with you since they also want the best for you.

19. Relationship Obsessive-Compulsive Disorder

Relationship obsessive-compulsive disorder (ROCD) is also known as Relationship Substantiation, a subcategory of OCD. It manifests when doubts about a relationship consume a person. Most people recognize it during significant relationship milestones such as moving in together or when they are about to get married. And if there is even a little doubt whether their partner is the right one or whether their marriage will last, it can cause the person to spiral.

OCD is known for having its ups and downs, and you might not even be aware of it as people are often quick to disregard what troubles them. Usually, OCD is triggered when a significant change happens or is about to happen. Marriage is one of these massive changes, and that is why ROCD might come to life at that moment.

A person who suffers from ROCD often questions his partner's motivation as well as his own. He must be sure that they are perfect for each other, and he will obsess about it. He often thinks, "Who will guarantee to me that he/she is the one" and he will continuously search for evidence to support the claim that his partner is the right choice. Such a person will continually ask his family and friends if they like their partner. He will exhaust himself by reading articles about the perfect relationship to acknowledge that he fits the picture.

Most people eagerly talk about a marriage planned for the future, but they can start questioning the relationship as the date nears. Coming up with reasons why they aren't a good match, delaying the marriage to find more proof that the choice is right. By no means does this mean that he or she doesn't love you anymore. ROCD happens for various reasons, and it's not always due to a lack of love.

Relationship OCD is no different from any other subcategory of OCD. They are all the product of intrusive thoughts that demand clarification, order, and confirmation. Most couples have similar views, and it is customary to question your relationship from time to time. It is entirely normal to feel different levels of attraction towards your partner during your relationship.

ROCD is diagnosed with anxiousness triggered by such thoughts and whose connection is literally hijacked by and no longer functioning correctly.

There are two types of ROCD that we can distinguish. One concentrates on the relationship, and the other is on your partner. Keep in mind that both types can occur at the same time. No matter which one you have, your ordinary life can be interrupted with the same intensity. When focused on the relationship, R-OCD can make you question whether your partner is the right one, or if the relationship will last, and if it will be happy and healthy. However, if it is focused on your partner, you might question their abilities and personality. You might wonder whether your partner is intelligent, attractive, or capable enough for your standards.

Symptoms

The difference between occasional and chronic doubt in a relationship is that everyone experiences it. It's just if ROCD is manifesting itself as a response to intrusive thoughts. A person suffering from this affliction will perform repetitive, ritualistic actions that are considered compulsive to relieve anxiety.

These Are The Most Common Symptoms Of ROCD:

- Seeking constant reassurance about your relationship or partner: compulsively asking others their opinion and views on your relationship. You may even want to ask your partner what they think about the relationship and love.

- Seeking evidence: An OCD person often needs evidence confirming that this is the right one. In other words, he needs proof that love is real. He will compulsively question himself whether he is attracted to his partner enough to validate the relationship.

- Extreme comparison: Compulsively comparing your partner to your ex or someone else in general. Some people can even compare the relationship to a fictional one from a movie or journal.

Another symptom of ROCD is the constant probing of your thoughts about your partner and relationship. You will examine them, observe them, and ask yourself if your emotions are real or strong enough.

When it comes to ROCD symptoms, it often feels like your brain's stuck on a loop. You behave irrationally, and even if you are aware of it, you probably lack control and cannot stop. Keep in mind that this condition still requires a great deal of research, as specialists haven't yet unlocked everything there is to know about it. However, the risks for developing OCD can be found in family genes or your childhood development.

Some believe that OCD is acquired through time; therefore, it cannot be unlearned. It is a physical problem with the brain's functionality, except the exact source of the problem is difficult to find to start treating it properly. Behavioral therapists have had success in reducing OCD symptoms and manage to influence their patients to take control of their lives once again.

Many will agree that the source of ROCD lies infrequent thoughts of the relationship when it comes to psychotherapy.

Thinking, "What if he is not right for me?" is an ordinary thought that occurs to everyone. But if you keep returning to this thought and over-analyze, this is referred to as habitual thinking. Your ideas count as experiences, and as you develop, your brain learns from experiences. Continually returning to this intrusive thought, you teach your mind, leading to behavioral problems.

Treating ROCD

Many people combine cognitive behavioral therapy, mindfulness training, and anxiety management training to overcome obsessive-compulsive relationship disorder.

Cognitive-behavioral therapy (CBT) will help with the obsessiveness you experience while having intrusive thoughts, and it will also help you manage your compulsive behavior. CBT can help you achieve balance in your thought processes as it will teach you how to reason and how not to give in to the urge to repeat the same harmful behaviors that follow ROCD.

Mindfulness training can teach you how to let go of your harmful, obsessive thoughts. As mentioned earlier, the whole ROCD problem lies in intrusive thoughts, and you need to learn how to manage them properly and let them go.

However, anxiety management training is an essential part of overcoming ROCD.

Learning how to manage the change in your behavior is playing a crucial role in the healing process. Treating ROCD is not easy, and it demands hard work and a great deal of thought and behavior change on your part. Keep in mind that this change might impact you negatively and even deepen your anxieties related to ROCD. For treatment to have full effect, it is vital to learn how to deal with change.

CBT, mindfulness, and anxiety treatment give even better results when combined with" exposure with response prevention" treatment. The goal of ERP therapy is to expose the patient to situations or thoughts that trigger their ROCD and prevent them from reacting in the ways they are used to. In time, the patient will face and successfully deal with the most feared situations that can trigger his ROCD.

If you notice any of the ROCD symptoms in you or a loved one, take it seriously. It is a condition that doesn't come easily to the suffering, and it is nothing to be ashamed of. If your symptoms are severe, seek professional help and even approved medicines that help treat ROCD.

20. Are You Feeling Insecure?

One of the most significant problems in which I see people fight is fear. This is mainly why I have devoted a great deal of my life to researching self-conscious thinking and perceptions with "conscious inner voices." It's not shocking that one of the most common self-attacks I have seen recorded in decades of study is, I'm different from everyone else. "It's incredible to feel left out and low about ourselves, with studies estimating that 85 % of people suffer from little self-esteem. Those of us who feel insecure may feel isolated, but we are in the majority.

One of the issues I have been grappling with in recent times is how current events influence oneself. Insecurity may be compounded when people spend a lot of time in their minds and alone. The longer they are alone, the more they slip into fear for others who feel uncomfortable about social or personal experiences. While our situations can be different, the ways to understand and resolve anxiety are the same. My approach to uncertainty mainly includes discussing two key concepts: attachment theory and the theory of separation.

Attachment Theory And Insecurity

Our attachment experience plays a significant role in the degree of comfort we feel in life, in our relationships, and within ourselves. The first patterns of connection that we had with our primary caregivers serve as a blueprint for how we expect relationships to function throughout our lives and inform our sense of identity. We are firmly attached to them if we feel protected, soothed, and seen by our parents or caretakers. However, if our parents can't cope with us and fix relationship fractures, we can build an unsecured attachment pattern. In infancy, unstable attachment habits are nervous and anxious, anxiously resisting attachment, and disorganized attachment.

A child with an Anxious-Anxious relationship can have an irregular parent who is more emotional than caring. The child will adapt by turning the volume on its needs and focusing on the parent. They try to get the parent's needs by grasping, screaming, or ordering. Since the parent is there emotionally sometimes and sometimes not, the child feels anxious, much as the parent wants to care about them, this pattern leaves a person uncertain whether they can rely on others. They internalize a feeling of fear and depression. As adults, you prefer to seek partners that are emotionally unreliable and circumstances in which you sometimes feel hurt. While this is difficult, your inner working model is familiar to you and confirms how others treat you. People also contribute to this process by continuous reassurance by seeking attention from their partners.

A child develops an evasive relationship if a parent is unable to fulfill their needs and emotionally inaccessible. The child adapts to escape the traumatic experience of voicing a necessity and having nobody respond by suppressing knowledge of their own needs. Since the child can't afford to see the parent as faulty and lose its protection, it falls like they don't matter, which is disgraceful. The child learns to control himself and to be self-parent. They will then grow up to feel pseudo-independent and burdened by other people's needs. They always look for a partner with "healthy" feelings and anxiety needs. This choice increases their internalized understanding of the market for them to take care of themselves and of the need for others who express themselves. However, an avoidant is always dangerous when they feel overwhelmed and cannot continue attempting to ignore their needs.

A child develops a disorganized relationship when a parent is frightened of them or when the child is frightened or confused and scared. Such a parent induces uncertainty without a solution. The child wants to go to them for protection, but they have to run when they're near. This leaves a child without a coordinated plan to meet its needs. As a result, they build the fear of others internalizing and, at the same time, the fear of being without other people. Their insecurities can feel daunting because they are traumatic.

These unstable attachment patterns, developed in our first relationships, often manifest in an unsafe adult attachment that significantly affects our romantic relations and parenthood and informs how we feel. Suppose we are more convinced to understand our fear individually. In that case, we must be prepared to go back to our history of attachment, which gives us vital clues as to why we believe, feels, and acts in our way of doing things, why we remain unsafe and why we always put ourselves and our needs into a negative light.

Separation Theory And Insecurity

The psychologist, and author Robert Firestone developed separation theory.

The theory shows how traumatic early childhood experiences, in conjunction with existential consciousness, lead people to psychological defenses. Defenses that suit real situations, e.g., denial, neglect, emotional deprivation, or harassment of a parent, which initially harmed a person's self, continue to harm or restrict the sense of self throughout their lives.

A child internalizes its parents' negative attitudes to them, and the complicated ways parents view themselves. Since a young child depends on the parent for survival, it feels too unsafe to break away from the parent's perspective or see its shortcomings. Instead, children internalize the negative behaviors and values of their parents as their own. For example, the child can see himself as unwanted or unlovable if a parent is misplaced or unavailable. If a kid responds as if he is too loud or insecure, he may see himself as an odd or burden.

A child's negative core beliefs form an inner dialogue, known as the essential internal voice. This "voice" becomes a lifelong critique, perpetuating most of his vulnerability. As we walk through various stages of life, we feel this filter. The critical inner voice adds to certain negative characteristics that suit an early self-image. When we pursue a relationship, our inner critic will say, "You're never going to find someone who loves you. If we become parents, it may say, "You can't deal with this. You 're too unattracted / bound / unsecure / unworthy / unworthy." When it comes to our jobs or aspirations, you can tell us, "You're not talented/capable/smart/noticeable." You're a horrible mother/father.

Even when it is a pandemic, the voice will reach us with a broad range of attacks that intensify our struggles. "You don't know what you are doing, what you are doing. You're not at this. Your children hate you. Your children hate you. You'll lose your job. You will always be lonely. You'll mess up and get sick. Whatever the situation we are in and whatever we say to you, it is worth remembering that the critical inner voice is the core feelings we have experienced or witnessed in ways that affect us very early in our lives. If we are to reinforce and go beyond these old beliefs, we have to consider and question them and how they are woven into our sense of self.

Looking at our history will help us shed light on our negative conception of ourselves. Knowing the root of our vulnerability will motivate us from the ground up to question them.

21. Social Anxiety, Fear and Relationship

Social Anxiety

You want to do your best to gain control of your anxiety. When you are anxious, it is harder to focus on what you need to do. You are worried about how every step you take in the healing process will affect your journey. Anxiety makes you rethink every decision, and you begin to focus more on the past and worry about the future. This causes you to fear what could happen when taking part in your process's specific steps. For example, over the last few months, you are not happy with the person you have become. You feel overly stressed, which causes you to lash out at the people you love the most verbally. You have a short fuse, so you want to start your healing process because part of your stress is all of your emotions. You have not worked through your feelings over the last few months, so they have continued to build up. As you reflect on the previous few months, you start to remember several of the arguments you and your significant other had. You retain all the times they threatened to leave you and how you told them that it doesn't matter to you because you are so unhappy with the way things are. You are now worried that you already drove your partner away, and there is no way to repair the damage.

Instead of talking to your partner and discussing your realization and working on healing yourself, you start to have panic attacks when they don't come home immediately after work. They used to always come home on time as you would have your evening meal as a family. Your significant other says they are working late, have a business meeting, or hang out with a co-worker. You start to assume that your partner is cheating and become more anxious about the situation. You wonder how you will bring this up and if your partner will be honest about what is going on.

Your anxiety makes it hard to talk to your significant other because you are afraid of the answer. You imagine the worst possible scenario. Finally, a few weeks afterward, you dare to bring up your concerns and discuss your plan to heal the relationship.

To your relief, your partner opens up and tells you that they never cheated on you, but they didn't always want to come home because of the way things have been.

Anxiety causes your emotions to go up and down, making it hard to control them. This is why it is essential to do what you can to turn your anxiety off. You will struggle with your anxiety from time to time. But, through strategies and focusing on what you can do to decrease your stress, you will guide yourself into a robust emotional healing process.

Fear

When it comes to starting something new in our life, we are sometimes a bit fearful because we don't know what will happen. This fear escalates as we go through anxiety and start to wonder if we are making the right decision. No matter who you are, there is always a little bit of fear when it comes to the unknown. Fortunately, it is still possible to work through and overcome this fear.

One of the first steps you need to overcome your fear to tell yourself, "There is nothing to fear." No matter what happens along your spiritual journey, you are working towards creating a better life. You are trying to reach your best self, and this is a crucial moment in your life. Anyone who strives to do their best, no matter what they are up against, is a healthy person and will accomplish anything they set their mind to. The key is to believe in yourself, as this will decrease your fear.

Another way to overcome your fear is by understanding that suspicion is reasonable. Like most people, you probably have a negative understanding of anxiety and believe that when you feel afraid, you are taking part in something that you shouldn't, or you need to be more cautious because of the way you are feeling. When you look at fear as a positive sign, you grow by becoming comfortable with a part of your life that you did feel uncomfortable with. You need to be painful to reach success. If you remain comfortable, you won't continue to grow, and you will be in the same spot for the rest of your life.

Empath Relationship

Close relationships are challenging for most people, whether they are an empath or not. A lot of effort goes into making a relationship work. It doesn't matter if you are friends, dating, or married.

Intimate relationships are especially challenging for empaths because they notice every shift within the person's mood. They see when their significant other is not telling them the truth or off within the relationship. Even if the reason your significant other is not acting like they usually do because of stress at work or within their family, it will still heavily affect you. As long as they communicate, you will understand that the problem is external, but this won't help your emotions. It won't keep you from feeling how they are feeling. You might find yourself struggling because you can't help them.

Another problem for empaths and intimate relationships is your home is no longer your sanctuary. You need to share it with another person, causing you to become overwhelmed as you don't know where to go to get your alone time. If you cannot get the time you need to recharge your abilities, rid the negative energy, and recharge, you will find yourself struggling mentally, emotionally, and physically. You might start to feel depressed or notice more negative thoughts. You can become physically ill.

This doesn't mean that you should stay away from intimate relationships. There is a lot of empaths who are happily married to their own family. The trick is you need to find a balance and continue to take your alone time—and as much as you need. This is harder when you have younger children, but by communicating openly with your significant other, you can reach this balance and find yourself living a healthy and happy lifestyle. Not every day will be perfect. Some days you will need a more extended break than other days. When these days come, you must take them without feeling guilty. This is easier said than done, but you must get to a psychological state where you can take time to watch a movie and not feel guilty about it because you know it is essential to keep your balance healthy.

22. Dealing With Anxiety When Repairing Relationships

It is no secret that we, the people, rely on social ties. Even if we say we're not at all social. People prefer to have friends and family with whom they talk stuff, also though it's as easy to talk about a trip to buy food. We work better with support. Our moods improve, and our ability to deal with stress also increases. Therefore, it must go without saying that any connection we meet in any way affects us, from relative foreigners to close friends and families. Taking the time to strengthen all relationships would boost the mood and build a better sense of well-being.

You should learn how to build partnerships and use these techniques more and more. Above all, we will discuss romantic relationships as these impact our mental health most. We will learn how to cope with the loss of a relationship that sometimes leads to anxiety or depression.

Why Does Your Emotion Relate To A Relationship?

If you're nervous or sad, you're concerned about what counts. Any partnership is put on the back burner. Your attention is on your issues and concerns. All this stress and distress exhaust you physically and emotionally, and the people who care about you fail to support you. If they are unsuccessful, they become depressed and powerless, causing them to step away from you. Set aside some effort to respond to the accompanying inquiries about a meaningful relationship in your life to see if depression or anxiety is harmful.

- Have I taken a friendship away? What are the ways?

- Did I get less affectionate? What are the ways?

- Did I get more critical or irritable? Which are the ways?

- Am I less empathetic or less complimentary? What are the ways?

As always, it's not black and white. There can also be other reasons why a relationship doesn't work.

Check with specialists in mental health, specialized in pair therapy. Digging deeper into your relationship: Have you ever heard a child say the first time you have a pet? They explain how well the animal is being handled. How well they can eat and walk and clean it up after it. So parents take care of the new burden their child has discovered and gone out and get a cat. The first week is excellent. The child does just the same as they say.

Nonetheless, by the end of a third or fourth week, the parents are more washed or fed and have to ask the pet to walk or take care of it in another way. The excitement of the animal and its enthusiasm are disrupted by life and complacency. It is not that this kid has gone astray, but rather that life has predominated. Relationships begin similarly. We look forward to sharing time with someone else and loving it very much. We laugh and congratulate each other, and then we intervene one day and begin to forget our duty. We fail to make arrangements or to call. The lack of consideration is responsible for the relationship. We build relationships with constructive behavior and words, and the techniques you learn will help you strengthen almost every relationship.

Communication is the foundation of which relationships are established. Excellent communication is essential for all our relationships because it is safe, and it keeps us free from stress. We are doing a few exercises to create such a healthy atmosphere. First of all, the Daily Bulletin is renamed. That is when you take the time to talk to your friend and listen to him. The goal is to enhance intimacy and should be done regularly.

- Check with your friend to decide when to sit and discuss the activities for 20 minutes.

- The target is regular, but 3-4 times is also excellent.

- Commit yourself to meetings and have them published so you can all see them.

- Let your partner continue and chat for 10 minutes.

- Ask questions, nod your head, and make short remarks to help them understand how they feel.

- After they have finished talking, try to summarize positively what they said.

- Ask your friend if you guess correctly, and if you don't, ask for clarity.

- Take time to share your day with your friend and ask them to obey the same rules.

Take the time to talk about how you feel before and after and how much more you understand each other. The second exercise reminds you of the power of congratulations. It's hard to think about other people when you're nervous or sad and how much you love them, but without mentioning that will make them feel unappreciated, and the relationship suffers. Taking a moment to compose your partner's top stuff you admire.

- Write down everything you love and respect your partner first. Include things such as skills, intellect, focus, support, etc., and be accurate.

- Compliment your spouse on the list you have created or create a new one at least once a day.

- Build a plan every day to accomplish this mission. Give yourself a habit of complimenting others.

After a few weeks of feedback, think about any changes in the relationship. If you can't think of anything, your friendship is in deep trouble with your partner. Having a broken partner can be devastating if a company is broken. Life is imperfect, and people are flawed. Often, death's suffering is due to certain factors, such as divorce, divorce, or a partnership that dissolves. In any case, the diagnosis of a loss induces stress and occasionally depression.

It is essential that you still take care of yourself when you lose a loved one. Make sure you eat and sleep and remain well because sorrows are both emotional and physical, and you're going to use all the energy to do so. Make sure you ask for assistance. You may look for help from friends and family, religious outlets, organizations voicing complaints, or experts in mental health. When coping with a loved one's death, you don't need to hole in the bed or resort to drugs that only make things more challenging but instead think about the person you've lost. Examine the relationship and the sense of the individual. This method leads you on.

Take the time to look at the following complaint questionnaire to help you discuss your concern. Taking as much time and don't try to answer questions. Expect to feel depressed or even sob, but please seek support if you think you can't handle the exercise at all.

- How was this person's life?

- What have you cherished about that person?

- What's been challenging about that person?

- What lessons have I learned from this positive and negative relationship?

- So what has changed in my life?

- What am I grateful for in this connection?

- What am I most upset about?

- What was this friendship I enjoyed?

Give the guy you missed a letter to close. Say whatever is in your mind.

It is irreplaceable to become warnings and the connections we share with them. That said, it is essential to pick up the pieces and move on and fill your life with meaningful relationships and activities after you experience a loss and take your time to grieve and recover. Take the time to help people out. It will make you feel better and more natural. Chat a little more. Again, it becomes social. Interacting with the people around you will undoubtedly help you to recover. Go out and do something good for you. Also, if you don't feel ready, try to do something that makes you happy. Enable yourself to rejuvenate.

23. Building A Secure Future

The Long Haul

Building healthy relationships is an ongoing, lifelong process. Even people who tend toward the secure attachment style will have ups and downs and will encounter new relationship dynamics that test their strengths. The best thing any of us can do is stay in touch with those parts of ourselves that still struggle with anxious or avoidant attachment and keep using the resources we need to heal. Understanding and healing your attachment insecurity has the potential to affect all your relationships positively.

Modern science doesn't yet know everything about the brain. Still, there is broad agreement that this complex organ mainly evolved to enable us to have relationships and communicate with others. It's natural for us to seek the support of others from birth throughout the life span. It's what our brains were meant to do. But attachment insecurity and learned behavior patterns of anxiety and avoidance get in the way of safety and trust in these relationships.

The journey to healing attachment insecurity is complicated and evolves. Romantic partnerships can bring up many of these issues and can be complicated most by attachment insecurity because of the degree of emotional dependence often found in these relationships.

Relationships have evolved to be too complicated, with immense choice in how we engage with others we trust, commit our time to, and cultivate emotional safety and security. Within this large arena of options, I invite you to remember your fundamental values regarding relationships of all kinds and call upon skills and tools to put these values into practice.

Healing The Anxious Self

If the ways your body and brain respond don't work for you, you have the power to make changes to align better with your relationship values.

One of your first steps is to find some acceptance for the thoughts, feelings, and body sensations that make up your experience of relationships.

Forgive the things you have done in the past that haven't worked or have even created hurt. Show yourself compassion when it comes to where you are in your development.

Here Are Some Relevant Steps Toward More Secure Relationships:

- Have patience with people while staying connected to your needs and wants

- Know that when people can't meet your needs, it's not personal to you

- Identify what attachment repair looks like for you and others

Desiree was a client who showed tremendous movement from attachment anxiety toward security. Looking back at her history, Desiree could tell that anxious attachment had played a role in every romantic relationship she ever had. Usually, she would get quite serious in a relationship with the hope that it would be "the one." But when her partners let her down, her behavior would turn more chaotic and blaming, eventually driving them away.

She was tired of this cycle and wanted to learn how to find what worked for her in relationships. She began therapy, read as much as she could on these topics, and talked to respected people in her community. Little by little, she was able to apply the ideas to her own life. She decided that she wouldn't enter into a severe romantic relationship until she felt more confident in her relationship skills.

This freed Desiree up to focus more on her community and friendships, and she began to feel it was possible to have a full life outside of the romantic partnership. She shared her needs and wants with people without feeling too bad if someone couldn't meet them. Your healing path may or may not look like Desiree's, but you may encounter similar themes with whomever you do your healing.

Healing The Avoidant Self

If you recognize avoidant attachment in yourself, and if it has harmed your relationships, the first thing to remember is that you're not to blame. These patterns were established long before you could make decisions, and without significant formative experiences to correct early injuries, you continued to engage in your familiar way.

Here Are Some Steps You Can Take To Build More Secure Relationships:

- Get comfortable with having needs and wants

- Practice sharing more about yourself with the people you care about

- Learn ways of working out differences with others

- Learn to repair with another person when they feel injured by you

Ali was a client who enjoyed success in managing his avoidant attachment style. Ali was a welder in a steel factory, a physically harsh environment where injuries and accidents were common. While handling a susceptible piece of equipment, he forgot an important step and sustained a severe injury that required rushing to the emergency room. After 28 stitches and some reflection, Ali identified feeling hurt that none of his coworkers asked how he was doing.

Ali's coworkers weren't callous people. It was a very supportive and team-oriented work environment. The primary reason Ali had not received much sympathy was that he had unknowingly trained them to expect deflection if they expressed care for him. By now, they had learned that there was no point. With any injury in the shop, big or small, Ali would write it as "no big deal."

After some time in therapy, Ali learned to recognize his specific needs, wants, and boundaries in his relationships. He found that when he relaxed more and shared himself with people, they opened up to him, too. He even got comfortable making requests at times.

Sharing your needs, vulnerabilities, and wants may not feel comfortable for you. You'll probably stumble or feel embarrassed. This is normal with anything unfamiliar. Feel some confidence that by committing to yourself and your relationship values, you'll create welcome changes.

Lasting Security

Lasting security in a relationship comes from the ongoing work you put into getting to know yourself and the people you care about. This is work that, for many, pays off in spades. You know, because you can begin to enjoy connections with people and lean on them when you are hurt or feel alone.

As you learn about and accept the feelings and thoughts that inform your responses, you'll also get more comfortable navigating them and making thoughtful choices based on the vision you have for your relationships. All this just takes some practice. For your hard work, I hope and believe you'll see that new and hopeful relationship experiences are possible.

Emotional safety and support produce lasting security, and now you are your own best consultant on what it's going to take to get it. Remember that getting things right in relationships involves experience and experimentation. You may find that you value a deep and intimate connection with one person. Or you may find that three best friends fulfill your vision for lasting security. Our brains are wired for reference, but there is no rigid formula for what that looks like. I encourage you to find whatever works for you.

24. Anxiety and Different Aspects of Life

Anxiety can influence an individual's life in many ways, including having effects on relationships with family and friends, their love life, and even work. Some people don't understand how anxiety function. Educating people about the mental condition is critical. Also, though anxiety can't be seen, it's real. Many people don't even think there are anxiety disorders and mental disorders. This doesn't necessarily go away just by accepting it, but it does help to get diagnosed and treated. For some instances, if left untreated, it can get even worse.

There are different sorts of tension issues, yet they all incorporate a similar kind of great dread that can prompt capacity and conduct issues. A few people are fundamentally influenced by social tension, affecting how connections are formed and set up. At the point when anybody has uneasiness in a relationship, it might impact the relationship. Relationship nervousness can prompt overthinking, questioning the relationship, scrutinizing your accomplice's emotions, contending, and focusing on the association. On the off chance that they're stressed over one thing they're doing, they will stress over it over and over during the day, sit up around evening time, stress over it, and spotlight on it. So getting tension isn't something to be disgraced for. Even though it might strain the relationship, there are manners by which the accomplice can help.

Being empathetic is crucial in handling people with anxiety disorders. Understanding that their experience with anxiety is unique to them, providing a listening ear, but most importantly, not pressing people or trying to force solutions on people. One simple thing that someone's partner can do is be considerate and patient with their significant others. Learning more about the disease will strengthen the bond between the two individuals. One should persuade their partner to seek out counseling.

Adverse Effects of Anxiety On Love Life

Nonetheless, anxiety should not come in the way of a relationship or place a strain on it to the point that it becomes difficult to enjoy.

You will love each other more deeply and communicate differently through knowing anxiety in general and how it affects both people in a relationship. Educating yourself and people around you can also alleviate tremendous tension. Most people have a couple of anxious thoughts. They are a normal part of being in a relationship, especially a new relationship.

Nevertheless, people with anxiety disorders or an anxiety disorder appear to have such nervous thoughts more frequently and more deeply. Their reviews take over and go straight to the worst-case scenario. The fearful thoughts cause signs of physiology, including shortness of breath, insomnia, and anxiety attack. Someone with anxiety can respond in a way as if the stress was a physical assault. Anxious thoughts often encourage you to behave in ways that stress you out and strengthen the relationship. Individuals with anxiety, for example, regularly test the loyalty of their partner by using vulnerable methods. For example, your partner is full of guilt that he's the first to start contact. He begins to worry that you don't like him as much as he/she likes you because you don't send out the first signal as often as he does. The fear is intensifying, and he starts to feel that if he didn't reach out first, you would never speak with him.

Unfortunately, people experience several anxiety-related behaviors in relationships. Being frustrated, irritable, overwhelmed, having difficulty concentrating, coming off as overly negative thoughts, and perfecting all the times become part of your life. And sadly, anxiety will affect your love life for those of us who are hoping to find love. It's terrible because everything seems so perfect, and you want everything to continue to be accurate, but you know that it's only a matter of time before things start to go wrong. This is how it feels like to be in a stable relationship for those of us with anxiety.

It's practically additionally encouraging when things start to turn out badly because your psyche has invested so much energy getting ready for a catastrophe that it's an alleviation to know you're not insane. Your relationship's destruction has consistently been sticking around the bend. Your uneasiness starts affecting your relationship for the more terrible, and it resembles you can't effectively stop it. When your relationship is in a challenging situation, the inclination you get is a more striking sort of tension that detonates into your psyche and feels substantially more extreme.

In any case, the thoughtful you get when all that is by all accounts fine and dandy is a moderate consuming apprehension that sits in the rear of your brain and makes a remarkably unpretentious sort of destruction on your mind.

Anxiety may trigger periods of panic, anxiety or overwhelming feelings, and a general sense of unease and stress. It can take over your thoughts and make many areas of your life bleed. If you feel a burden on your relationship, anxiety may have a part to play. Your fear or your partner's put your relationship in danger? Here's how and why stress can ruin your relationship with your partner:

Anxiety induces fear or concern that can, in a given moment, make you less conscious of your actual needs. If you're concerned about what could happen, it's hard to pay attention to what's going on.

Nervousness breaks your inward voice. Any individual who seems, by all accounts, to be on edge may think that it's hard to convey their actual emotions. It may likewise be challenging to keep up reasonable limits when requesting the consideration or space required. Since encountering uneasiness is awkward, you may subliminally endeavor to delay their experience. Then again, nervousness may lead you to feel that something should be spoken about promptly when a brief break can be gainful. On the off chance that you're not voicing what you think or need, at that point, tension gets more noteworthy. Furthermore, if you hold them in, your feelings can winding reeling. You could get disappointed and cautious.

Anxiety may make you behave selfishly. Since pressure is an overactive reaction to fear, often someone who experiences it may concentrate too much on their worries or problems. Your concerns and fears can bring undue pressure to bear on your relationship. You may feel you need to think about protecting yourself in your relationship, but it will prevent you from being caring and open to your partner. If your partner has anxiety, you can also build up anger and respond in selfish ways. The behaviors we have and the experiences are infectious. It is especially challenging to keep the stress levels under control when the partner feels nervous, frustrated, or defensive.

Unhealthy anxiety levels keep you on the emotional edge all the time. Anxiety causes you to dismiss non-hazardous things and avoid things that might benefit you.

It can also stop you from taking adequate action to change something that hurt you in your life because it makes you feel hopeless or stuck.

The sentiment of satisfaction requires a feeling of insurance or freedom. Tension causes us to feel either unnerved or impeded. A mind and body molded to pressure will likewise have a lot harder time appreciating closeness and sex. Contrary considerations and fears sway an individual's capacity to be available inside a relationship and conceivably drain the delight out of a second.

Adverse Effects of Anxiety On Family And Friends

There are a variety of ways anxiety can affect one's family life. Specifically, the symptoms one can encounter during an anxiety disorder can involve symptoms such as irritability, stress, lack of healthy sleep, and focus issues — this may impact one's relationships with family members or one's ability to do one's work effectively. It hinders your communication with others.

Anxiety disorders are often co-occurring with other severe psychiatric disorders, particularly familiar, depression, and drug abuse. And when you have an anxiety disorder, you are at a considerably higher risk of developing one of the two other conditions that significantly affect relationships and work. Anxiety can place a lot of pressure on relationships, which can become very isolating. Friends and family may also feel depressed or anxious, and they don't want to see you hurting, but they don't always know how to help.

Depending on the symptoms you encounter, anxiety can affect relationships in a variety of various ways. To others, it can cause them to rely excessively on their loved ones. Some may isolate themselves to fear being a burden. Here's how anxiety can ruin your relationship with your family and friends:

Anxiety may often cause you to become excessively dependent. Their fear may make them worried about being alone or facing other circumstances by themselves. Stress can also create a person to doubt their decisions, which can lead to over-dependence as well. People with anxiety may have a strong need to be close to their friends or spouse and maybe looking for constant support. This can cause social interactions to overthink, causing them to worry about someone not reacting quickly via social media.

Some people have anxiety avoid relationships (like being upset or irritated with a loved one) to prevent negative feelings. It can be challenging to open up to those you are close to and be vulnerable to. Because of that, though you are striving for closeness, others may view you like a cold stand-off, making it extremely difficult, and often impossible, to sustain and establish new ties.

People with anxiety sometimes feel anxious or irritated, and people around them may feel the stress. When someone has pressure, others sometimes don't know how to react to it. This stress can cause connection problems and communication problems in relationships.

Adverse Effects of Anxiety On Work-Life

Anxiety can badly hit your work-life. Because when you start to lose your essence, it will affect all aspects of your life. Here's how pressure can affect your work-life:

You can feel mostly uninspired and unmotivated to do pretty much anything when you have anxiety issues. This insanity feeling will make socializing difficult, holding a job, or finding some pleasure in the hobbies you used to enjoy. Those items can, of course, affect your social life as a couple and also your mutual finances.

If you struggle with anxiety or depression, it may feel like an achievement, sometimes just getting out of bed in the morning. It's important to celebrate the tiny steps you take when you're dealing with anxiety or depression. You can't do the things other people can do as quickly. At the same time, taking positive steps to strengthen your mental health is equally necessary. Incapable of interacting, those coping with depression or anxiety sometimes encounter feelings of isolation even though they have a supportive and caring partner. Some may feel their partner doesn't understand what they're going through and can't talk about their mental health.

Living with anxiety and depression is hectic and severe. It is exhausting both mentally and physically and can leave you feeling powerless and sad. Living with anxiety is incredibly hard when you have to wake up daily and got to work. It creates serious focusing issues, and you find it hard even to do standard stuff that you used to do without even things too hard before.

25. Anger Issues

Dealing with frustration/anger in a partnership has challenges, as it can quickly change a situation's dynamics. If a person has an emotional reaction, they are possibly responding to your behavior. An adult can have frustration issues, but they may not know that they make the relationship difficult. Anger also happens because there is a breakdown of contact or empathy between the two parties. Often, somebody gets the blame for the offense that emerges when, in fact, both the companions play a part in the cause.

Understanding Anger

Although rage is a feeling experienced by individuals within context, some research shows that it can arise in relationship periods where some things are not understood or resolved. Aspects refer to attitudes and acts displayed during a dispute or conflict, categorized as rude, unreasonable, or other damaging behavior types. Some behaviors may cause a negative trigger, which adds fuel to one's frustration. Anger concerns that persist as the issue's emphasis are not where it has to be, because it's yet to be resolved. Talking about anger issues with a couple's counselor can reflect the source of anger and how husbands and wives can work together productively to manage it.

We all know how wonderful it is to love unconditionally and emotional tranquility with your companion; it's not about anger! Yet anger is a normal part of life and unavoidable, particularly when two individuals are closely engaged in sharing experience. One of the most significant problems confronting a pair is how to cope with rage, both their resentment towards their companion and the irritation of their companion towards them.

Yet first of all, what is rage/anger? This is a widely underestimated feeling. Anger is not, on one aspect, a destructive emotion. Most people find it evil or unethical and believe that being upset causes them to become the wrong person. Some think anger is the reverse of affection and believe that rage expressions have no room in an intimate personal partnership. Another common yet inaccurate assumption is that by being angry at your partner means you're hateful to them. In truth, being angry isn't harmful or mean.

Feelings of anger are seldom right or wrong. In the Dalai Lama's wise words, if a person never shows rage, I assume that something is off. He isn't okay in the brain.

Getting mistreated by their intimate partner evokes resentment, and the anger will cause the mistreatment to reciprocate, ultimately contributing to a cycle of harmful actions and frustration.

Destructive behaviors can initiate anger in intimate relationships. Let's all assume the following scenario: Partners A and B have financial difficulties. One day, A arrives home from the office to discover that B enjoys a very pricey alcoholic cocktail. Instead of offering B an opportunity to justify, A turns to disruptive activities (e.g., name-calling).

That may intensify the loop of frustration at this juncture is the precise interpretation of A's actions by B. Is there a strong possibility that B would interpret the destructiveness of A's actions correctly? Hey. Romantic partners are excellent at recognizing conflict-related reaction types for each other, according to studies. And B can quickly see whether A is negative or offers positive feedback.

A Warning

When you're in an abusive situation, so your safety is the most valuable issue. Be sure you are safe before seeking to get support with your partnership. When your partner is in some form physically abusive to you, then it's necessary to separate yourself from the association. That doesn't suggest there's no chance of fixing the friendship, so you should not go back into the partnership before counseling is done and improvements are made. It's not worth taking a risk on your safety.

That's valid about your behavioral and emotional wellbeing, too. Most individuals can remain in marriages where their mate is mentally or psychologically, taking out their frustration instead of physically. You do not need to be in such a partnership. Your mental and emotional well-being is just as crucial as your physical health.

Receiving Anger

When your companion gets mad at you, it's normal to feel frustrated. If anyone is upset at us, we all get the same knee-jerk reaction, we feel furious. Our response is rapid and irrational:

"Don't get upset with me! Close your mouth. I wouldn't like to hear what you say! Simply, rage creates rage. And that is very clearly not dramatic. Don't miss that initial frustration, ever. Otherwise, it would keep smoldering and harm relationship contact.

You increase that personal power because you don't encourage yourself to be fooled into becoming something you don't want.

Rage may be harmful to relationships, as you might have already learned. An unhappy companion's aggressive attitude and actions will sap your resources, making you feel depressed and unheard of, and damage not just your well-being but the partnership's well-being. That being said, if you can communicate with an unhappy companion skillfully, the relationship will turn drastically. Here are a few useful approaches to combat an upset girlfriend.

Neutralize And De-Escalate Emotionality

If you attempt to manage an upset companion, they can become aggressive and more non-compliant. It's foolish to get upset in reaction to a companion's anger; it's best to let other individuals get upset and understand that they can ultimately cool down. The calmer you stay, the sooner their fury can subside.

You de-escalate the scenario in this way. The main aim of de-escalation is to reduce mutual tension and channel animosity into improved cooperation.

Being Respectful And Assertive

To behave assertively is the practice of taking a role in which you may convey your desires openly and politely while taking into account the thoughts and wishes of your companion as well. You are optimistic, frank, and accessible when behaving and communicating in an assertively polite way. Around the same time, you motivate your mate to bear their share of accountability by being tactful. Assertively, you allow them to reach their portion of the liability.

Encourage Positive Communication, Acknowledge, And Confirm

People also behave angrily when they fear they are overlooked, are not taking seriously, or are not respected. They can feel frustrated and ignored.

To stop inflaming the frustration, it's best to listen to them carefully before you're confident they feel respected and acknowledged. Go undercover to seek to grasp their basic desires to affirm your thoughts and perceptions. By affirmation, we express approval to each other. It does not mean that they comply with everything. Instead, it considers and takes into account the viewpoint of your partner. The secret to acceptance is to be aware and honestly seek and learn. It's trying to listen to their and your perspective, sticking with them instead of driving them further or ignoring them. The other aspect of the confirmation represents just what you think, e.g., "What I think you are saying is...Is that true?". This will be achieved in a simple, rational, and caring way without judgment or decision.

Practice Tolerance And Kindness

Beneath rage is usually more profound and more fragile feelings, such as anxiety, depression, or discomfort, which might be less apparent to your companion. Anger acts as a defensive barrier for a brief amount of time, which helps the companion feel secure and in charge. And it affects them from inside, in the long run. That's why it's necessary to have compassion and step away from guilt and suspicion against your companion.

Patience will act as both a cure to anger between you and your companion. It includes being wise as rage emerges. It's just waiting, not communicating, or doing something immediate or reactive. Patience and humility are the cornerstones of constructive thinking and human interaction.

Choose Your Fights And Think Long-Term

The term "choose your fights" does not only refer to today's military; it is also applicable

to angry partnerships. Military officials may be able to lose individual battles to "win a war." Usually, they don't spend time and money on others; they cannot win. Similarly, as people have various values, viewpoints, desires, and aspirations, partnerships may be a battlefield where vigilance practice is often a wise tactic.

If you wish, you will consider a variety of issues to disagree with your companion over. But to be cautious, leaving that which concerns least, will be to your advantage.

Know, arguing for whatever dispute you have is neither wise nor realistic. You might win the debate, but your partnership can eventually be undermined.

Monitor And Understand The Causes Of Your Behavior

Being responsible is acknowledging the position of being upset with an unhappy companion, and worrying about your behavior can cause frustration. It also involves knowing what allows you to act in the manner you do. The more you are aware, the less aggressive and the more positive you will get. For you, your family, and your partnership, the outcome can be more excellent health.

If you know that you've played a part in worsening a conflict, be respectful, and consider your position. Your ownership can reduce friction and allow your wife to take responsibility for it as well.

Make Sure Your Partner Is Relaxed

When the mental status of your companion is strongly overloaded, the cognitive function may be affected. There's no use in solving the dilemma as long as the frustration persists. Give room to relax the negative emotions and generate a logical dialogue.

When you're all relaxed and united, discuss the problem that contributed to aggressive behavior from your companion. They could be open to listening and learning at this moment. Don't hesitate to add the maxim to yourself, too. When triggering, the mental or upset components take a moment to cool down. Rage drives frustration, and relaxation fosters a peaceful environment.

Influence Over Control

Don't dwell on wanting to transform your companion around. You simply can't. However, you should persuade your mate and show them your position's benefits. By developing a supportive atmosphere conducive to collaboration rather than domination, you will affect your companion.

You might have heard the saying, "You can catch more honey flies than vinegar." If you handle your companion with sugar, you can get them closer to you and closer to knowing how you experience and why you think that way. That will improve the odds of productive results.

If you follow the above techniques, you can be surprised to see how quickly the love changes for both you and your companion and how your partnership flourishes. Partners in a perfect universe should take turns to get angry. Even we get mad at the same moment in the actual world. This is when it is necessary to do maintenance.

26. Secret Strategies For Handling Insecure Partners

1. Dump Friendships That Genuinely Pose A Threat To Your Relationship

You might need to take out specific individuals from your life on the off chance that they give your accomplice enough motivation to feel unreliable. You may have that one companion who has earned infamous notoriety of being an urgent adulterer. He/she may dress provocatively, drop indicates continuously, and by and large attempt to hit on you. This can be sufficient to have your accomplice smoldering and can be an adequate motivation to take out the companion from your life.

When there's sufficient explanation or sensible enough desires for you to abandon somebody for the advancement of your relationship, don't spare a moment to do it. Guarantee this doesn't turn into an example; however, their requests don't get nonsensical over time. Do it just in situations when you impartially feel that your accomplice is legitimized in feeling compromised or uncertain.

2. Jettison The Insecurity Triggers

Stay away from the desire/weakness triggers at whatever point you can by attempting to be touchier to your accomplice's sentiments. In the end, when you realize, something troubles him/her, put forth a conscious attempt to cease from doing it. Abstain from playing relationship games was to like yourself; you deliberately cause them to feel shaky. For example, if you realize they get tense about plainly coquettish conduct (anyway innocuous it might appear to you), attempt to abstain from being a tease around them and make them the emphasis on your consideration. Luxurious, liberal commendations on them, enlighten everybody regarding something remarkable they did and continue showing indications of warmth/friendship through your non-verbal communication.

3. Support Accomplishment Of Personal And Professional Goals

Since unreliable sentiments are regularly profoundly established in feelings of insufficiency or low confidence, helping your accomplice set and achieve objectives can be an excellent method to build their fearlessness. It very well may be anything from shedding pounds to chipping away at a provoking new task to pursuing a public talking class to making YouTube recordings – anything that encourages them to enjoy a sentiment of individual accomplishment. When they like themselves, they are less inclined to get tenacious and continue requesting approval from you.

It helps move the concentrate away from "Am I commendable?" to "Amazing, and I've done this. I should be brilliant." It gives them a valuable objective to focus on instead of being fixated on your whereabouts. As an accomplice, empower their accomplishments (anyway little) with veritable recognition. Rouse them to set and achieve much greater objectives that help their confidence.

4. Leave Them Alone A Part Of Your Buddy Gang

Desire or possessiveness frequently comes from a profound situated sentiment of the instability of not being "sufficient" or "tantamount to xyz." Eliminate these emotions by including your accomplice more in exercises arranged with your companion circle or social gathering. This will guarantee him/her about your life by and large when he/she isn't with you. Instead of keeping them speculating or dubious, make your public activity more open and available to them. This will build straightforwardness and trust inside the relationship and progressively reduce the aches of instability.

5. Try not to Lie To Avoid Questions

If you mostly end up at the less than desirable finish of unlimited inquiries and allegations, you likely could be enticed to mislead get away from these unmerited showdowns. Nonetheless, this can accomplish more harm than great over the long haul. On the off chance that your accomplice finds that you've been misleading him/her, they might be considerably more persuaded that you have something to cover up instead of accepting that it is his/her activities that have made you lie.

Take, for instance, there's a co-worker your partner just doesn't like for some reason, and you have to collaborate with him/her on an important project, which needs you both to stay up after work. The partner questions you about your extended hours, and you avoid mentioning the co-worker to escape the avalanche of questions that will follow. It appears too much of a hassle to make them understand. Instead, you simply say you have your bosses from the headquarters located in another country visiting, which requires everyone to stay up late for meetings.

6. Tell About The Elephant In The Room

It helps to talk to a green-eyed partner bluntly, openly, and compassionately about his/her feelings. Do not merely gesticulation off their behavior as weird or denunciate them of being silly. It will barely make them more cautious about their insecure or jealous behavior, toting more significant fuel to the fire. When people are permitted to share their feelings in a supportive and positive environment, it leads to better problem resolution.

Insecurity is often triggered by fearful thoughts, which ironically cause the very thing they dread. Discounting your partner's fears makes them feel more misunderstood and frustrated.

7. Seek Professional Help

Getting yourself out of a persistently possessive relationship can be a challenging proposition. However, do not let the fear of alone getting the better of you. Being lonesome is better than staying in a toxic and controlling relationship.

Counselors or behavior therapists can help you overcome the damage of being at the receiving end of a jealous or insecure relationship. They can tackle your negative feelings and help you come to terms with ending a bitter relationship. You may also need the help of a support group if you have suffered physical or mental abuse in an insecure partner's hands. Damaged emotional health can affect your future relationships and overall personality. Acknowledge the issue and move on without letting go of your self-respect.

8. You Cannot Play Mr. /Ms. Fixit All The Time

While you can help your partner cope better with their insecurity by showing empathy, understanding, and compassion, you cannot fix it for them. It is merely so much you can do about it; however, eager you are to help. Let your lover know that though you will support their effort to combat jealousy/insecurity, and you will not give in all the time to avoid ugly fights.

Tell them that your role is only to fill the disconnection gap, if any, between the two of you. Assure him/her that you can work as a positive team to tackle their insecurity without taking the entire blame on you. While you will do everything in your capacity to show understanding for their issues, it is only him/her who has to ultimately fix the problem by consciously changing their thoughts and behavior patterns.

9. Admit You Screwed Up And Rebuild Things

It is natural for your partner to feel jealous or insecure if you have betrayed them in the past. You cannot expect them to come out of it overnight, and you may have to pay the price of your betrayal by being more patient, reassuring, and answerable until they are at ease. Reassure them, spend more time with them, make them your priority, do the little things they cherish, participate in fun adventures together, take some time out to travel, do romantic dinner dates – anything that makes him/her feel appreciated and wanted again. Though it will not be easy for you, reassurances and sincere actions will go a long way in establishing your loyalty.

10. Give It Some Time

They have not spent enough time with you to realize how different you are from an evil ex-lover. This may lead them to be more sensitive and suspicious of your actions until they get to know you well and begin to trust you. Do not immediately label them paranoid or over-possessive. Give them sufficient time to get over their feelings and start charging people again. Be there for them. Spend time hearing them out attentively. Involve them more in your social life. Eventually, they may get over their insecure feelings and trust you completely.

11. Avoid Comparisons

How many times have we been tempted to compare our partner with someone who fits the picture of our ideal mate? Or with an ex-lover?

Or a parent? It is relaxed to fall into the trap of comparisons as a means of expressing precisely what you are looking for in him/her. However, even well-meaning comparisons can be downright hurtful for your partner's ego. He/she may feel inadequate and belittled. It may lead to more significant damage by inducing a feeling of insecurity or "not being good enough" in them. Do not ever try to measure their worth by comparing your partner with someone else. Try to highlight the unique characteristics that made you fall in love with them, even when they focus on the negative.

12. Demonstrate Your Love And Belongingness In Public

While jealous and insecure people do this all the time, if you do this for your jealous/insecure partner, it may make them feel more assured and confident about the relationship. Unsure folks tend to be highly territorial. If you show them off when you are in public by holding their hand or kissing them to establish that they are yours, it may do your relationship a world of good. It does not take much to look at how proud you are to have them in your life. Your pride in him/her can go a long way in making your partner feel more secure and less fearful in the relationship.

13. Avoid Succumbing To Unreasonable Demands

Do not create the mistake of isolating yourself from friends without any good reason just because your partner does not like them or is unreasonably suspicious of your association with them. Once you start giving in to their demands, it will only encourage them to wield a more significant influence about where you go, what you do, and whom you talk to. Do not succumb to this pattern of emotional imprisonment.

Take complete responsibility for your actions rather than denying them. Instead of saying you weren't with your friends just to please your partner, say you weren't doing anything wrong, and it's normal to go out with friends. Be assertive without being insensitive. If you think there truly is a basis for your partner's suspicion, try and talk to them about it to clear it rather than escape it. Never feel guilty about having a good time with other friends or co-workers without your partner.

14. Manage Retroactive Jealousy Diplomatically

Romantic partners of people suffering from retroactive jealously never have it easy. They are frequently questioned and scrutinized based on their past.

They are asked for detailed explanations about past relationships, sexual history, and other unproductive elements that have no bearing on the current connection. There seems to be an amplified obsession with their partner's past relationships. Do you find yourself at the receiving end of retroactive jealousy or insecurity? Have in mind that nothing you do or say can "solve it" for your partner. How many ever details you to offer or recount the exact events of your past relationships or even your opinion about how you view them – it may never be enough resolving the issue.

27. Loving A Person with Anxiety

Relationship and love demand that we get involved in our partner's life, which means we always have to be supportive and loving. If you have a partner with one or more anxiety types, you are already aware of how it can influence your relationship and life. Anxiety comes in many forms, and there is no magic pill that can help. Stress is also an individual experience that can differ in many ways. We can make a list of things to help our partner when they have an anxiety attack that varies from person to person. You should know how to recognize the symptoms and learn how to neutralize an anxiety attack by relying on experience.

Your involvement in your partner's journey of learning how to live a life free of anxiety is of great importance. When it comes to sudden panic attacks, you can do several different things to help distract your partner and ease any suffering. When it comes to chronic anxiety, you are the one who will get involved in exposure therapy. There are specific strategies you can take into consideration when it comes to each type of anxiety. You will improve your relationships' quality, strengthen the bond you have, and confirm your love and devotion to your partner.

Acute Anxiety

Acute anxiety happens out of the blue. It can be caused by different things, specific situations, or other people you and your partner meet. It transpires suddenly, and there is no time for planning and taking it slow. You need to be able to react at the moment and to know how to assess the situation. Understand what is happening, what your partner is going through, and develop the right way to neutralize the anxiety. There are four periods you can take to be supportive and helpful in case of acute stress:

1.   Be calm, be compassionate. If you are not, you won't support your partner's needs at that moment. If you give in to anger, frustration, or anxiety, it won't help. It can even make things worse. You also need to consider not to give in to your partner's anxiety and accommodate it. In the long run, this is not helpful. Instead, offer understanding, not just solutions.

2.   Assess your partner's anxiety. What level is it? What are the indications and signs of an anxiety attack?

An anxiety attack can hit with a different strength each time. You required to be able to recognize it to choose actions appropriate to the given situation.

3.   Remind your partner of the techniques that helped with past anxiety attacks. Whether it is breathing or exercise, your partner is probably aware of their success in neutralizing anxiety. But in the given situation, maybe he or she needs reminding. Once they are on the right path of dealing with stress, your job is to provide positive reinforcement. Give praise and be empathetic once your partner executes techniques that will help with an anxiety attack.

4.   Evaluate the situation. Is your partner's anxiety attack passing? If it is, be supportive and encourage your partner to continue whatever he is doing to lower his anxiety. If it halts at the same level or increases, you should start the steps from the beginning and develop different techniques and strategies to help your partner with an acute anxiety attack.

Chronic Anxiety

To address chronic anxiety, you might have to try out exposure therapy, as it is considered the golden standard of treatment by many people. Usually, it takes the guidance of a professional therapist to try exposure therapy. But, if the level of your partner's anxiety is not severe, you might feel comfortable enough to try it on your own. In this case, you have to guide and learn how to be a supportive person for your partner.

Exposure therapy works by creating situations that trigger your partner's anxiety. This will help your partner learn how he or she can tolerate certain levels of stress. Your partner will learn how to reduce anxiety and how to manage it in given situations. Over time, you might be surprised how your partner knew to enjoy conditions that made them anxious.

You have to start with the least challenging situation and progress slowly and steadily towards more challenging ones. Don't push your partner to the next level until they are ready. If anxiety isn't decreasing in the first challenge, it's not time to go to the second.

For example, let's about your partner has a fear of heights. He or she wants to overcome this fear and be able to climb the buildings last floor. How will exposure therapy look in this case?

1.   Tell your partner to look out the window from the ground floor for precisely one minute.

2.   Climb to the second floor together with your partner. Remember that you are not just an exposure therapy guide; you also need to support it. Make them look out the window from the second floor for one minute. In case of anxiety showing up in its first symptoms, remind your partner to do breathing exercises to lower its impact.

3.   Once your partner feels better, they should try looking out the window again.

4.   If no anxiety presents itself, you should leave your partner's side. They need to be able to look through the same window, but this time without you.

5.   Climb to the third floor and repeat steps three and four. When your partner feels ready, continue to the fourth floor, sixth, and so on. If your partner's anxiety is too high, don't hesitate to stop. The first session doesn't need to take longer than 30 minutes.

6.   Each new session needs to begin with the last comfortable floor your partner experienced. You don't need to always start from the ground floor, as your partner progresses, feeling no anxiety when looking through the window of the second, third, even fourth floor.

7.   Take time. Your partner will not be free of the fear in just a few days. Be patient and continue practicing exposure therapy in this way until your partner can achieve the goal and climb the last floor.

8.   The goal of exposure therapy is not just to get rid of fear and anxiety. It should also teach your partner that he or she can control and tolerate discomfort. Your partner will have an opportunity to practice anxiety-reduction techniques in a safe and controlled environment, with you in the support role.

Specific Disorder Interventions

Under the support of a trained therapist, the two of you will learn how to approach it in the best possible way. Your partner's therapist might ask you to join in a few sessions, and he will teach you how to help better your partner in situations that elevate anxiety.

If your partner is not diagnosed, but both of you suspect he might have a particular disorder, advise your partner to visit a doctor. Self-diagnosing can lead to mistakes, and you will make the wrong choices in approaching your partner's anxiety.

Panic Disorder With Agoraphobia

If this is your partner's diagnosis, you two probably already have a pattern of behavior designed to accommodate your partner's anxiety. You probably follow your partner to social events, and you are the one who is in charge of running errands outside of the house. This accommodation is counterproductive in the long run. You show that you care, love, and support your partner, but it prevents him or her from experiencing a full life. Your partner needs to learn how to overcome anxiety. You may approach panic disorder with exposure therapy, so your partner becomes less dependent on you:

1.   Choose an errand that your partner thinks he can handle himself. It can be shopping, going to a doctor's appointment alone, walking a dog, etc.

2.   Plan what errands are more challenging for your partner and add them to the list. Write them down as "to be accomplished in the future." It is essential to work slowly but keep a clear vision of what needs to be accomplished.

3.   Work together on slowly accomplishing the first task on your list. If it's going shopping alone, accompany your partner a few times, so they are accustomed to the environment. When he or she feels sure enough to go alone, let them. Encourage and support their decision.

4.   Once your partner accomplishes the task, be there to discuss his experience with it. Listen carefully and address any issues that might arise. Encourage your partner and keep track of his progress.

Generalized Anxiety Disorder

The behavior of people with GAD is similar to that of people who have OCD. They have fears about certain things, and these fears are not comforted by reassurance. GAD usually creates concerns that we all have. It can be about finances, health, and school. But people with GAD will overblow the proportion of these fears and influence their daily lives.

If your partner is diagnosed with GAD, you know how simple problems we face every day can sound like total catastrophes. Your partner probably assumes the worst possible end of certain situations.

People will GAD often express physical discomforts such as headaches, stomach pains, or muscle soreness. This can influence your intimate life and add up to anxiety. When one partner suffers from GAD, the other usually joins in for a couple's therapy. This is because GAD is always creating underlying problems in the relationship that need to be dealt with. A therapist can educate a couple about GAD and examine what is causing the anxiety. GAD can be developed because one of the partners feels they are not allowed to make significant decisions. He or she may feel like his partner is neglecting their opinion.

It often happens that people with this affliction develop a constant feeling of inadequacy. They deem they are not good enough for their partners and that they never will be. When this happens, they usually try to overcompensate and make everything perfect so their partner can love them. On the other hand, some may feel nothing they can do and no point in trying. They underperform, reinforcing their feelings of inadequacy.

If your partner suffers from GAD, the best way to help is to join the therapy session and discover your relationship's underlying problems. Learn how to deal with them. It can be anything from money concerns to sexual dissatisfaction or just communication problems. A therapist will teach you both techniques that will help you and your partner change your thinking. This involves recognizing the thoughts that cause anxiety. Once identified, you will have to challenge those thoughts and assess the likelihood of anxiety-provoking events even happening. Help your partner practice alternative beliefs and listen to the therapist's advice on how else you can influence your partner's GAD.

28. The Areas That Most Impact Anxiety

Anxiety Triggers

Certain areas of your life may trigger anxiety. The following are some common reasons why you may start to feel anxious. Keep these triggers in mind to discover what parts of your life might be causing you the most stress and, as a result, causing you to be snappy or uncommunicative with your partner. Anxiety stemming from any of these areas can and will impact your relationship if you are unaware of your feelings. People commonly project what they feel in other parts of their life onto their relationship, hurting that relationship in the process.

One of the main areas that people feel anxiety is work or school. People need to make money and create a path for their future. Accordingly, there is a lot of burdens to succeed in professional environments. Plus, making money is often a necessity for survival, which only heaps the pressure on. With all this in mind, it's no spectacle that causes people to get stuck in their heads and feel unable to cope with their workplace duties. Your job probably gets overwhelming, and that's normal. Still, you don't want to bring these negative feelings home with you and inflict them on your relationship, getting angry or upset at your partner when those work stresses have nothing to do with your relationship.

Relationships beyond the one you have romantically can be massive trigger points for many people. Whether it is your relationship with a friend or a family member, sometimes things can get tense, causing you to have anxiety related to those outside relationships. Those feelings in external relationships can also start to creep up on you when you're with your partner because those insecurities and doubts you have with other people are fresh in your mind.

Another area that causes distress is the way your body looks. Thus, with so much focus on looks, even in a secure relationship, you may begin to have doubts about not looking good enough. You may worry that people think less of you because of what you wear or how you do your hair.

People judge others based on these things, but anxiety pathologizes this fear until you are so obsessed with how you look that you can't focus on anything else.

Believe it or not, diet can impact your anxiety levels. Research has suggested that your mood affects the foods you crave, but it has also shown that what you eat can influence your anxiety levels. For one, significant dietary changes can cause increased levels of anxiety, so don't make drastic nutritional changes overnight. Further, while the impact of diet on individuals varies significantly because of different eating patterns and feelings associated with certain childhood foods, high-fat diets tend to reduce anxiety. In contrast, high sugar diets can increase. Of course, that's not to suggest that you should start only eating fat and eliminating sugar because the best results are found in balanced diets. Most importantly, if your body has the nutrients it needs, you will feel clearer, brighter, and be able to resist anxiety. Physical health translates to better mental health.

Drug use, including caffeine and alcohol, can also cause anxiety. Again, like with diet, that doesn't mean that you should cut coffee and alcohol entirely, and you very much shouldn't stop taking any prescribed medications, but it is still something to be aware of. Both prescribed and illicit drugs could shift the chemical balance in your brain and make you more prone to anxiety. When starting new drugs, monitor how you are feeling. If you start feeling more spikes of pressure as you begin a new drug, you may want to ask your doctor about potential alternatives or turn to a psychiatrist to help you with your anxiety.

Illness can be another factor in anxiety. Mental or physical ailments can leave you worrying more than is healthy. A person with cancer, for instance, is likely going to have some concern about their condition. Around forty-five percent of people with cancer show symptoms of clinical anxiety, which is a staggering number. Chronic diseases like IBS may also show increased anxiety levels in people, proving how triggering illnesses can be anxiety. Further, mental illnesses can often be comorbid, so someone with depression or other mental conditions could have increased odds of pressure. Accordingly, don't neglect your feelings regarding medical diagnoses because an illness can make forging a relationship even harder with all the complications it provides.

Negativity, in general, will naturally cause anxiety. If you're a glass-half-empty kind of person, you're probably more jaded and more anxious.

You'll tend to look at your partner with this same kind of cynicism, making it hard to establish trust. Those who are persistently negative struggle to look at the world and not be afraid. Negativity is a perfect spot for anxiety to crawl into. Luckily, just recognizing when you are in a negative headspace is a significant step forward, and positive thinking is pretty easy to curate with time and practice.

Arguments are another one of the leading causes of anxiety. They don't have to be full out yelling matches to be harmful either. Even just a disagreement with a coworker can lead to you coming home irritated and feeling worried about your situation. Unresolved arguments are especially anxiety-inducing because they fester. If the views happen with your partner, for obvious reasons, double the strain is put on your relationship, but having arguments with someone else could still result in you picking fights with your partner. This could because you're just feeling irritated, or it could be because you think disempowered with the other person you're fighting with but know that you can safely argue with your partner without immediate consequences. A yelling match with your boss could never happen, while a yelling match with your partner won't singlehandedly destroy the relationship. However, arguments can be harmful if you don't learn from your mistakes.

Solving Anxiety Triggers

While you inevitably will have things in your life that trigger anxiety in you, you don't have to let those triggers ruin your ability to handle stress and cope with your issues. There are ways to manage your anxiety and prevent some flare-ups, even if you cannot avert anxiety altogether.

An excellent first step is to determine what triggers you and address the root cause of your triggers. There's a whole list above outlining some of the common ones, but anything that causes a disturbing feeling in the pit of your stomach can be a trigger. These triggers will often relate to your past traumas. Think of the times you've felt the most helpless and afraid. Those events should give you a better idea of what your triggers are. Triggers could be little things that you barely consciously consider. For example, maybe a smell of perfume that someone you'd rather forget always wore causes a visceral reaction, or perhaps confrontations with your boss make you feel like a small child being yelled at by your father. It can help to go to your trusty journal during this step. Write down times when you feel peaks of anxiety and see if you can find overlap of causes for that anxiety and connect these causes to past hurt.

When anxiety takes hold of you suddenly, don't forget to breathe. Stop and let yourself live and give your brain a bit of a rest too. It seems like a waste of time to stop to breathe when you could charge through your work, but if you take that time for yourself, you will ultimately be more productive and better able to handle the work you have in front of you. If you can get your anxiety under control, you will be more productive and feel less burnt-out when you come home. As a result, you'll be able to spend after work time with your partner and be more present instead of feeling like an overworked zombie.

Another easy change is to limit your alcohol and coffee intake. Both substances change the way your brain works like illicit drugs would as well. Coffee, for example, is a stimulant. Accordingly, the impact it has on your body can feel like a fight or flight response and make you feel even more anxious. So, maybe instead of drinking three cups, you can try just to have one. Alcohol, meanwhile, is a depressant, but it can also be detrimental to your anxiety levels. Alcohol can help you calm down and relieve some of the stress you are feeling, but with long term use, the impacts become lessened, and you end up less able to handle the anxiety independently. Further, excessive drinking has many mental and physical symptoms that can cause additional stress rather than less stress. Thus, while substances can make you feel good temporarily, they may make you more anxious.

An exercise is an excellent option for people who feel like they have a lot of pent-up energy due to anxiety. Suppose you feel like a shaken soda bottle ready to explode at any interaction. In that case, physical activity can improve your mood by sending a surge of feel-good chemicals through your body and letting you use some of that anxious energy for a better purpose. Some studies have found that exercise reduces people's chances of having depression or anxiety by twenty-five percent. For those who already have anxiety disorders, anxiety symptoms were reduced an average of twenty percent just with routine physical activity. Accordingly, even for those with less severe anxiety, exercise can still ease the worry. Plus, working out makes your body healthy, which gives you less to worry about when it comes to your health. You don't have to try extreme activities or even intense ones. Anything you can do to get your body moving will suffice. Find something that challenges you, but it also enjoyable.

Give meditation a try.

Many people think that meditation sounds silly, but it doesn't have to necessarily be the stereotypical image that comes into your mind of a yogi humming and sitting with their legs crossed on the floor. Yoga can be a prodigious way to meditate and be mindful, but it isn't the only way. Meditation is solely the process of becoming aware of yourself and your body and reconnecting with your emotions, and allowing them to exist without constantly worrying about them. It will enable you to be mindful, which means that you are present and wholly at the moment rather than bogged down by outside concerns. Sixty percent of people who try meditation and stick with it over an extended time reduced their anxiety levels within a year. Meditation can also be useful for your heart, blood pressure, insomnia, depression, and even PMS symptoms, which means that it can help improve areas of your life that might otherwise cause you even more stress.

29. Couples Improving Relationships And Marriages

The most imperative relationship you will ever have in your life is your marriage. It is a sacred bond developed between you and your spouse, and it is meant to last your entire lifetime. Most people take pride in their marriages because they have found the perfect soul mate who completely understands them.

A marriage can be happy if there are mutual trust and respect; however, this does not mean that things cannot get better for the couple. A couple of things should improve their relationship and marriage to make the experience even more exciting.

Have you considered showering together regularly? It might sound small, but this single action can make your marriage far more exciting. Sharing a shower experience will allow you to develop closer intimacy with your partner and enjoy their presence even in awkward situations.

You do not have to plan to shower together, and the spontaneous suggestion of the two of you jumping under the water together is likely to excite both of you. Taking a shower does not necessarily have to lead to sex, but it will enable both of you to spend some precious time together.

You should also spend time playing games together and working on building your intimacy. Your partner should be somebody who you enjoy doing light activities with that both of you are interested in. You will be surprised, but simple exercises have the propensity of improving your relationship immensely.

The activities that you do together do not have to be complicated because playing board games, taking nighttime strolls around the neighborhood and even visiting a museum are all activities that can improve the relationship between a couple.

It is always nice to show your partner affection when you are out in public, such as holding hands and kissing him gently on the cheeks. It offers extra commitment on your part and the fact that you are very proud of your partner. Giving your peck of approval in public will go a long way in strengthening your relationship together.

There is nothing erroneous with showing your affection in public, even if you have already grown used to kissing each other every morning. Public love increases somebody's comfort in a relationship, and it is a sign to the rest of the world that you are together and enjoying your relationship.

Some couples have developed a routine of waking up together very early in the morning to spend quality time together before work. There is no recovered way of starting the day, such as this, because you can do anything in the early hours, even if it is just talking in bed before setting off to work.

You will be surprised how comfortable your day will be, although it might subject you to be sleeping early when you return home. Either way, you will not get interrupted early in the morning, and it is an excellent time for you to recombine with your partner in the stillness of the early days.

Be very encouraging with your spouse, whether in their professional life or handling something difficult in their lives. Showing encouragement is a sign of positivity, and this will endear your partner to you in an incredible way.

When you continually support their work, they feel a closer connection to you like no other person. There is no more incredible feeling than knowing you have somebody in your corner who is ready to encourage you even through the thickest of problems.

How many periods do you tell your partner, "I love you?" Well, you will be surprised that most married couples do not say it that much often, and it always has negative ramifications. If it is too vigorous for you to tell your partner that you love them every once in a while, it probably shows that you do not love them.

You will be surprised that a relationship on the brink of collapse can be improved immensely merely by the couple telling each other of their love. It is a very comfortable feeling, and it confirms that there is nobody else significant in your partner's life other than yourself.

Many people simply establish not understand the power of a simple conversation, whether it is small talk or not, because it builds on the love between them.

It is possible to make healthy memories with him even though you have endured tough times in your relationship by setting aside time to talk to each other. This can be an excellent time to solve pertinent problems affecting the two of you so that you can move the relationship forward.

You should also spend some time reading together because tranquility often is the best time to think. You will find yourself sharing a lot with your partner when you have some quiet time to yourselves regularly. Whether it is novels or newspapers, reading time can set the tone for the appropriate environment to interact.

A relationship will always improve tremendously if both of you understand the value of each other's time. It is essential to respect their interests as much as they will yours, and this interaction together will always improve a relationship even if it has endured several difficulties along the way.

These useful strategies can be implemented in most marriages to help them overcome common problems affecting couples. The advice should prompt you to take action and never sit around complaining about your spouse when you can take action yourself.

It is necessary to point out that action is always needed to improve any relationship as long as there is love between them.

30. Analyzing And Attacking Anxiety

Walk down the street, and one in four of the people you pass with either has an anxiety disorder or may encounter one at some stage in their lives. And about half of the people you meet will suffer to one degree or another with anxiety, while they may not have a full-blown anxiety disorder. For several decades the prevalence of anxiety disorders has increased, and no end is in sight.

The world is watching in panic, like disasters, terrorism, financial crisis, pandemics, violence, and war endanger a home and family security. Anxiety creates domestic chaos, ruins relationships, creates workers to miss work time, and prevents people from living whole, healthy lives.

Anxiety includes feelings of anxiety, concern, anticipation, and fear, and it is the most serious of all the so-called mental disorders. In other words, if you have unnecessary anxiety, you certainly aren't alone. And, over the years, numbers have risen. At no time in history have extra people been tormented by fear than it is now. Why? For what?

Life has never been as hard as it is now. Workweek grew longer instead of shorter. Broken and mixed families generate increased manageable stresses. Real-time computer screens and tv news carry the latest horrors to your living room. Chronic violence, fighting, and corruption are published in newspapers, forums, tweets, and magazines. Terrorism has traversed the world, rising to new heights. The representation of these modern plagues by the media involves full-color photographs of unprecedented graphic detail. Let's face it, Selling terror.

Unfortunately, as overwhelming as the world today is, only a fraction of people suffering from anxiety seek care. This is a concern, as pressure causes emotional pain and depression, physical strain, and even death. Stress takes a significant body toll and can even lead to suicide. Stress is costing society as a whole, to the rate of billions of dollars.

When people talk about the feeling of anxiety, you can hear any or all of the following descriptions: When my panic attacks start, I feel tightness in my chest. It's as if I sink or suffocate, and I start sweating; the anxiety is unbearable.

I sound like I'm going to die, and I'm going to have to sit down because I may be sick. / I was still painfully shy. I want friends, but it's just too awkward to call anyone. I guess I'm feeling like someone I'm getting will think I'm not worth talking to.

Every day, even on weekends, I rouse up with anxiety. I've been worrying all the time, ever since I lost my job. Often I think of going to sleep when it's terrible and never waking up.

I've had hallucinations and endless images running through my head since my accident about glass shattering, spinning tires, and spinning passengers. I am so irritable and jumpy that I can hardly get through the day.

I'm so afraid of flying that I won't be able to drive, even though I want to.

I'm so concerned about germs and waste that I wash my hands about 30 times a day. I'm just not going to pause.

Anxiety occurs, as you can see, in all sorts of emotions, attitudes, and feelings. When your stress starts to interfere with daily life, you need to find ways to ease your concerns and worries.

Tabulating The Costs Of Anxiety

Costs on fear. This affects the sufferer mentally, physically, and financially.

Yet this is not stopping there. Anxiety also puts a psychological burden on everyone.

Stress, worry, and anxiety affect relationships, family, and jobs.

What Does Anxiety Cost You?

If you have an anxiety disorder, you'll know the expense of nervous, depressed feelings. Anxiety feels pitiable. But do you know that in other ways too, untreated anxiety runs up a tab? Higher blood pressure, headaches of stress, and gastrointestinal symptoms can affect your body. Indeed, new studies showed that certain forms of chronic anxiety disorders alter the composition of the brain's structures.

A toll on your children: parents with anxiety have anxious children more often than not.

This is partially due to biology but also because children are learning through observation. Anxious children can be so overwhelmed they won't be able to pay attention in school.

Fat: Anxiety and stress boost the stress hormone called cortisol.

Cortisol allows the abdominal region to store fat, thus increasing the risk of heart disease and stroke. Heat also contributes to eating more.

More hospital trips: This is because people with anxiety also experience physical signs that are alarming. Besides, anxious people every worry about their health a lot.

Issues with relationships: People with anxiety sometimes feel irritable. Often they physically withdraw, or do the reverse, and cling to their partners dependently.

Downtime: Missing people with anxiety disorders happens more often than most, usually as a temporary attempt to quench their pain.

Adding Up The Cost To Society

Anxiety cost the world a lot of billions of dollars. A study by the U.S. government suggests stress costs more than depression, schizophrenia, or any other emotional problem. The yearly tab is valued at over $65 billion.

In 2002, the UK spent 32 billion pounds (about $53 billion) on mental health services, a large portion of which was spent on anxiety-related issues. Also, countries that pay less on mental health services are incurring high anxiety disorder costs. These expenses include often decreased productivity — often due to health conditions made worse by anxiety — continually Drugs reduced productivity. But the financial loss arising from downtime and treatment expenses does not include the dollars lost to drug abuse, which many of those with anxiety disorders turn to relieve their anxiety. Therefore, anxiety extracts a tremendous toll, directly and indirectly, on both the individual who encounters it and on society at large.

Recognizing The Symptoms Of Anxiety

You do not identify whether you have an anxiety disorder or an anxiety disorder. This is because there is a wide variety of symptoms involved with anxiety.

Every person has a slightly different constellation of those symptoms. And your particular constellation will decide what sort of anxiety disorder you can have.

For now, you should know that, in the form of thoughts or opinions, specific symptoms of anxiety occur. Many symptoms of fear occur in bodily sensations. Many signs often occur in various kinds of nervous behaviors. Many people show anxiety symptoms in all three forms, while others view their anxiety only in one or two places.

Thinking Anxiously

People with anxiety usually think differently from the ways others do. If you experience approval addiction, you're probably thinking anxiously: if you're an approval addict, you're concerned a lot about what other people think of you.

- Thinking in the future and expecting the worst: you think about all that lies ahead and expect the worst possible result as you do so.

- Magnification: Those who magnify traumatic things are typically more depressed than others.

- Perfectionism: When you are a perfectionist, you believe that every mistake is a complete failure.

- Low concentration: Routinely anxious people report struggling to concentrate their thoughts. Short-term memory often still suffers.

- Running thoughts: thoughts in a current of almost uncontrollable anxiety and concern race through your mind.

Battling Anxiety In Your Relationship

Thoughts have a substantial effect on your emotions. Your emotions also affect your thoughts at the same time. For battle anxiety, you need to be aware of both your thoughts and feelings.

The following true story from our lives shows how profoundly thought affects the way people behave.

We took a cruise some time ago to reward ourselves for having completed a big project.

We sat on deck chairs one evening and watched a beautiful sunset: bright red and orange clouds melted into the deep blue sea. Ever so slightly, the breeze picked up, and the ship rolled gently. We sat comfortably, watching the scene peacefully and the cradle-like motion. We reflected that we have never felt so at ease in our lifetime.

The way we felt influenced our feelings or the way we perceived the weather a lot. A state of calm happiness turned into anxious fear while the weather hadn't changed by itself.

The goal is to become a detective of thought, capable of uncovering the ideas that lead to anxious feelings. We're teaching you how to collect facts and put your theories to the test. We help you see how thoughts cause your anxiety all too quickly, and we're giving you validated strategies to turn your nervous ideas into calm thoughts.

Distinguishing Thoughts From Feelings

Psychologists also interview their clients to find out how they feel about their lives about the latest events. Clients often respond with the way they think of the events rather than the way they think. Others know how they feel, but when it comes to what they believe, they are stumped. We address in the following segment why people frequently end up out of contact with their emotions, opinions, or both. Instead, we're exploring how your ideas and feelings can be controlled.

Blocking The Blues

People often have difficulty recognizing and marking their emotions and feelings, especially negative ones. The complexity is essential for two reasons.

Firstly, it also affects feelings. Everyone should like to experience intense sorrow, grief, anxiety, or fear. One easy alternative is to suppress feelings entirely, and there are some inventive ways to avoid emotions. Unfortunately, most of these approaches can be destructive: some workaholic: some people are busy all the time instead of worrying about what disturbs them.

Alcoholism and substance abuse: when people feel bad, addicting their feelings with drugs and alcohol can provide a temporary, artificial emotional lift, leading to addiction, ill health, and occasionally death.

One tactic for not thinking is fooling yourself by believing nothing is wrong. Denial is also considered a cognitive mechanism because repression is done beyond the people's consciousness, but the effect is almost the same.

High-risk habits like sexual promiscuity and compulsive gambling can all drive away anxiety for a while.

Distraction: athletics, sports, hobbies, television, internet surfing, and many other activities that mask bad feelings. Distraction can be a positive thing. Only when distractions are unnecessarily used to cover up emotions and stop them become issues.

The second reason people cannot define, convey, and mark emotions is that they're told that they "shouldn't" have those feelings early. Parents, teachers, peers, and relatives are bombarding children with texts that "do not feel." Note the following "don't hurt" messages you've always received before: Big boys, don't cry; don't be a girl!

31. Impacts of Anxiety

There are moderate to the severe impact of anxiety over the relationships. They all are more towards the extreme of negativity concerning the bonding and connectedness in the relationships. They ultimately end up getting more hurt and shattered. Nagging, doubts, suspicions, and assurances will drift the two apart.

How Anxiety Will Impact The Relation?

When you're nervous, then you realize how deeply it can affect any part of your life. You follow the office where you find it difficult to concentrate. It follows along when you're socializing and nagging you back home. But the worst of these maybe is how anxiety will impact the bond.

Now that's where it's getting very distracting. Firstly, to date, there's the difficult task of having confidence. Such things are not precisely approved by anxiety, and therefore can make coupling feel like that of an unlikelihood. (How are you supposed to meet someone? Are they going to be Cool with your awkward ways?). So, even once you have a mate, the problems will always hang on and could even get much worse.

When anyone deals with anxiety problems socially, they are less inclined to go with them, take an interest in them, or consciously partake in events with their spouse. That may mean that date evening is the no-go. As well as going to travel as a pair? Not likely.

Factually, anxiety might also turn you to feel jealous and paranoid, even though you're trying hard to not. The beliefs of anxiety sufferers may not be founded on evidence, but they can't 'shut off' the tension. This can cause stress among you and your spouse and won't always lead to blissful relationships. For this reason, it is particularly why identifying such anxiety-induced issues, just like those mentioned below, could be helpful. If you know about all the possible ways anxiety could impact your bond, then it will be much convenient to sort out the problems as a pair.

Anxiety can affect your interactions in a variety of ways based on the signs you experience.

It may cause someone to be reliant on their beloved for some, while others may detach themselves for the paranoia of humiliation or become a hardship for others.

We should go into some of the growing forms the generalized anxiety disorder influences the partnerships.

Neediness Could Be A Perennial Issue

Anxiety induces unnecessary tension and insecurity, and you shouldn't fault yourself for becoming insecure. Just note that neediness will trigger any partnership tension. Your partner needs you to be present there for them, and just they will only provide so much help. When they cannot get through any time (and how will they manage it?), you'll both eventually feel irritated.

Dinner Dates That May Be Discontinued

Had been your partner giving up on the date night? This could be they think that if you go, you'll just say no, or even be unpleasant. For their side, it's a rational presumption but not necessarily what you want. When that's the situation, make sure to talk up, rather than just sit around and feel left out.

Disputes Fueled By Envy Prevail

Accusing your companion of deceiving once, and they'll typically want to ease your concerns. However, blame them fifty times, and you folks might have a discrepancy on your side. After protecting themselves against perceived questions regarding their conduct, they would be tired and feel threatened and not respected. It makes perfect sense that they would feel this way but be able to work things out.

Disputes Happen Regularly

With all of that anxiety-induced strain that it's no mystery, you could perhaps discover yourself getting into fights or beginning arguments out of nowhere. In partners, it might imply some sort of continuing to act out that's harmful, rapidly making assumptions, or making choices that won't bring desired results. Telling yourself to slow down (as well as a step away) will improve if you see that occurring more frequently than not.

You Are Always Worried

Besides fearing if your spouse will cheat, you may also worry that your spouse will want to move on and that the entire relationship will go ablaze. This concern is often unfounded, but even so, the anxious person cannot stop. Despite knowing that anxiety is the reason, you and your spouse are likely to feel frustrated and frustrated; and that's never great at all.

Interaction Often Is Not The Safest

Communication is challenging enough in a "usual" partnership. Add fear to the equation, and it can seem almost tricky. Part of the issue might be being able to express emotions about how fear influences everyday life. "In other terms, even the friend doesn't even have anxiety, and it may be very challenging for them to" see what's going on with their minds. If that is the case, there will be expected to be confused as well as circular debates.

Sex Can Move Into The Subject Of The Old Days

There should be no question that psychiatric disorders influence sex appeal. Depression could even end up making you neglect sex, but anxiety can lead you to think it over. Or, it can make you completely freak out or make a person feel isolated. If the case might have been, your spouse might feel insulted, and you might wind up feeling anxious.

You Folks May Not Find Any Friends With Each Other

The formation of a group of shared friends is one nice thing concerning relationships. But that is difficult to occur if you have anxiety, mainly if it was the social type. Your spouse could be out with her or his buddies in town when you're worrying at home.

The Anxiety Could Even Begin To Spread

Invest sufficient time mostly with your companion, and you would eventually continue to enjoy the same things, dress up similarly, and finish the sentences of each other. This is kind of cute. Till it touches on some common anxiety, your companion will get pulled down along with you and have the same fears and worries. Indeed, that's never purposely done, but this can occur.

Valuable Outings Sound Unlikely

You'll have to join many nuptial parties, baby showers as well as holiday parties as a pair. That's strenuous sufficiently, but the anxiety could even make everything worse. Individuals are experiencing social anxiety end up in total discomfort in these cases. This doesn't allow evenings just for pleasure or pleasant memories.

"The Fam Meeting" Will Never Take Place

You are too nervous to function and overly concerned about going out together with your mates. And how do you trust your future in-laws to retrieve the courage? Well, you just can't. When you hit the crucial stage in your relation in meeting the relatives, don't be shocked if the entire thing fails.

And when anxiety becomes active, quite much anything will sound fucked up in a bond. That's why remaining by one's side is vital and weathering the stuff together. A touch of comprehension will be moving a significant way.

Becomes Quite Reliant

Anxiety may also lead an individual to become too dependent. Their concern could make them uncomfortable about being alone or facing certain circumstances alone. Stress may often trigger the individual to doubt any choice they undertake, which may contribute to over-dependence.

Because of that, anyone with anxiety will have a strong need to remain near to their friends, relatives, or spouse and will remain searching for continuous validation and encouragement.

This overreliance can trigger social experiences to overthink, causing them to stress about others not reacting immediately by telephone and social networking.

People who depend excessively on interpersonal relations can trouble communicating effectively and strikeout in terms that are harmful to their ties. It might emotionally and physically lead friends and relatives to maintain their distance.

Social Solitary

On the contrary, specific depressed individuals separate themselves and quit interactions to prevent destructive emotions (like being upset or irritated with a buddy or significant one).

It may be daunting to be open to others you are nearest to and be honest with. Just because of that, although you are striving for closeness, others may view you as a distant, stand-off, or emotionally inaccessible. This makes it very challenging, and even unlikely, to sustain and establish new partnerships.

Chronic Tension

Persons who become nervous sometimes feel stressed or irritated, so those around them may sense the tension. If someone has anxiety, others sometimes don't know what to say to it and may seem to step over eggshells with that person.

This stress can trigger interaction issues and communication problems in interactions.

General unhappiness

Life with depression is a tested and established phenomenon.

Depression may influence any aspect of everyday life and leave you feeling as if you don't realize who you are.

Every day feeling terrible, unimaginative, or lonely is daunting for both you and your partner. This is hard to endure a sense of unhappiness every day, even like it is difficult to fall into a relationship with somebody sad all the time.

Existence is a roller-coaster ride made of highs and lows, but more highs than lows will bring a happier life. You can gain traction of your anxiousness and gain back power of your daily existence by seeking marital therapy and by appointing your doctor.

Your romantic life is deteriorating

The intimate bond with your partner is essential for your marriage to succeed.

Getting romantic is what puts you, the body, mind, and soul together. Research suggests that people who have an active, balanced sex life in bodies produce oxytocin. The mystical molecule is accountable for interacting, morale building, and tension relief. Oxytocin also leads to the resulting interpersonal familiarity.

Unfortunately, research demonstrates that mental illness (or taking medication) can significantly affect a person's intimate relationships, living standards, and mental health. It also has the potential to influence one's love life.

Depression has also been shown to decrease libido, reduce sexual arousal, slow or reduce orgasm potential, and cause erection problems.

If your love life fails, the remainder of your bond is likewise.

Partners might not be quite as close as loving or as confident as one another. It can also leave an unimportant feeling for one partner and might even entice an individual to deviate from the relationships.

Living uninspired

You may feel completely unexciting as well as unproductive to do reasonably much everything when you're down. This insanity feeling can make socializing, keeping a job, or finding any joy in the leisure activities you used to cherish.

Such issues will, of course, affect your life outside of work as a partner and also your mutual finances.

When you struggle with depression or anxiety, it can seem like an achievement, sometimes just having gotten out of bed every morning and clean your teeth. It's essential to appreciate the tiny steps you consider taking when dealing with anxiety or depression.

Do the stuff that familiar people can do is not as convenient for you.

At the very same point, proactive steps are equally necessary for improving your mental well-being. Starting marital counseling with your partner (or have taken a web-based married class) could even help you understand your ailment more deeply. It could also assist your spouse know how to act around you, resist trigger points, and show compassion for the feeling you have.

Conclusion

Nervousness doesn't need to crash your life or the life of your accomplice. Assume you are seeing someone uneasiness is an issue. You should breathe easy in light of realizing that nervousness manifestations can be overseen adequately in different manners, easing the hold that restless considerations have on your relationship. Part of what makes anxiousness so challenging to manage in relationships is that many people do not understand what anxiety is, rendering the simple act of recognizing it a difficult one.

As the reader has learned, anxiousness impacts millions of people worldwide at any given time, with some estimating that as many ten percent of the population will experience an anxiety symptom in a given year. Anxiety can be described as an emotion categorized by excessive worries or fears. This anxious emotion allows a class of disorders referred to as anxiety disorders to be defined. These disorders are all characterized by the experience of anxiousness, although how the feeling manifests may differ from one condition to them another after that.

Perhaps the most well-known anxiety disorder is what psychologists refer to as generalized anxiety disorder. This is the disorder that some people are referring to when they talk about anxiety. However, it is estimated to account for slightly less than fifty percent of all cases of anxiousness. A common category of disorders characterized by pressure is specific phobias. Specific phobias are associated with excessive fear around a particular object or trigger, like crowds, spiders, or speaking publicly.

The initial step to effectively managing nervousness in the relationship setting is instructing yourself enough to comprehend the condition and how it might surface in a relationship. This permits you not exclusively to move toward the nervousness in your connection from the stance of information. Yet, it additionally allows you to show compassion toward your accomplice's tension since you comprehend it better and have a thought of where it might be coming from.

Being entirely taught about concern necessitates that you have an essential comprehension of tension issues. Albeit numerous connections might be described by the overall uneasiness related to summed up nervousness problems, different conditions like frenzy issues, explicit fears, fanatical urgent issues, or post-horrible pressure issues have unusual manifestations that make managing them an unforgettable experience. The goal is not necessarily that the reader should know how each disorder should be addressed, but at least to recognize what type of anxiety their partner suffers from and be aware that different anxiety types should be managed differently.

Although it has been observed that this condition does frequently run in families, it has also been found that anxiety appears to be more common in Western countries than in developing countries (in addition to other notable demographic trends). A potentially important cause of concern is the dysfunctional relationships that some men and women may experience in their youth. This is the idea behind attachment theory: the model shows how children learn how to interact with other people and their environment based on their primary caregiver relationship. As this focuses on relationships, understanding the role that attachment plays as a possible cause of soon anxiety can allow the sympathy that a partner shows for their significant other to become genuine empathy.

Anxiety can be treated successfully, providing relief for the millions of men and women in relationships and out of them that deal with anxiousness. Anxious symptoms can be treated with medication, but it can also be treated successfully with therapy, dietary changes, and natural remedies. These natural remedies include things like herbs found in the environment, inositol, and transcendental meditation.

This would not be effective in dealing with anxiousness in relationships. If it did not provide the reader with tips, they could follow to help them maintain their relationship in the face of worry. It is not easy dealing with anxiousness either as the individual suffering from it or as the anxious individual's partner, and this is a concept that this recognizes.

An important fact to know about anxiety is that it usually does not go away on its own. If stress is left untreated, it will persist, potentially derailing the anxious individual's familial and romantic relationships and preventing them from forming new, enduring ones. The goal here is to help the anxious person's partner become more supportive, which may be so crucial for that person that it can change the course of their life. Anxiety can be beaten, but it will take effort, and reading this was the first step in your accomplishment of this important work.

Part 2

COUPLES THERAPY FOR RELATIONSHIP

Introduction

Couples therapy or couples counseling is a form of therapy focused on helping couples overcome problems that are getting in the way of a functional and loving relationship. Couples therapy is a bit different from couples counseling. Some people suggest that treatment signifies the fact that something is wrong. Counseling facilitates dysfunctionality in relationships and is usually focused on counseling couples in the pre-marital stage. However, the two types of therapy for couples are not that different. Both have the ultimate goal of helping the team overcome their issues and improve their relationship before it is too late. 'Too late' would represent a stage in a relationship where a couple is no longer able to communicate and come to an agreement on whether they should work to save their relationship or just go separate ways. Couples therapy represents a combination of talk therapy and techniques, exercises, and worksheets that help the couple overcome their differences, resolve their conflicts, retrieve functionality to their relationship, and improve their overall quality. The main objective is to increase awareness and enhance the knowledge that the couple has about themselves as individuals, their behavioral patterns, their relationships, and all the things that are not working well. Established awareness and increased knowledge then lead to creating a positive environment for conflict resolution, signifying successful completion of the couple's therapy. Couples therapy is a long process that takes gradual steps towards leading couples to resolve their issues and improve their relationship. Since it is rather tricky for a couple to agree to observe their problem objectively, a third party often makes the process a lot more constructive and comfortable. In the couple's therapy, the third-party represented is a psychologist, counselor, or therapist, preferably specialized in relationships. However, this guide aims to enable you and your partner to come to a resolution without the need to attend therapy sessions. This guide will act as an intermediary towards aiding you in resolving your conflicts and improving the quality of your relationship by proposing helpful and efficient techniques and exercises as a part of couples' therapy; our guide will act as a third party in this case scenario, while you and your partner need to be ready for mutual support and cooperation for the therapy to succeed. One of the most critical conditions that need to be fulfilled is cooperating and being patient until the first improvement results are noted.

Patience, motivation, cooperation, and mutual love and respect you have for each other should help you get through even the most challenging periods of your relationship. However, it must take two people (and an intermediary) to work towards a successful resolution of your relationship problems, which means that both, you and your partner, have to agree that couples' therapy is precisely what you need and what you are willing to get involved in.

All You Need To Know About Couples Therapy

Couples decide to start with therapy and ask for advice for numerous reasons and motives, while many of these reasons revolve around seeking improvement in the relationship between the two. Common problems in the focus of couple's therapy are trust issues, various dysfunctionalities in the relationship, communication problems, lack of individuality and individual growth in relationships, and many different problems that could bring a relationship into jeopardy and eventually towards an end. Couples who manage to realize that they are having some sort of a problem that can make them lose one another usually try to solve the problem by themselves, attempting to get to the bottom of what went wrong. Still, often this situation requires a third party that could act as a medium between a couple and brings a dose of ultimate objectivity. This objectivity should help the couple understand each other better and grow awareness of each other's behavior patterns, about their relationship, and about themselves as individuals. So, to conclude, couples decide to try with couple's therapy for many different reasons. However, the ultimate motive is always the same: learning, increasing awareness and objectivity, and finally resolving issues. Couples therapy is usually conducted by a certified therapist to whom the couple confines the problem.

In contrast, the therapist develops techniques, exercises, and worksheets to strengthen their relationship and resolve it. In this case, our guide should act as an intermediary between you and your partner while having the same objective as a couple's therapist: to help you resolve any potential issues that might be getting in the way of a functional and happy relationship. However, formerly we get to the part where you will need to get involved with your partner in various persuasive worksheets and exercises. You need to learn a thing or two about couples' therapy.

Why Couples Go To Couples Therapy?

Even in cases where people are meant to be together and are functioning relatively well in a relationship, different factors, usually external experiences and situations, could make any relationship more complicated than it needs to be. External factors such as stress, lack of time for each other due to busy work schedules, lack of couples' privacy, and problems at work can create conflicts that might be difficult for the couple to resolve by themselves. To be able to determine what went wrong in their relationship, a couple needs to consider objective reasons and legitimate arguments, as well as analyze the situation from an objective point of view, which is often too difficult for both sides because strong emotions, both positive and negative, are included in the equation. That is how couples decide to turn to counsel. Couples therapy or counseling for couples can help the couple overcome their relationship problems by growing awareness of their relationship and their partner and themselves as an individual. Counseling should also improve the relationship and strengthen their weak points; the only catch is that both parties need to cooperate to work, as couples therapy cannot be attended only by one party. This case would indicate that the other party is not very much interested in working on improving the relationship, while also might not be able to see that there is a problem that can jeopardize their relationship once the conflict/problem evolves to the point where it can't be neglected or overseen. Many people are mistaken into believing that couples therapy is reserved for couples who have decided to get a divorce or are working on separation. However, once the relationship gets to this point, the damage is nearly or fully unrepairable. That is how couples are advised to seek a counselor as soon as they can notice that their conflicts are getting in the way of their everyday functioning, to the point where constant conflicting becomes unbearable.

32. Types Of Relationships

Anxiety regarding relationships is more common than you believe. Everyone has had some understanding of that, but the fear was mild.

It is here where the trouble ends as it is debilitating. If uncertainty regarding relationships prevents you from getting the relationships you desire, you have to do something about it.

Friendship Anxiety

We need to feel valuable to everyone. Another reason that's happening to us is in comparison to other people. Have you ever been part of a community of people, had the need to abandon the party for one purpose or another ... and when you quit the community ... people you believed you were friends with didn't want something to do with you anymore?

It can be a source of insecurity around relationships when it is about having new friends. Social Anxiety Disorder triggers anxiety concerning intimacy.

Effects Of Anxiety On Friendships

Anxiety in all forms — not restricted to social stress — can have many impacts on friendships. People don't understand what we're going through, particularly when we're trying to express how stress affects us, and that may trigger gaps and rifts to form.

However, what's crucial to note is that you're not necessarily alone in this, and it's not a verdict on you. Anxiety doesn't make you a terrible friend; it just makes you someone for whom intimacy may be a little different from what's considered "natural." A good friend would recognize that, acknowledge that, and support you for who you are. We mentioned some of the improvements and disparities between ordinary people's comfortable relationships and those with anxiety:

Annoyance

But you don't want to keep wondering if you're irritating since you know the problem can be frustrating on its own.

Delayed Response To Messages

Replying to an introductory message will take you a long time because you don't want to get across the wrong direction. You don't want the response to be too brief and spoil the discussion until it gets started, but you don't want to tell too much and over-share by mistake either.

Prone To Cancelling Of Plans

The comfort of staying home just lasts a second, and then you continue to fear that no one will ever invite you out again because you're never turning up. The final thing you want is to say you're not involved in going out with those who matter the most to you.

Disposition To Quietness

If your friend asks you to dinner with an extra individual you didn't know was coming, you could clam up. Perhaps you feel awkward. You could not attach a single word to the discussion, so while you are just nervous, you'll end up sounding nervous.

Feeling Of No Real Friends

And if there are people in your life that genuinely care for you, that reach out to you on weekends and settle you down when you're angry, there's always a piece of your subconscious telling you they're not your true mates. You are suspicious because you doubt your worth. It creates you feel as if there is no chance anyone can ever like spending time with you.

Resorting To Distancing

You're scared of looking rude and also frightened of getting hurt, so you're pushing people away. You don't think about yourself. They keep the other party focused on the topic so that they never know too much about you.

Tend To Leave Parties Early

Often it is too difficult for you to socialize, so you need to leave before the night finishes. You really can't stop it.

Fussiness About Future Meetings

If you know precisely when you're meeting and where you will turn up and who else should be present, you're not likely to commit to arrangements. You're not in for shocks. I appreciate seeing a schedule drawn out in advance, so I realize what you are walking into.

Difficulty In Indulging In Conversation

If you're relaxed with others, you have a tough time seeking something to speak to them about. You know what you want to ask. This is why you find that establishing new relationships is too challenging.

Avoid Parties And Gatherings

You're not typically involved in heading out to wild gatherings and packed clubs. You'd just hang out with a much smaller group of people in someone's home.

Start Sending Embarrassing Messages

You should talk to your friends through your stress attacks on how much you are dealing with and how you need their support. But once you're comfortable again, you'll feel humiliated by all the comments you've posted and wish you could take them back.

Friendships Are Stronger

Even though there are times when you feel like the world's worst friend because you take too long to rewrite text and cancel plans, the truth is you are loyal. You are pretty good. You are kind of a sweetheart. It takes you a while to feel relaxed with new people, but they're a companion for life until you find them.

Reaching Out Becomes Challenging

Never contact anyone. You're scared if you do, then you'll annoy people. And you've missed a lot of friends, so you've been too afraid to spend the night in your own house.

You're thinking at home how they want to see you because it seems like you don't want to be approached by them. It's so lonely for you.

You Become Clingy

The insecurity makes you believe the friends are not your friends, which leads you to read so much into any single item. Any slight rejection from a missing response or a rejected invitation is a tragedy for your anxiety.

The individuals you're referring to, while they're not responding by email, you're going to worry whether you're doing the incorrect 'stupid' or speaking too often. Yet if you give a particular tone, they'll say you're clingy.

You're just preoccupied with having too much for anyone. You are so clingy that friends walk away without a word from your life.

Start Avoiding Friends

You ignore your friends because you believe they only have you as a part of the deal that comes with your wife and baby.

You prefer to separate yourself pretty much. You don't hang out too much with people because you never reach out to them, and they seldom reach out to you.

Leads To Ending Of Friendships

We avoid accepting or even care enough to check on you after rejecting invitations. You thought you had plenty of friends. Anxiety has told you that it isn't real.

Anxiety continues to drive out your friends since you're becoming nervous. Making plans is hard for you and holding them. When invites to cancel or to decline are still made, people finally give up.

Family Relationship Anxiety

When you think about it, a family is a community of individuals with whom we can be the most secure. Often, however, our harshest observers and opponents may be relatives. Picture a social scenario where you will get a break and where everybody is seated around the table. It is a time of peace and affection, and cooperation for individual families.

It is not right for many. Excessive smoking, critique, judging, unreasonable aspirations, or a mixture of those can occur in a family gathering. It is challenging in that sort of situation, and an individual might also have formed a defensive mechanism to defend themselves.

And when you are worried about going to family gatherings, you may experience anxiety.

Romantic Relationship and Anxiety

If you need to realize that you are in a sentimental relationship or not, at that point, thinking about it relies upon what you mean by "sentimental." Technically, genuine affection is made

Closeness

It is the active constituent of your relationship. This is the point at which you can lessen and be your actual self around someone else, sharing your most profound contemplations and sentiments, trusting the other, knowing the person will reliably be steady and will stay quiet without double-crossing you.

Enthusiasm

It is the physical segment of your relationship. This is the longing to contact, kiss, hold, have intercourse, and so on

Commitment

It is the intellectual component of the relationship. When problems arise, you work through them, and you stay together, no matter what.

And being in a romantic partnership typically implies the two parties concerned are familiar with each other (emotional closeness). They are potentially sexually active to some level (passion), but what converts romance into true love is the introduction of fidelity- the determination to stay loyal to each other and willingness to take critical steps to make the partnership succeed. You live in delusion without the decision. You feel that love is what you need, and nothing else counts. It is possible only when you fully commit to another that the cornerstone for a genuinely lasting partnership is established. Understanding that you are genuinely dedicated to your partner will increase the degree of commitment and love you have for your spouse.

When you're still in a relationship and feel insecure about it, many issues might happen. If you move in the partnership on eggshells: Question yourself why? Is there a legitimate motive?

Is there any actual or verbal abuse? When you can't see it because someone you know is claiming it's there, listens to it.

When there is no violence, is there internal concern regarding the relationship? Is it a product of how you speak about yourself, the films you see in your head, and the emotions you feel?

If those fearful thoughts contain a constructive meaning for you, such as "Get out, you're in an unhealthy relationship that ruins your self-esteem," be alert.

Whether you're moving back into the realm of relationships owing to a divorce, a break-up, or just thought you're a complete newbie at it … it doesn't have to be loaded with anxiety.

There are other feelings linked to anxiety, such as embarrassment, guilt, and fear.

33. Some Behaviors That Can Kill Your Relationships

When you love someone with toxic behaviors, you may not be able to notice with ease. This is because your feelings make it even more challenging to spot. Furthermore, some relationships start healthy but subsequent change into toxic ones without you even noticing. For this reason, you need to learn to spot the harmful behaviors that can transform a healthy relationship into one, which is unhealthy. This way, you can find accurate yourself if you exhibit these behaviors or call out your partner if he or she is.

They Never Care About What You Are Going Through

A toxic person has a reputation for always sharing their problems with you each time they have one, and they still expect you to be of help. They, however, do not give you any attention when you need them to solve a problem.

They Make Frustrating You A Habit

It is not a break from the norm for interpersonal relationships to have a bone of contention because of the different interests and opinions of those involved. But people with toxic attributes always seem to find a way to ensure you have negative feelings. They do this by either making you feel some guilt or making you angry. If you always go through some imbalance with your emotions whenever you are around someone, there is a considerable likelihood that this person is toxic.

They Are Always Ready To Discover Your Flaws

Everyone has a flaw or something imperfect. However, with the right person around, we can become better people and improve ourselves. But, If you have someone around you who is always ready to tell you about your flaws without noticing the things you have accomplished, that person is toxic. Instead of trying to help you improve, this person keeps using your weaknesses to tear down your confidence and self-worth.

Your Feelings Are Not Important To Them

As individuals, we all have a bit of empathy. This is a vital attribute that allows us to consider others. However, toxic people lack this attribute. Instead, selfishness is a significant attribute for them. This is one reason it is effortless for them to put other people under pressure to get whatever they want. Toxic people are all about things that are in their favor and are not interested in making sacrifices of any kind. Due to this, they use various techniques to make moves contrary to your beliefs and values.

They Make You Have Doubts

It is not wrong to have people who let you know the flaws in your plans or decisions because you can improve your techniques. But certain people only notice risks and make you doubt your dreams. These people are not precisely cautious. They are merely people who are not ready to get out of their comfort zone and want others to stay in their comfort zone. Therefore, they have a reputation for coming up with uncertainties in projects that they are involved in. If your partner is exhibiting the sort of behavior that makes you forgo your dreams, then it is an extremely harmful behavior.

They Keep Crossing Boundaries

Toxic people have no regard for the rights of those around them. This is one reason they keep going over the line endlessly. It appears like they always carry out tests to see how much you can take. They keep getting into your space, taking your time, and also want you to give them attention each time they request it continually. Failure to do things their way means they will manipulate you emotionally to make you feel some guilt.

They Do Not Like Change

In many instances, if we have to keep up with some relationships, change is one thing that has to occur. When two people are in a relationship, for things to work the way they should, the two people involved in the relationship will have to go through some changes. However, if one person is ready to change, but the other is unwilling to, it is best to stay out of such a relationship as the other party is reluctant to make things go smoothly.

34. Habits Of Successful Couple

Do you find yourself going through a string of failed relationships while those around you all seem to be happy and content in their marriages? Do you ever stop to surprise what they are doing differently? Perhaps you have now found yourself with a partner you feel you could build a future with and want to do your best to make things last.

We have taken a look at behavioral traits that can damage relationships, but what about the behaviors that strengthen them? What are the secrets of those couples who have made their relationships last for twenty, thirty, forty years, or longer? Is it merely a case of learning to put up with your partner's challenging behaviors? Or is there much more to it?

Couples therapists agree there are several vital traits present in successful relationships that all couples should aspire to. Let's take a look:

Forgiving One Another

Developing the ability to forgive your partner freely is essential for developing when improving our relationship.

But what exactly does it mean to forgive deeply and freely? Many of us have never stopped to consider precisely what forgiveness entails. We think of it as a vague concept of letting go of wrongs committed against us, forgetting, and moving on. But true forgiveness is about far more than only moving on. Genuine pardoning includes not just relinquishing the wrongs done to you, however supplanting the hurt it caused with something positive, for example, getting sympathy, empathy, and, on account of our life partners, profound love.

Many of us have the incorrect belief that forgiving someone means allowing them to get away with whatever they did to us. But this is simply not the case. Forgiving someone does not mean we are not forgoing our need for justice, an apology, or reconciliation. Forgiveness is separate from the three things. For example, receiving an apology necessarily mean a person is forgiven. And forgiving a person does not mean we are obliged to reconcile with them. Forgiveness is a place we must come to independently of these three elements.

Another common misconception is that forgiveness is a sign of weakness, but this is simply not the case. True forgiveness can be immensely challenging to give and requires a great deal of inner strength. As I'm sure you will agree, this is as far as a weakness as one can get.

Forgiveness can be considered as having two elements: decisional and emotional. Decisional forgiveness occurs when we consciously move from ill will towards a person to wishing them well. We no longer wish for bad things to happen to the person who has hurt us, an essential first step on the journey. This is most often the most straightforward element of forgiveness to manage.

But emotional forgiveness goes much deeper. This type of forgiveness occurs when we can actively move away from the negative feelings the wrongdoing invoked in us and replace them with far more positive emotions. This part of forgiveness often takes time, as it is human nature to dwell on negative emotions, and even when we feel we have moved on, they have a tendency to return when we least expect it. This is especially prevalent when our spouse has committed significant wrongdoing against us, such as telling lies or being unfaithful. Sometimes even the smallest trigger can lead us to recall events we thought we were over.

In all likelihood, you are mindful of the link between stress and physical ailments. Anxiety, worry, and resentment are linked to a wide range of illnesses. Chronic anger puts us into a constant fight-or-flight mode, which causes changes in heart rate, blood pressure, and immunity. But the decent news is that there are also links between forgiveness and improved mental and physical health. When we forgive, we release the stress associated with our negative feelings, which leads to reduced anxiety, depression, and other mental illnesses.

Forgiving your partner for their wrongdoings also sends out a powerful message. When you do so, you make them aware that you know they did not intentionally set out to hurt you, as there is love between the two of you. This is an essential first step in letting your relationship mend.

Complimenting Your Partner

Regularly complimenting your partner is a simple way to show what you value in your loved one. It contributes to your spouse's positive self-esteem and provides a focus on all that is good about your relationship.

But while complimenting your partner when the two of you alone is excellent, the relationship can be further strengthened by making these positive comments in front of others. And this needn't be a showy declaration of all that is wonderful about your spouse. Simple throwaway lines to friends and family such as "My husband made a great dinner last night" or "She always picks up the phone when I call" can go a long way to maintaining closeness and a sense of appreciation within a relationship.

Focusing On The Positives

All interactions have their ups and downs, even the strongest and most loving ones. But for a relationship to be happy and prosperous, the joyous moments must outweigh the negative. Successful couples make a habit of pointing out the positives within their relationship. They thank each other for kind words or actions, give compliments freely, and congratulate one another on their successes.

Similarly, couples tend to be stronger when they laugh a lot. This is a powerful trait that helps prevent life from becoming weighed down with stressors. Of course, all couples will face severe issues throughout their life, but being able to face challenges with a sense of humor can be a powerful asset.

Understanding Each Other's Differences

Most often, the cracks that form in a relationship are the result of two clashing personality types. We can easily interpret our partner's behavior as an attempt to create conflict or start an argument. But more often than not, disagreements arise because different personalities approach situations in different ways. Something we see as just a normal part of our day-to-day behavior may drive our partner mad; for example, if one habitually messy partner fails to put their clothes away at the end of the day. The tidy partner might misconstrue this as their loved one deliberately being lazy or disrespectful, while for the messy partner, it was merely a subconscious reaction with no deeper motive.

Successful couples invest time understanding who their partner is, what drives them, what irritates them, and what is important to them. When we progress a deeper understanding of our partner's inherent personality traits, we make it easier to avoid conflict and handle disagreements more effectively when they arise.

Expressing Interest In One Another's Lives

While you and your partner must have independent interests, one of the traits of successful couples is their ability to show interest in their partner's lives. It includes areas such as work-life, friendships, family, and hobbies. Ask questions regularly and listening intently to the answers.

This also goes a long way to assure you that you are comfortable with the part of their life that you are not involved in.

Letting Each Other Know When They Will Be Home

Of course, in any healthy relationship, there will be times when couples are apart. And a specific trait shared by many successful couples is that they consistently let their partner know when to expect them home. While it may seem petty or unnecessary, the simple act of calling or texting to let your partner know when you will back help build a sense of trust and security within a relationship and helps eliminate anxiety and worry.

Flirting With Each Other

Flirting is one of the keys to maintaining an active sex life and a connected and loving relationship outside the bedroom. Even – and especially – for couples who have been together for many years, flirting is a powerful way to show your attraction for your partner and keep the spark alive. When flirting is no longer present, the relationship runs the risk of becoming stale and mundane, both in and out of the bedroom.

Don't Fight Dirty

All couples fight, even the strongest ones. But those in successful relationships ensure that, when things get tense, they do not resort to name-calling, put-downs, or digging up the past. Even when you and your partner disagree, respecting one another is vital.

Developing Both Shared And Individual Interests

While successful couples have many things in common, they also have their interests. To thrive as a couple, it is essential to develop shared hobbies and passions, but equally crucial to allow one another space to follow their interests.

To develop your shared interests, think back to what drew you to your partner in the first place. In all likelihood, you can pinpoint some things you have in common, which can develop into shared hobbies – if they have not done so already. These interests can be as simple as watching a movie together or as complicated as accompanying each other on the trip of a lifetime. Sharing interests and hobbies with your partner allows you to connect in new ways and create fresh memories of your lives together.

And when it comes to individual interests, successful couples make room for each other's unique hobbies and passions. They show an interest in each other's love, asking questions, and actively listening to the answer.

Going To Bed At The Same Time

Differences in schedules and sleeping patterns can make this a challenge for many couples. But to strengthen your relationship, try to make adjustments so you and your partner can go to bed at the same time several times a week. The act of falling asleep side by side while experiencing skin-to-skin contact is incredibly effective at strengthening a relationship's bonds.

Taking Time To Connect

Conversely, successful couples carve out time to truly connect, no matter how busy life gets, and no matter what is going on in the rest of the world – or on their social media feeds. These moments of connection can be as simple as going for a walk, chatting over dinner, or even doing the dishes together. It's not the activity that's important. Instead, it's the fact that you set aside a specific time to be together.

35. How We Communicate

Communication is necessary for your relationship to thrive. Without it, the love and fire in your relationship will grow cold and dead. Communication is like oxygen to a relationship. Most people think effective communication is all about merely listening actively, but there is so much more to it.

Thanks to the science of psychology, we understand that the differences in communication between the genders are partly due to both genders being kept apart while growing up. Since girls mostly hang out with girls and boys with boys due to societal norms and cultures, there can be a disconnect in understanding how the other gender processes stuff and communicates how they feel. It's almost always a case of little boys playing with trucks and little girls playing dress up or dolls.

Communication Isn't Just Verbal

Communication is not only verbal, however. It is also essential to understand that non-verbal cues differ for both men and women. Of course, the facial expressions for many situations will remain the same as the typical grimace when anyone, male or female, bites into a slice of lemon instead of the smile that follows a bite of a homemade lemon meringue pie.

There are seven types of non-verbal cues. Knowing how both genders use these cues will change how you and your spouse communicate with each other for the better. This way, you can become more aware of your lover's goals, hopes, needs, and fears, with little or no misunderstanding. Let's take a look at what these non-verbal cues are.

Physical contact: Regardless of genetic makeup, males and females communicate very differently through touch. While for men heavy slaps on the back and rough nudges are a way to display camaraderie, power, influence, and dominance, women take the much gentler route of offering a hug or reaching out to pat the other person's shoulder to show compassion, or simply refraining from touch when not in the mood or angry or wronged in some way.

Thanks to science and a lot of research, we now know that touch causes oxytocin release, which automatically generates the couple to share the communication to feel better about themselves and in one another's a company, no matter how terrible their days have gone. Sometimes it is not Advil you need, but a great big hug.

Facial expressions: The human face is a wonder. There are 43 different facial muscles in the beginning, capable of many words — the closest and most recent estimate being approximately 10,000. This makes human facial expression one of the most important non-verbal ways we communicate.

More often than not, women use a lot of facial expressions. There is eye contact or the lack of it. There's nodding the head and pursing of the lips — a lot more compared to men. In addition to having many facial expressions, women are often better at reading facial expressions, thanks to their intuitive and evocative nature. If you doubt this, try telling a lie to a female. For the most part, it won't take long until you're found out.

Paralinguistic communication: Have you ever wondered why a word or sentence can imply several different things depending on the way it's said? You either know of or have had some experience with a little something called paralinguistic communication if you have.

Also named "paralanguage," it is the study of voice, tone, and the various nuances and cues accompanying words when they are said. They represent aspects of communication that go beyond words. There are many things to consider when speaking of paralanguage, including fluency, pitch, accent, speech rate, and modulation. You've also got to keep track of cues like hand gestures, body language, eye movements, and the like.

Paralinguistic communication is essential, as the more you understand it, the less likely people will be able to hide the truth and cover up emotions around you. This is an excellent thing because once you know the actual problem you're addressing with your spouse at any given point in time, it's easier to address the real issue and not the second reason they give you.

Body posture: Since men usually tend to command more personal space than the female folk, they are more likely to align their bodies in such a way that their feet are more spaced apart, with their arms placed farther apart from their bodies when they are upset or feel challenged.

On the other hand, females retract and keep their arms close together with their feet crossed when they feel intimidated, afraid, or averse to a particular person or situation.

You want to be careful when you're interpreting body language. Always pay attention to the context in which you observe it. Don't assume your wife is upset with you because she's hugging herself — it could just be frigid outside for her.

Causes Of Miscommunication In A Relationship

He versus she complex: While women use communication to build relationships and intimacy, men don't understand the logic behind using so many words. Many men believe that communication should have a clear goal, and they see no use in communicating if they are not allowed to fix anything.

If a woman tells her spouse about how she feels overweight and finds it difficult to lose the post-baby weight, a typical male response would probably be along the lines of, "I have the number of a great personal trainer," or "Why don't you cut down on all those fries?" These comments may sound like an insult to her body image, but he genuinely feels he is offering advice. All the woman wants is to be told she is beautiful no matter what the scale reads.

Active or passive listening? It is a Herculean task to get most men to listen without coming in with a solution or their feelings about an issue. Another issue would probably be just how much to say in a given situation. Just how much is too much? Before a man answers a question or narrates an occurrence, he has sifted through the events in his mind. In the end, he only winds up telling the aspects he feels connected to the story.

The reverse is the case with the opposite gender. Women use the power of words to comprehend their experiences and emotions fully. There are times when a woman may not understand what she is feeling and why she feels that way until after she has talked about it. This is why the wickedest thing you could do is not respond when a woman shares her feelings and thoughts with you. You may assume you're paying attention, which should be enough, but that's not the case. You should show that you do indeed understand her by putting yourself in her shoes and feeling what she feels, too.

These differences in communication would explain why a man becomes withdrawn and retreats to a spot where he feels safest (man cave, anyone?) This man cave serves as a mini-vacation spot without the extra expenses incurred with tickets and such. In the safety of his own space, he sorts out his emotions and tries to comprehend what he is feeling.

This withdrawal period can leave his spouse wondering if she is at fault in some way or if she is losing him. That's not necessarily the case. When confronted with an incredibly tight or difficult situation, women would value the support and some level of care and nurture from her significant other, as she would use words to communicate and try to process her feelings.

Avoiding Misunderstandings

Now that the complex nature of communication has been established, and I have made it clear that gender differences only add to this complexity, I want to point out that all this does not mean men and women are incapable of getting along. They can. It's merely a matter of practice and a willingness to understand one another.

The overall purpose of improving communication in your relationship or marriage is to adapt to one another's communication style, rather than try to change the other person completely. Here are some facts you need to be aware of if you want to practice effective communication with your significant other:

1. Recognize that communication has different and distinct styles, and each has its strengths and weaknesses. Understand these and don't be quick to find faults or point accusing fingers.

2. Try not to fit into or feed the stereotypes that exist with gender differences. Understand that the environment plays a massive part in the way to respond verbally or nonverbally.

3. Be aware and get information concerning the different communication styles to control your response to each one effectively. Recognize the different types that exist, and adapt fluidly to each one.

36. Dialogue In Relationships

Everyone aspires to have an incredible, dazzling, and memorable conversation. For this, it is crucial to know how to start a great discussion, continue it excitingly, and end it smoothly.

Steps For Having A Remarkable Conversation

Purpose

You should have a clear goal. Just like you never drive to a new place without knowing the address, you should not engage in a directionless conversation. Indulging in an interaction without a suitable game plan can be compared to driving without being suitably equipped with a map.

If you wish to have a dazzling conversation and get dates and business connections from your meetings, you should identify your aim before going to events, parties, and conferences.

To be a good conversationalist, you must prepare, practice, and execute like an excellent athlete to win. Therefore, you should set your goals, know something about those you are going to meet, and do sufficient research to be well-prepared for the occasion.

While doing this, see if you can answer these questions regarding the event.

Who is the host of the event?

When is the event, and what is the schedule?

What type of people will be there?

Why are you going there?

It is all right to have superficial reasons for going there, such as to get new customers or to enjoy time with others. It will enable you to have a purpose while talking with people. Everyone likes people with directions. The goal is contagious; it gives confidence and enhances influence.

The Right Approach

Meet people with the right attitude. Approach them as a friend and not as a foe.

Maybe you think that people make their first impression only when they start talking. However, this is a wrong notion. The first impression is made even before that. When the other person sees you for the first time, they notice your confident and open body language.

You should give the right signals to being friendly. For instance, your hands should be visible, and your shoulders relax. You can smile and greet people.

Use The Technique Of Bookmarking

You can use this technique to mark or emphasize certain parts of your dialogue to create deeper connections.

Bookmarks are verbal markers that make follow-up easy and give you a topic you can talk about after.

Types Of Bookmarks:

Future events: While speaking about conferences, if a person you like mentions that they will attend a meeting in a few weeks and you are also going, you might say that you will be there too and it would be nice to have coffee together after the speeches. You can bookmark it in this way and follow up subsequent.

Interesting incidents: When you talk with a person, and some funny or interesting thing occurs, you can bookmark it and use it after. For example, if you were chatting with someone in the park and you opened a packet of cookies to offer to the other person, and a dog jumped in the middle and sat between both of you, touching your hand with his paw, you might both be surprised by the dog's sudden appearance. Perhaps the dog stayed there and refused to move until he had finished all the cookies, then went away and returned with a ball. The dog put it in front of you, wagging its tail, as if saying, "Thank you." You can bookmark it and laugh about it whenever you share some edibles in the future.

Some similarities: Sometimes, you may come to know certain things simulator both of you. For instance, you may meet someone who has two elder brothers who are two and five years older than them, just like you.

You can bookmark it and say that you are lucky to find someone in a similar family situation and understand what it is like to be the youngest in the family and live with two elder brothers.

Sharing things: When you are talking about articles, journals, or videos and someone shows interest in them, you can bookmark it. For example, you can say that you will send them the link to have a look. It may prompt them to share some of their favorite stuff with you.

Look For Something Exciting

After you start talking, it is necessary to keep the dialogue engaging, so you should look for some conversation sparks. That is what most charismatic people do. They ask questions, introduce topics, and put forth ideas that light up the conversation and kindle excitement.

Try to find what the person is excited about and talk about them instead of chit-chatting in a directionless manner and having awkward lulls during the interaction.

Usually, the topic that triggers dopamine makes a person feel excited. So it is excellent knowledge to bring up an issue that enables a person to experience joy.

Some examples of sparking questions are:

- Do you have any plans for a big vacation in the subsequent few months?

- Have you been working on something exciting recently?

- Have you seen any exciting movies recently?

- Are you pursuing some hobbies that you are passionate about?

Nonverbal Cues

Raising the eyebrows is an enjoyable trick of nonverbal communication. Almost in all cultures, people raise their eyebrows when they come across something interesting. So if you notice this unspoken cue during a conversation, you should understand that the topic arouses the individual's curiosity, and he may be interested in discussing it.

For example, you engage in a casual conversation about sports. When you mention a famous individual player who studied in your school, the other person may raise their eyebrows. You can guess that he is a fan of that person and talk more about him and hold an interesting conversation.

Tell Enchanting Stories

Stories make a conversation more captivating. People tend to grasp an idea and remember things more easily with the help of stories or anecdotes. But you should not monopolize the conversation and give a chance to the other person to tell his story as well.

Mutual Interaction

Do not hold a lopsided conversation. Even if you tell great stories or exhibit excellent body language, if you do not allow the other person to participate equally, they might avoid talking to you.

There should be reciprocity in a conversation. When a person shares something, they hope that their speaking will share a similar story. Likewise, when they ask a question, they hope to get a proper answer. So whether you are the speaker or the listener, make sure that there is equal give and take on both sides.

Another mistake to avoid when engaging in a conversation is to show that your experience is slightly more than the other person. Do not try to outdo someone. For example, if the other person says that they did not have a good day, you need not say that your day was worse. Or, if they say they have traveled to five countries, you do not need to tell you have been to ten countries, even if you have. Give the other person a chance to revel in his happiness.

End Smoothly

Ending the dialogue on the right note and making a good last impression also has much significance. You can use the bookmarks you have made earlier for ending your conversation. That means you can touch upon something interesting that you came across during the interaction. Use whatever subject applies to you at the time.

Recollect And Analyze

It is quite possible that when you return home after a date or event, you may be exhausted and wish to go straight to bed.

However, it is advisable to recollect all that took place. You can do this while driving home, talking to your roommate or spouse, or writing a journal.

Try to answer these questions:

- What are the things that went well?
- What did you learn?
- Who is the person you should follow up with?

Recapitulation will help you to learn from your experience and polish your social skills.

Conversation Starters

You can use various starters to begin a conversation.

For example, you can say something about the wine or the venue.

These icebreakers serve as a building block in forming relationships, be they short or long term. When we come upon someone new, we can't start by talking about your daughter's upcoming wedding or how much you enjoyed the latest Netflix flick. These are subjects reserved for those you know well.

To converse with someone you don't know, a comment about the weather is always a good opener that can lead to further conversation. If the person is wearing a sports hat or jacket, and you know something about that particular sport, then you've got a great conversation starter. Sports lovers love to talk about sports.

A sincere compliment is always a great way to strike up a conversation. You must be genuine because of pretentiousness notice. You don't want to alienate the person. Give them a chance to expand on the conversation by telling you something about whatever it was you complimented. It will include the principal in a more engaging conversation.

A psychological trick first described by Ben Franklin is to ask for a favor. For some reason, human nature perhaps, when someone does a favor for another person, it sparks a connection and makes the person more open to conversation. You don't need to ask a stranger anything elaborate.

Something as simple as "Can you tell me how to get to room 200?" or "Can I borrow your pen for a moment?" is all you need to say. Most people will be happy to oblige.

Another excellent opening remark is what to say about your location. For example, if you're attending a conference and see someone you'd like to converse with, you can point something out and comment on it. You could mention the seating arrangement or ask where the coffee locates, etc.

If you're in an office setting, you can mention a painting on the wall or construction taking place outside or anything you see that can spark a discussion. Don't be shy. Most people will respond and be happy to engage in conversation with you.

Asking for someone's opinion is a form of flattery and is a sure way to begin conversing. You can start by saying, "Excuse me, I'm not from here. Could you recommend a good restaurant?" or "I see you have a Starbucks coffee. Do you know how their lattes are?"

All of these things, and more, can open the door to a conversation and a lasting relationship. Even if you never reencounter the person, you likely had an enjoyable exchange and one that made your day a little better.

37. The Adverse Effects Of Non-Existent Communication On A Couple

Relationships rely on communications to succeed. If just one person has terrible communication skills, it can negatively affect the relationship drastically. That is why understanding what necessary communication is will be extremely helpful in improving and growing your relationship. Although people communicate daily, most of us don't think about how we do it and what communication entails. We all have our unique habits, and we likely share similarly on a day to day basis. We will learn the basics of communication, learn about how communication skills affect your romantic relationships, and learn about some guidelines for couple disputes. If you have any predispositions about your communication skills or your partner's, scrap that now and begin re-learning.

Communication Ground Rules

The ground rules of communication are relatively simple and describe in two words; open communication. Depending on who the person is that you're in a relationship with, they may have higher or lower EI skills. Being able to communicate openly is the best way to avoid any assumptions and misunderstandings. To understand the importance of ensuring open communication in your romantic relationships, I will teach you how communication skills can affect your romantic relationships.

How Communication Skills Affect Your Romantic Relationships?

Communication skills play a crucial role in your romantic relationships. Without proper communication skills, you might as well flush your relationship down the toilet.

If you are a good communicator, this means you can;

1.   Listen effectively and actively

2.   Observe your thoughts and feelings

3.   Know when a response is not needed

4.   Observe other people and practice empathy

5.   Form thoughtful and appropriate responses according to your observations of yourself and others, through empathy

By preparing all of these things, you can connect with people on a deeper level through understanding. You can share information with people effectively and receive information as well. These five points are beneficial in all types of relationships. Relationships are all about connection, and the connection is challenging without being a good communicator.

How Bad Communication Affects Relationships?

If you are a person who brawls with good communication, you may find it difficult to interact with people in professional and personal settings. If you cannot listen to the people around you and cannot express yourself through verbal communication, reaching mutual understanding in your relationships will prove quite tricky. Observing your thoughts and feelings and explaining these to other people through writing or speaking, for example, is very important, and being unable to or ineffective at this can lead to miscommunications or misunderstandings in your relationships.

Bad communication is not always in the form of mean words, exchanges or voices raise. In most cases, inadequate communication is a lack of communication. When certain things are not acknowledged or said, both begin to assume things about one another and conclusion drawing. Avoid lousy contact in the relationship; over-communication use in said. By over-communicating your intentions and thoughts, the receiving person begins to understand your style of communication and thought processes. The more they acquire about what goes on in your head, the less they will misinterpret you. It is especially crucial at the beginning of relationships, as that's where the most significant learning curve is. It holds not only for romantic relationships but for professional, personal, and familial relationships as well. Just like how you probably have a strong understanding of how your best friend thinks and communicates, you should know that you have a weak sense of the way your new coworker thinks and feels and vice versa.

To avoid any misunderstandings and arguments, be sure to over-communicate to leave no room for misinterpretations. Once you and the other person have developed an understanding, the two can form your communication style that works for both parties.

Fighting In Relationships Is A Form Of Communication

Fighting now and then is inevitable, but the way that you fight is the important part. Fighting is a type of communication that involves both verbal and nonverbal communication. If you are the form of person that screams and yells when you are fighting, you are likely not listening to the other person actively, and this may be something that causes problems for you in your relationship. Being able to fight healthily is an integral part of communication in relationships. There are many different ways to fight, and you can employ empathy to observe and understand the way your partner fights to respond accordingly. Some people turn quiet and will not speak when they are fighting. While this is not an effective form of communication, recognizing this in another person will help you become a better communicator by understanding how your partner fights. You can reply in a way that will lead to a resolution and a strengthening of the relationship. If your partner becomes quiet and will not engage in dialogue during a fight, you can use empathy to understand that they may be feeling angry and hurt and may need some time to process their emotions before sharing them. You can opinion something like, "why don't we take thirty minutes apart, and then revisit this after." By doing this, you show your mate that you understand what they need and that you are willing to give this to them. You are not lying down and admitting defeat; you are merely using your communication knowledge to choose the most effective way to communicate in your relationship. It is a sign of mature and effective communication. By giving your partner this time to themselves, they may come back after those thirty minutes willing to discuss calmly with you and communicate effectively. By approaching arguments in this way, you will examine the situation as progress, respond accordingly, and choose the most effective communication type.

Communication Guidelines For Ideological Disputes

Almost every single couple in the world has experienced its unique ideological disputes. It is unavoidable as no two people will be the same. The key to moving past conflicts that arise from different ideological stances is to listen to the other person and try to understand where they are coming from. Although the two of you may never agree on a particular topic, listening to the other person makes them feel heard and understood. Listening does not mean agreeing, but it certainly does make the other person feel valued. It goes the same for your partner, as well. They don't necessarily have to agree to all your ideas; they just have to listen to them and try their best to understand.

The problem with listening to different ideas sometimes is that a person may merely just be hearing you but not listening to you. You may listen to the individual words that a person is saying, but this is not the same as understanding the sentences they are saying and the entire concept further if you are hearing. But not listening, you likely would forget what the person had been talking about just a few short minutes after the conversation.

When you are only hearing someone and not listening to them, it is a type of violent communication. When you and your partners have ideological differences, violent communication usually is the starting point for further disputes. When a person begins to used violent communication, most of the focus is on the self. Using this type of communication is usually more concerned with their ideas, how they are presenting themselves, and how they want to get what they want more than anything else. Due to this, they are likely only hearing the other person but not putting any effort into really listening and understanding it.

Instead, nonviolent communication uses during discussions of each other's ideologies. Listening is critical in these discussions. Since nonviolent communicators are concerned with the well-being of the people they interact with and play a part in improving this well-being, they place importance on listening and understanding the person to know how best they can contribute to the betterment of the other person.

Another place where this becomes important is when listening to your internal monologue. At this point, you are so used to your inner monologues and thoughts that you may not notice most of the time. When it comes to hearing and listening, you want to ensure you listen to your thoughts rather than just hearing them. Doing this will help you become aware of how you talk to yourself. Are you using violent communication when you speak to yourself, ridiculing, shaming, and judging yourself? It may be something that you notice by listening to your thoughts. By becoming aware of your internal voice, you will also begin using nonviolent communication with yourself. It is just as important, if not extra necessary, to speak to yourself in a gentle and understanding way.

When you can listen to yourself and your partner in a nonviolent manner, you can slowly begin to understand their views regardless of how different they are. The definition of the word understanding includes words sympathetically, aware, forgiving, tolerant, and feelings. It means that listening and learning go hand in hand. The best way to develop an understanding is by listening, asking thoughtful questions, and concentrating.

38. The Most Common Mistakes in Communication to Avoid

One thing that you will note is that a simple bad habit is what gets couples into trouble. Once your marriage is on a rough patch, it gives room for negativity to grow. It is when issues begin to escalate because both spouses repeat their mistakes over and over again. But the most crucial question here is, "what are these common communication mistakes we should look out for, and how do we fix them?"

Mistake 1 Yelling At Your Spouse

It expects that when we are angry, we tend to raise our voice mainly because anger stirs up so much tension. As that tension begins to build up, the body looks for ways to release or express that anger. One of the fastest ways to expel that is by yelling at your spouse.

Many people fail to realize that they are only causing more trouble than relief by yelling at their spouse. When you unleash that tension, it may feel good at first. However, notice that the sense of satisfaction you draw from this act is only short-lived. There is a high likelihood that everything you say when burning with anger will only add more fuel to the fire.

It is essential to understand that yelling often tends to unleash many healthy and negative emotional feelings. It does not solve the problem you are trying to communicate because what will take center stage is personal feelings. It is this very emotion that will capture the attention of the listener.

Mistake 2 Having A Competitive Attitude

Look around you, can you see the competition going on? I guess your response is Yes! Well, the truth is that competition is all around us. You are probably watching a football game, getting ahead at your workplace, preparing for a job interview, or even preparing some Christmas displays in the neighborhood, among others. All these are forms of competition that someone will always be striving hard to win.

There are clear areas of your life where you are probably trying to get ahead, and your marriage may be one of them. You need to realize here that both spouses are considered losers when one of you is a winner.

The little cooking competition in the neighborhood may be ok, and you probably will rib each other out with all the cookout winning predictions. But the integrity is that that is just about it! You have to understand that anything that is not mutual and playful can create walls between the two parties.

In some instances, you will find yourself creating a case at the back of your mind and then creating a very long list of bullet points for the disagreement you envision with your spouse. The truth is that you may win all these arguments. However, you do not realize that you are exhausting and demoralizing your spouse more than anything else in the world.

Mistake 3 Making Marriage About Me Instead Of We

Is there are chatter going on in your mind? Ever stopped to listen to what it has to say? In most cases, it focuses on you. It is interested in what you like, how you messed things up, what you have coming up on your schedule, what your expectations are, and so on.

Naturally, there is so much bias in this chatter because it is mainly from your perception of things and how you perceive the situation. But one thing that you must ask yourself is what does a conversation about your spouse say? Is it about how much fun you will have then what you expect from them, what mood you are in, and so on?

Most of the time, when we allow our selfish desires to get ahead of what our relationships and marriage needs, then we lose the point. You must start shaking off that self-centered view so that you can see the bigger picture.

Mistake #4 Splitting Housework Evenly

You may already be asking yourself what could be wrong with splitting house chores 50/50 between you and your spouse. You need to understand that you are opening yourselves to keeping scores when you do this.

What happens when you feel that your spouse is not taking a fair share? The truth is, there are times after you will think that you are taking up lots of the work at home while your spouse gets to relax and watch a movie! Trust me when you start feeling like there is unfairness in how to work share between the two of you, you open the door for anger and resentment.

Openly Discuss Who Does What

You both must talk about who does what openly. Who will cook, clean, maintain the house, cars, and care for the children, among other vital activities in your household? The thing is, when you feel that work divides mutually based on an agreed-upon approach, each one of you feels that their contribution is highly valued.

Mistake #5 Setting Unrealistic Expectations For Your Marriage

According to research, most therapists have revealed that what kills most marriages is often the failure to accept what they are, their spouse, and marriage what they are. You met your spouse, dated, fell in love, and got married, right? But the problem comes in when we think that the only thing that keeps marriage standing is love and respect. But really, it is communication and acceptance that does. It is the glue that holds your marriage together!

Marriages are not perfect. They are very far from anything excellent. Some storms will threaten to tear your marriage apart if you let them. However, when you communicate effectively with your spouse and accept your union as it is, you will get that it is not always wine and roses. You will be able to weather the storms together, and that is what will strengthen your union and keep you going for as long as you both live.

Mistake #6 Thinking That Sexual Issues Do Not Matter

It is essential to a reminder that sex is a critical component in many marriages. It means that you both have to be on the same page as far as your sexual intimacy is concerned. If you have issues in your sex life, then you have a huge problem.

However, understand that most of the sexual issues couples go through are treatable, but you both have to be willing to seek medical or mental health help from professionals. When you take the time to identify the problem, you will also be able to fix these difficulties, hence making sex better. Fixing sexual intimacy issues can fix other issues in the marriage as well. The main reason for this is that it is tough to be distant from someone you connect to.

Mistake #7 Anger Issues

In a relationship, you need to be careful about your anger and keep it in check. You need to realize that when you allow anger to get the best of you, then the chances are that you will hurt your relationship so badly.

When one of you cannot deal with anger issues effectively, it opens the door for so much damage. Therefore, you both must learn how to successfully deal with anger to eliminate the possibility of building up and becoming a weapon that can hurt your marriage. Talk to your therapist about it to identify the root cause of your anger and nib it at the bud before it grows out of hand.

Mistake #8 Expecting That Your Spouse Will Read Your Mind

There are periods when we have all made the mistake of thinking that our spouse knows what we need, even without telling them. We assume that they can read your mind and see what you think because you are both married. You think that because you had a rough day at work, they can tell that and hug us. We believe that he will wash the car because it is filthy and will use it the following day.

Well, one thing that you have to note is that this is close to impossible. What you are doing is just allowing yourself to be resentful if your spouse fails to do what you expected them to "in your head."

The Best Thing That You Can Do Is To Be Transparent With Them.

Simply give your spouse all the information they need. Do not expect them to know things they cannot see if you have not told them. Simply tell them that you have had a rough day and would not want to be bothered. Tell them to remember to wash the car on their way home because you will be using it the following day.

Mistake #9 Parenting Differences

We all have our philosophies about parenting. There is something that you believe in as far as parenting and will always want to adhere to that line of thought no matter what, right? The fact is that too many parental parenting disputes stem from the fact that both parents have different views on what proper parenting should or should not be.

For instance, you may prefer to allow your kids to make mistakes and then face the consequences naturally, while your spouse prefers a more proactive way of preventing children from making mistakes in the first place. This kind of difference is what brings about conflict in marriages.

It is important to note that when your parenting style is different from that employed by your spouse, it can get to you and, at its worst, bring about destruction. If you are not careful, this may drive a wedge between you and your spouse creating distance between you and your children.

Mistake #10 Financial Disagreements

It does not matter how much money a couple makes because when there are financial disagreements, the marriage is on fire! Financial problems can lead to a considerable conflict irrespective of whether a couple is in debt, has no budget, cannot agree on their expenditure, among other issues.

When you got married, you understand that each of you came into the marriage institution with their money attitudes. If there is no clarity on how much money is to be saved, spent, earned, and used, you head for so much trouble.

Mistake #11 Underestimating small changes

Have you been through a change in marriage before? How did that affect your marriage?

The truth is, when you get married, there are so many changes that will happen. Interestingly, couples tempting to look at the changes and blame their spouses for the outcome. In other words, small changes can be the reason why there are resentment and bitterness in your relationship.

You will often hear a spouse asking their partner to quit their job to take care of the growing house chore demands or childcare, among others. Yes, so many chores at home can be overwhelming when both of you are working. The secret is for you to consider smaller changes that you both can compromise to help better the situation.

39. How To Master And Control The Emotions And How Emotions Affect Your Partner?

Imagine your usual morning. You wake up looking dissatisfied at the arrows on the alarm clock. Then, enjoying your first cup of morning coffee, you think that everything is not so wrong. Enjoy the boss's praise. Be disappointed by the bad news. It's only one in the morning, and the contrast of emotions we experience at one time may seem like a swift swing.

Feelings are a fundamental aspect of our life. If we like it, it is human instinct; what encompasses us incites an enthusiastic reaction. In doubt, this response promptly follows the occasion, which is why compelling feelings are regularly called "streaks" and can be either immensely useful or forcefully damaging. How do these responses influence us? Furthermore, for what reason do we need feelings?

In scientific terms, an emotion is a condition associated with evaluating the importance of the factors acting on it for a person. It does not mean that all things and events around us will cause strong reactions, but only things and events related to our needs and interests. The mechanism of the emergence of emotions is as ancient as humanity itself. And no other than feelings is a mechanism for regulating a person's relationship with the outside world. The first reactions experienced by men in practice are no different from those experienced by prehistoric people.

Every single one of us probably saw how distinctively we could respond to critical occasions. Something causes us fervor or imperativeness, or then again, outrage or scorn. If something pushes us to make a prompt move, we can't stay quiet and act smoothly. Different occasions and wonders appear to hinder us; we are in a detached contemplator, and maybe we are losing power. Subsequently, we can presume that various feelings can both give us energy and remove it.

If We Hadn't Experienced Emotions

There is an opinion that the more emotional we are, the more problems we create for ourselves. However, would we have gotten rid of problems if we had not experienced emotions at all? Let's look at such a hypothetical situation. Along the way, we find ourselves an angry bull. The natural feeling, in this case, is fear. Fear will trigger immediate action that will allow us to avoid this danger. The absence of fear here can have severe consequences. And it turns out that the right emotions at the right place at the right time will become a defensive reaction, a call to action, and a way to activate the energy.

Luckily, it isn't regularly to the point that we need to face such apparent peril. Yet, looking at the situation objectively, our response to wonders of little significance might be misrepresented, and the outcomes of this end up being eccentric. Recall how frequently you could express an excessive amount to family members, supervisors, and partners in the hearts. Individuals who realize how to control their feelings can undoubtedly control us, which is a considerably more severe risk. It is fundamental not exclusively to have emotions yet to control them and contain them for reasons unknown.

But there is one critical point in this process. Do not confuse control of your emotions with suppression.

Control And Suppression Of Emotions––What Are The Differences?

Sigmund Freud, who needn't bother with a different presentation, stated: "Shockingly, the quelled feelings don't kick the bucket. They were quiet. Also, they keep on affecting the individual from the inside." The impacts of such an effect, too bad, are a long way from positive. We regularly move the antagonism from such burdensome states to different parts of our lives. We can succumb to kids, spouses, or outsiders basically because we stifled outrage when conditions didn't permit us to discard it. Having the option to oversee feelings, we could transform negative energy into good or, if nothing else, unbiased force. In any case, a quiet life determines sooner or later after finding an exit plan. If this is the case, how do we figure out how to manage our emotional state, but it is insignificant for ourselves and others. In this case, it expects.

How To Control Your Emotions?

Several techniques will help you deal with your feelings. Sometimes, for various reasons, we have to hide what we feel. Obedience, good manners, and prevailing cultural norms dictate a specific behavior pattern that sometimes contradicts what we think. Sometimes, too strong a reaction does not allow us to convey what we want to say and what feelings we are trying to express to the interlocutor. And in this case, we have to get together. Where do you start so that you do not succumb to your own emotions but take advantage of them?

Exercises For Controlling Emotions In Psychology

Of course, this will require effort from us. But the result of this work will be to manage emotions and self-control in every life situation.

Everyone knows that a good mood in the morning can lead to a good feeling throughout the day. Allow yourself a few minutes after waking up to stay in a relaxed environment, banishing thoughts of all problems, and thinking about the beautiful things that the day can bring. Do not watch the news; do not cling to the family. Remember that their day begins now, and there is no need to ruin it.

A straightforward but handy tool is the smile. And the first person you smile at is yourself. Stand in front of the mirror. Take a few unfathomable breaths, look at yourself, and smile with all your heart as the dearest, dearest person. Give your favorite affirmations; find a reason to brag now. As trivial as it may appear to you, it will undoubtedly lift your spirits, and this is a guarantee of calm and partiality. Keep a smile on your face throughout this exercise, even if you habitually want to stop doing it.

During the day, you may have anything to happen. The quiet state will not cause much damage. We offer straightforward strides for overseeing feelings. Another well-known fact is that chuckling is the best medication. It supports the state of mind as well as the general tone of the entire life form. During giggling, the progression of oxygen to the cerebrum increments, and it starts to work all the more effectively. Merely a couple of moments of authentic giggling can supplant a few hours of unwinding. After such a beneficial impact, negative feelings will be a lot simpler for us to survive if the reason for giggling can't discover without incredible trouble, at any rate, evaluation, an amusing circumstance, or story.

If your negative emotion is directed at a specific person, connect your imagination. Imagine it in an absurd costume. Remember that if you laugh, it is harder for you to get angry—positive emotions counteract the negative ones.

Another strategy is to carry the circumstance to ridiculousness mentally. For this situation, you have to understand your feeling, comprehend why you are encountering it, and intellectually build up this circumstance, ideally make sudden entertaining ends or present the best outcome. This methodology won't tackle the issue. However, our errand is to evade negative feelings—can be illuminated with insignificant exertion.

These simple techniques can be used as an emergency tool when you need to take control of emotions here and now. But sometimes it can be a lot more complicated, and the technique, in this case, will require more serious effort.

Distance Yourself From Emotions

An adverse reaction can sometimes be so intense, so painful that it can adversely affect your mental and physical condition. Such an aspect may be, for example, a feeling of intense fear or annoyance when something is out of your control. In this case, the ability to watch everything from the outside will help. Acknowledge your emotion, say, "I'm angry (angry, angry) because..." Find the cause of this feeling and imagine watching yourself; see how your emotions affect you. An outside observer's role will help you focus not on the stimulus but yourself, your reaction, awareness of its nature, and its consequences. Being aware and expressing emotions will help you find the fastest way to eliminate them. Your focus on observation will help you to get rid of unpleasant feelings. Maintaining balance and self-control will become a routine and straightforward practice for you if you exercise a little.

40. When Conflicts Concern The Financial Sphere?

When a man and a woman are living as a couple, or when they have a wedding project, it is rare to hear them discuss the topic of financial management. However, according to several studies, the monetary question is at the origin of several divorces. It's nice to love each other, but it does not pay for shopping, cinema, or traveling in Beijing. So how do you manage your money in a relationship? Of course, as there is no one way to be in love, there is no miracle recipe for managing one's finances with one's life partner. That may be why we sometimes see great relationships that end in violent conflict because of money. Thus, to avoid those money management problems which are a real wasp nest for your marriage, here are some tips.

Set Priorities

It is perfectly reasonable and understandable that everyone can have different habits and desires in a couple's life than the other. And it is customary to try to answer them reasonably, without penalizing one or the other. It notes that experience as a couple requires a certain number of choices, even sacrifices. It's, therefore, imperative to know how to make choices while considering each other's desires.

Also, it is vital, and above all, to define the way of working together, to establish a budget, even prematurely, and to think about savings and investments. It is usual for couples to divide their daily tasks to make their lives easier. However, it's essential to talk about it and choose a line to follow regarding your financial strategy. You probably have joint projects that require individual and collective sacrifices on which you will have to agree. Listening is the best way to getting along.

The three healthy ways of spending in a relationship: The couple's financial management is a spectrum built around three methods: equity, half and a half, and pooling. There is a brilliant idea when both of you agree. Fairness means that everyone participates according to their income. Sometimes, one spouse earns much more than the other or has special needs; therefore, they contribute more than the latter, which is unfair.

Half and a half are the methods that will prevail when both couple's members have the same financial personality (debt, leisure, income). They will share the expenses. Pooling is acting without regard to who pays what. The couple serves as a single entity in revenues and expenditures.

Communicating With Your Spouse

Even if one decides to have separate accounts and finances, it is essential to talk with one's spouse about investments (loans and outstanding debts). And this is all the added important since a standard account has been created. You should not have financial secrets. Having secret accounts could be the source of unpleasant surprises if one of the two partners disappeared or is deceased. An obnoxious assumption but still possible, being aware of the dead's reports and accounts, simplify the survivor's life.

Create A Common Account

To put into practice the three healthy ways of financial management, couples will have to choose how they will manage their money in a financial institution. This comes down to three choices, too: joint account, a separate account, or both.

Separate accounts allow seeing clearly in the expenses and contribution of each. Each spouse can, therefore, bear his share of responsibility, and the balance is quickly found. However, this solution may sometimes not be optimal. A couple is also a two-person adventure that involves a lot of shared expenses. Tracking can become complicated. The joint account makes it easier to keep track of the couple's expenses. For those who wish to pool their money, this can be the right solution. That said, the joint account requires more control and consultation to avoid unpleasant surprises. But, while maintaining absolute autonomy and a personal financial space, it is possible to spend together on joint projects. This is the best of both systems but also concentrate on their faults. It will require more logistics.

Creating a standard account makes it possible to simplify each one's participation in ordinary expenses and the follow-up of the costs and the budget. Then you have to feed the bill for the regular costs. Each spouse has, of course, the freedom to keep a personal account, which he can manage independently by keeping a discretionary income.

As for the management of this account, we must allocate the funds to the common priorities. We must also try to be rigorous, but without depriving ourselves of everything. This would mean that if one spouse needs something that does not jeopardize the couple's finances, the other spouse should allow him or her to buy it.

Once you have made the financial decisions, you can go about your relationship without worrying more than you need to about money. In the end, good accounts make good relationships.

Balancing The Budget

Achieve and maintain a balanced budget by dividing ordinary expenses based on each person's income. As an illustration, if one of the two spouses earn 10,000 euros while the other earns 5,000 euros, the one who makes more should assume two-thirds of the domestic expenses. In contrast, the other one would pay just the remaining third.

As soon as the couple's situation evolves, it is necessary to adjust and adapt to the budget. This is, for example, the case when the family is growing or when buying a house. Moreover, not living beyond one's means is an excellent way to reach a balanced budget, evoked just above, to build precautionary savings and reserve an investment capacity.

But we must at all costs limit purchases on credit and, above all, question its consumption habits. Small daily and recurring expenses can be nice sums for which you could find a better use.

If one of the spouses is thrifty while the other is a spender, try to find the balance by defining each task's tasks. In other words, it is imperative to establish who does what. The ideal would be a good manager who deals with the management of high finances. But communication must remain, that the decision-making remains shared and that the other can assume other responsibilities in the couple.

Also, even if you do not have investment projects, a financial advisor can help you. You can start with your banker, for example. To be satisfied with your only banker is, however, not judicious. The best thing in finance is still to be trained. You could be autonomous and keep control of your investments.

Contrary to what you can imagine, it is not so complicated. And many sites and blogs are very well done and provide sound advice.

If not wholly independent, training will also help you better understand your financial advisor's advice and suggestions, ask relevant questions, and be surer of your choices.

Money can be a source of trouble and discord in your marriage. Take the lead, and these tips should help you.

One last tip: do not hesitate to address the subject, even if you fear being taken for someone interested. In any case, the question of money will come sooner or after. So, go! Moreover, by explaining your approach, doubts will be lifted. And then you will pass for someone responsible and proactive.

41. Working To Improve Your Relationship

Anger And Forgiveness

Forgiveness involves voluntarily letting go of negative feelings toward someone who has caused you to suffer in some way. Some people point out that forgiveness doesn't mean forgetting what happened or excusing terrible behavior. Ultimately, when, how, or whether to forgive is a personal choice that can only be made by the person who suffered the harm.

If you're thinking about how to salvage the relationship when the confidence has fallen, you're likely to feel furious, jealous, wounded, mistrustful, and a variety of other negative emotions. When you're the one who lost the faith, you feel bad and ashamed. You may also want to accuse your wife or excuse your actions. All spouses need to focus on reconciliation in this case.

You're not only going to wake up one day and feel good about pardoning your wife. Forgiveness is a matter of thought. It's a series of little acts – accepting faults, exercising total integrity, and putting your partner first – that add up over time. Forgiveness is doing a job.

When you are a trust-breaking partner, you will take full responsibility. Be mindful of how badly you upset your partner and give them the support they deserve. Place the partner first, so don't slip into a trap of self-denial. If your faith is lost, take some space, but keep talking. Let your partner know what you essential to restore your relationship. First of all, never give up on that.

Relationships are complex, and work is needed.

Relationships just don't occur.

Relationships are all about our lives.

To have good, happy, affectionate, pleasant relationships, you must understand forgiveness and confidence in relationships.

Other relationships are more shallow, like the person with whom you speak while shopping at the grocery store or people you see only in the church on Sundays. Foundation Some connections are more profound, like maybe neighbors and your hairdresser. Many relationships are much more complex–partner, parents, kids, grandchildren, close friends, etc. That relationship, regardless of its degree, is affected by our choices. Some people were hurt if you made poor choices in your life. We will never harm ourselves if we say something terrible, neglect others, choose to be dishonest, or go the wrong way. Since everything we do affects someone, relationships can be very tense and need reparation. This is one of my favorite topics because I have been through the restoration of relations that I didn't think I ever hope to close again.

I have a personal experience of witnessing the magic of repairing relationships with the people I love most on earth. The connection could not remedy because the other party has no part to cooperate with you. But it is also possible to solve the worst case. Don't give up hope.

One goal in relationships is to know that you are unable to take over the other person. If you hurt somebody-make modifications, don't apologize-make changes. Don't try to justify what you have done-make changes. This is the right thing to do, and it is the thing that keeps you know that you are doing what you can to restore relationships, to the extent that it depends on you.

Responsibility You have no power over whether the other party wants to accept the modifications, but recognize that it does not mean that you accept their apologies. This means that you take 100% responsibility for who you are in the relationship. Note, I said I was in a relationship, not in a relationship. These two things are very different. You need to understand and accept the disparity in the two for you to have healthy ties. The other person must assume the role of reconciliation and obligation alone. You cannot forgive or trust them again; you can't ignore them. More often than not, when they see consistent, honest perseverance in your actions, they will forgive and trust you. In the relationships you have, you are responsible for you. This also refers to the other person; they are liable IN the relation.

Forgiveness and confidence are two of the most challenging things in relationships. Forgiveness does not depend on faith, but trust relies very much on forgiveness. If someone hasn't pardoned you, they probably won't allow you to earn your trust.

And somebody can forgive you, but they can never trust you again. Whether or not they select to charge you again is beyond your control. You're going to live in a constant loop of chaos if you try to control what can only be their judgment.

As an act of humility, we forgive others. Matthew 18:21-22 says: Then Peter came to him and said, "God, how much longer shall my brother sin against me and I forgive him? Up to seven times?" Jesus said to him, "I do not say seven times to you but until seventy times seven times." This doesn't mean it will be cold, and it can be almost impossible in some situations in our humanity.

If we invoke the strength and courage of the Almighty, the "impossible" is entirely possible.

On the other hand, confidence is something people have to win within themselves—many, many scriptures talk of believing in the Lord. Psalm 40:4-" How satisfied is the man who has made the Lord his faith and has not turned to the arrogant or the deceiving. "I love this verse because Our God loves us so much that He would never hurt us by orgy or error, but by men.

You don't start trusting someone for what they say; because of what they do consistently, you trust them.

Choices The other Scripture Psalm 41:9 says, "I have lifted his heel against me even my close friend, whom I had confidence and who ate my bread." No, you will find that the Lord cannot be trusted, but that people may and will fail us sometimes. If you've lost, you're going to have a choice. The first choice is to forgive the person for what they did. This is a formidable alternative because feelings that tell us if we ignore them always confuse them, and we open up again for the same hurt potential. This is not so, however. Because you choose to obey God and release your heart's pain to begin healing, it doesn't automatically mean trusting again. When you decide to trust, the potential to be hurt again exists.

Practice wisdom in trusting others. Their deeds represent their heart's truth. Do not listen to their terms. Listen to their words. Easy to say names, but facts tell the real story.

To forget, it doesn't mean to try to ignore the crime, no matter how many times you forgive. Nor does granting forgiveness to anyone trying to gain your faith mean you have to forget what happened in the past.

The fact is, for a good reason, we don't forget. Our memory protects us and helps us to heal. Time can aid in lightening the wound, and it can even fog the memories, but it doesn't erase memories.

Freedom

Enter freedom of forgiveness. Space Your own heart is when you want to be loyal and forgive others. The bitterness and resentment of unforgiveness just hold you in slavery. The bondage that will steal your joy, peace, and life from you.

Forgive and set yourself free immediately — confidence over time and healing.

Communication Goals

A good relationship requires that both parties be mutually caring, respectful, supportive, and loving.

This requires both to be honest and communicate their needs, feelings, likes and dislikes, concerns, vulnerabilities, and insecurities.

When the anxious partner suppresses their needs and gets upset with the partner for not meeting unspoken needs, it triggers a cycle of mistrust and discontent.

You must make yourself vulnerable to be fully in the relationship, and you can do so by opening up to your partner, trusting that they have your best interest at heart.

You cannot expect your partner to know your needs intuitively, what triggers old feelings, or how it makes you feel. You must talk about it.

If you find it hard to trust, this may be extremely difficult for you – find a trusted friend or a therapist that is not emotionally invested in your relationship to practice with, to help you sort through your thoughts and needs.

This, of course, entails that you spend time figuring out what your needs are, why, and if your partner can reasonably meet them.

You must figure out what you have to take responsibility for in taking care of your own needs and what you can expect your partner to do for you.

Talking openly will help you shift your internal negative model and change your brain (via neuroplasticity) to a more positive stance and help you integrate these new experiences into your life.

Secure people can take comfort in each other, express their feelings, and ask for help. During stressful times they can discuss problems calmly. Even if they do not stay exceptionally calm, they understand that the conflict is temporary and does not affect the relationship. They trust each other and manage conflict appropriately without letting it take over their relationship.

You must practice good communication and learn to master topics that scare you by breaking them into smaller portions. For example, if you are anxious about your future together, try to talk about things in the immediate future before bracing the longer term. Practice these conversations with yourself in the mirror, your teddy bear, your best friend, or your therapist until you are more confident.

Exercise: Communication

See the list of questions in your Emotions Journal. Pick one or a few of these for dinner conversation, pillow talk, or any time you find suitable.

These will help you get to know your partner better, understand each other's vulnerabilities and hopes and dreams, and help you build intimacy. You can make up your own too, for example:

Who did you look up to most as a child?

What did you do if you got scared when you were little?

Who would you love to have as a dinner guest, living or dead, and why?

What is the one thing you need me to do for you if you are upset?

Build Your Future Together

As you both keep getting to know each other, you will surely come to see each other's flaws. Improving yourself will take some time, and it's apparent that it needs to be constant. If you feel like your efforts are not yielding any fruit, don't despair; sooner or after, your partner will see that you want to improve the relationship.

Every little thing that you do to nourish and strengthen the relationship today will add and make it more substantial in the future.

Try to show affection to your partner. Be respectful of what he thinks of your actions. Be mindful of his needs. Communicate openly and frankly. Show your love with little acts that will make your day and his brighter. Let him be your closest confidant.

42. Sexual Sphere - How To Create More Intimacy

I took my first sex therapy class in graduate school in the late 1980s. I had little to no discomfort discussing sexual issues, so I was confident I would have all the answers to treat couples' sexual dilemmas in therapy. Unfortunately, despite my sex-positive attitude, I learned that couple sexuality is a complex, multifaceted, ever-evolving, and vulnerable area between couples. I would have to step back, increase my patience and knowledge base, and honor the nuances that arise in couples' sexual relationships.

I have studied that when it comes to sexuality, emotional safety is often preeminent. Minority populations who don't identify with a heterosexual majority might need special care because they have continually developed shame from rejection or had traumatic experiences while developing sexual identities. Whenever addressing sexual issues, I work very hard at emotionally attuning to the couples to help them formulate their process of increasing their mutual responsiveness and discovering a pathway to a mutually satisfying sexual relationship.

In a large majority of my relationship therapy cases, if sex does not come up as a problem area in the first few sessions, it will eventually come up after. That's because there is such a high correlation between general relationship happiness and sexual satisfaction. I view sex as a sort of litmus test that will eventually reflect the overall relationship's challenges. Emotional intimacy and sexual intimacy seem to influence each other in long-term romantic bonds reciprocally. Sexual engagement usually becomes part of the couple's negative cycle, particularly in the typical case of differences in sexual desire.

Finding Intimacy

Sexuality is a central component of adult romantic attachment bonds. Sex researcher Dr. Barry McCarthy (Barry McCarthy) found that in a good relationship, about 15% to 20% of love is attributable to the sexual relationship, while in a bad relationship, 50% to 70% of distress. Because of sex, this shows that sex is usually an important area of negotiation in any long-term relationship.

Research indicates that great sex doesn't happen by accident; couples who report high-quality sex also prioritize this part of their union. When teams understand its place in the attachment system and learn to cultivate safety and authentic empathy, they set the groundwork for positive sexual relationships.

There are many reasons couples have sex in long-term relationships, such as reassurance, recreation, reproduction, expressing affection, bonding, and stress management. Sex is associated with several physical health benefits, and it prompts our body to release oxytocin, a hormone believed to play a part in couple bonding.

Sex is considered part of the adult romantic attachment system. The anxious and avoidant tendencies that show up in insecure relationships will commonly play out in the sexual relationship. Thus, uneasy partners can seem aggressive, coercive, and demanding about wanting sex, or they may rigidly require a certain level of emotional connection before sex, which compromises security in the other partner. Avoidant partners can seem emotionally disconnected during sex, or sex might be the only form of closeness they pursue in the relationship regardless of emotional connection. Both scenarios can compromise a sense of safety and comfort when it comes to sex.

Since sex is a form of exploration and plays in a relationship, secure attachment is often necessary for both partners to feel comfortable with sexual risk-taking. Sexual arousal is also fostered in an environment of low anxiety, where individuals feel accepted. Any attachment distress will often hinder individual and couple sexual activity and quality and exacerbate conditions like erectile dysfunction and sexual pain disorders. Conflict introduces insecurity in partners, so when couples are stuck in negative patterns, sex is highly likely to be compromised.

Dr. Sue Johnson conceptualizes three sexual styles in couples, directly related to attachment: Sealed-off sex, solace sex, and synchrony sex. Sealed-off sex is characterized by a focus on "sensation and performance," devoid of emotional connection, and shows up often as a strategy used by avoidant individuals. It is essentially a detached approach. Solace sex is the term used to describe the pattern of anxious individuals seeking soothing primarily through sexual activity, mainly if they can't get reassurance about their worth through emotional means. Synchrony sex is the term used to describe mutual risk-taking, openness, and responsiveness in an exchange where couples can bring their complete selves to the sexual relationship without fear of being judged or criticized. They can risk-take without fear of rejection and, in turn, attune to their partners to communicate loving acceptance.

Peak Sexual Experiences

There's no question that we live in a sex-centric society where we are bombarded by messages for how to have "The. Best. Sex. Ever." Many of the messages offer advice on positions, techniques, toys, and other mechanistic features of sex. Dr. Peggy Kleinplatz and her colleagues studied what couples report as far as peak sexual experiences. They released the findings in their article, Magnificent Sex. They found that regardless of sexual orientation, most people say that their peak experiences are related to elements of sexual accessibility, responsiveness, and engagement. These elements are all alluded to in synchrony sex and overall adult attachment processes. Empathy came up repeatedly among research respondents as the main ingredient for great sex. In long-term relationships, couples benefit from accepting the reality that sexual satisfaction naturally waxes and wanes. The acceptance of less-than-ideal sex can ease anxieties to make room for future positive sexual encounters.

Deepening Intimacy

What exactly is "sex" anyway? For years, the sex therapy field has identified the problems inherent in equating "sex" with orgasm. Early sexual response models incorporated orgasm as an end goal, but there are many sexual interactions independent of orgasm that may or may not lead to orgasm. Dr. Kleinplatz and her colleagues also found that couples didn't necessarily equate their optimal sexual experiences with orgasm. They pointed out that sex was overall associated with a "mind" exercise. Many activities can be perceived as sexual. In particular, they asserted that kissing was frequently viewed as an erotic exchange. When couples focus too heavily on orgasm, it can harm the sexual relationship. Focusing on orgasm can increase anxiety about performance, which is a paradoxical barrier to sexual engagement. Focusing on orgasm as an outcome prevents people from being fully present in their sexual activities.

Couples also sometimes underestimate the power of warm, supportive touch for physical connection. Dr. Julianne Holt-Lundstad and colleagues found that increasing intentional courteous communication between couples reduced stress.

Since increased pressure negatively impacts empathy, and empathy is a crucial ingredient for good sex, couples who recognize the power of this kind of activity will likely lay the groundwork for better sex.

Besides setting aside time for an intentional warm touch, couples can increase safety by disclosing beliefs and emotions around sex in an accepting environment. To share experiences and to feel understood allows for risk-taking and vulnerability in sexual communication and behavior. I commonly give couples a series of questions related to sex just to invite a conversation. The main guidelines for this type of exchange are that partners must have their own opinions and emotions. When recalling questions, partners can watch for their emotional responses and practice deep breathing to stay regulated. Also, identifying the emotional reactions and fears that make them feel vulnerable can help regulate any reactivity.

43. Rebuilding Trust In Relationship After It's Been Broken

I have already talked about the overwhelming fear of betrayal. Some people find it hard to handle the fact that their partner has broken their vow of trust. It doesn't matter if you have been married, or if you have been living together, or even if you are starting your typical journey in the world as a couple. Breaking someone's trust is always a hurtful situation. Recovering from that is not still a given, making things a lot worse. So now, let's forget about theory for a while and concentrate on the action. What happens when trust is broken? How do you deal with it? Is the relationship long gone, or is there a way to survive this together?

There is no easy answer here. There is no easy way out, nor should there be. This is a severe breach of trust that has taken place. Betrayal comes in various forms, and they all hurt. One of the most popular and dramatic ways, of course, is infidelity. When you find out that your significant other has cheated on you, how do you cope? Do you try to let go and move forward? Do you suppress your memories, or do you choose confrontation? There are other forms of betrayal, but here we will focus on infidelity, as it encompasses all the details that make it hard to trust again.

Let's be clear: this is one of the worst things that can happen in a relationship. Not only does it shake you from the ground and leave you speechless, but it can also feel as though everything you have worked so hard to achieve so far has been canceled out. All these moments you spent with your partner now seem to matter a little less. You second doubt everything, even the most straightforward decisions. Moreover, you are playing the same images over and over again in your mind. This is your coping mechanism to identify the exact turning point: the point when things could not be reversed.

How come you didn't realize that? What are you, blind? These are just a few of the questions, which will be running through your head non-stop. You will be trying to see through your partner's lies, realizing that you have been lied to when you called them and asked if they were

237

coming home for dinner. All the phone calls, the late hours at the office, all the excuses for not sleeping in, all this will be put under scrutiny. Perhaps this is the worst aftereffect of a betrayal. Even if it was a one-off thing, trust has been breached. This cannot change easily. Some people claim that it never switches back to its former state, as faith can restore 100 percent.

One thing that you need to commend yourself on is the fact that eventually, you saw the red flags. Although it may have taken you a while, in the end, you saw through the lies and exposed your partner for who they were. All this time, perhaps you have been troubling yourself in search of evidence. Maybe you have been staying up all night, trying to think clearly. You may have been making excuses, justifying their behavior time, and again. All this should not haunt you, as it is not your business to be overly suspicious.

It is necessary to allow yourself some grieving period. In the beginning, you might be filled with rage and anger. You will want nothing more than to smash things, yell and shout at your partner, call them names, and probably eat uncountable amounts of ice cream and cake. All this will be washed down by abundant alcohol, for sure. However, after all, this intense period is over, what are you going to do? You need to allow yourself some space. During that time, you will grieve. It is true, you have invested emotionally in a relationship, and now you feel let down. You think that something has broken inside. Unless you mourn, you will not fully comprehend the extent of your sorrow.

After having dealt with the pain and suffering, after grieving for the betrayal you have experienced, it is time to move on. The relationship is pretty much in your hands. I assume that you are facing a dilemma as to whether or not a relationship can be mended. Can you heal the wounds? Nobody can tell you that for sure.

Nevertheless, it is good to know how, if you are willing to try. The most important thing to remember in this case is the fact that you should see it as a clean slate. Otherwise, your efforts are doomed to fail sooner or after. You need to separate the past from the present, whether you are in a new relationship or decide to start over. View it as a fresh start and don't dwell on the past.

Talk to your partner about this endeavor. Unless you are completely transparent and honest with each other, this is never going to work.

Share what you both expect from this experience and talk about your insecurities. You will both be hurt. This is a given. So you need to prepare the ground to start rebuilding the trust that has been breached. If you both want this to work, you will make it happen. It will take time, it will be painful, but eventually, you will get there.

Can The Relationship Be Mended?

You are now trying to rebuild trust, which is a huge thing. It goes without even saying that every case is different. As a result, you must be clear from the start. You will structure this relationship from scratch, addressing all issues, and making it clear what you can and cannot tolerate. For example, where do you stand regarding monogamy? Is it something that interests or hates you? If you want to make this relationship work in the long run, you need to be honest. No more clouds in your skies, no more raining on your parade.

Then you should make sure to take advantage of the opportunity given to you through this unpleasant experience. Although not every betrayal is caused by a problem that the couple faces, it is constructive to ask about the signs you should have spotted. What is it that drove your partner to do such a vile thing? What caused them to act in a way that hurt you? More than that, does he acknowledge that you injured, or is he trying to lower the value of the real betrayal? Besides, when you have all the info, you can modify your behavior accordingly and reduce the probability of suffering from the same thing twice.

If I had to choose just one element, which would make or break the rebuilding of trust, this would be love. Without love, there is no way you are ever going to make it to the blissful moments of the past. It is a colossal transition you are going through, and love is the only thing that will keep you together. However, you cannot rely solely on love. The second element that I would recommend having, to ensure that the whole experience is as breezy as possible, is responsibility. You both need to take partial responsibility for the betrayal. It is only fair that you discuss it further, but the general notion is that you should both be held accountable for what has happened.

I know this might fill you with rage right now, but trust me. This can be a bitter pill to swallow, but you will thank me after. If this does not happen, and you insist on blaming your partner, you will not have any chance to succeed. You will beat around the bush for a while until you realize that you have reached an impasse.

So take a deep breath and be the bigger person to give your relationship a fighting chance. Either of you must enter this experience with a sense of inferiority.

Then, as you will get to see for yourself, you must regain control over the situation. One of the most challenging things to acknowledge is that things have gone out of control. You could not anticipate what happened, and this is tearing you up inside. To gain some control back, you are welcome to establish some ground rules. For example, you can schedule a time and a place to talk about betrayal. Besides, it would be best if you opened up with no strings attached, without any restrictions or judgment. When you talk about your feelings, you need to be honest and expect the same level of honesty from your partner.

Part of accepting your fair share of responsibility is to apologize. You need to come across as sincere, which is essential to the healing process. Respectively, your partner needs to apologize, and then you both have to accept each other's apology. It sounds pretty simple and straightforward, but in reality, it can go horrible. To avoid that, again, try not to be judgmental or criticize what has already been done. There is no use in crying over spilled milk. After wrapping up and proving to each other that you are sincerely sorry, you will have to formulate a plan. In this way, you will prevent future breaches of trust from taking place.

Now, if you are the one who has suffered through the betrayal, then you need to consider some other matters. To begin with, you must be clear as to avoid humiliating your partner. You are angry, but you should go above and beyond to restrain yourself if you want this process to pay off. Besides the apparent betrayal, there are things about your partner that you do not like or appreciate. Are they mere complaints, or do they form the ground for constructive criticism?

After having done all that, and after having completed the process with your significant other, it is time to make a decision. Do you have what it takes to forgive them? This is directly correlated to your partner's attitude. Do they seem genuinely motivated to change? Have they regretted the fact that they betrayed you or that they got caught? There is a vast difference, and you can tell if you look closely. They might have agreed to go down that path with you, only to avoid feeling guilty. This is not the kind of attitude you should be searching for. On a side note, whatever happens, you should seek help.

A professional will listen to what you have to say, but also a support group of friends or family network will do. You are wounded, and you need to lay off some steam. Otherwise, all these negative thoughts and feelings will be piling on, and they will end up haunting you.

44. Disagreements About Parenting

The reason why we are often returning to conflicts and disagreements, and ways to resolve these problems, lies in the fact that many couples are struggling with negative communication in terms of being unable to effectively and efficiently resolve their disagreements. The key to resolving negative communication is establishing equality in the relationship and focusing on understanding your partner's perspective rather than brainstorming how to defend your ego from being attacked by your partner. When you decide to give trust and receive trust, you also need to be ready to understand that giving trust means that you will also have confidence in the fact that your partner is not trying to attack you just for the sake of making you feel bad. In case both partners are aware that there is a problem that needs to be solved and the possibility that they are responsible for the problem, it will be easier to resolve conflicts and disagreements. Accepting that your partner's dissatisfaction is not attacking you but instead challenged to work together with your partner towards solving your problems creates a healthy environment where both partners can express themselves. Communication in relationships is one of the critical components of a healthy relationship and connection between you and your partner, which is why you should try to approach every conflict with calmness and readiness to communicate with your partner so you could solve the problem together. The inability to find an agreement and resolve disputes may also create negative communication, which appears as a side effect of prolonged miscommunication. It may seem to both partner like everyday communication is no longer possible. Negative communication can be any form of communication that makes one or both partners feel depressed, discontent, insecure, hurt, and offended. Communication in relationships is not only limited to verbal communication - instead, your tone of voice matters, as well as your body language and facial expressions. To escape the zone of negative conformism where negative communication has become an everyday asset that the couple uses as a standard way of communicating, you need to make an effort. That effort can include a daily routine where you and your partner will share your thoughts and everyday experiences, i.e., how was work, how was your day, did something happen, etc.

You can agree on having dinner together or having a morning coffee together, so you would be given more room for openly communicating with your partner positively. Negative communication and negative behavior patterns are conditioning loss of connection and, eventually, a break up if not taken care of in an appropriate way.

To make conflict resolution more effective even when there is a fiery argument set between you and your partner, you may agree as a couple on arranging a set of rules for conflict resolution. Creating a set of rules may help you set limits that both partners may decide on when fighting. What should be off the limits, and what you can rely on during an active conflict? You may agree not to allow offenses, yelling, and swearing oaths. You and your partner may also agree that your competition will revolve around looming issues – you will not use your partner's past "faults" to win the argument. Moreover, your conflicts shouldn't revolve around winning or losing an idea, but rather on solving the problem together. Openly talking, using facts, and avoiding offensive behavior is the best way of resolving a conflict.

Differences In Parenting Methods

When it comes to married couples, who had become parents, and couples with children, conflicts may arise due to parenting methods' differences. It is difficult to come to an agreement when your philosophies on how to raise a healthy and happy child are different. However, this needs to be done to preserve the peace in your relationship and your family and ensure that you can provide a healthy and constructive environment for your child. Agreement and planning are the key strategies in this case, as both partners need to overcome their differences in this case and think of what is best for the child from an objective point of view. "What is best for the child" may sometimes be used as an excuse by one of the parents (partners) to manipulate the other parent into accepting their perception and philosophy on how to take care of the family and your child – this sort of behavior is damaging. It can be considered as a way of manipulating. One should never use a child to impose a set of values.

Moreover, each parent has a role. Although these roles have many shared characteristics, the role of mother and father is still different so that each couple may raise a healthy child despite active differences. What is needed in this case is setting a set of rules that both parents can agree on.

This is where you will be practicing the skill of compromising and asking for a compromise. Another thing that will come as more than handy is using facts and logic to find the best solution for forming shared parenting methods. For example, when deciding when your child should be punished or praised, both parents need to be able to conduct the same way and agree on the same set of rules. If you decide that angry crying in public due to not getting the toy your child wanted to regard as something "bad" and "punishable," both parents should stick to that decision. In case one parent said "No" to the toy and the other "Yes" without having regard for one another's decisions, the child may get confused or find a way to use the gap between your parenting methods to test your limits and get what he/she wants. If not overcome and resolved, these differences may seriously damage the relationship you have with your partner, breaking the connection between you and creating more problems that may eventually result in an entirely dysfunctional relationship/family. The agreement, clear communication, and support are the essential qualities that should help you align your parenting methods with your partner's parenting philosophy. You need to have in mind that you are always stronger together, and as a couple, regardless of the type of problems you and your partner may have.

45. Couples And Spirituality

Along with finance, sex, and parenting, another critical issue in couples' therapy is spirituality, or, more specifically, religion. Historically, people have turned to religion to be told who to marry. Although this is no longer the case for many cultures, our faith and spirituality can still cause disagreements between you and your partner and your family.

Religion

Mainly if you come from a religious background, it can be difficult for your family to accept a partner who is of a different religion to you – or indeed, a partner for whom religion is not a big part of their life. But as the world becomes smaller and we embrace other cultures more and more, there is no guarantee we will fall in love with someone from our race or religion.

When it comes to religion, its effect on a relationship goes deeper than merely determining whether or not you will attend church on Sunday. Religious beliefs can play a part in choosing how to raise children, how you relate to your family, how you celebrate holidays, and even where you live and work.

But interfaith relationships – or a relationship between a believer and an atheist – are not necessarily doomed to fail.

Respect Each Other's Beliefs

One of the critical steps to overcoming any disagreement is respecting and understanding your partner's perspective. Remember, in this case, and it's fair to agree to disagree – the important thing is that you can openly discuss your views with one another without passing judgment. This is especially critical in spirituality and religion, as those who identify strongly with a particular faith often attach a part of their identity to their beliefs. And by criticizing their trust, you are, by extension, attacking them.

Share In Each Other's Religion

Your partner's religion can be an essential place to practice this. While it is a key to give your partner space to practice their religion as they see fit, you can create a deeper connection between the two of you by participating in their faith from time to time. Remember, you don't need to be a believer to be a respectful observer. Consider going to church, synagogue, or mosque with your partner from time to time or attending a religious celebration. This helps you understand your partner on a deeper level and goes a long way to show them you accept this intrinsic part. It can also be particularly beneficial if and when you have children – if your children choose to follow in your partner's religion, you want to be able to share in this aspect of their lives.

Allow Time For Your Partner To Adjust

Even if your partner seems particularly willing to embrace your religion and all it entails, allow them time to adjust to changes. Acknowledge that introducing him or her to a new religion can raise questions and cause them to feel unsettled. Give your partner time to adjust to any changes, and be there to answer their questions.

Accept That It Could Be A Deal-Breaker

Sometimes it may be necessary to acknowledge that, for the devoutly religious, a partner who does not share their beliefs can be a deal-breaker. If you find yourself being cast aside for your partner's religion, acknowledge that it is not about you but rather about their deep-seated beliefs – beliefs that were in place long before you came along. In this case, please do not try to change your partner's mind, as this may cause long-term conflicts between you and your family. Instead, respect their decision and move on.

Broader Spirituality

These days, many people have a broader view of spirituality than just religion. Spirituality can encompass our relationship with the universe and our higher self, our relationship with the planet, and our beliefs surrounding the human soul, along with many other things.

And while it is not necessary to share the same spiritual beliefs with your partner, it can lead to a deeper connection at all levels when you explore your spirituality together.

Increasing Our Spiritual Connection With Our Partner

To increase the spiritual connection between you and your partner, you must first be clear on what spirituality means to you. You must understand who you indeed are and what you want in life.

To do this, take some time to reflect on the following questions:

What are my beliefs regarding life in general?

What do I believe in terms of spirituality and religion? How important are these elements in my life? How essential are these elements in a relationship?

What do I believe concerning God or a higher power?

Am a devoted to a particular religion or spiritual path? How committed am I to this path? How important is it that my partner shares this path? How will the decisions I make in this area affect my family (and the wider community)?

What daily rituals do I have regarding prayer, devotion, or meditation? How non-negotiable are these?

Once you have taken the time to understand your thoughts surrounding these crucial issues truly, ask your partner the same questions. Be sure you know the answers to his or her questions and the underlying reasons behind these answers. Sometimes, talking openly about these matters and understanding the reasons behind your partner's beliefs can be enough to deepen your spiritual connection truly.

If you and your partner have spiritual beliefs that align with one another's, you might consider designing a daily spiritual practice that you can both share. For example, you might choose to meditate together at the beginning and end of the day. The simple act of sitting in silence together can be a fantastic way of deepening your connection.

What To Do When Your Partner Doesn't Share Your Spirituality

But what do we do when spirituality plays a large part in our lives, yet it is not something that our partner values? For many couples, this can become a valid point of conflict as those trying to build an interfaith relationship. And just like interfaith couples, one spiritual and one non-spiritual partner does not necessarily spell the relationship's end.

The key is respect and understand. Challenges can arise when one partner not only doesn't share their spouse's spirituality but fails to understand why they have such beliefs in the first place. They may seek to make fun of their partner's thoughts, seeing them as too "new age" or "fluffy."

But the steps outlined above to help interfaith couples navigate their relationship can also be applied in relationships in which there is one spiritual and non-spiritual partner.

If you are the spiritual partner, consider ways to share your spirituality elements with your spouse without forcing them to alter their beliefs or engage in anything that makes them uncomfortable. This may be something as simple as reading them a passage from your favorite spiritual journal or asking them to sit with you for a five-minute meditation.

If you are the non-spiritual partner, firstly acknowledge that your partner's spirituality likely makes up a large part of their identity. Please recognize that you are mounting a personal attack on them by mocking or criticizing their spiritual beliefs. While you should not be expected to adopt your partner's beliefs or practices (unless, of course, you choose to), agreeing to learn more about their spirituality shows you accept and respect a crucial part of your loved one. This serves to deepen the connection between you and encourage you to share more of your lives.

46. Strategies And Secrets To Improve Couple's Communication

Regardless of whether it is a relationship with your better half or even your friends, there will be some challenges. Different factors are essential for the success of a partnership or even a long-term relationship. However, a necessary element of all is communication. The lack of proper communication skills can effectively ruin any relationship you have in life with anyone. It is quite vital to effectively and efficiently communicate what you want, need, feel, or desire with your partner for your relationship's health. The lack of proper communication often creates misunderstandings and feelings of resentment. These things can quickly ruin your relationship. The good news is that you can also improve your communication skills with any other gift in life.

General Tips For Better Communication

Active Listening

There is a difference between hearing what the other person says and actively listening to them. At times, you might even listen to what your partner says, but you may not be fully present while doing so. You might be distracted with something else or react to any strong emotions they display. In regular conversations and especially during any heated discussions, you might impatiently wait to express your thoughts or wait for your chance of a rebuttal. You might be impatiently thinking about all the various ways in which you can respond to them while they are still speaking instead of actively soaking up what they are saying and then responding after. When you do this, you do not pay much attention to what your partner is saying because you're engrossed in your thoughts.

Now, with any talk about the concept of being an active listener, you must make a conscious effort to slow down your thoughts and listen to what your partner is saying, not just with an open mind but an open heart as well. Like most things in life, this is easier said than done. However, your intention is what matters, so this will be a starting point.

If for some reason, you don't have the concentration to listen actively and openly to what others say, then you can put the argument or conversation on hold until after. Another simple way to work on becoming an active listener is by sharing your feedback. You merely need to restate or paraphrase whatever your partner says toward the end of the conversation to demonstrate the fact that you have been listening to what they were saying.

The conversation dynamic can shift positively when your partner knows that they are being seen and heard. That said, I'm not suggesting you have to agree with everything they say, but you can effectively improve the communication in your favor by showing that you understand them. Even if you sound a little transparent while doing this, it is okay. At least you are making an effort to get started. For instance, you can say something like, "... did I understand this correctly?" Or "it seems like you are upset with me for not doing..."

As with any other skill in life, you can become an active listener, but it takes time and effort. You cannot develop the skill without practice, so start practicing your skills of becoming an active listener. The more you get, the better you will be, and the easier it will be for you. During an initial couple of weeks, active listening might not come naturally to you, but you will get the hang of it after a while.

Open-Ended Questions

"Do you ever stop talking and ever listen?" or "I wonder if you will ever clean up without me asking?" You might have used such rhetorical questions at some point or other with your partner. Well, do these seem like great conversation starters to you? I'm sure even you would agree that this is not the best way to start a healthy conversation or a dialogue. Sure, when you are frustrated, upset, or annoyed, these might seem like pretty good things to say in that instance. However, for the health of your relationship, these are good for you in the long run. By making such statements or asking such questions, you are essentially putting your partner on the defensive once again. Once this happens, the scope for healthy discussion goes down the drain. Instead of transferring any unpleasant emotion into the conversation, start using open-ended questions. For instance, if you are unhappy that your partner doesn't clean up, instead of the rhetorical question mentioned above, try using an open-ended question.

Instead of saying, "I wonder if you will ever clean up without me asking!" you can say something like, "I could certainly use more help around the house. What can we do about it?" or "It would be nice to get this all cleaned up quickly. What can we do?"

Internal Editing

While you are communicating with your partner, you must make a conscious effort to avoid resorting to any form of personal criticism. It means you must refrain from displaying criticism either verbally or through your body language. So, don't resort to any putdowns, insults, negative criticism, or indicate undesirable body language such as eye-rolling or dramatic sighs. The minute you start being critical of your partner, you are immediately shifting into the defensive. Once your partner gets defensive, whatever the topic of conversation was, it is most likely to turn into an argument or a nasty fight. When you put your partner on the defensive, it significantly harms the entire conversation. It not only limits how much you listen, but the conversation will escalate out of anger, and you might both end up hurting each other with the things you say.

Keep Calm

Whenever you are engrossed in discussion with your partner, ensure that you keep calm. If you stay calm, the chances of a conversation spiraling out of control and turning into a massive argument will decrease. If you want, you can break from the conversation and then revisit the issue when you feel more emotionally stable and calm. Not just you, encourage your partner to do the same as well. It is better to have a discussion when you and your partner are emotionally stable and not volatile. You must also become conscious of any internal self-talk in your mind while conversing with your partner. For example, let's suppose you are in disagreement. Does your internal self-talk increase your ability to calm yourself down, or does it make you even more irritated? If you notice that this internal self-talk seems to be fueling the fires of emotional distress, it is time to change it. While in the middle of an argument, if you catch yourself thinking, "the last time we fought, the things they said hurt me," or "this is what they always do, and it is unfair," then stop yourself immediately. By engaging in negative self-talk, it will only worsen the situation at hand. Don't do this and, instead, try to replace all this with calmness. Once you are calm and no longer seeing red, you are better positioned to express yourself and understand your partner.

Work on self-soothing whenever you are upset. For instance, maybe you can go for a short walk or even take a timeout and physically remove yourself from the room your partner is in. This helps ensure that your emotions are in check, and you're the one in control of them. A conversation will be quite productive when your emotions are balanced and your mind is clear.

Being Gentle

If there is a problem that bothers you, you can freely state the reason. While doing this, you must be gentle with your partner. Don't blame your partner, but instead talk about what you feel and have experienced. When communicating questions, please pay attention to the tone used. Using a mutually respectful manner, you can start a constructive dialogue and open up communication lines between you both. Keep in mind that the style you use must not be aggressive or passive. Once again, if your partner detects any hints of criticism or passive-aggressiveness, the entire conversation will come to a startling halt.

Incorporate "I" Statements

The best way to own your feelings while communicating with your partner is by using "I" statements. Instead of pointing out your partner's mistakes, concentrate on expressing how you feel because of their actions. The most common phrases you can start using are, "I feel," "I want," or "I need." For instance, saying something like, "I feel bad that you said ____." By doing this, you are effectively preventing your partner from becoming defensive while expressing yourself. It will also make your partner more self-aware of their behavior. This technique also encourages you to express yourself, your thoughts and emotions, more clearly.

Perspective

Your perspective essentially determines everything you feel and think. For instance, you might say that the glass is half empty, while your partner says the glass is half full. No matter what you think, the amount of water, or any liquid in the mirror will remain the same. So, why not believe this is true from your partner's perspective. After all, the content of juice is the same, and your partner isn't wrong. Placing yourself and your partner's shoes in any situation makes it easier for you to view things from their perspective.

Once you understand where they're coming from and why they are saying what they say, it becomes easier to understand them. It can also trigger feelings of empathy for you. The extent to which your relationship can be successful depends on whether you can accept influence from your partner or not. At times, all it takes is a mere shift in perspective to resolve a dispute.

Understanding

We all want to be understood, but one thing we all fail to do is understand others. You must first try to understand what the other person says before you demand that you are understood. This is a simple technique you can use while engaging in conversations with your partner, family members, friends, colleagues, or pretty much anyone in your life. As human beings, it is an inherent tendency or desire to be understood by others. Take a moment and think about all the times you've said, "No one understands me," or "You don't understand what I'm trying to say!" For a healthy, loving, and successful relationship, you and your partner must understand each other. For a moment, don't emphasize your need to be understood, and instead, shift the focus to understand them better. This simple shift in the way you use your attention helps clear a path for fresh communication and positively shifts the relationship's dynamic.

47. Some Example Of Conversation And Dialogue In Different Day Moments

Each day you want to deeply understand your partner, how they view life, and their deepest thoughts. Sometimes you feel like you have talked about everything, and the spark is fading. Here are conversation starters that will light that fire or rekindle it.

1.   Would you describe yourself in one word?

2.   What are you currently worried about?

3.   What will you never do in your life?

4.   What are you willing to fight to the death for?

5.   What is this that you repeatedly do, you do not like it, but you still do?

6.   What makes you uneasy?

7.   What do you miss most about your past?

8.   What is your biggest challenge?

9.   What are your current life goals?

10.   What have you ever given up on?

11.   What do you feel is your purpose in life?

12.   What plans do you have for your future?

13.   Who do you consider to be your family?

14.   Who is your best friend, and how did you meet?

15.   What music do you love listening to, and why?

16.   Do you think you could survive to live in another country, and what country would this be?

17.   Which culture do you find fascinating?

18. Do you believe that your dressing defines you?

19. If you could choose to be anything in this world, what would you be

20. What if your animal spirit?

21. Have you ever lost something or someone important to you?

22. What is your understanding of love?

23. What gives you joy?

24. Does your job make you happy?

25. If you did not have to worry about money, what would you do for the rest of your life?

26. What do you consider to be your strengths?

27. If you could meet one significant person or celebrate, who would it be

28. What is the most exciting, adventurous activity you have ever done?

29. What you ever had an illegal crush on? A forbidden passion has feelings for someone you shouldn't have.

30. Do you look forward to date nights, or would you instead spend the evening at home?

31. What are your favorite social media site?

32. What is your most embarrassing moment, and how did you respond?

33. What is the biggest mistake you have made, and how has it impacted your life?

34. If you could spend the whole day with two historical figures, who would you choose and why?

35. What is the most useless item you have bought?

36. What is the largest purchase you have ever made?

37. What is the most remarkable thing anyone has ever said or done for you?

38. If you are given a chance to change anything about yourself, what would you choose to do?

39. Who was your childhood hero?

40. Who was your favorite teacher, and why?

41. What is the highlight of your day? This is a question you can ask every day?

42. What season do you enjoy most, and why?

43. If you were to pick the desert or the tundra, where would you live in for a year?

44. Who is your favorite actor or actress?

45. What is the best show or concert you have seen live?

46. Who is your favorite musician, and which single do you love most?

47. Who is your least favorite actor or actress?

48. Which brand do you enjoy listening to?

49. Which color do you like most?

50. What your favorite meal and beverage

51. Which is your least favorite meal or beverage

52. What do you do in your free time?

53. Do you like dancing? If yes, what type of dance?

54. Do you enjoy entertaining other people?

55. If you had only one more day to live, how would you live it

56. What would you love your last meal to be?

57. Would you prefer living in the city, on the coast or in the country?

58. Have I ever embarrassed you publicly?

59. What is one thing I do that ultimately drives you insane?

60. What did I do today that made you feel special and appreciated?

61. Apart from my looks, what else do you love about me?

62. What is the best way for me to show how much I love?

63. How do you know when I am upset?

64. What do you like most about my body?

65. Which family member are you closest to?

66. What did your family teach you about love and relationships?

67. How does your family settle conflict?

68. Do your parents influence the decisions you make?

69. What did you admire about your parent's behavior towards one another?

70. What does my family do that makes you uncomfortable?

71. What has always been your dream job?

72. Have you ever been fired?

73. What is your definition of being successful?

74. How would you spend your vacation?

75. What characters do you hate in a person?

76. What about you makes you proud?

77. What do you regret missing out on?

78. Are you happy with the company you keep?

79. What music instrument excites you

80. What was your most embarrassing fart?

81. What is your understanding of death?

82. What are your rules in life?

83. What movie or journal would you wish to experience?

84. If you had a friend with similar characters to yours, would you maintain them?

85. What petty things do people do that annoy you?

86. What is your darkest secret?

87. Who is the most irritating person?

88. What have you always struggled with?

89. What calms you down?

90. What is the craziest thing that happened to you in school?

91. What is the most traumatic thing you've gone through?

92. Where is the scariest place you've been to?

93. What is the state of the world right now?

94. What is the biggest betrayal you've experienced?

95. What makes you unique from the rest?

96. What lesson did you learn the hard way?

97. Which of your personalities should you work on?

98. What words of wisdom do you walk with?

99. Tell me about your near-death experiences.

100. How do you vision your perfect life to be like?

101. Which friend have you not communicated with for a while now?

102. Do you have any pretentious character?

103. Who do you look up to?

104. What are the healthiest and unhealthiest times of your life?

105. What do you think you were born to do?

106. What do you like doing when alone?

107. How would you want people to remember you?

108. What don't you fear that others find frightening?

109. What is your take on morals?

110. What animal do you fear most?

111. What major scandal have you been involved in?

112. Do you think you can handle prison life?

113. When was the last time you cried, and why?

114. What is your take on trust?

115. What do you regret taking for granted?

116. What was the most significant opportunity you had?

117. What question do people often ask you?

118. What is the saddest experience you've gone through?

119. What do you look forward to most in a day?

120. What time of the day do you like most?

121. Do you work well under pressure?

122. What is the most challenging favor someone has asked you for?

123. What habits do you still have from your childhood?

124. What is the best or worst character you've inherited from your parents?

125. What school subjects did you like and hate the most?

126. What toy did you love most?

127. What new hobbies would you want us to try together?

128. What is our greatest strength as a couple?

129. How much time and space would you prefer in this relationship?

130. What makes our relationship unique?

131. How do you vision us ten years from now?

132. Where do you want to live after retirement?

133. What adventure would you want us to go?

134. What would I do that you cannot forgive?

135. What are your relationship goals?

136. When am I sexist?

137. What is the most embarrassing that has happened to you during sex?

138. Would you want us to have children? When and how many?

139. Do you think having kids will affect our relationship?

140. What weird food combinations do you enjoy?

141. What new cuisine would you like to try out?

142. Do you think aliens exist?

143. What would be your reaction if you ever see an alien?

144. Which movie can you rematch severally without losing interest?

145. What crime are you likely to be convicted for?

146. What is that one thing that will always be fashionable?

147. What older people's behavior do you have?

148. What is the most precious thing you broke?

149. What is the spiciest dish you have ever eaten?

150. Which body part can you sell at ease?

151. What do you think is the cure for hiccups?

152. Which mythical creature do you have a connection to?

153. What do you look at when judging someone?

154. If someone was to narrate your life's story, who would you prefer?

155. Which smartphone app do you like?

156. Which quotes inspire you most?

157. What joke do you know by heart?

158. What is the funniest prank you have ever carried out?

159. Which charity do you think is most deserving of money?

160. If you could talk to a ghost, which would it be?

161. What would you make them do?

162. What game can you play for hours?

163. Which movie left you in suspense?

164. Which music would you recommend me to listen to?

165. Which world-famous monument would you want to see?

166. What are you most addicted to?

167. What has been your most wicked revenge plan?

168. Who would make for the worst roommate?

169. What is your worst meal?

170. If you were kidnaped and all they offered was your worst food, which is fresh of your best food but thoroughly spoilt, what would you choose?

171. What is the worst thing you have done just to achieve your goals?

172. Which songs make you nostalgic?

173. Who would you have instead acted as the main actor and actress in the titanic?

174. What is a ridiculous lie you have said?

175. When was the last time you lied?

176. If you were given the ability to shapeshift, what will you be?

177. What animal or plant species do you think should be renamed?

178. How would you rather die?

179. Which new language would you want to learn?

180.   Which is your favorite restaurant?

You should ask these questions with an open mind, and you should not be mad if some of the answers given are not what you wanted to hear. These questions will have to follow up questions, and you will find both of you engaging in the endless charter.

48. How Couple Therapy And Marriage Counseling Can Improve Relationships?

Couples therapy is intended to explain the personality discrepancies between people in a relationship to solve problems more efficiently. Couple therapy is a fast, solution-centric approach that describes and takes the outcomes into account clear and achievable recovery objectives. Couples therapy allows couples to develop relationship enhancement approaches.

The pair therapy approaches to teach you how to take constructive chances in establishing a romantic relationship. Opportunities for personal development persist throughout the lifespan. Individual development contributes to healthy, engaged ties. Couple therapy encourages relational development that allows people to feel more connected. People gain trust when they feel confident to expose to their partners the darkest, most private self. The best way of obtaining a successful outcome is to partner with an accomplished specialist, including a licensed marriage counselor and a family therapist.

Which Kinds Of Issues Are Dealt With In The Consultation Of Couples?

Psychotherapy for couples deals with everyday issues in relationships, including inadequate communication, difficulties getting along, and boundary conflicts with other family members such as parents or grandparents, parental disputes, or financial stress. Couple counseling teaches couples a more caring and compassionate way of living.

Employment or job, financial, and child and family problems are the pressures that modern society imposes on a relationship. Through marriage therapy, people learn how to cope with daily challenges without damaging their relationship. Through psychotherapy, couples understand that we are all imperfect and that we all have human flaws. Couples in counseling understand that we can harm one another and learn strategies to avoid it as much as possible. Partners in the therapy process feel that they have a safe place to identify harmful behavior.

People learn good communication skills in relationships to apologize for and to express sorrow.

How Long Do People Live In Pairs?

Counseling for couples is structured to deal with unique issues. In 10 to 12 sessions, problems should be detected on average, and practical behavioral approaches start to effect. The number of sessions is adjusted according to the couple involved and their specific problems.

Many couples want to work with the therapist to develop new skills and successful approaches. They know that cognitive instruments that lead to a more productive partnership can be taught. When a few put into practice what is learned during the original sessions, they are inspired to "learn more" because they see that they have a happy life with their partner. Couples frequently initiate marital counseling in a situation of crisis. If heavy emotions begin to withdraw, the psychotherapist and the couple will begin the real learning work and develop other skills and strategies to strengthen marriage or relationship.

Why Do You Use A Marriage And Family Therapist (MFT) For Counselling And Psychotherapy For Couples?

Marriage and family care practitioners, who have a certificate in marriages, family dynamics, and psychotherapy, are specially trained. These experts diagnose and treat a wide variety of emotional and psychological problems among people in a relationship.

A marital therapist is professionally trained to listen and unbiasedly examine the problems posed by partners. The couple's friends and family are always caring and want to help. Still, their deep emotional involvement in one or both partners leaves them unable to consider the relationship dynamics critically. After the first session with a successful marriage therapist, it is very typical for couples to have "hope" in their relationship that they do something good.

Can I Become A Better Listener By Offering Advice To Couples?

During couples' therapy, people learn different methods of responding to the needs of their spouse.

Effective listening strategies enable people to build their partner's empathy, understand better, and strengthen their relationship with their partner. Relationships and relationships are improved and cherished when people learn to listen to each other.

Psychotherapy for couples includes instruction in dispute management, the removal of miscommunication, and painfully hurt emotions. Any unavoidable partnership causes issues. You should listen entirely to your partner's needs through counseling. An accomplished marriage therapist, a family, and couples may help people develop their communication skills uniquely.

The therapist will help you keep track of a question while working on it. You learn to avoid "making a case" by carrying insignificances that can only cause others' suffering. Couple counseling can help establish dialogue surrounding a difference of opinion that leads everyone to a suitable solution.

Why Is Counseling Couples Going To Help Me Overcome My Marital Conflicts?

Then, the therapist should help develop a secure, warm, and trustworthy relationship for both parties. So you meet with the therapist to grasp the conflict's existence. Conflicts also occur when partners vary in intent or expectation in a relationship. The therapist helps you and your partner consider each other's needs and learn new ways of interacting to overcome the conflict.

An experienced couple therapist may help couples build communication skills to strengthen dispute resolution techniques that can be developed over time. People develop an improved willingness to listen to the other person's views, although they may not agree to the specific question. In a non-critical and non-confrontational manner, the marriage therapist will demonstrate successful and reliable ways of communicating negative emotions like hurt and rage. The efficient resolution of disputes leads to couples becoming more substantial and more secure, strengthening their marriage.

Is Therapy For Couples Effective?

Many studies indicate the importance of therapy for couples. The vast majority of people in pair counseling show a change in their understanding and relationship.

Couple therapy does not only allow people to remain together very effectively. Nevertheless, as each person in the relationship continues to grow and evolve, they progress to more efficient, constructive contact and successful conflict resolution outcomes outside their relationships in their lives. Person therapy is not a passive "done" for a person, but a "service" with the psycho-therapist. The counselor and the couple have joyous communion to achieve positive outcomes.

Couple counseling is an efficient way of recognizing the relationship's spouses' actions and allows a sufficient resolution of relationship problems. A couple of counselor deals with some different problems and helps couples learn to work together more lovingly. Couple counseling varies in length to provide ample room for different issues in connection. Professional marriage and family therapists are highly qualified professionals who can promote impartial and comprehensive care for a couple. Those attending marriage therapy learn some skills for better listening and dispute resolution. Overall, people find that couples therapy is successful and that their well-being and relationships are strengthened overall.

49. Couples Therapy Exercises For Improving Communication

Viable communication is the lifeblood of any relationship. For some couples, merely figuring out how to convey emotions, resolve conflicts, and offer with one another is a challenging endeavor. Utilizing a couple of necessary couple's therapy practices for communication can do miracles to support you and your accomplice manage issues and develop nearer. Learning communication skills that can allow you to appreciate the marriage or relationship you have wanted continuously is significant. Setting up a superior discourse with your accomplice and figuring out how to share your sentiments and address issues with less conflict will be conceivable to make a healthier, more robust, and all the more emotionally satisfying.

Using Positive Language

Couples therapy activities can extend your emotional bond and allow you to manage muddled circumstances and issues without lashing out or contending. Utilizing positive language when you speak with your accomplice might be the absolute best approach to make an increasingly successful emotional discourse. It is all too easy to wind up baffled, especially if your relationship has hit an unpleasant time. Bending over backward to embrace a positive and empowering tone during your discussions can turn what might have generally turned into a warmed contention into an open door for positive development and progress. Being excessively basic or receiving a negative tone might cost you numerous chances to sustain and strong. This activity, when polished after some time, can allow you and your accomplice to develop nearer.

Communication Exercises To Build A Lasting Relationship

Learning and applying couples therapy practices for communication can do a lot to reinforce your relationship. Managing touchy issues and sensitive issues can be a strenuous endeavor.

Tools and activities that will allow you and your accomplice to share and convey what needs to be more readily can demonstrate an essential piece of making a healthier and more satisfying relationship. Poor communication might do unmistakably something other than restricting your capacity to manage common issues. Activities intended to make communication quality instead of risk can help guarantee a more drawn out and more positive relationship. Figuring out how to improve as an audience and rehearsing the skills that will allow you and your accomplice to develop nearer makes it feasible for you to appreciate another degree of understanding and gratefulness for one another.

Active Listening

Numerous couple's therapy activities are based around rehearsing skills that will improve you and your accomplice audience members. Undivided attention is intended not just to make it easier to banter about touchy issues but also to develop your understanding and valuation for your accomplice. When rehearsing undivided attention, it is significant for the speaker to stay focused on a single idea or point. For the audience, focusing on sharing their accomplices' point of view while endeavoring to find new bits of knowledge about how the person thinks and feels can be of incredible advantage. Regardless of what subject is being examined, the most significant piece of undivided attention is to do it with persistence and love. Tending to how your accomplice feels instead of merely responding to what your accomplice says is essential for successful communication.

Learning To Grow Closer

Individuals change and develop after some time, regularly in manners that are amazing or startling. Being in a long haul relationship can make it easy to ignore new features and aspects of your accomplice's character. Couples who think it's challenging to acknowledge who their accomplices have developed into will likely experience difficulty imparting. Couples therapy works out. For example, learning undivided attention skills and sharing emotions uninhibitedly can enable you to build up a superior feeling of who your accomplice is. Indeed, even the most agreeable endeavors could be bound to disappointment if you can't understand and identify with how your accomplice's advantages and passions may have changed after some time.

Sharing Emotions Freely

Numerous couple's therapy practices for communication are intended to diminish conflict and make a progressively successful path for you and your accomplice to share what you are feeling. When it is challenging to examine emotions without starting a contention or causing a battle, working through issues and differences may also be unimaginable. Talking about what you need to have a sense of security when sharing how you both feel can be useful. For some couples, having a specific time or spot to examine significant issues or take a shot at the structure, better communication may have any effect. Set aside the effort to ask your accomplice what might make that person feel progressively useful when sharing your emotions. At that point, put these ideas energetically to help guarantee that your future endeavors to improve your relationship are as successful as conceivable.

Taking A Trip Together

Keeping up relationships requires a great deal of diligent work, which is why it is significant for you and your accomplice to unwind and loosen up. Masterminding an outing with your accomplice can give you chances to take a shot at structure excellent communication while having some good times. Following a similar everyday practice or remaining in a safe environment can eventually cause a relationship to stagnate. Sharing time in another condition will allow you and your accomplice to make new recollections while alleviating the pressure that could be making communication unquestionably progressively tricky. It's also regular for couples to go on couples withdraws where your outing's very purpose is to improve your relationship.

I Feel

Expressing your sentiments in a manner that is easy to understand can be a precarious endeavor. Starting your announcements with "I feel" can give couples a progressively powerful approach to organizing their considerations while offering the audience data more comfortable to grasp. This is one of the numerous couple's therapy practices that can handle sensitive issues that can prompt contentions. By isolating how you feel from the original conditions and occasions being examined, you can support your accomplice feel not so much guarded but rather more ready to tune in.

50. Tips And Tricks To Maintain Your Emotional Wellbeing

Ego is the most dangerous thing in relationships; eliminate your ego to get a neutral perspective.

The term ego refers to when a partner in a relationship feels the entitlement of things to be done their way. People develop ego because they think they are superior to others. In a love relationship, when you turn and let your ego make crucial decisions in your relationship rather than your spirit, this will lead to manipulation as a means to give and receive love. This is because the ego does not have any relationship skills. Whenever you try to protect yourself, ego resorts to fighting, sarcasm, depression, aggression, intolerance, blame, resentment, distrust, frustration, rude gestures, and self-doubt.

Choices that we make out of our ego end up being the very obstacle to our relationship and love life. This, in turn, ends up being ego battleships instead of the committed relationship between two persons.

For natural love in a relationship, there is no need for manipulation to receive or give love. One's spirit loves, and it is capable of loving with no conditions or expectations. Our spirits also utilize the relationship skills of wisdom, acceptance, forgiveness, apologizing, being creative, responsible, understanding, and discerning.

The following techniques can help you learn how to let go of your ego:

- Practicing letting go and forgiveness. One of the most powerful tools that will help you in letting go of your ego is to practice forgiveness. You need to learn how to forgive people who hurt you and also learn how to forgive yourself. By forgiving, you will accept, let go and keep moving forward to achieve your set goal. Forgiveness will allow your soul to remove the negativity in our inner being and allow a new wave of happiness in our soul.

- Practicing being transparent. One of the most significant articulations that I realize we have all run over in our day by day schedule is, "reality will liberate us." Holding onto reality will stifle the feelings that will cause you to create discouragement and tension.

Being straightforward will consistently give you an unmistakable opportunity to be associated with yourself instead of attempting to be something you usually are not. Figure out how to disapprove of the things or matters that don't increase an incredible value, acknowledge and open your arms to things that welcome a positive effect on your life.

- Learn to Surrender Your Need to be always in control. When you let your ego control your love relationship, it will always make you conform to things or Statue that is not part of your natural being. By doing so, you do things that you are not used to doing, and when you lose one of the things that you have created to make yourself what you want, you will realize that all the other things that you identify yourself with will fall like dominos and this will lead to you losing your happiness. Do what makes you happy as a person, be curious, and be a risk-taker. Take a challenge every day, do something that scares you, and notice that you will start to feel happy in the small things you do.

- Having silent moments to yourself and enjoy it. Create a daily routine that reminds you of how special you are and why it is beautiful for you to be yourself. In the same daily routine, perform an act of self-love and enjoy doing it. Five minutes every day for you to be alone and in silence. Sometimes in silence, you may find answers that in noise or voices can never find.

- By rehearsing appreciation. Make time for yourself consistently to consider all the encounters, exercises, and slip-ups you have accomplished in your everyday life and be grateful to each one of those. It is about the difficulties we face and how we respond to them, causing us to succeed and be upbeat throughout everyday life. Individuals who are consistently thankful will feel more adored and empathetic than individuals who are reliably not appreciative of any deed since they live in the discipline. This is the right place for the conscience to flourish and other melancholic musings. Indicating gratefulness will likewise show you the magnificence of life.

The Battle Of Love Versus Ego

As human beings, we all have an ego within us. All we need to do is to learn to control our ego and not to let it control our lives. Letting your ego go unchecked can cause tremendous turmoil in your life, especially with our closest and intimate relationships. Having negative emotions, such as fear, jealousy, and anger, are all ego products. We all have two opposing forces that battle against each other in our inner being. In a battle, each side always has its plan, idea, and suggestions. The forces are always opposite one another. These two forces in us are the force of Ego and the force of Love. It is upon you to choose which one will control or govern your life.

How The Battle Unfolds

1.   The force of ego. This kind of force makes you decide with the help of your ego rather than your spirits. The negative thing about the force of ego is that it has no any relationship skill. Instead, it uses manipulation to receive love and give love. The force of ego makes one fear that loving will result from hurting, and it also creates a fear that if you love so much, you will abandon the concept of ego, that is, self-protection and separation. Ego Love is a mirror of the desire and need of the lover and not the loved one. This kind of love only rests on one partner's mercy, the partner being manipulative to receive the love. It asks them to be something that they cannot possibly be. That is what you want them to be, rather than what they are. This practice leads to disappointment and disillusionment that will lead to resentment. All in all, the Genesis of all these things will lead to a relationship's breaking up.

2.   Force of love. This is a force that drives us towards good deeds. It ensures one to be always sensitive and kind at all times. It admonishes you when you are neglectful and unkind to your partner or people close to you. There are no demands placed on the other partner than the Ego Love in this kind of love. This is because, in this Love force, there are no demands. With no demands on this kind of love, there are no expectations from any party. This kind of love takes the ego out of our hearts; it controls every aspect of our life and every move we make, creating beauty and joy wherever we go.

How you can deal with a person with a huge ego

1. Do not be afraid to be a little rude to someone you know has a big ego.

2. Try not to make any sense of their behavior; this is because someone with a considerable ego tends not to make any sense.

3. When they do not even agree with you on standard facts, please just don't try to argue with them.

4. When you are in a conversation with a huge ego, talk facts, not emotions.

5. There is a need to cut some phrases from your speech. For example, do not try sentences with: I feel..., I think..., I just.... and I sort of...... This is because such phrases will automatically make you sound less superior to them.

6. At the start of any conversation with someone with a huge ego, you should adjust your attitude not to expect a crappy talk.

7. Always do not take it personally if they tend to use vulgar language or abuse you.

51. Frequently Asked Questions

What Are Our Main Issues?

The things that issue the most to one mate routinely seem, by all accounts, to be inconsequential to the after that. At the point when you're seeing someone, prompting meetings can focus on these likely clashes. Ask your life partner what the individual accepts are the essential issues between them and what should be conceivable to fix the situation. For example, your mate may figure you don't hang out, and you could cure this by discovering ways you can acknowledge time with one another even more as often as possible. To find courses of action, you ought to at first perceive what the issues are.

What Issues Are Most Important?

Discover what your spouse considers are the most significant issues and work on those first. You ought to also air your perspectives on what you think the most significant problems are with the goal that you two can take a shot at them together.

Is It Precise To Say That You Are Seeing Someone New?

If your spouse has begun thinking about separation, see whether there is another person in the image. If there is betrayal, discover from your spouse what is inadequate in your relationship that prompted another person's sentiments. Brain research Today notes that six out of ten miscreants never get captured, so if your spouse is deceiving, you may well not know.

What Is The Real Purpose Of Couples Therapy, And For What Reason Is It Useful?

Couples therapy can incorporate a wide range of objectives and differing procedures. In such a manner, it's less like aspirin and increasingly like a serving of mixed greens, with numerous discretionary and differed fixings.

Therefore, I will clarify the objectives for couples treatment as I do it, utilizing the treatment strategies I expound on in my article From Conflict to Resolution.

Couples come to treatment because they are miserable, usually because they have been unsuccessful at settling their conflicts. Therefore, they have either separated emotionally because of their differences or have turned out to be excessively factious.

In the two cases, the specialist's essential employment helps move the couple from conflict to resolution. That generally requires:

1.Guiding the couple through a success win critical thinking procedure to the decision of every one of the issues they have been trapped in.

2.Teaching skills so the couple can handle their resulting differences cooperatively all alone—no more need either to separate from one another or to battle.

3.Learning skills for keeping the emotional tone between them upbeat and adoring. No more outrage, melancholy, or nervousness. Parts all the more sharing of fondness, thankfulness, embraces, and grins.

4.Gaining bits of knowledge into the youth birthplaces of their dangerous propensities and counteracting other unnecessary emotional reactivity.

Couples therapy is useful to the degree that it achieves these four destinations with the goal that the couple can appreciate a communitarian (not any more battling), friendly (counting sexually close), dependable, and long-cherishing organization.

What Are The Insider Facts For Causing A Couples Therapy To Succeed?

A compelling couples' specialist guides customers with a firm hang on the reins, so no negative associations bait a couple of the friendly and helpful way of agreeable shared critical thinking. As soon as one accomplice talks, for example, in a way that is basic or controlling instead of clever, the advisor intercedes to interfere with the exchange on a community track.

Compelling specialists encourage skills so the couple figures out how to talk prudently, listen responsively, and resolve differences in a manner that reliably prompts arrangements that please the two accomplices.

Compelling specialists show outrage the executives, so the accomplices figure out how to expel themselves from a circumstance in which tempers are getting too hot in exchange for remaining beneficial and sheltered, quiet themselves down, and then without a moment's delay, come back to continue their endeavors to discover common understandings.

Viable advisors clarify that every spouse's activity in therapy concentrates on their learning and development, not to attempt to get the other individual to change.

A compelling advisor empowers occasional brief thinking back in the back view reflection of how each accomplice educated propensities that are currently risky. However, the vast majority of the treatment focuses on settling current conflicts and showing better communication skills for what's to come.

The successful specialist encourages the couple to chat with one another. The advisors' responsibility is to urge and mentor better skills with the goal that the accomplices figure out how to determine their very own issues. It isn't to have each accomplice gripe to that person and then fill in as judge or concoct answers for the couple.

Have You Ever Considered Having An Affair?

As indicated by the aftereffects of an MSNBC overview, about one of every five grown-ups has undermined a present accomplice. If your spouse has thought about deceiving, discover why.

What Are Your Expectations of Counseling?

Ask your accomplice what the person anticipates from marriage mentoring. If your spouse goes into mentoring with similar any desires for sparing the marriage that you do, at that point, there is a decent possibility you can work things out.

What Are The Reasons You Want To Work Things Out?

Ask your spouse what the reasons are for making the marriage work. If the reactions base on love and duty, the odds are you can cooperate to reconstruct the relationship. If the response has to do with remaining together for the kids or the number of bills you share, you may need to reconsider the relationship.

Are There Any Past Conflicts We Should Agree?

It's hard to push ahead if there are dubious clashes. Not only will the past keep coming up in future conflicts. It's hard to gravitate toward someone on the off chance that you are up 'til now incensed about something they did. See whether there are any dubious issues and work on them.

Do You Feel You Can Communicate With Me?

One of the most significant aspects of a relationship is communication. If you can't converse with each other easily, you will always be unable to work through future issues. Find better approaches to improve contact with each other without judging or blowing up.

Do You Feel Accepted?

See whether your spouse feels loved and acknowledged by you. It's imperative to have the support and considerably increasingly critical to pick up acknowledgment from those you love. If your spouse feels undervalued, you need to chip away at discovering approaches to show your thankfulness for the relationship.

Do You Aspire A Divorce?

If you are focused on that, your relationship has shown up at the last defining moment. One of the most apparent marriage tutoring questions is whether you ought to stay together. But on the off chance that you both give a definite yes to isolate, it justifies accepting a wound at tutoring as a way to deal with save your marriage from detachment. Partition isn't happy or unassuming, so you should make certain without question you are set up to give up before making that step since it's hard to turn around once you make that decision.

What Type Of Love Make You Feel?

Inquiring as to whether you are cherished is one of the essential marriage tutoring questions. It's anything but difficult to fall all through sentimental love, yet the affection in a veritable marriage runs further. On the off chance that your life partner has significant and enduring kind gestures for you, by then, it's defended, regardless of all the difficulty, toward chipping off at the relationship. The issue begins when you quit disapproving by any stretch of the imagination.

Do You Trust Me?

Trust is one of the most critical variables in any relationship. If your significant contrast struggles to trust in you, you will imagine that it is not easy to relate on any level. As shown by Psychology Today, paying little brain to how dubious your relationship with your assistant has transformed into, it's never past the point where it is possible to revamp if the two people are glad to work at it.

How Can I Acquisition Your Trust Back?

The lone critical component in picking up the trust is absolution. Perceive if your accomplice has figured out how to contemplate you because of things you have done. Figure out how to discuss needs and emotions and offer your reasons for what you did. Ask for pardoning and clarify why you will never rehash your mix-up. Allow your spouse to reveal to you what you need to do to recover trust.

It Is Innocuous To Say That You Are Satisfied With Our Intimacy?

Almost all couples experience an adjustment in science, but the most significant inquiry is how you feel about it. If the science is dead, your accomplice might be inclined to looking elsewhere. Attempt to discover approaches to revive the flash, for example, sharing fantasies or going on a marriage mentoring retreat.

How Do You See The Future?

Question your spouse about how the person in question perspectives what's to come. It is harmless to say that you are incorporated into vision, or is your accomplice increasingly worried about discrete expectations and dreams? If you are as yet a piece of things to come, your spouse hasn't relinquished the relationship.

Have We Tried Everything?

If you have made it to marriage mentoring, odds are you have quite recently begun to take a shot at your relationship. One of the most significant marriage mentoring questions you can ask your spouse is, "have we taken a stab at everything?" Focus on why you became hopelessly enamored in any case and examine ways you can recover that feeling.

It Is Harmless To Say That You Are Willing To Change To Make Improvements?

Both of you must be happy to work at the relationship to make it work. One of the most supportive marriage mentoring inquiries to pose to your spouse is whether the person in question is eager to advance each push to improve things, as long as you are set up to do likewise.

What Is Couples Treatment And What Is Couples Directing?

"Couples treatment" and "couples directing" usually mean something fundamentally the same as. There is no distinction between them on a reasonable level.

The primary setting where it makes a difference what the session is called is a legitimate one; in certain spots, you should have a different certification or permit to rehearse "therapy" that is more difficult to acquire than the certification or authorized to work on "guiding."

Regardless of whether you call it couples therapy or couples guiding, this sort of commitment with a qualified proficient furnishes couples with a chance to work through their most difficult or emotionally challenging issues.

These issues can run from straightforward communication issues or significant differences to substance abuse issues and mental issues (Bonior, 2017).

52. What Is EFT?

Emotional Focused Therapy uses acupressure and psychology to help improve a person's emotional health.

Even though emotional health tends to be overlooked, it plays a crucial part in a person's physical health and ability to heal. It doesn't matter how devoted a person is to maintain a proper lifestyle and diet, and if they have emotional barriers standing in their way, they probably won't achieve the body they want.

You can, most of the time, apply EFT directly to your physical symptoms to find relief without working through the emotional contributors. However, you need to figure out and work through the emotional issues for a powerful and lasting result.

EFT's premise also understands that the more emotional issues you can work through, the more emotional peace and Focused you will have.

With EFT, you can eliminate limiting beliefs, increase personal performance, improve relationships, and have better physical health. Let's be honest; everyone on Earth has at least a couple of emotional issues that they are holding onto.

EFT is straightforward to learn and can help you in areas such as: achieving positive goals, eliminating or reduce pain, reduction of food cravings, and the removal of negative emotions. And that's just the beginning of what it can do for you.

EFT is based on the meridians of energy that have been used in traditional acupuncture to heal emotional and physical problems for more than five thousand years, but without using needles. Instead, it uses simple tapping of the fingertips to move kinetic energy into a specific meridian while thinking about your problem and speaking an affirmation.

The use of affirmations and tapping the meridians can help clear the emotional block from the bioenergy system. This then helps to restore the body and mind balance that is needed for optimal health.

Many are wary of this practice at first, mainly the thoughts of electromagnetic energy that flows through the body. Then are others that are taken aback by the theories of how EFT tapping works.

You need to understand that with this technique, you will be tapping with your fingers. Several acupuncture meridians live on your fingertips, so when you touch, you are using the energy in your fingertips and the energy of the area you are moving.

Traditionally, the tapping is performed by the index and middle finger and with one hand only. You can use whichever side that you want.

Many of the tapping points are on either side of your body, so that means you can use whichever side you want, and you can switch sides during a taping session.

You can also modify the practice by using your fingers and both hands to create a gentle, natural curved line. The more fingers you use, the more acupuncture points you will access. You will also cover more area to hit the points easier than with a couple of fingers. It's also essential that you take off any bracelets or watches that you may be wearing.

Affirmation Statements

Another important part is coming up with the affirmation statement that you will use.

Traditionally, the phrase is something like, "Even though I have this (fill in the blank), I deeply and completely accept myself."

You would fill in the blank with a short description of the negative emotion, food craving, addiction, or other problems that you are experiencing.

You can also use the following variations. All of the following are great to use because they use the same raw format. Meaning, they acknowledge what the problem is and create acceptance despite the problem's existence. Those are the things that are important in creating an effective affirmation.

The traditional one is easier to remember, but feel free to use one of the following. "I accept myself even though I (fill in the blank)" or "Even though I (fill in the blank), I profoundly and deeply accept myself."

You can also use "I accept and love myself even though I (fill in the blank)."

Some interesting facts about affirmations are that:

You don't have to believe your affirmation sincerely; all you have to do is say it.

It's more effective to say it with emphasis and feeling, but just saying it will still do the job. It's better to speak it out loud, but if you are in public where you need to mutter it or do it silently, it will be just as effective.

You can tune into your problem by merely thinking of what it is. If you don't tune into your question, which creates energy disruptions, then EFT will not be sufficient.

Advice And Caution

You should only ever do what feels right for you. Never enter into any physical or emotional waters that could be threatening. It's your job to make sure you stay safe in this setting. You can quickly seek professional assistance if you need to.

Here is some advice before you dive into EFT.

It would be best if you were super-specific with your language when you use EFT.

You have to be completely tuned into your issue. Many times, if you are dealing with something harrowing, you will try to disconnect from your feelings.

Because you are working with energy, it is essential to pay attention to a cognitive shift. You will know when one has happened because you will reframe the problem. When you see the problem from a different angle, you will likely be surprised or have a new insight. This is great when this happens, and it may open late valuable insights.

Make sure you stay well hydrated. Water helps to conduct electricity, and you are accessing electrical energy when practicing EFT.

EFT Application Range

The only thing that can limit what EFT can do for you is your imagination.

Experienced practitioners and the EFT originators worldwide, amongst them, are psychotherapists and psychologists, have used EFT on several different issues.

This means that they have used emotional issues, where it works the best and for physical problems, with surprising success, whenever there is an emotional component or related traumatic experience.

But that's not the only thing, and EFT is also an excellent tool for personal development. It can help eliminate self-imposed restrictions that prevent people from experiencing abundance, great relationships, wealth, and happiness in their lives.

In EFT's short history, it has already been able to help many people with many common emotional problems, including:

confusion, grief, guilt, and almost any other emotion you can imagine

self-doubt

inner child issues and negative memories

all types of phobias and fears

depression

frustration and anger

anxiety and stress

The fantastic thing is that the benefits don't end there. EFT tapping isn't just limited to getting rid of painful emotions.

It can also help improve your health by:

- increasing feelings of wellbeing

- helping insomnia

- relieving feelings of pain

- reducing physical cravings, for example, for chocolate and cigarettes

It can enhance your effectiveness in the things that you do, including:

giving you the confidence to speak in front of a crowd and with the people that you are not able to communicate with at the moment

- improved personal and business relationships
- improved performance in sports, job, and any other areas of your life
- Make your quality of life better, including:
- encouraging spiritual and personal growth
- giving you the courage to try things that you have wanted to but were afraid to
- removing blockages that have kept you from having a life that is full of love and joy

There are many examples of people who have quickly recovered from emotions that have bothered them for years and sometimes decades, using EFT.

It has been something that people turn to for help when nothing else has been able to help them.

It has also successfully helped reduce several physical systems such as insomnia, back pain, and headaches. EFT's power is at its best when the physical symptoms are also linked to anxiety and stress.

The developers of EFT had reported a success rate of 80 to 100 percent when it came to emotional problems. When it comes to physical ailments, the percentage of success is somewhat lower. Most of the time, EFT effects are permanent and, if they aren't, you can easily repeat the process if needed.

It works quickly and is gentle. People can often release emotions like stress, anger, anxiety, and fear in one session, a few days, or a couple of weeks compared to months or years in traditional therapy.

One of the best things about EFT is the fact that it is so versatile. When you master the skills that it takes, which aren't hard, it's almost like developing your superpowers.

You can use these tools in pretty much any situation. Like if you have a big presentation to give at work or you're going in for a job interview, you can use EFT right before to help calm down your nervousness. It doesn't require anything special, yet it works wonders and can be used anywhere.

53. Non-Violent Communication

Stuff is bound to flare up in your relationships. There will be times when things become so thick people cannot see eye to eye, and this is when nonviolent communication (NVC) will come into play.

NVC prevents conflicts from taking place by establishing a foundation of respect and trust when people communicate. The beauty of NVC is that even at the point when you feel most angry and ready to flare up and when your initial response will be overboard because you were angry, NVC causes you to act in a trusting and respectful manner, without a hint of passive aggression that typically causes resentment and distrust.

By definition, NVC is a communication framework designed to reduce conflict and tension among the people. It provides us with a lens that gives us an entirely different perspective of the world. It also changes how people express themselves to others, connect and communicate with others, and how they empathize with them. Essentially, NVC enables you to create a better, higher quality connection so that people may enjoy being in a relationship that has mutually beneficial outcomes.

Below Is A Few Of The Features Of An NVC:

1.   Peaceful Resolution Of Conflicts

Conflicts are a normal part of interacting and relating with other people. Still, the important thing is to resolve them peacefully and productively, and this process requires some considerable time, support, and lots of practice. Peaceful conflict resolution engages both parties and has them working together to de-escalate, process, and resolve a conflict situation.

In this case, rather than confronting each other or burying the conflict as a whole, feuding persons are encouraged to demonstrate courage by opening up to each other regarding the conflict and how it affected them. They are also asked to show compassion to each other's side of the story, empathizing with the other party's experiences or interpretation of the events.

Thirdly, the parties are asked to work together, in collaboration, to process the conflict and to come up with a resolution plan.

Here are the guidelines that help to chatter the way as you work towards resolving your conflict in a peaceful, healthy, and kind way, even in very tense circumstances:

Remain calm: remember that you control your emotions and not the other way. You must be able to manage your anger emotions before you can help another person manage his. Whichever method you use, from breathing deeply to others you may have up your sleeve, the idea here is to keep your emotions under wraps long enough to allow a negotiation

There are no winners: sometimes, the conflict will revolve around a ridiculous issue of little or no consequence. For example, don't get caught up in conflict regarding a football match that happened or even one that is going to happen. Although fans can be very passionate, the players determine which team wins and which ones lose by playing in the field. As fans, you have to sit back and watch. Don't lose your peace over things you have no control over, especially those that do not require your participation. Also, do not fear to submit to another's opinions regarding issues like these because they do not influence your life in the first place.

Give the audience to the other party: If someone makes you part of an uncomfortable conversation, allow them to speak as much as they need to. Acting disinterested or interrupting them while they will not work in your favor only aggravates the situation. Remember that the person is not rational at the time, and he can pull you in that direction. Therefore, give him time to get everything off his system, and eventually, things will calm down.

Do not engage in verbal insults: when resolving a conflict, be watchful of your tone and the words you use. Avoid abusive or angry words; let your inner voice do the work. Audibly speaking profanity, screaming, and using hateful language only escalates the conflict.

Maintain a safe and comfortable distance: If you fear that the situation could quickly deteriorate and turn physical, keep a safe distance from the other person. This will keep the person from attacking you or from interpreting your physical moves as offensive postures.

Therefore, keep your distance and do not give room for the other person to feel threatened.

2. Reconciliation After A Conflict

After a conflict, reconciliation allows parties to return to working together to build the society and achieve shared goals. Parties must begin to move past their divided opinions into a shared future. Reconciliation is meant to restore the relationship between people to allow for future engagements and collaborations. Unfortunately, reconciliation can be quite tricky, mainly because there are so many setbacks and failures involved, depending on the conflict's depth. However, the only real failure would be if the parties involved did not consider reconciliation.

3. Secrets Of Mediating Knowledge

There will be situations where the only thing feuding parties can agree on is that they need a mediator's help. The mediator ought to be a neutral party, whose role is not to judge and declare the winner and the loser. His goal is to help the parties come to an understanding.

Mediation takes place in two stages. The first stage is the joint session. Mediation begins by holding a meeting that lets the mediator in the prevailing situation. The parties present their facts, and each side indicates what its ideal resolution of the situation would be. The mediator also needs to have all the information regarding the conflict and where it has gotten.

The second stage is the caucus stage, and in this one, the mediator is obliged to hold separate sessions with each party. The meeting's details should be highly confidential, but for the statements that the first party would want to be repeated to the second party. The mediator then collects each side's interests, including information about the concerns and needs that the dispute is affecting.

Once the second stage is done, the mediator begins moving from one party to another, collecting proposals and suggestions that the parties believe will equally satisfy their interests. Ultimately, a solution is reached. Sometimes, it will be a one-sided victory, while other times, it will end in a 'win-win' situation.

4.   Making Bad Thoughts Disappear

When evil thoughts plague your mind, closing your eyes as tightly as you can do not shut them out. The thought or the feeling keeps popping up, over and over. The thoughts could be of a disturbing story you heard on the news, nagging self-doubt, or thoughts of your relationship that went sour. All these thoughts make you miserable and cause you to feel imprisoned by your cruel mind.

You must remember that blocking out the negative thoughts is an effort in futility because the thoughts rebound one way or another. Then, when your guard is down, the thought comes back with the vengeance of a battalion, and suddenly, all you can think about are the negative thoughts. However, it is possible to block out the negative thoughts and not have any rebounds; you only need to remember two things.

The first is that blocking the thought is difficult, but just because it is difficult does not mean that you need to think about it. Your brain is not out to get you with the negativities. Stop thinking about the difficulty of letting the thoughts go because it gives the thought more meaning and importance, making it even more challenging to get rid of.

The second step is to know how to handle negative thoughts when it shows up. The solution is to plan, in advance, what to do when the thought comes to mind. Some opt to ignore it while others choose to replace the negative thought with some positive ones.

5.   Using Positive Language

Language is quite a powerful tool, and how you express yourself affects how it is received, whether positively or negatively. Positive language is so useful it is used to convey even bad news. It also elicits cooperation and reception, unlike negative language that arouses confrontation and argument. In your daily communication, positive language helps project a positive, helpful image while negative language projects a destructive image.

You must have come across a naysayer in the course of your life. A naysayer is a person who criticizes ideas, always having an opinion about why an idea won't work. Sometimes, the naysayer won't even have a negative attitude. He or she will speak using words or a tone that implies negativity. If you have been around someone like that, you know just how annoying and mentally fatiguing a person like that can be.

6. Being Honest

Honesty is one of the most exact values to practice, yet it can take you to heights you never imagined. It can also make you so fulfilled, happy, and successful better than any other virtue. Trust honesty to rip through deceit and lies. As a noble human being, honesty should be one of the foundational pillars of your core principles and values in life.

By definition, honesty is not just about telling the truth; it is also about being real with yourself and others about who you are on the inside, what you like, and what is most important to you if you will lead an authentic life. Honesty empowers you and causes you to be more open to having consistency in your delivery of facts. It also sharpens your focus and perception, allowing you to see the things around you with greater clarity.

If you are not honest, you certainly are lying or being deceitful. Lying is terrible, whether you are deceiving yourself or others. Whenever you lie, you fool yourself into believing the things you're saying. You also begin to dig a ditch of hypocrisy that only gets bigger with time. A liar confuses himself and others around him, losing all credibility and possibly putting himself in harm's way.

7. Creating Feelings

One of the most significant discoveries of my life has been that my feelings are the product of my thoughts all day. If your thoughts focus on the positive side of life and bright, happy things, you are bound to feel happy about yourself. This shows that if you master your thoughts throughout the day, you will have mastered your feelings.

More than anything, you want to have a happy life by being happy with who you are and accepting others for who they are. Positive feelings cause you to feel good, energetic, determined, and able to take action to pursue and achieve what you want. They improve your relationship with others and make you likable.

8. Making And Receiving Good Praise

When it comes to motivating the people around you or motivating you, offering praise and recognition can positively affect. We all feel good when others praise us. This kind of recognition brings up feelings of pride, pressure, and raises a person's self-esteem.

This is because praise releases a burst of dopamine, the feel-good hormone that controls pleasure and reward centers in the brain. The result is a good feeling that could change the trajectory of a person's life, change his self-image, or, at the very least, brighten his day.

54. Showing Up In Love

Whether you've decided to stay and continue working on the marriage or decide to leave the marriage, your following step is to show up in love.

What It Means To Show Up In Love

To love and to be loving to our partners is an action, a choice we make. But when we engage in the action of loving to receive love in return, we're starting from a place of what we can get rather than what we have to give. Relationships tend not to work very well when we're attempting to get something from someone else.

So love, of course. Take the actions of loving toward one another, but do so because it feels good to love, not to get something in return.

Love because it's your true nature to love.

Love because it's who you are.

Love because it's all we're here to do, and it's the whole point of our lives.

Society would tell you that your purpose in this life is to grow up, obey your parents, get good grades, get an education, get a job, own a home, take on debt, start a family, pay bills, be kind and loving toward those that are kind and loving toward you, try not to get too sick, and then eventually die of old age.

I would argue that your purpose is to come here into this life to love and allow yourself to be loved and grow and allow others to grow as well. Some of those other things happen, of course, but the whole point is to love and grow in the midst of it.

Show Up In Love Whether You Choose To Stay Or Go

Showing up in love seems logical when you've chosen to remain in the relationship. You keep tending to the garden of your relationship, applying the tools so that you're better able to communicate and grow closer and more connected over time.

You manage your mind to show up in the relationship as the woman you want to be. Please choose to be loving even when he doesn't deserve it. Choose to be loving to yourself by setting healthy boundaries. Choose to love so that you can feel good in the relationship, lining up with your decision to stay and evolve the relationship, so it feels good again.

Showing up in love when you're choosing to leave the relationship is a little less intuitive. That's because we've been taught that you must hate him as a pretext for leaving the relationship. If you had a love for him, then you would stay, right? After all, there's not a story written or a movie made that does not have a villain in it. So our minds go looking for the villain. And we think that either we're the wrong person in this story or he is.

What if no one is wrong? What if you're both entirely and deserving of love and understanding? What if you're both good people, and the relationship itself didn't work for one or both of you? What if the relationship wasn't supposed to last forever, and now it's complete?

When you start to look at it through that lens, you truly can unwind a marriage lovingly and peacefully. I tell my clients that a year or so from now, you will look back on this time in your life – this difficult time of walking away from a marriage – and you're going to want to be able to say, "I'm proud of how I handled that. It was not easy, but I'm proud of myself for how I showed up during that difficult circumstance." Let that goal of looking yourself years from now in the mirror guide you through this process. Every time it gets difficult to be loving, that thought of looking back on this time and wanting to feel good about how you handled a difficult situation will change how you react and move through this.

Just because most people don't do divorce lovingly and peacefully doesn't mean that it's not possible. Most people don't have the tools you now have. Most people act out in hurt and anger, feeling punched, they want to punch back, and what I'm inviting you to do is put your weapons down. The fights about who was wrong and needed to change have all been had...likely hundreds of times. Now is the time to intentionally dial down the drama and get clear about what's important to you because not everything you will fight about will matter in a few years from now. (I had a client whose husband was battling her for the dinner plates and flatware when they divorced; I promise you will not care about the dinner plates a year from now...let him have them.)

If you're willing to walk away in love, you will:

Not have to endure months (or years) of hatefulness toward the person you once loved. (A loving act for yourself.)

Not unintentionally force your children to navigate not having Mom and Dad in the same room together at graduations, weddings, the first birthday party of your first grandchild...all because the two of you couldn't be emotional adults through this process and now despise one another. (A loving act for your children.)

Give your future ex-husband the best opportunity of finding his happiness. You may not realize it now, but you do want that. If he's happy, he's not tormenting himself about you. If he's happy, he's moving on with his life. If he's the father of your children, I promise that you want him to be happy, healthy, and thriving in his life for the benefit of your children. (And that is a loving act for everyone.)

My ex-husband moved on very quickly after I left. Although it's a broad generalization, men do tend to move on quickly after a marriage ends. There are many philosophies on why this happens, but mostly because men do better personally and professionally when they're in a relationship.

I had a client this afternoon told me that her husband went out on a date last week, and they had only decided to separate less than two weeks ago. His priority wasn't figuring out new living arrangements or how to tell the kids. It was setting up an online profile and going on a date.

But having been on the other side of that myself, what I can tell you is that it brought me a great deal of peace to think that my ex found someone that thinks he's utterly fantastic. He's not a wrong person, undeserving of love. (I don't believe that anyone is undeserving of love.) He just wasn't my person, and I wasn't his. It was long overdue that we told the truth about that.

If I know anything about love, I do know this: we all want to be loved. To have love, you need to become love. You need to become the one who loves. Not love pointed at you, but love was flowing through you. And when you do that, you'll never have a shortage of it in your life. And to love and to be loved is the whole damn point.

Our Greatest Teachers

At this point, you realize that I have numerous educators: Wayne Dyer, Elizabeth Gilbert, Rob Bell, Elizabeth Lesser, Marianne Williamson, Byron Katie, and Abraham-Hicks.

On the off chance that you need to realize where to locate the most noteworthy profound instructors for your life, look no farther than your nearest, most close connections.

Dissimilar to customary instructors who are there to bestow astuteness, our nearest connections are there to uncover all the pieces of ourselves that we would prefer not to see, show us absolution and acknowledgment, and expose our convictions about our capacity to adore and be cherished. They are there to assist us with recuperating our injuries. At times they give the vital difference we have to get clear about what our hearts want.

- They will show us how our judgments of them are just a mirror to the pieces of ourselves that we're not yet ready to own

- They will bring to light all of our underlying fears that have not yet been addressed

- They will demonstrate just how many expectations and conditions we place on our love and allow us to rethink those conditions

- Our marriages will show us how we've learned and applied the same unhealthy behaviors we saw at home growing up into our current relationships

- They will most certainly teach us about forgiveness

- These closest relationships will show us the correlation between the depth of emotional pain and the depth to which we're willing to love. And when that emotional pain brings us to our knees, it will force us to walk through it to get to the other side of it

- Your relationship with your life accomplice will, without a doubt, instruct you that it is just through extraordinary trustworthiness, trust, and weakness that you will, in reality, discover incredible closeness, enthusiasm, and love

The individuals in our carries on with that we open the most profound pieces of our souls are there for us as our most noteworthy otherworldly test and our most remarkable profound instructors. They're divine blessings to free us up to the more profound realities of what our identity is and to move us to turn into our most noteworthy and best form of ourselves. Nobody will challenge us how our beloveds will, and nobody will show us more ourselves.

55. Why Couples Battle?

An eminent investigation of vessel wellbeing directed in Framingham, Mass., happened to raise its 40,000 members what subjects were conceivable to cause struggle in their relationship. Women's issues above-including children, housekeeping, and money, made the principal issues in their connections. Men aforementioned their contentions with their accomplice ordinarily fixated on sex, money, and relaxation. Even though the rundowns were somewhat extraordinary, the truth of the matter is that men and young ladies colossally care about consistent issues: money, notwithstanding, they take care of their time from work (housework or recreation) and compromise the pressure of family life (kids and sex).

Money

Sometimes cash issues become wedding problems.

Studies show that cash is systematically the foremost common reason for conflict in a very relationship. Couples with money issues and debt produce have higher stress levels and are less happy in their relationship.

Why will cash cause conflict? Money fights ultimately aren't significantly about finances. They a couple of couple's values and shared goals. An individual who overspends on restaurants, travel, and fun stuff usually desires to measure within the moment and ask for new adventures and change; a saver is hoping to shop for a house someday might most price stability, family, and community. Money struggle is an estimated gadget for your relationship's well-being and a marker that the 2 of you're out of the set on some of your most central qualities.

David Olson, an employee old at the University of the American state, examined 21,000 couples and known five inquiries you'll have the option to raise to look out in case you're monetarily viable along with your accomplice. We concede to the best approach to pay money. I don't have any issues concerning; notwithstanding, my accomplice handles money. I am content with our choices concerning reserve funds.

Significant debts aren't a haul

Making money selections isn't tough.

Dr. Olson found that the happiest couples agreed with a minimum of four of the statements. He also found that couples failed to see eye to eye on three or more statements were more likely to attain low on overall married happiness. Debt tends to be the largest offender in marital conflict. It is a fantastic supply of worry and stress. As a result, couples who will concentrate on cash issues and cut back their debt might discover that they need additionally resolved most of their marital problems.

Here's some parting recommendation for managing your cash and your relationship:

Be honest about your paying: It

s astonishingly common for two individuals in a very relationship to slug however they spend their cash, actually because they apprehend it's a sore purpose for their partner. Researchers decision it "financial unfaithfulness," and once it's discovered, it represents a massive breach of trust within the relationship. Surveys counsel secret disbursal happens in one out of 3 committed relationships. Buying garments, pocket money on a hobby, and gambling are the three most-cited varieties of secret disbursal that cause conflict in a very relationship.

Maintain some money independence: whereas two individuals in a very relationship have to be compelled to be honest with one another regarding however they pay their cash, it's a decent plan for either side to agree that every person has his or her discretionary pot of cash to pay on no matter they need. Whether or not it's a daily manicure, garments searching, an excellent bottle of wine, or an elaborate new bike -- the purpose is that simply because you've got different priorities as a family doesn't mean you can't sometimes feed your indulgences. The secrets to agree on the number of discretionary cash you ever have, then kept quiet once your partner buys the latest iPhone simply because.

Invest in the relationship. After you do have the cash to pay, pay it on the connection. Take a visit, head to dinner, and see a show. Pocket money on new and shared experiences may be a sensible investment in your partnership.

Children

One of the additional uncomfortable findings of relationship science is that the malicious result kids will wear antecedently happy couples.

Despite the popular notion that kids bring couples nearer, many studies have shown that relationship satisfaction and happiness generally plummet with the primary baby's arrival.

One study from the University of Cornhusker State faculty of Nursing checked out married happiness in 185 men and girls. Scores declined to begin in gestation and remained lower because they reached five months and twenty-four months. Alternative studies show that couples with two kids score even not up to couples with one kid.

While having a baby makes oldsters happy, the money and time constraints will add stress to a relationship. When the birth of a baby, couples have solely regarding third the time alone along as they had after they were unfruitful, in line with researchers from Ohio State.

Here's the excellent news: A minority of couples with kids — regarding twenty % — manage to remain happy in their relationships despite the youngsters.

What's their secret? Prime 3 predictors of a cheerful wedding among oldsters

- Sexual Intimacy
- Commitment
- Generosity

So there you've got it. The key to actual parentage is to own innumerable sex, be trustworthy, and be generous toward your partner. In this case, generosity isn't money — it's regarding the sharing, caring, and type gestures you create toward your partner each day. After you are attempting to survive the chaos of raising youngsters, it's the microscopic things — like delivery your partner occasional, giving to select up the cleansing or do the dishes, which will build all the distinction within the health of your relationship.

How To Build Resilience In Midlife?

Make It Last

Here are some suggestions for a way to strengthen your relationship supported by the findings of various studies.

Stay Generous

Is it accurate to say that you are liberal toward your accomplice? In any case, usually makes one absolute love? Or then again, do seemingly insignificant details for your accomplice like bring them espresso? Men and young ladies who score the best on the liberality scale are far more likely to report "upbeat" relationships, following an investigation from the University of Virginia's National wedding Project.

Do You Have a Generous Relationship?

Here are four queries researchers from the University of Virginia's National wedding Project accustomed live generosity, high levels of predictive of a stronger relationship.

Use Your Relationship For Private Growth

Finding a partner who makes your life additional fascinating is crucial to consider sustaining an extended relationship.

Gary W. Lewandowski Junior., a faculty member at Monmouth University in New Jersey, developed a series of queries for couples: what quantity has been together with your partner resulted in your learning new things? What quantity has knowing your partner created you an improved person?

Assessment

Do You Have A Property Marriage?

Take this quiz to live what quantity your relationship expands your data and make you feel sensible.

"People have a basic motivation to boost the self and raise who they're as an individual," Dr. Lewandowski says. "If your partner helps you become an improved person, you become happier and additional happy within the relationship."

Be Decisive

How thoughtfully couples build selections will have an enduring result on the standard of their romantic relationships. Couples who are decisive before the wedding — on purpose shaping their relationships, inhabitancy, and coming up with a marriage — seem to own higher marriages than couples who merely let inertia carry them through major transitions. "Making selections and talking things through with partners is vital," mineral above K. Rhoades, a relationship scientist at the University of Mile-High City and author of the report. "When you create an intentional associate call, you're additional probably to follow through thereon."

While the finding could appear obvious, the fact is that several couples avoid real decision-making. Several couples inhabitancy, as an example, failed to sit down and mention habitation. Usually, one partner had begun disbursal longer at the other's home, or a lease terminated, forcing the couple to formalize a system.

Showing intent in some type — from coming up with the primary date to inhabitancy, to the marriage, and on the far side — will improve the standard of a wedding to be told additional, examine the science behind "The Decisive wedding." "At the individual level, apprehend who you're and what you are regarding, and build selections once it counts instead of rental things slide," Dr. Stanley aforesaid. "Once you're a handful, do constant issues in terms of however you approach major transitions in your relationship."

Nurture Friends And Family

Here and their couples become fixated on the association that they neglect to the position in their loved ones' associations. Scientists Noemi Gerstel of the University of Massachusetts, Amherst, and Natalia Sarkisian of Hub of the Universe staff have discovered that hitched couples have fewer connections to family members than the unmarried. They're less inclined to choose or therapy relations and less presumably to associate with neighbors and companions.

The problem with this trend is that it places associate unreasonable burden and strain on the wedding, says Stephanie Coontz. She teaches history and family studies at The WA faculty in Olympia, Washington. "We usually overload wedding by asking our partner to satisfy additional wants than anybody individual will presumably meet," writes Dr. Coontz. "And if our wedding falters, we have got a few emotional support systems to fall back on. To strengthen a wedding, think about asking less of it, suggests Dr. Coontz. Meaning leaning on alternative relations and friends for emotional support from time to time. Support your partner's outside friendships and luxuriate in the respite from the stress of the wedding once you're not alone.

See A Rom-Com

It sounds silly; however, analysis suggests that seeing a sappy relationship moving-picture show created in Hollywood will facilitate couples estimate issues within the universe. A University of Rochester study found that couples who watched and talked regarding problems raised in movies like "Steel Magnolias" and "Love Story" were less probably to divorce or separate than couples in the same management cluster. Astonishingly, the "Love Story" intervention effectively kept couples along as two intensive types of wedding medical care.

Talking two or three moving-picture show isn't coming to illuminate crucial issues in a very wedding. In any case, the discoveries signal the significance of correspondence in a very wedding and discover chances to talk concerning your varieties. "A moving-picture show might be a non-undermining on account of kicking the discourse correspondence off," Ronald portrayed above D. Rogge, a partner teacher of logical order at the University of Rochester and the lead creator of the examination. The best films to begin useful correspondence show various highs and lows in a very relationship. additional films used in the examination grasp "Couples Retreat," Date Night," "Love and elective Drugs," and "She's Having a Baby." Avoid motion pictures that glorify connections like "Restless in Seattle" or "When Harry Met Sally." Even however, some of the proposed films are clever and not almost sensible. The objective is to rapidly "get an exchange moving," said Dr. Rogge.

56. Most Couples Come To Therapy Too Late

There is one final truth I feel I must reveal. I hate this one. It makes me want to sink into my therapist's chair and drop my head in defeat. When I encounter a couple struggling with this truth, it makes me wish I had magic wands, lotions, and potions that could turn everything around.

But I don't—and so this is the reality, the terrible truth: most couples come to therapy too late.

When I encounter a couple who has waited too long to come to therapy, I find myself sadly wondering, Why now? Now, when you have wounded each other so badly, now, when you have lost respect for each other, now, when this has been going on for so long—why are you just now coming in?

Unfortunately, they are usually coming in because one person has finally thrown in the towel. They have given up, emotionally and sometimes even physically, and their desperate partner has been left scrambling and begging, "Please, at least try therapy!" So they come.

And I can see the sad truth, which is that the partner is only coming to say they tried. "See, we even tried marriage counseling, and even that didn't work! What else do you want me to do?" The partner has already checked out, and often there is nothing I can do about that. Believe me, if I could change that by standing on my head while singing "The Star-Spangled Banner," I would. But your best chance for change comes when you start early enough, while you still have respect and love for each other somewhere deep down inside. Don't wait until it's too late.

What About Counseling?

How do you know if it's time for counseling? There is no definite answer—but I do know that your marriage does not have to be in turmoil or crisis for counseling to be of help. If you are feeling disconnected, unloved, uncared for, or emotionally unsafe; if you feel little confidence in your ability to talk about difficult things as a couple and find some resolution; if you are starting to feel hopeless, lonely, depressed, anxious, or helpless when it comes to your marriage—if any one of these things is happening, counseling can help.

If I called my husband to ask him whether I should take our daughter to the doctor when I suspected she was developing an ear infection for the hundredth time, he would give me the same response he gave me the first ninety-nine times: "It can't hurt. You might as well find out if there is anything more to it." The same thinking applies here: it can't hurt. Just as almost everyone occasionally falls under the weather, no marriage is perfect. Suppose you start feeling nervous about some aspect of your marriage. In that case, it's almost always worth coming in for a "checkup" to determine whether that aspect is worth worrying about or whether your dynamics might require a little tweaking.

When seeking help, it's essential to know that not all therapists can help you in the ways you need. I'm not trying to discredit any therapist out there—there are many different types of issues and clients I'm not the most qualified to work with. Instead, I refer these clients to therapists who are more qualified. You have to find someone who specializes in the problems you're having. I see many clients who have tried going to all sorts of therapists to work through their marital woes. But that is like going to a general practitioner instead of an oncologist to treat cancer— and while general practitioners may be amazingly knowledgeable and helpful about lots of different things, they aren't cancer specialists. Similarly, not every therapist has been specifically trained to deal with marital strife. It's a specialty.

To find a specialist, ask around. Talk to your primary care physician, your OB-GYN, your dentist, your dermatologist—heck, you could even ask your florist. Better yet, talk to your friends. You will be amazed at how many of them have seen a marriage counselor at some point or know someone who has.

As I have mentioned, I am a massive supporter of Dr. Sue Johnson's emotionally focused couples therapy (EFT). Check out some bios and profiles of therapists in your area. Call them. Determine their availability. Make an appointment. And if you don't have a positive experience—if you don't walk away feeling like the therapist "gets" you or your relationship, or don't feel you are being understood and listened to—find someone else. Sometimes you have to shop around to find a good fit. That's okay. You probably didn't jump in and buy the first car you test-drove, either. This might take a little effort, too. But it's worth it.

And it's worth commitment, too. Whatever you do, don't go to couples therapy a mere three times and say, "It's not working; nothing is changing; we must be irretrievably broken." That's like going to the gym and saying after three sessions, "It's not working! I haven't lost the weight, and I still don't see a six-pack." It's like saying, "He went to five golf lessons, and he still can't sink the putt! He still hits it into the woods like he always has, and sometimes he even misses the ball altogether!" Of course, he does! Golf is challenging—frustratingly so. I started taking lessons years ago, and on most days, I still can't play worth a darn. But at least I'm out there, swinging and missing and then trying again.

It's not uncommon for a couple who has been struggling for fifteen years to come back after five sessions and say, "It's not working; he's not even doing anything different!" Whoa, Nelly! He has been doing things a certain way for fifteen years in this marriage, with probably another fifteen years of the same madness before he married you. Making positive changes takes work, my friends—but it's your marriage, for goodness' sake!

I'll never stop being amazed at how much money a couple will be willing to spend in a contentious divorce. At the same time, they balk at the idea of spending even a fraction of that on marriage counseling to give themselves a chance. If your marriage is on the rocks or in shambles, it's going to take some work and sacrifice to fix it. So if you want to save your relationship, don't take that big trip this year. Take a break from fancy dinners, and use that money to do something different. Use it to find someone who can help.

How To Handle Your Kids?

If you believe your marriage is in danger of failing, you need to make fixing it a top priority. You need to make it more important than playing in your weekly tennis match or getting your kids to their soccer game. After all, watching their mother and father handle the pain and heartache of a divorce would be far more devastating for your kids than missing a game, or five—or even all of them.

There is no harm (actually, quite the opposite is true) is going to your kids and saying, "I'm sure you have seen Mommy and Daddy fighting. Well, we are going to talk to someone who can help us. Because we love each other so much, we will let someone help us be better husbands and wives. And I hope that if you are fighting with your husband or wife one day, you will let someone help you, too! It's so important!

"So, because of this, we are going to let you ride to and from your Friday soccer games with your friends, and we are going to have to miss those games. Just for a little while, until we learn how to make our home a happier place. We love you so much, and we are willing to do anything to make sure our home is happy. I can't wait to hear all about your game! Go get them!"

If you want to save your marriage, you need to make sacrifices until things have turned around. Then you can take the big trip, go to the fancy dinners, and cheer on your kids at their soccer games. And it will be a lot more fun, I promise.

The best thing you can do for your kids—more important than signing them up for soccer or dance class, more important than reading bedtime stories or helping them with their homework, more important than making sure they have perfectly matching outfits to wear for those family portraits that will adorn the front of this year's Christmas cards, which you are secretly hoping your friends and family will look at with envy, thinking, Now, that is a cute family!—more important than all these actions is showing your kids what a healthy marriage looks like.

Notice I didn't say, "Showing your kids what a happy marriage looks like." I didn't say your kids need to see marriage as something that's all smiles and sunshine. I said, "Showing your kids what a healthy marriage looks like." A healthy marriage can include conflict. Mistakes. Mishaps. Misunderstandings. Miscommunication. But it should also include a joint mission to try harder, learn new things, work through conflict, and talk things out.

Your marriage should be the center of your family. And if you are religious, then God should be the center of your marriage. Do you know what this means? If God is the center and your marriage is succeeding, this means your kids are in third place! Third! Don't operate as if they are first.

If your instinct is to say, "I may be a crappy husband, but I'm a great dad"—impossible! You may do some fantastic things for your kids; I do not doubt that. But the most amazing act of fatherhood is to respect your children's mother. Love her. Do it openly, even when it's hard, even when she acts unlovable because she is so exhausted from all she does for your family.

Wives—you may joke and say, "My husband and I haven't talked in weeks, months, or years. But who has time for that? I've got three kids to raise, swim lessons to get to, dentist appointments to make, and school supplies to purchase. And tomorrow is school picture day, and I need to go online and pay seventy dollars for overnight shipping to get that perfect Hanna Andersson dress so that everyone can look at my daughter and say, 'Mom, you did so good, she looked so adorable!'"

Guess what? She looks adorable because she is. She could wear a grocery bag and look adorable because she is that darn cute. Now grab your best hand-me-down out of the closet, set it out for tomorrow, and go snuggle with your husband! Let him know he is more critical than buying perfect clothes that your son will ruin within minutes when he jumps in the first mud puddle he sees.

57. Verbal Abuse

Verbal abuse emerges from nowhere inside a relationship. It gets ever more pessimistic and deceptive, causing people to wonder whether they are even punishing themselves on the losing end or overreacting. Usually, verbal assault arises in privately-owned places where nobody else may intervene and eventually becomes a natural communication mode. For those who endure it, verbal abuse is often despised, and in the self-esteem, it chips away, making it difficult to reach out to a companion. Some citizens who experience it rationalize the abuse in their minds and don't even realize it's an unacceptable form of communication. Yet this would not make us on the losing end any less stressful on the feelings or distressing. In general, verbal aggression is an instrument for maintaining control and power over others. There are a variety of different forms that verbal aggression can be, making understanding even more difficult. First, verbal harassment includes being exposed every day to name-calling, feeling constantly belittled or demeaned, and being targeted to the silent treatment of a spouse. If you can't tell if your partner is either funny or belittling, here are a few say-tale signs that your relationship is weakening.

These Are The 11 Most Prevalent Forms Of Verbal Violence To Watch Out For In A Relationship:

1. Showing Disdain

A sarcastic speech and a slight sarcasm should not be a standard aspect of partnerships between the partners. It also may only be the mate's regular source of laughs. It can start nice, that's why it often goes unnoticed, and however, depression or condescension is terrible in the time.

For instance: No wonder it's your weight still not looking okay, but look how really clean your tray is!

2. Blaming Your Partner

The accusation is one of the common forms of verbal harassment, with the effect that a person is continuously punished for one's actions rather than taking liability for it.

That may include prosecuting an offender for activities they had little to do about, prosecuting the victim's partner for the behavior.

You are the reason we cannot get on time. And now see what you did to me, are the instances.

3. Name-Calling

Probably the most easily recognizable form of verbal abuse is this. That entails calling names and continuously getting screamed at. Arguments that sometimes turn to yelling in a confrontation and using insulting language are also signs that the spouse's partnership is anything but secure. Partners in a healthy relationship back from a fight or attempt to speak about the issue. In a verbally violent relationship, the perpetrator will yell until they have what they desire.

Example: Your idiot, you've just made me furious.

4. Showing Manipulation

Identifying a dominating personality may always be simple, especially when one is continually manipulating their partner to do things that they are not delighted about. Deception can be hard to detect by contrast. It may be subtle, such as turning around situations and putting the burden on the offended individual.

Example: You would not tell that if you loved me or you would not do that.

5. Useless Argumentation With Your Companion

Those are also signs of a bad relationship when the companion continually argues with you and clashes if they see an opportunity or whether talks and arguments begin to go round and round in circles, leaving you tired and frustrated. Those on the other end of these kinds of disagreements tend to feel like they stay on eggshells and avoid getting back to the same topic over and over again. We don't always have to decide over anything in a relationship, so it should be decided mutually. Instead of an atmosphere of one using another or engaging in discussions, you'll never win. If you seem like you're still on the brink and walking with your friend on eggshells, or if all of those habits seem ancient to you, you might be in an unhealthy relationship. Sometimes, if something is wrong with your trustworthy mates or family telling you, please listen. They will see something you cannot perceive or hear it.

Remember, by setting boundaries. You can learn to respect yourself in a relationship and be honest about how it makes you feel.

6. Mortifying Comments

This is risky if a partner makes mortifying comments regarding your ethnic origin, race, background, and religion, past in general, to drag you down. This would not need to be systemic, as if it happens once, it will occur again and not be reduced. A partner who respects you, who beliefs you're not going to exploit something inherent about you to push you down.

As examples: You women, crying like meaningless screaming for nothing. And I am not surprised, and you're Asian, you are all doing that.

7. Throwing Criticism On Your Partner

When asked on occasion, it's cool to offer constructive feedback. It's nice to be truthful with your companion. Nevertheless, belittling and constant resentment of a beloved other is not healthy, and over time will result in a drastic loss of confidence and self-esteem.

Example: Why are you so disorganized? I may rely on you to ruin our nights out, several times.

8. Using Threats

While this might be a convenient one to recognize, but that is not always the same case. Threats may be delivered in a way that makes them seem like not that bad or in a way that makes you wonder that you've understood it correctly. But the risk is a threat, and a loving companion doesn't turn to them to get their real way.

For example: If you're not doing this, you might find that your cat's out of the house. And I am going to damage myself if you will leave me tonight.

9. Accusing Your Partner

Repeated accusations resulting from intense jealousy are often a form of verbal attack. Being regularly accused of doing something often leads an individual to start worrying if they are doing something wrong, either dressing or talking too much, respectively.

Examples: When I was chatting to your boring teammates, I caught you trying to hook up with your boss again. And I believe you fool me.

10. Gaslighting On Your Partner

Gaslighting involves discounting a person's wishes and telling them either their feelings are false and meaningless. It is a pervasive form of emotional abuse and, hence it can be indirect, highly manipulative, often goes unnoticed. Gaslighting can make you feel isolated and powerless to express your experiences. Gaslighted people sometimes capture themselves. They're embarrassed for acts that they never did.

For example: Why do you rely so hard on almost everything?

11. Withholding

A partner will often walk away from conflict, opting to encourage the dust to settle down and engage in a more constructive conversation without feelings flaring up. Although it is a sign of a healthy partnership, the silent penalty, which is not, was sometimes called withholding. Whether they don't get what they need or ignore you completely, withholding will entail your partner declining to answer your calls.

Example: You're discussing restaurant options because you do not want to go for an alternative for your spouse. They leave the place and refuse to talk to you because they think you're not good at them.

58. Four Stages Of Marital Conflict

Consider the four stages of marital conflict and save your marriage partnership.

Throughout their novel The Seven Conflicts, authors Tim and Joy Downs say the couple who never learn how to deal with their conflicts effectively begin a sequence of phases that can inevitably kill them.

What Is Marital Dispute?

A marital dispute is not a pure difference of opinion. Instead, it is a sequence of incidents that were mistreated to harm the marital relationship seriously. Issues of marriage have festered to the point where stubbornness, pride, resentment, hurt, and hate hinder marriage's successful communication.

Nearly all marital severe discord has its origin in selfishness on the part of one or both parties. Saving a marriage requires denying selfishness, giving up ego, forgiving hurt, and putting aside bitterness; these steps are becoming more difficult, so it is best to stop the spiraling downward of marital conflict.

Preventing marital conflict is the best way of doing marriage work. Marriage preparation is accompanied by premarital therapy. Suppose that doesn't happen, then immediately after the wedding. In that case, marriage relationship therapy will provide couples simple marital dispute resolution techniques that can be used before marriage issues get out of control.

Marriage is a partnership in which trust is developed over time, as devoted partners set aside their desires for their partner's good and build skills to sustain a healthy and open relationship.

Who Gives Rise To Marital Conflict?

As mentioned above, egoism is the crucial cause of marriage disputes. Another way to mean this is that marital problems arise when one party thinks it has its way. While one has personal interests, a choice that often affects the marriage demands that one's self-interest prevail.

Could any relationship succeed if one party continually gets his or her way? Not.

If the marriage partnership succeeds, then giving up self-interest is something to which couples have to become accustomed. Sacrifice is finally a pleasure and not a burden.

But it's not just giving in and never getting your way. The marriage partnership grows deeper as partners lovingly share and explore their desires, often displaying a willingness to compromise while genuinely working together to possess the best marriage solution mutually.

How marital conflict impacts marriage relationships If husbands and wives are unable to resolve their disputes, as indicated by the four stages of marital discord, they collapse into repetitive conduct patterns. Recognizing that all these stages are unstable is significant. The negotiation stage and agreement may appear promising, but it will disintegrate without commitment and a clear understanding of the challenges and obstacles that have to be addressed.

When correspondence about marriage breaks down, feelings get hurt, emotions run high, and solutions seem out of control. The harm multiplies when marital disputes and children are living in the same household.

Four Levels Of Marital Dispute In Which Marital Discord Increases:

1. Have It Your Way.

Couples newly married and unable to overcome their differences correctly prefer to seek to settle problems by avoiding conflict. Without ever resolving the core problem, they cede together. If you fight against your husband, you will slowly find yourself uncomfortable and change your attitude to the resulting point.

2. Have It My Way.

When couples have depleted themselves by disregarding their own needs, they regularly change the contrary and start demanding that their needs are presently met. A spouse who has held her sentiments to herself will abruptly understand this has prompted her anguish and may begin communicating her musings and perspectives at each chance. However, unfortunately, this stage doesn't work either as a couple start butting heads.

3. Have It Our Way.

The third stage includes trading off and dealing with one another. The pair may at first be excited about their new correspondence style. However, energy blurs gradually. For marriage, accomplices face additional time limitations and worries from their child-rearing, monetary issues, and chaotic timetables. Between an ineffective compromise style and the can weights of life, couples can begin to question their relationship during this time.

4. Have It The Way You Like.

This stage represents a sense of resignation. Couples are overwhelmed by the constant disputes and may even feel discouraged that all the unresolved issues will ever be resolved. If you are at this point, then you need expert guidance on marriage.

Good Marital Communication

Marriages due to disagreement should not have to end up this way. Couples should work through their problems with good communication and dispute management skills, rather than ignoring or dragging out the issues. Begin finding new ways to interact with your husband if you identify one of your marriage's unpleasant phases. If you're unsure where to start, check out the library for a few journals, read articles online, or talk with the famous couples you know. Try attending a marriage therapist to help teach you constructive approaches if the conflict appears to go unresolved.

Conflict is a recurring feature of almost all ties. This can be a significant source of tension, too. Hence it is crucial to find a resolution to most conflicts. It sounds like a simple assumption, but sometimes people are suppressing their frustration or only 'going along to get along.' Others believe they are causing one by resolving a dispute and just staying silent when upset.

It is, unfortunately, not a balanced long-term approach.

Unresolved conflict within the partnership may lead to frustration and another unresolved conflict.

But more critically, continuing conflict can potentially have a detrimental effect on your well-being and life. Sadly, conflict resolution can also be challenging. In reality, attempts at conflict resolution, done poorly, may make the conflict worse.

Researcher John Gottman and his colleagues, for example, have been researching how couples compete and can predict which teams will go on to divorce by analyzing their dispute solving skills — or lack of them.

(Clue: Couples who are continually reprimanding their accomplice's character, or closing down during contentions instead of working through clash in a proactive, deferential way, should lookout.) For the individuals who weren't naturally introduced to a family where impeccable compromise aptitudes were displayed every day (and the number of us was?), here are a few rules to compromise more direct and less unpleasant.

Get In Touch With Your Feelings

Just you are interested in an essential aspect of dispute resolution — knowing how you feel and why you feel so. Your feelings may seem clear to you now, but this isn't always the case. You feel upset or resentful at times but don't know why. You often believe the other person doesn't do what they 'should' do, yet you don't know precisely what you expect from them, or whether it's even sensible.

Journaling can be an essential way to contact your own emotions, opinions, and desires so you can express them to the other person more effectively. This cycle often brings up some pretty massive issues, and psychotherapy can be helpful.

Using Journaling

Hone Your Listening Skills

How effectively we listen is critical for successful conflict resolution as to how effectively we express ourselves. If we are to conclude, it is vital to consider the other person's viewpoint, rather than just our own. In reality, making the other person feel heard and understood can often go a long way towards a conflict resolution. Effective listening also helps you close the distance between the two of you, realize where the difference is, and so on.

Sadly, active listening has not been acknowledged by anyone. It's normal for people to believe they're listening when they're just formulating their ensuing answer in their minds, thinking to themselves how wrong the other person is, or doing something other than trying to consider the viewpoint of the other person. It's also customary in your viewpoint to be so protective and stubborn that you can't only hear the other person's point of view.

59. Importance Of Communication In Relationship And How To Reconnect With Your Partner

You must be both interested in good contact in your partnership. This needs you to be genuinely interested in what your partner says and responds in kind. You should also show your feelings plainly, for a stronger relationship. This lets him know exactly what's happening to you, which fosters a deeper connection and a better relationship. Nevertheless, this relationship is not a static object. It moves through its ups and downs through the different stages. What are these stages? Let's take a look. Let's take a look.

The Six (6) Stages Of A Relationship

According to life and organizational strategist Tony Robbins, the six (6) phases of a partnership are clearly defined.

1. Love And Passion

This is the step when your partner is the only thing on your mind. The chemistry between you is correct, and you are invested in your partner's success. All your acts are designed to lose yourself and help you achieve them.

2. Not Enough Romance

You both love one another, but you sense a void deep within. You wish your partner could fill this, but you can't.

3. The Relationship Of Convenience

The romantic dimension has dissipated in the third stage as the relationship progresses. This is not so much devotion, not so much passion. However, you cannot separate yourself because you have other ties to keep you from doing so. You're living with the family (when you have children) or because it's too difficult to get rid of mutual financial obligations and responsibilities. "You may live together with your partner, and you may be happy, but there's no profound emotional involvement. There may be tension among you because either of you feels very loved or willing, or each one of you can find ways to satisfy the majority of your needs. Whether you focus on work, hobbies, family (other than your partner), friends, etc., most of you are probably in Position Three. What is challenging is to believe your partner is the right person— not lovely enough to get excited, not bad enough to quit.

4. Planning Your Escape

In stage 4, the relationship brings you no pleasure. In reality, you still think of how wonderful life would be if you weren't with your current partner. If you think about this, you probably have considered planning an exit strategy.

5. You Have A Relationship But Don't Want To Be In A Relationship

In the fifth stage, you want to communicate with someone. Despite your past partner's achievements, you still hope to find the right person to complete it.

6. You're Not In A Relationship, And You Don't Want To Be In One

You've given up relationships now. You don't want to let anyone come close to you. You've had a bad experience, and you don't want to ruin it. Which level do you feel at the moment? Write it down. Write it down. Sensitivity is the first step towards any positive change.

The Six (6) Human Needs In Relationship/Marriage

Here is a breakdown of the six human needs:

1.   Certainty: You must make sure in your relationship you are relaxed, i.e., you have enjoyment free of pain. However, for some people, particularly those who long for spontaneity, it can be monotonous and boring to make sure that everything is perfect.

2.   Variety: It is the need for variance and variety ety "spice things up" and keep things more exciting in the relationship. You want variety and tasks that exercise your emotional and physical scope.

3.   Significance: It feels good to know that you are essential, unique, necessary, and desired.

4.   Love / Connection: This is the need for a deep connection with another human being and a sense of true belonging.

5.   Growth: "If we stop growing, we die," it was said. It is vital in every facet of life-spiritual, emotional, and intellectual-to continue to grow.

6.   Contribution: This is the ability to go beyond one's own needs. As Tony Robbins says, "All things in the world benefit or are destroyed outside itself." Whether it's time, money, energy (or all three), it's all worth it and makes you feel like a whole person. Which of these six human needs are your first and second motivations? What's your partner like? Problems arise when in our relationship, we do not meet each other's primary and secondary needs. Now that you know the phases and human needs in a relationship, I hope you have found out where the partnerships and interests (and your partners) fit into the scheme. Let us take a look at the things that one or both of you most likely do.

Why Couples Argue

There are many reasons why couples fight and argue about differences in in-laws, quality time spent together, or jealousy. However, there are three main reasons for disarraying any relationship. Let's look at those. Let's look at those.

1.   Sex: There is typically a disconnection at some stage in this type of intimacy. Perhaps your partner is not as open as you are in your bedroom or vice versa. You may not also be happy that you feel you deserve.

2.   Money: Couples fight for money, too. Your costumes might not represent your partner's. Such discrepancy also leads to tremendous disagreements, which can even end the relationship.

3.   Kids: Children are another major topic that creates a divide between couples. The preference of parenting style, in particular. You may be strict in your parentage, but your partner is more relaxed. If children gravitate to the lenient parent, the more demanding parent may feel tired of being the "bad guy." This could then lead to discord and a sense of being left out or unbearable. Even before the rugrats are

born, fights will begin. For example, you might like your grandma to name your child. Still, your partner may prefer to use "northwest" as an individual celebrity couple did. You may have differing opinions, even though you are not parents, whether or not you both want children, what religious or cultural system they are taught, or how you want them to be educated. All these communications must be answered as soon as possible.

How Communication Works In Relationship

Many in troubled relationships say,' We don't talk anymore.' They probably mean that they don't communicate any more effectively. The truth is that people still connect. Sometimes two people who treat each other quietly interact with each other.

The Five Traditional Forms Of Marriage Communication:

1. Emotion

2. Touch

3. Spoken or written communication

4. Context of the situation

5. Non-verbal physical expression (facial expressions, expressions, gestures, behavior, etc.)

It is easy to concentrate only on words, but only a fraction of the information pairs share.

60. Maintaining Your Relationship

Creating and maintaining relationships comes easy for partners that have a good relationship with each other.

When partners genuinely enjoy being in the same space, conversing, communing with each other, and coexisting with each other, their relationship becomes effortless and smooth.

This also gives them a better understanding of each other's behavioral traits and quirks, which helps them predict each other's behaviors and understand why their partner behaves a certain way and guides them in acting accordingly.

Relationships with partners existing on the same wavelength and in total sync with each other are more likely to be long-lasting and successful than relationships with partners that do not have a strong sense of relation.

Being in a state of harmony with one's accomplice helps robust correspondences as accomplices who are in a state of harmony with one another can comprehend both verbal and implicit messages being gone across through non-verbal communication.

When accomplices don't relate with others appropriately, it is simple for accomplices to be absent to one another's sufferings and issues on the off chance that they are not verbally shared.

This could make an individual feel desolate even in the relationship and become genuinely removed from his/her accomplice.

For accomplices to fabricate enthusiastic closeness and reconnect their relationship, accomplices need to inspect their relationship level and pose inquiries. They have private, informative discussions on the best way to develop their associations with one another.

How Do We Relate With Each Other?

To build emotional intimacy and reconnect relationships, partners have to find a means of relating better with each other. For partners to build intimacy, there is a need for a sense of closeness and interdependence between them, which can only be built when partners relate on a deeper level together.

To reach this level, partners need to ask questions about what drives them, where they feel the most safety, their history and experiences, and other factors that make him/her uniquely different from every other existing human being.

Every human has different vibes to them, different ways to get comfortable.

Some feel much relaxed and open only when they outdoors and one with mother nature's gifts.

Some people feel more of themselves when they listen to music and other forms of art.

It's just a matter of finding the 'it' for them.

You may find that they talk about that specific thing a lot. They like to be around it a lot or bring a certain level of peace and enthusiasm whenever they are around it.

Creating better relations with one's partner is a two-way street; both partners have to be willing to deepen the connection and communication between them to enhance a deeper level of intimacy and emotional connection.

Notwithstanding, certain gestures go a long way in getting your partner to relate and connect better.

Using Positive And Motivation Words During Conversations.

When we utilize complimenting words on our accomplices and eventually people around us, it will, in general, draw out their best sides. It causes them to feel reformist and vital. This can go far in guaranteeing a steady relationship. In any event, when confronted with difficulties from the working environment, cultural weight, it is fundamental that they accept there's somebody who might consistently trust in them despite. As the colloquialism goes, "positive vibes can just yield positive natural products."

- Endearing nicknames /pet names

Adults have found this to be very useful. Using nicknames for yourselves can help bring out the 'child-like' instincts in all of us. It makes them feel young again, playful, attractive, less tense, and unforgettable.

- Having shared memories and experiences

This involves planning and doing things together, going on vacations, planning special treats and dates for just you both, doing silly but less dangerous pranks on each other, video blogs, etc. owning something together gets the bonding hormones flowing.

- Respecting individuals' point of view and opinions

Whenever arguments arise, be it severe or not, it's always essential to understand their side of the story. Trying to prove difficult will only give the impression that you are more apart and hardly find common ground. This is discouraging for any relationship, even if the love started strong. Common arguments and disagreements can build up over time.

- Thoughtful gestures like giving surprising and unnecessary gifts

The act of gift-giving has been the most effective way of showing your loved ones that they matter and unique.

It is imperative not to underestimate the simple gesture of giving, more so, if it's a thoughtful gift, something they have always dreamt of having, something they love, and even surprising those with newer packages can be a way of opening their hearts.

How Do You Keep Connected And In Sync With Each Other?

All relationships require efforts, commitment, and patience to stay alive and work.

It is easy to drift apart and lose the emotional connection between them when partners get too comfortable with each other and stop trying to keep the emotional connection intact.

For partners to stay emotional connection even when they are physically apart, there needs to be a level of trust and emotional security between partners that allows them to rest easy even when they are thousands of miles away from each other.

When partners have a complete sense of closeness, belonging, and togetherness, it helps them feel secure in their emotional connection because they know that no matter what happens, his/her is on the same team as them.

Different partners have different relationship dynamics. I.e., what works for Mr. A in his relationship might not work for Mr. B in his relationship.

This is a result of individual and behavioral differences.

Thus, different individuals in different relationships have different ways of staying in sync with his/her partner, based on their behaviors/personalities and the type of relationship they have.

Partners can be informed how best to stay in sync with each other by asking questions and initiating intimate conversations. However, there are general universal tips that can be used to maintain sync between partners.

Here Are Some Useful Tips;

- Spend quality time with your partner

Planning and spending some time alone with your partner regularly will help you both stay connected and feel special because quite often, as time goes, by we get entangled by work, raising a family, and social duties, and so we forget that it's essential to keep the spark alive. You need yourselves of all the fun things you both did before all the extracurricular activities came into play.

Sitting face to face and close to your partner regularly can help bring solace.

- Stay communicated

Whether short or long-distance relationships all require adequate communications because communication makes your partner important, it keeps them updated on what you are going through at every point in time. It's complicated to get back on track once the bridge in communication is broken and left unattended.

This is the most vital part of every relationship. Make it a habit of telling your partner what you are going through and not making them guess. According to Lawrence Robinson, "if you have known each other for a while, you may assume that your partner has a pretty good idea of what you are thinking and what you need. However, your partner is not a mind reader. While your partner may have some thoughts, it is much healthier to express your needs directly to avoid confusion.

- Give and take

A relationship is a give and takes business. When you recognize what's important to your partner, it brings wholeness to him/her. It shows a measure of goodwill, thoughtfulness, and a sense of devotion. Always giving to others at the expense of your own needs will only build resentment and anger

How Deep Is Our Emotional Connection?

In romantic relationships, the level of emotional depth and dependency between both partners determines that relationship's strength. Communicating with your partner does not guarantee that you do understand what he/she is going through, and often, partners may feel like their significant other listens out of a sense of duty, not because they genuinely care or feel the way they do, which could lead to him/her feeling small and insignificant.

Emotional depth is being able to listen, interpret, and sensitively respond to feelings that arise in your partner, others around you, and ultimately yourself.

This is the ability to show empathy, to 'feel into' someone else's experiences to know what it feels like to be them.

That level of interdependency gives both partners a sense of reliability, true friendship, and a deep intimate connection built over time. This and empathy take time to become insoluble because significant factors affect the level of transparency and vulnerability needed between partners to achieve the desired emotional depth and intimacy.

We often want our partner to talk to us about everything and be the first to share their emotions whenever they were going through something positive or negative. Still, we also understand that no human being was ready-made as specific factors such as early/childhood environmental factors, prominent life-changing experience and events, gender, and gender roles as dictated by society. An individual's background and culture can affect and influence an individual's perception and personality, which dictates the individual's ability to understand, empathize, and form emotional connections with his/her partner.

61. Sex Therapy

There is a myth that sex is the most incredible experience for most people in today's culture. That is why sex with anyone, anywhere, anytime, will always be an experience. Wonderful and orgasmic. This myth is ever sold to us, especially in theatres where sex is portrayed as a country-breaking experience, even when two people who have had sex only met a few minutes before. The physical part of sex is all that is appeared in vast numbers of these experiences. The truth of the complex, enthusiastic, and mental procedures that cause or suppress desire and orgasm is never mentioned.

Problems In Sex

Much work has been done to study the reasons why many men and women have very unsatisfactory sex. In the 1950s, Masters and Johnson conducted numerous scientific and clinical studies on humans' causes of desire. Masters and Johnson have no doubt shown that sexual reactions are as sensitive to conditioning as other animal or human behavior. Sexual working in creatures and people is effortless to disturb by penalizing external stimuli and is particularly vulnerable to learned inhibitions or distortions. In the 1970s, therapists refined this vision of sexual response, based on arousal and dysfunctions of orgasm, to consider a lack of desire as an essential factor in treating many sexual disorders. Shere Hite (1998), in Hite's report on female sexuality, reported on his groundbreaking research on male and female sexuality, based on thousands of detailed questionnaires completed by people in the United States. USA Hite has found that many women feel that sex is not comfortable because men usually spend too little time in foreplay and do not understand a woman's need to wake up entirely before having sex. Sexual intercourse. Many men have recognized that old stereotypes of a real man during sex contribute to considerable frustration and a lack of sexual pleasure. The feeling that someone loves emotionally and cares about a partner is also a prerequisite for most people to have close and satisfying sex.

Most people at one time or another experience a lack of pleasure or a lack of sexual desire. Our moods, emotions, fatigue, and anxiety levels, and hormone levels can make this happen on occasion. It is likewise hard for an individual who has been adapted for quite a long time to accept that sex is "bad" or thinks that their body is unacceptable to suddenly feel entirely at home to express their emotions through their sexuality. Sex is the most natural activity globally, but we have to accept that problems can frequently arise because we were brought up in a very unnatural environment. People will also feel compelled to adhere to film standards for sexual performance, saying, "everyone is having a good time, so what about me." Many people experience fear, shame, shame, and personal inadequacy when they encounter problems related to this very own area of their lives. Subsequently, it is evaluated that the number of people who come for treatment is significantly lower than the actual frequency of sexual problems. For those who continuously enjoy the sexual side of the relationship, especially those who are ultimately afraid of having sex but still want to be sexually active, several therapies are available to help overcome these problems. The most common sexual difficulties in men are impotence or erectile dysfunction, inability to ejaculate or organic male dysfunction, and premature ejaculation. In women, the most common problems encountered are frigidity or dysfunction of arousal, dysfunction of female organs and vaginismus, or involuntary spasms of the vagina. A lack of desire can occur in both sexes. It is estimated that about ten percent of all women have never experienced an orgasm of any kind.

Psychotherapy And Couple Therapy As Part Of Sex Therapy

Specialized therapists offer sexual therapy to help couples overcome the sexual problems they may experience. For sex therapy to be successful, both parties must commit to attending the sessions, doing their homework, and trying new techniques for at least an agreed initial period. Individual psychotherapy can be vital in helping a person talk about their fears, negative conditioning, or past traumatic experiences that can inhibit desire, excitement, or the ability to let go and permit themselves to have an orgasm. By seeing each person separately, the therapist can help clients speak more openly about their feelings and experiences in the relationship. Their desires and fantasies are also explored. Several sessions with each couple will help the therapist access the causes of the sexual problems that arise. Excitement problems are often due to a lack of foreplay or knowledge about what excites a couple. In couple therapy, communication needs to be open between couples regarding their sexual preferences, as this is a crucial way to help them better understand their individual needs.

It should be noted that the needs of both people are just as urgent. Also, unless the two involved care about each other and want to be together, sexual desire and pleasure will never be affected.

Therapies To Overcome Sexual Problems

Sex therapy involves several stages, and the couple is encouraged to practice each step in the privacy of their own homes. First, they are asked to massage and pet themselves. They are then asked to kiss and kiss, to touch body parts, including the genitals. The following step is the stimulation of the genitals and breasts in women. Self-stimulation can be a learning and sharing process useful for both parties, followed by manual masturbation for each party. If a woman is unable to achieve an orgasm using these methods, a vibrator can be used. When both people feel comfortable and fully aroused, sex can be attempted. The problems that arise at each stage are mentioned at weekly meetings, such as areas of the body that a particular couple does not like to be touched. Sex therapy, in its most successful form, leads to higher open and effective communication, both emotional and physical, between the two parties.

What Happens In Sex Therapy?

Most people need a lot of courage to call a therapist. It usually takes even more to call people a sex therapist. Most people know what happens in psychotherapy when watching TV shows or movies where a character goes into therapy. But there is not much that happens in the office of a sex therapist. Given all the shame and guilt of having sex, it is no wonder that it is difficult for people to imagine what is going on without feeling upset or even upset. Sex therapy is similar to any other psychotherapy session. The customer (or patient) talks about their set of experiences and involvement in an issue. The advisor causes them by placing things in context or making concrete recommendations for change. No contact (aside from incidental embraces whenever mentioned by the customer) and absolutely no nakedness or sex.

The course of sex treatment likewise takes after other psychotherapy. Most sex specialists request that customers round out an underlying affirmation structure. The strategies are extraordinary. However, the sexologist typically needs to know some data about you, including why you request help and what you have had the option to determine the past issue.

The advisor additionally needs to know you all the more for the most part. For instance, a specialist has to find out about their connections, their work, and something about the family they grew up with.

In sex treatment, the advisor frequently needs to comprehend what you found out about sex and who instructed you. On the off chance that his family had never mentioned sex and his folks rested in various rooms, he instructed him sex, though by implication. Or on the other hand, your folks may have been available to sex. However, you waedded an accomplice who knew then to no about it. Likewise, you may have learned sex adversely; Maybe your first sexual experience was alarming or pitiful, which is a horrible method to become more acquainted with sex.

The therapist will also want to know your current sexual experience in your relationship. Do you like sex? Do you hate it, or do you think it's "disgusting"? Does it work as it should, or do your sex organs work? Is sex painful for you? Do you watch a lot of porn, or do you have sex with strangers? Do you have an unusual interest in sex, such as fetish behavior? Do you and your partner have different ideas about sex? Do you even have trouble with that?

If you are in a relationship, the sexologist will observe what is going on in your relationship outside the bedroom. If there is a lot of conflict or stress, the therapist will want to help you learn better ways to make your relationship more enjoyable and facilitate work on a sexual problem. Sometimes there is no conflict, which is not a good sign; this usually means that one or both partners are upset but not ready to "shake the pot" for fear that the relationship will collapse. In this case, the sexologist should encourage the married couple to talk about their problems to have a more real connection and understanding. Sex therapy generally involves recommendations for activities, from a joint meeting to a discussion that encourages you to associate or exchange a sensual touch. Sex therapists often recommend reading about subjects so that you have the most current knowledge and that you can dispel any myth that hurts you. It is also tactical to know that sex therapists must be licensed in the country where they practice. A sex therapist can be a psychiatrist with a medical degree, a psychologist with a Ph.D. certified clinical social worker with a master's degree marriage and family therapist, or a licensed professional counselor and then a master's degree. Only one state, Florida, requires that a psychotherapist have additional training in using the title "sexologist."

However, all psychotherapists must be educated, trained, and advised on ethics to treat a new or specialized population.

There are a few associations that can support you in finding a sex therapist. The largest is the American Association of Sexuality Educators, Counselors and Therapists, or AASECT. You can also ask your doctor or psychology service at your local university to refer you to a sexologist in your area.

Can Sex Therapy Lead To More Satisfied Older People?

The short answer to the last question is, "I bet you can!" The most extended answer is usually not the first tool when you want to improve your love life. Most people are intrigued by the idea of sex therapy, but they have no idea what it entails, what clients and therapists do, and they fear that the first step is always to remove their clothing.

Conclusion

You need to know that this is going to take some time and some work. It also depends on how bad things have gotten between you and your loved one.

That said, I don't want you to quit. You need to ask yourself if your love is worth fighting for. So you must be willing to put in the work. Set your ego aside and allow a chance for your love to get back to where it was, or even better. I hope you know how much it matters for you to be willing to understand each other as a couple.

I will tell you one thing: Just because it's going to take some work, it does not mean it has to be all drudgery. Spending time with your lover, checking on your relationship can be very enjoyable! If you allow yourselves, you will notice you're growing closer and closer to one another, day after day.

If there is one thing I would like to stress, make loving a daily business. You know you can't just skip work whenever you feel like it, for whatever reason — not if you hope to keep having a roof over your head and food to eat. So, in the same way, get serious about your relationship. No one is wired to be alone. This person has chosen to be with you. The least you could do is to be the best version of yourself that you can be for them. It's always worth it.

I highly recommend that you figure out the best ways to show your partner that they mean a lot to you every day. Don't just show them you love them the way you're used to showing it. Show them in ways that they can understand. This means getting to know what your lover loves to feel and experience so that they know you really and truly love them. Even in loving, it is possible to be selfish. Don't assume just because you're showing them love in your love language that they know it all the time. Step outside of yourself sometimes so you can love them the way they truly want and deserve to be loved.

Another thing I need to stress is that there is no such thing as the perfect human being. Beyoncé is a goddess, and she is flawless, but only Jay-Z's therapist would know what's going on with them. What I mean by this is that you should not put undue pressure on your partner for not always being one hundred percent Prince or Princess Charming.

Sometimes things happen, they get stressed out, or they forget. In times like these, do lovingly recall all the good they have done, the good that is still in them. Be there, loving, patient, gently nudging them back to the person they indeed are.

If you think you're going to make any headway by whining about the fact that things are no longer the way they used to be between you two in the beginning, then you've got another thing coming. Don't whine. Do something. Be proactive about your relationship and getting it back on track. Your partner might have the same feelings about you, so why don't you take the lead in bringing back the spark? Don't wait. Just act! Your partner will appreciate you and love you for it even more.

Love is not a race. It's a journey. It only ends when death does you part. At least, that's how it should be. That is how two people come from a headspace that says no matter what, I love this person, and we will always get through whatever life brings out away.

When you're in love, honestly and selflessly, you come to realize that there is no mountain high enough and no valley low enough, just like the song says. There is nothing two people determined to be together cannot overcome. Know that, and you're more than halfway towards having the relationship most people only ever dream of but never actually experience!

I guess you could say we have cracked the code to make the honeymoon last a lifetime. Takes a lot of work, but it's worth it. I only have one head. Last time I checked, so did my partner — and I checked just a couple of minutes ago. If we could take our relationship to where it is now, then so can you.

I am rooting for you and your spouse or partner one hundred percent. There is no doubt in my mind that you both can be a lot better than you already are together. Are you willing? Are you open? Then that's all you need. Put in the work, and watch the good times roll with each other. True love is no myth. But it is no walk in the park either. Maybe not at first. However, once you build those loving habits, and realize you're both in this for better or worse, then there is absolutely nothing that could get in between you two. Ever.

Part 3

COMMUNICATION IN RELATIONSHIP

62. What Is Anxiety?

Anxiety is an emotional state, pleasant or unpleasant, associated with a state of alert and fear against all outside; generally, it is an "exaggerated" reaction to the real situation. This emotional state includes not only the individual subject but also the people around him. This emotional state's symptoms are nervousness, apprehension, insomnia, apnea, ease of crying, palpitations, weakness, and stomach cramps.

According to the great psychoanalyst S. Freud at the onset of anxiety, there are internal tensions or "battles" within the individual who have not had a resolution. Generally, all individuals run into feelings of anxiety, which - if adequately motivated - remains a transitory sensation with a positive effect; vice versa, anxious episodes that arise without real justification due to incomprehensible and non-affective reasons are at the origin of excessive reactions characterizing pathological or harmful anxiety. In most cases, pathological anxiety is accompanied by "panic attacks," acute crises characterized by fear, palpitations, and disordered and animalistic behaviors. Instead, the so-called "phobias "Are attitudes of real fear but not objective for contextual situations, or animals or objects. Treatment of anxiety includes:

- Pharmacological treatments for overt pathologies, when anxiety is due to organic disease.

- In the case of "situational anxiety," it is necessary for the individual to overcome that difficult moment by himself. Eventually, he can use hypnotic-sedative drugs for short periods.

- In the case of "chronic anxiety," long-term drug therapy with hypnotic-sedative drugs is used, possibly associated with psycho-therapy.

What is an Anxiety Diagnosis?

Anxiety is not a simple diagnosis. It is not caused by bacteria that can be detected in blood tests. It takes many forms or can also accompany other medical conditions.

To diagnose anxiety, a comprehensive physical examination is necessary. This can help your doctor find or rule out other diseases that may cause your symptoms or be masked by these symptoms. A complete personal medical history is also necessary for your doctor to make an accurate diagnosis.

During the Physical Examination

This will help if you are completely honest with the doctor. Many things can cause or be affected by anxiety, including:

- Certain diseases

- Drug

- Alcohol consumption

- Coffee consumption

- Hormones

Other medical situations may cause symptoms similar to anxiety. Many signs of anxiety are physical symptoms, including:

- Heart of Racing

- Shortness of breath

- Trembling

- Sweating

- Chills

- Hot flashes

- Chest pain

- Twitch

- Dry mouth

- Nausea

- Vomiting

- Diarrhea

- Frequent urination

Your doctor may perform physical examinations and order various tests to rule out medical conditions that mimic anxiety symptoms. Medical conditions with similar symptoms include:

- Heart attack

- Angina pectoris

- Mitral valve prolapses

- Tachycardia

- Asthma

- Hyperthyroidism

- Adrenal tumors

- Menopause

- Side effects of certain drugs, and such as drugs for high blood pressure, diabetes, and thyroid disease

- Quit certain medications, such as medications used to treat anxiety and sleep disorders

- Drug abuse or withdrawal

Diagnostic Test

It is suggested that you complete a self-assessment questionnaire before taking another test. This can help you determine if you have an anxiety disorder or are responding to a situation or event. If your self-assessment leads you to believe that, you may have an anxiety disorder, your doctor may ask you for a clinical assessment or a structured interview with you.

Your doctor may use one and more of the following tests to assess your anxiety level.

Zung Self-Rated Anxiety Scale

The Zung test is a 20-item questionnaire. It asks you to evaluate anxiety on topics such as the following from "very little time" to "most time":

- Tension

- Anxiety

- Trembling

- Heartbeat

- Faint

- Frequent Urination

- Nightmare

After completing the test, a well-trained professional will evaluate your answers.

Hamilton Anxiety Scale (HAM-A)

The Hamilton Test was developed in 1959 and is one of the earliest anxiety scales. It is still widely used in clinical and research environments.

It involves 14 questions that score emotions, fears, tension, and physical, mental, and behavioral characteristics. Professionals must administer the Hamilton test.

Baker Anxiety Scale (BAI)

BAI can help you assess the severity of anxiety. You can take the exam. Professionals can also take it.

Social Phobia Scale (SPIN)

This 17-question self-assessment can measure your degree of social phobia. You rate the anxiety level of various social situations from zero to four. Zero means no anxiety. Four indicates extreme anxiety.

Pennsylvania Worry Questionnaire

This test is the standard widely used measure of concern. It distinguishes social anxiety disorder and generalized anxiety disorder. The test uses 16 questions to measure the generality, excess, and uncontrollability of your problems.

Generalized Anxiety Disorder Scale

A seven-question test is a screening tool for generalized anxiety disorder. In the past two weeks, you have been asked how many times you have been troubled by irritability, nervousness, or fear. Options include "not at all," "a few days," "more than half a day," or "almost every day."

Yale-Brown Obsessive-Compulsive Disorder Scale (YBOCS)

YBOCS is used to measure the level of OCD. This process is a one-on-one interview between you and the mental health professional. You select the three most disturbing items from the symptom checklist and then assess their severity. The system will then ask you when you have some other obsessive-compulsive disorder or obsessive-compulsive disorder in the past. According to your answer, your mental health professional level, your obsessive-compulsive disorder is subclinical, mild, moderate, severe, or extreme.

Diagnostic Criteria

The diagnosis of anxiety depends mostly on your description of the symptoms you are experiencing. Mental health professionals use the "Diagnostic or Statistical Manual of Mental Disorders" (commonly called DSM) to diagnose anxiety and other mental illnesses based on symptoms. The criteria for each anxiety disorder are different.

DSM lists the following standards for generalized anxiety disorder (GAD):

- Excessive anxiety, worrying about many things most of the time, at least six months

- Hard to control my worries

- Three of the following six symptoms appear: restlessness, fatigue, irritability, muscle tension, sleep disturbance, and inattention.

- Symptoms that seriously interfere with your life

- Symptoms are not caused by the personal psychological effects of drugs or medical conditions.

- Symptoms are not caused by another mental disorder (for example, panic disorder for an upcoming panic attack, anxiety due to social disorders, etc.)

Diagnosis of Childhood Anxiety

Childhood and teenage years are full of new and frightening experiences and events. Some children learn to face and accept these fears. However, anxiety disorders can make it difficult or impossible for children to cope with.

The same diagnostic criteria and assessments as adults also apply to children. In the DSM-5 (ADIS-5) interview schedule for anxiety and related diseases, your doctor will interview you and your child's symptoms.

The symptoms of children are similar to those of adults. If you notice signs of anxiety or any anxiety or worrying behavior that lasts more than two weeks, please take your child to see a doctor. There, you can check whether they suffer from anxiety.

Some studies have shown that anxiety may have a genetic component. If someone in your family has been diagnosed with anxiety or depression, please evaluate your child as soon as you notice symptoms. A correct diagnosis can lead to interventions to help them manage anxiety as a child.

What to Do If You Are Diagnosed with Anxiety

Focus on managing anxiety, not eliminating or curing anxiety. Learning how to best control anxiety can help you live a more fulfilling life. You can prevent anxiety symptoms to avoid reaching goals or expectations.

To help manage anxiety, you have several options.

Drug

When you and your child are diagnosed with anxiety, your doctor may refer you to a psychiatrist who will decide which anxiety medicine is the most effective. Adhering to the recommended treatment plan is essential for therapy to work effectively. Try not to delay treatment. The earlier you start, the better the effect.

Treatment

You may also consider seeing a therapist or joining a support group for people with anxiety disorders so that you can talk about anxiety publicly. This can help you control your worries or gain insight into the source of anxiety.

Lifestyle Choices

Find positive ways to reduce stress. This can decrease the impact of anxiety on you. Some things you can do include:

- Exercise regularly.

- Look for hobbies that attract or occupy your mind.

- Participate in your favorite activities.

- Keep a daily log of thoughts and activities.

- Create short-term or long-term plans.

- Socialize with friends.

Also, avoid alcohol, nicotine, or other similar drugs. The effects of these substances can increase your anxiety.

Communication

If possible, stay open with your family and close friends. It is not easy to talk about any mental disorder. However, the more people around you understand your anxiety, the easier it is to convey your thoughts and needs to them.

Anxiety Relief Techniques

- Stick to the treatment plan suggested by your psychiatrist.

- Think of seeing a therapist or joining a support group for people with anxiety disorders.

- Discover positive ways to reduce stress, such as regular exercise or keeping a daily diary.

- If possible, stay open with your family and close friends.

- Avoid alcohol, nicotine, and other similar drugs.

- Focus on managing anxiety, not eliminating or curing anxiety.

What is Normal Anxiety?

At the essential level, anxiety is an emotion. State that emotion is the subjective state of existence. It is usually related to feelings, behaviors, thoughts, and physical changes.

Like all emotional states, the intensity of anxiety is also different. For example, we might say that we are happy. A more robust expression of the same emotion may be a pleasant experience. But unlike the emotion "happiness," which has different words to convey these different intensities (for example, the intensity ranges from happiness to happiness), anxiety is a single word that describes a wide range of emotional intensity. At the very low end of the intensity range and anxiety is normal or adaptive. At the high point of the intensity range and anxiety can become pathological and maladaptive. Although everyone feels anxious, not everyone has the same intensity, frequency, or duration as people with anxiety disorders.

Normal Emotions of Anxiety and Fear

Anxiety and the fear of close relatives and cousins are considered emotions. Although there is considerable overlap between the two terms, there are some critical differences. Fear is usually considered the main emotion. On the contrary, anxiety is regarded as a secondary emotion, which means avoiding fear (including avoiding stimuli that produce fear). The main emotion is the emotion that can be recognized by facial expressions. Observers can easily understand the main emotions, and they can exist in different cultures. These main emotions are happiness, anger, sadness, fear, surprise, and disgust. Outside observers cannot easily recognize secondary emotions such as anxiety. Secondary emotions are usually considered internal private experiences.

The most important difference between fear and anxiety is the schedule. Fear is the response to the current dangers that currently exist immediately. On the contrary, anxiety refers to the anticipation of specific potential threats that may or may not occur in the future. In other words, fear is a response to the immediate danger, and anxiety is related to the threat expected in the next moment. Anxiety reflects the expectations of fear and represents an adaptive attempt to prevent situations that cause fear. In a state of anxiety, people are getting ready and ready to deal with future problems or dilemmas, and they expect that these problems or dilemmas will cause specific harm if they cannot be avoided. In this regard, anxiety is a normal and beneficial emotion.

Emotions are just a normal part of the human experience. Therefore, they are neither good nor bad.

What happens afterward determines whether we experience a particular emotion for good or bad, that is, changes in our feelings, behavior, thoughts, and physiology. At this point, when you may be thinking: "What are the benefits of fear and anxiety? Are these emotions not painful?" Well, the answer may be shocking, but fear and anxiety are basic emotions. If it comes to human survival and achievement, anxiety and fear motivate us to take necessary actions. For example, imagine a young mother and her child are crossing the road. The mother suddenly realized that they were driving towards the upcoming car. Imagine what would happen if she didn't feel the slightest fear. Presently imagine a law student preparing to take the bar exam so that he can become a lawyer. What if he is not worried about passing or failing the bar exam? If there is no fear and anxiety to prepare for automatic action, they are in danger of suffering some terrible negative consequences. Therefore, although the experience of fear or anxiety can sometimes be unpleasant, we can see that without these essential emotions, our situation would be worse.

What Is the Nature of Anxiety?

Like sadness and anger, anxiety is one of the three primary emotions that cause many problems when you lose control. Several people who have trouble in social situations struggle with it to some extent. This is one aspect of shyness, and of course, this is the main factor of social anxiety.

It is easy to describe anxiety quickly. It causes physical, mental, and behavioral symptoms. Physically, someone may have a faster heartbeat, tremble, start to sweat, feel pain, or dry mouth. They may feel fear, worry, and distraction psychologically. Emotions make people want to get rid of anything that makes them feel that way. They may also be at a loss. That's a summary, but anyone with an anxiety disorder knows that there are many nuances besides this one:

Socially, The Worst Effect of Anxiety Is That It Makes You Avoid Things You Shouldn't Avoid

Anxiety is not good. At the highest level, this isn't very comforting. When anxiety is caused by a specific situation rather than general life stress, it forces you to avoid these things. Its logic is elementary.

It tells you: "When you are in certain situations, I will appear, and you will feel terrible. If you do not adapt to these situations, I will not look up, and you will feel good."

The problem is that this response often runs counter to your long-term interests. If someone is anxious about an obscure situation, it won't affect them much, but they are usually nervous about the ordinary things they want to do. They want to go to parties, share opinions with friends, or invite someone to hang out. Avoidance makes people miss essential parts of life because they try to prevent themselves from feeling uncomfortable. They may eventually rearrange their lives into lonely, sterile ruts, so they don't have to face fear.

What an anxious person needs to do is face anxiety and learn to deal with it. Following the siren's call for avoidance is a bit like a drug addiction. If someone is addicted to cocaine, even if it is not easy to withdraw and recover, they need to get rid of it. However, their addiction tells them: "If you haven't made Coke for a long time, you will start to feel uncomfortable, so as long as you stay tall, you won't have this problem!"

Avoidance Can Lead to A Vicious Circle and Aggravate Anxiety

It works like this: Certain things make people feel anxious. They want to avoid this situation, either to escape the existing situation or decide not to take action they are considering. By escaping, they kept in mind the fact that the situation they had avoided was terrible. They may feel more anxious next time and even want to leave there. Not only that, but they feel relieved when they give up the urge to avoid, which reinforces this behavior.

People Can Partially Avoid Certain Situations Through Safe Behavior

Safety behavior is a kind of behavior of people that can put them in a situation that causes anxiety and protects them from all the shocks they worry about. Some examples:

People who are nervous at a party may consider drinking as a safe behavior.

Alcohol will dull his nerves and prevent him from feeling all the anxiety. It also provides a convenient prefabricated excuse for any mistakes he may make.

A woman who is afraid of flying may still travel by air, but only if she brings a bottle of quick-acting anxiolytics. She does not accept it but needs to know that she has it just in case.

A person who is afraid of driving may be able to keep up with the steering wheel, but only if he must plan his route and make sure to follow alleys and paths.

Safety behavior may be more subtle. A woman who is mildly anxious in social situations may be able to talk to others, but only if she insists on a neutral topic. She does not reveal any more in-depth personal information about herself. If she exposes herself to the premise of sharing her true self, she will be too nervous.

What Causes Anxiety?

Anxiety disorders are not caused by a single factor but by multiple factors. Other factors also play a role, including personality factors, life difficulties, and physical health.

Family History of Mental Health Conditions

Some people with anxiety disorders may have genetic anxiety tendencies, and these disorders can occur in the family. However, having a parent or close relative experiencing anxiety or other mental health conditions does not mean that you will automatically develop anxiety.

Personality Factor

Study shows that people with certain personality traits are more prone to anxiety. For example, perfectionists, children who are easily flustered, timid, suppressed, lack self-esteem, or want to control everything, sometimes experience anxiety in childhood, adolescence, or adulthood.

Persistent Stressful Event

As a result of one or more stressful life events, anxiety conditions may arise. Common triggers include:

- Work pressure or job changes

- Change life arrangements

- Pregnancy and childbirth

- Family and relationship problems

- A major emotional shock after a stressful and traumatic event

- Verbal, sexual, physical, and emotional abuse and trauma

- The death or loss of a loved one.

Physical Health Problems

Chronic physical illness may also cause anxiety or affect the treatment of anxiety or the physical disease itself. Common chronic diseases associated with anxiety disorders include:

- Diabetes

- Asthma

- High blood pressure and heart disease

Some physical conditions can mimic anxiety conditions, such as overactive thyroid. Seeing a doctor and performing an evaluation to determine if there is a medical reason may help your anxiety.

Other Mental Health Conditions

While some people may experience anxiety disorders independently, others may experience multiple anxiety disorders or other mental health conditions. Depression or anxiety often occurs at the same time. It is essential to check all these conditions at the same time and get help.

Substance Use

Some people who feel anxious may use alcohol or other drugs to help them manage their condition. In either case, this may cause people to have substance use problems and anxiety. Alcohol and drug abuse can exacerbate anxiety, especially when the effects of substances diminish. It is also essential to check the conditions of the use of any sense and get help.

How Does Anxiety Affect the Body?

Anxiety affects physical and mental health. Both have short-term and long-term effects on the body and mind. Although many people know the effects of anxiety on mental health, few people are aware of physical side effects, including digestive problems and increased risk of infection. Anxiety can also change the functions of the cardiovascular, urinary, and respiratory systems.

In this article, we discussed the most common physical symptoms and the side effects of anxiety.

Symptoms

People with anxiety disorders experience a series of physical and psychological symptoms. The most common ones include:

- Feeling nervous, nervous, or fearful

- Restlessness

- Panic attacks in severe cases

- Rapid heartbeat

- Shortness of breath or hyperventilation

- Sweating

- Trembling

- Fatigue

- Weakness

- Dizziness

- Difficult to concentrate

- Sleep problems

- Nausea

- Digestive problems

- Feeling too cold or too hot

- Chest pain

Some anxiety disorders have other symptoms. For example, OCD also causes:

- Obsessed thoughts

- Compulsive behavior designed to reduce anxiety caused by thoughts

- Temporary relief period for coercion

The Effect of Anxiety on The Body

Anxiety can seriously affect the body, and long-term anxiety can increase the risk of chronic physical diseases. The medical center suspects that anxiety develops in the amygdala, which is the brain area that manages emotional responses.

When a person becomes anxious, stressed, or fearful, the brain sends signals to other parts of the body. These signals indicate that the body should be prepared to fight or escape.

For example, the body responds by releasing adrenaline and cortisol (many people describe it as stress hormones).

When confronted with a combative person, the fight-or-flight response is useful, but it is not helpful during job interviews or speeches. Similarly, maintaining this response for a long time is not healthy.

Some of the way's anxiety affects the body include:

Breathing Changes

During periods of anxiety and a person's breathing may become rapid and shallow, called hyperventilation.

Excessive ventilation allows the lungs to absorb more oxygen and quickly transport it around the body. Excess oxygen can help the body prepare for battle or flight.

Excessive ventilation can make people feel that they are not getting enough oxygen and my pant. This can exacerbate hyperventilation and its symptoms, including:

- Dizziness

- Feel fainted

- Dizziness

- Tingling

- Weakness

Cardiovascular System Response

Anxiety can cause changes in heart rate or blood circulation throughout the body.

A more active heart rate makes it easier to escape or fight, and the increased blood flow brings fresh oxygen or nutrients to the muscles.

When the blood vessels narrow, this is called vasoconstriction and affects body temperature. People often experience hot flashes due to vasoconstriction.

In response, the body sweats and cools down. Sometimes this may be too effective and make people feel cold.

Long-term anxiety can be detrimental to the cardiovascular system and heart health. Some studies have shown that anxiety can increase the risk of heart disease in otherwise healthy people.

Impaired Immune Function

In the short term, anxiety will increase the immune system's response. However, long-term anxiety can have the opposite effect. Cortisol can prevent the release of substances that cause inflammation and shut down the immune system that fights infections, weakening the body's natural immune response. People with a chronic anxiety disorder are more susceptible to common colds, flu, and other types of conditions.

Changes in Digestive Function

Cortisol prevents processes that the body considers unimportant in combat or flying situations. One of these blocked processes is digestion. Also, adrenaline reduces blood flow and relaxes stomach muscles. As a result, people with anxiety disorders may experience nausea, diarrhea, and stomach upset sensations. They may also lose appetite. Some studies have shown that stress and depression are related to several digestive diseases, including irritable bowel syndrome (IBS). A study showed that 30% to 40% of IBS participants also suffer from anxiety or depression.

Urine Reaction

Anxiety and stress increase the need to urinate, and this reaction is more common in phobias. The need for urination or uncontrolled urination may have an evolutionary basis because it is easier to escape with an empty bladder. However, the link between anxiety and increased desire to urinate remains unclear.

Complications and Long-Term Effects

Anxiety can cause long-term adverse effects. People with anxiety disorders may experience:

- Depression

- Digestive problems

- Insomnia

- Chronic pain

- Difficulties in going to school, work or socializing

- Lost interest in sex

- Drug abuse disease

- Suicidal thoughts

Treatment

Anxiety disorders can be highly cured, and doctors usually recommend a combination of the following methods:

- Drug

- Treatment

- Support Groups

- Lifestyle Changes Involving Physical Activity and Meditation

The doctor may recommend one-on-one or group counseling. Cognitive-behavioral therapy is a strategy that can help people view events and experiences in different ways.

What Is A Panic Disorder?

Panic disorder occurs when you experience repeated unexpected panic attacks. DSM-5 defines a panic attack as a sudden attack of intense fear or discomfort that peaks within a few minutes. People with this disease fear panic attacks. You may panic when you feel sudden, overwhelming terror for no apparent reason. You may experience physical signs such as a beating heart, difficulty breathing, and sweating.

Maximum people experience one or two panic attacks in their lives. The American Psychological Association reports that 1 in 75 people may have panic disorder. The characteristic of panic disorder is that you will continue to worry about recurring panic disorder after experiencing at least one month (or more) of continuous attention or worry that another panic disorder (or its consequences) will occur again.

Even though this disease's symptoms can be overwhelming and frightening, they can be controlled and improved with treatment. Seeking treatment is an essential part of reducing symptoms and improving quality of life.

What Are the Symptoms of Panic Disorder?

The symptoms of panic disorder usually begin in adolescents under 25 years of age. If you have experienced four or more panic attacks or have experienced a panic attack and then live with the fear of recurring panic disorder, you may have panic disorder.

A panic attack produces a strong sense of fear, which begins suddenly and without warning. An episode usually lasts 10 to 20 minutes, but symptoms may last more than an hour in extreme cases. Everyone's experience is different, and the symptoms are generally various.

Common symptoms associated with panic attacks include:

- Racing heartbeat or heart

- Shortness of breath

- It feels like you are suffocating

- Dizziness (vertigo)

- Dizziness

- Nausea

- Sweating or chills

- Trembling or trembling

- Changes in mental state, including illusory feelings (unreal feelings) or depersonalized feelings (separation from yourself)

- Numbness or tingling in hands and feet

- Chest pain or tightness

- Worried you will die

The symptoms of a panic attack usually occur without an exact cause. Often, symptoms are not proportional to the degree of danger present in the environment. Since these attacks cannot be predicted, they can severely affect your functionality.

What Causes Panic Disorder?

The cause of panic disorder is unclear. Studies have shown that panic disorder may be genetically related. Panic disorder is also associated with significant changes in life. Going to college, getting married, or having your first child are critical life transitions that can cause stress and lead to panic disorder development.

Who Is at Risk of Panic Disorder?

Although the cause of the panic disorder is unclear, information about the disease suggests that certain people are further likely to develop the disease. According to data from the National Institute of Mental Health, women are twice as likely to suffer from the disease as men.

How Is Panic Disorder Diagnosed?

If you experience the symptoms of a panic attack, you can seek emergency medical care. Many people who experience a panic attack for the first time think they have heart disease.

During the emergency room, the first responders will perform several tests to see if heart disease causes your symptoms. They may perform blood tests to rule out other conditions that may cause similar symptoms or perform an electrocardiogram to check heart function. If your symptoms have no emergency basis, you will be referred to your primary care provider.

Your primary care provider may conduct a mental health check and ask about your symptoms. Until your primary care provider diagnoses panic disorder, all other medical conditions will be ruled out.

How Is Panic Disorder Treated?

The focus of panic disorder treatment is to reduce or eliminate symptoms. Qualified professionals can treat this, and in some cases, can also be achieved by medication. Treatment usually involves cognitive-behavioral therapy. And this therapy teaches you to change your thoughts or actions to understand your attacks and control your fears.

Medications used to treat panic disorder can also include selective serotonin reuptake inhibitors (SSRIs), a class of antidepressants. SSRIs prescribed for panic disorder may include:

- Fluoxetine

- Paroxetine

- Sertraline

Other drugs sometimes used to treat panic disorder include:

- Serotonin-norepinephrine reuptake inhibitors (SNRIs), another class of antidepressants

- Antiepileptic drugs

- Benzodiazepines (usually used as tranquilizers), including diazepam or clonazepam

- Monoamine oxidase inhibitors (MAOIs), another type of antidepressant, rarely used due to rare but severe side effects

- In enhancement to these treatments, there are steps you can take at home to reduce symptoms. Examples include:

- Keep schedule

- Exercise regularly

- Enough sleep

- Avoid stimulants such as caffeine

What Is the Long-Term Outlook?

Panic disorder is usually a chronic (long-term) condition and may be challenging to treat. Some people with this disease do not respond well to treatment. Others may have periods of no symptoms and periods of severe symptoms. Most people with panic disorder get medicine to relieve their symptoms.

How to Prevent Panic Disorder?

Prevention of panic disorder may be impossible. But you can reduce your symptoms by avoiding alcohol and stimulants (such as caffeine and illegal drugs). It is also helpful to inform you if you have symptoms of anxiety after experiencing distressing life events. When you are troubled by something you have experienced or been exposed to, please discuss your primary care provider.

What Causes A Panic Attack?

As with most mental health conditions, research has shown that many factors can increase an individual's sensitivity to panic attacks. The impacts of these factors vary from person to person.

At Priory, our professional panic attack treatment experts can help you determine the root causes and triggers of panic attacks, enabling you to develop future health coping strategies and take measures to achieve a comprehensive and sustainable recovery.

Genetics has been found to play an essential role in determining the likelihood of a person suffering from a panic attack. Research shows that having first-degree relatives (such as parents or siblings who have suffered a panic attack) makes you more likely to have a panic attack at some point in your life. Other causes of panic attacks can be divided into psychological, pharmacological (related to the use and effects of drugs), and environmental factors.

The psychological causes of a panic attack may include:

- Chronic stress

- Existing mental health conditions, such as anxiety, depression, obsessive-compulsive disorder (OCD), or post-traumatic stress disorder (PTSD)

- Phobia-a person may have a direct panic attack when exposed to a fearful object or situation.

- Lack of self-confidence-increasing evidence supports the view that people suffering from panic attacks communicate or interact with others passive.

- Inferiority

The pharmacological causes of panic attacks may include:

- Alcoholism, drug use, or drug withdrawal

- Drug side effects

- Excessive caffeine intake

Environmental causes of panic attacks may include:

- Chronic physical diseases, such as cancer

- Suffer significant personal losses, including bereavement or breakdown of the relationship with a romantic partner

- Significant life changes, such as unemployment, becoming a parent and moving

- "Maintenance" behaviors, such as avoiding situations or environments that cause panic, anxious/negative self-talk, dysfunctional beliefs, and faint feelings

What Are Fears and Phobias?

After a long and slow climb, the roller coaster hesitated for a second on the steep peak. You know what is going to happen. It cannot be avoided now. It's time to hang on the armrests, sweaty palms, fast heartbeat, and get ready for a wild ride.

What Is the Fear?

Fear is one of the basic human emotions. It is registered into the nervous system and functions like instinct. From the moment we are babies, we have the necessary survival instincts to fear when we feel dangerous or insecure.

Fear helps protect us. It keeps us alert to danger and prepares to deal with it. In some cases, feeling fear is natural and helpful. Fear is like a warning, warning us to be careful.

Like all emotions, fear may be mild, moderate, or vigorous, depending on the person's situation. Fear can be short-lived, or it can last longer.

How Fear Works

When we feel danger, the brain will immediately respond by sending out signals that activate the nervous system. This can lead to physical reactions such as faster heartbeat, faster breathing, and increased blood pressure. The blood is pumped to the muscle groups to prepare the body for physical preparation (such as running or fighting). Sweating the skin keeps the body cool. Some people may notice sensations in the stomach and head, chest, legs, and hands. Certain physical sensations of fear can be mild or strong.

This answer is called "fight-or-flight" because this is precisely what the human body is prepared to do: fight the danger or run away quickly. The body remains in this fighting state until the brain receives a "completely cleared" message and turns off the response.

Sometimes fear is triggered by some startling or unexpected event (such as a loud sound), even if it is not dangerous. That's because the fear response is activated immediately a few seconds faster than the thinking part of the brain can process or evaluate what is happening.

Once the mind has enough information to realize that there is no danger ("Oh, that's just a balloon explosion-howl!"), it turns off the fear response. All of this can happen in a few seconds.

People's Fear

Fear is the word we use to express our emotional response to something that seems dangerous. But the word "fear" is also used in another way: to name something a person usually fears.

People are afraid of things or situations that make them feel unsafe or uncertain. For example, people who are not good at swimming may worry about deep water. In this case, fear helps because it warns the patient to stay safe. Someone can overcome this fear by learning how to swim safely.

If fear can warn a person to stay safe in potentially dangerous places, it will become healthy. But sometimes fear is unnecessary and can cause more caution than the situation requires.

Many people worry about public speaking. Whether it is a lecture class, speaking at an assembly, or reciting lines at school events, talking in front of others is one of the ordinary people's fears.

People tend to avoid situations or things they worry about. But this does not help them overcome their fear-in fact; it may be the opposite. Avoiding something terrible will exacerbate fear and keep it fearful.

People can learn and gradually adapt to the things or situations they worry about, thereby overcoming unnecessary fears. For example, people who can fly despite the fear of flying will get used to unfamiliar feelings such as takeoff or turbulence. They learned what to expect and had the opportunity to watch what others did to relax and enjoy flying. Facing fear gradually (safely) can help someone overcome fear.

Fears in Childhood

In childhood, specific fears are usual. This is because the fear may be a natural response to uncertainty and vulnerability, and many things experienced by children are strange and unfamiliar.

Young children are often afraid of being alone, strangers, monsters, or other terrifying fictional creatures, and fear of the darkness. School-age children may feel scared when a storm comes or when they first stay overnight. As they grow and learn, with adults' support, most children can slowly overcome these fears and get rid of them.

Some children are more sensitive to fear and may be challenging to overcome. When fear persists beyond the expected age, it may indicate that someone is too scared, worried, or anxious. People whose fear is too strong or lasting for too long may need help and support to overcome the fear.

Phobia

Phobia is an intense fear response to specific things or situations. When suffering from a phobia, fear is out of proportion to potential danger. I feel dangerous because fear is so extreme for people with phobias.

Phobias make people worry, fear, frustrate, and avoid things or situations they fear because the physical sensations of fear can be so intense. Therefore, phobias interfere with everyday activities. A person with a dog phobia may be afraid to go to school if he or she sees a dog on the way. People with elevator phobia may avoid field trips if they involve taking elevators.

If the weather forecast predicts a storm, a girl with thunderstorm phobia may be afraid of going to school. When the sky turns overcast, she may feel very painful and fearful. People with social phobia are terrified of speaking or interacting in public places. They may even be afraid of answering questions in class, making reports, or talking with classmates in the lunchroom.

Feeling that phobia is accompanied by intense fear can be exhausting and frustrating. Lost opportunities can be disappointing because fear makes you shrink. Fearing things that others don't seem to have problems with can be confusing and embarrassing.

Sometimes people laugh at their fears. Even if the person making fun of does not mean being unfriendly and unfair, making fun only worsens the situation.

What Causes the Phobia?

When someone has a horrible experience of something or a situation, a sense of fear arises. A small brain structure called the amygdala (pronounced uh-MIG-duh-duh) records experiences that trigger strong emotions. Once something or situation triggers a strong fear response, the amygdala will trigger a fear response to warn the person every time it encounters (or considers) the event or situation.

In exceedingly terrible circumstances, after being injured by Ung, bee phobia may occur. For that person, looking at pictures of bees, observing bees from a distance, or even walking near flowers where bees may be present can trigger phobias.

However, sometimes there may not be a single event that causes a particular phobia. Some people may be more sensitive to fear due to their inborn character traits; specific genes are inherited or experienced. People who had intense fear or anxiety in childhood are more likely to have one or more phobias.

Phobia does not mean weakness or immaturity. This is a reaction that the brain learns to protect people. Just as the brain's alarm system triggers false alarms, it generates intense fear in proportion to the situation. Because the fear signal is so strong, people are convinced that the danger is more significant than it is.

Overcome Phobia

People can face fear gradually and learn to overcome phobias. It was not easy at first. This requires willingness and courage. Sometimes people need the help of a therapist to guide them through the process.

Overcoming phobias usually starts with listing a long list of people's fears in order from worst to worst. For example, for dog phobia, the list might start with what the person is least afraid of and such as looking at a dog's picture. Then it will work until the most severe fears, such as people standing next to petting dogs, petting dogs on leashes, and people walking dogs.

Gradually, with support, the person tried every fear situation on the list-once, starting with the smallest fear.

This person was not forced to do anything but worked hard every time before he felt fear until they felt comfortable, and it took a long time.

The therapist can also show people with a dog phobia how to approach, raise, and walk the dog and help them try it. People may expect terrible things to happen when they approach a dog. Talking about this also helps. This can be a great comfort when people discover that what they worry about has not become a fact.

The therapist can also teach relaxation exercises, such as specific breathing patterns, muscle relaxation exercises, or soothing self-talk. These can make people feel comfortable and bold enough to face the fears on the list.

When someone adapts to a fearful object or situation, the brain will adjust its response to overcome the phobia. Usually, the most challenging part of overcoming the phobia is the beginning. Once a person decides to do it and gets the right guidance and support, the surprising fear quickly disappears.

How to See Yourself in A Positive Light

How we view ourselves plays a significant role in our lives. We all make mistakes. Maybe you made a mistake that made you feel sorry for yourself. Someone may point out that you already know this insecurity very well, but now you feel very rubbish. Especially under the considerable influence of today's social media, our dislike of our functions is easy to be troubled. So, as the title implies, we will discuss several ways to look at ourselves more positively!

If you are depressed, you tend to focus on yourself, insecurities, and how bad you feel. When you are in that sad bubble, it isn't easy to see what other people are going through. But try it. Try to do something for someone. When you consider helping others, your focus will not be on negative emotions. The famous artist Conan O'Brien once said: "Be kind, things will happen." Wise words! When you are kind to others and help them, you will also help yourself, because positive emotions should replace those nasty negative emotions.

Another way we can reduce our negative emotions is to confuse our daily work.

Small things like going to work along the same route every day may cause depression. Therefore, switch it. Try different routes or use other forms of public transportation to get to work. Or visit the places you have always wanted to go to. Breaking the routine can refresh you and open your eyes to different lifestyles. Likewise, it will distract you from the negative thoughts that disappoint you and transform your views into happier ones.

Also, social media can have a critical impact on our self-image. Nowadays, when we scroll through Instagram or Twitter, we see thousands of photos of people living in different people groups. Social media has many positive aspects, although it can also be harmful. It is easy to compare yourself with the "ideal" women or men who seem to be shaped by social media and society. For example, a person may not feel beautiful because their body is different from some Instagram models or do not get as many likes and comments as others. Have you felt this way before? This may damage a person's self-esteem and image, so we should do our best not to compare ourselves with others. Remember, everyone is beautiful, and our ways are different. Accept it!

When we feel negative, we can purely focus on our limitations and what we think we are not good at. Although the critical question is, what are you good at? Take out a notepad and start listing your skills and attributes. Consider your qualities; maybe you are a good person or a creative person. You can even ask close friends and family members what their hobbies are for you. Also, what have you achieved over the years? It may not seem beneficial to record these positive things, but it does. When you remember that people like your qualities and the great things you have done in your life, it can help you feel good about yourself again. Keep this list so that you can revisit it when negative emotions recur.

All in all, sometimes, all of us feel inadequate or even worthless. We make mistakes. However, we should not just stay on our limitations and errors but should try to learn and learn from them and shift the focus to our lives' climax and good life. Let us pop that sad bubble today!

63. Anxiety in Relationships

How to Overcome Insecurity in A Relationship?

Our interpersonal relationship feels insecure from time to time; this is entirely normal. However, some people feel like this most of the time, so that both partners become overconsumed. Knowing how to handle and manage the insecurity in a relationship can truly differentiate the relationship's flourishing and failure.

Signs of Insecurity in The Relationship

Insecurity in a relationship may be like:

- Always troubled that your partner will leave you

- Feel you don't have enough

- When your appearance or behavior is imperfect, think over and over all the time in the relationship

- It feels like a fraud destined to be exposed

- I feel bored, overweight, stupid, ugly...

- Feel you are not worthy of lasting love

- Often feel inward and ashamed.

- Desire to get attention and peace of mind, but it seems hard to be convincing even if you get it.

- Switch back and forth between doubt, anxiety, anger, and internal

- Jealousy can lead to unhealthy thoughts and behaviors, such as excessively questioning a partner's whereabouts, infringing on privacy, and controlling behavior.

When we have a relationship with a person who has strong feelings, these feelings can worsen. The more significant the relationship is to us, the more we think we lose. Here, our insecurities become very uncomfortable, exacerbate anxiety, fear, suspiciousness, anger, and other unpleasant and unhealthy emotions.

What Causes Insecurity in Interpersonal Relationships?

Fundamentally speaking, insecurity usually comes from a deep sense of inadequacy. It is generally believed that we are not enough. We are flawed, ugly, or not worthy of love. Often, this feeling of "low value" comes with one or two of these unhealthy patterns-severe inner critics and the belief that others will love us only when we act in a certain way.

No matter what standards are adopted, actions must be strong, fun, compliant, enjoyable, beautiful, hardworking, and staying with others at all times. We might think that this is the only way for our partners to stay. Sometimes, it even feels like cheating our partners to love us. It may not be obvious, but somewhere between the two lines, we may worry that they will leave once they discover our true colors.

On the other hand, and we may feel powerless before internal critics continue to insult us. It may be so embedded in our daily self-conversations that we don't even know how much it affects our overall self-esteem.

The Impact of The Past on Our Current Relationship

All these beliefs are usually the product of our early experience. They come from using limited resources to interpret and integrate these experiences into our belief system to the best of our ability. Some examples of these early experiences might be:

- The attachment style we developed with the primary caregiver was later transferred to other relationships.

- The primary information we receive from the environment makes our deep beliefs about ourselves, others, and our overall life tailored.

- Observe the relationships around us and "learn" what we absolutely should and shouldn't do to avoid harm

- Harmful experiences, such as rejection, neglect, or humiliation by people we care about

Although it is easy to blame the insecurity on the partner's behavior, the truth is that in most cases, the insecurity in a relationship does come from within us. Indeed, building relationships with people who regularly judge most of our work will shake our confidence. Tolerating repeated criticism and seldom getting love or appreciation from our partner will increase our self-doubt. But be aware that words increase, not creation. It is best to remember that others cannot make us feel or act in a certain way. Only our thoughts and beliefs can.

Will Insecurity Destroy Relationships?

It is perfectly normal to feel insecure occasionally. It sometimes brings benefits even in small amounts, because it may inspire us to devote more energy to our partnership. Long-term self-doubt can negatively affect our mental health and interfere with our interpersonal relationships.

One of the critical elements of a successful romantic relationship is the actual connection between partners. The real connection comes from authenticity, and authenticity requires us to show our fragile side publicly. For this, we need to believe that even if there are loopholes, we are still beautiful and worthy of love. In other words, we must adapt to our identity, at least to some extent. Long-term insecurity may prevent you from becoming yourself entirely and prevent you from having a sincere relationship with your partner.

Constant worries in a relationship may exhaust you and take away your peace and happiness. The obsessive-compulsive disorder makes your head a genuinely uncomfortable place instead of enjoying the journey and giving quality time with the people you love and care about. Just like this is not painful, if you let your insecurity get out of control and affect your behavior, this may lead to a series of harmful interactions between you and your partner. You and your partner are not satisfied, and the relationship will suffer Influences.

How Modern Life Causes Anxiety (And How to Do It)

Although many things in modern life can make our daily work more comfortable, many aspects can cause lasting anxiety. Of course, we are within reach, with countless worlds of information and thousands of applications, but is this a good thing? Are people in the past easier than us in some way? I mean, anxiety is about 400 BC, ask Hippocrates. Yet did the ancient Greeks have to deal with Instagram or decrypt the decrypted text messages (or lack of text messages) from someone he dated last night? Do not.

The following are some familiar sources of stress in modern life, and more importantly, what measures you can take to deal with these stresses.

Trigger 1: Open Office Plan

The cubicle is not super fun, but neither is the open office plan. The concept is relatively new and aims to make employees feel better at work. Research shows that this is not necessarily the case.

On the first day working in a magazine with an open office plan, I found myself hyperventilating and suffering silently at my desk. The boss is only one foot away from me at the shared table, and I have always been within the editor's sight. It's not that I'm slacking off, it's just that I still feel like I'm being watched!

The open plan increases the pressure we feel in the office. Didn't you see other people taking a lunch break? Well, guess you shouldn't either! Didn't you see anyone leaving at 6 pm? Well, if you stop at 6 on the decimal point, you must be a lazy person, right?

How to Do

For better or worse and sometimes the only way out is through customs. You may be stuck at the same desk in the same office for a while. I hope that, over time, you will gradually adapt to this situation.

For me, a great help is to find a friend in the office where I can be completely open or honest about my anxiety.

She fully understands, but it keeps her comforted. Similarly, when an employee left, the table was not in the center of the room, I suddenly popped up and claimed it immediately. Make a difference! As for lunch or punctuality, if it starts to affect your happiness, you may have to bring it to your boss or human resources department.

Trigger 2: Compare Yourself with People in The Media

It wasn't until I saw the influx of celebrities that they closed their lips (coughing, Kylie Jenner), that I was unaware of my "little" lips. Suddenly, because I don't have puffy pillow-like lips, I feel that I am not sexy enough, not sexy enough. My heart is distressed for all the beautiful friends who think that my condition is not good enough. I send a photo in the group chat saying: "I need Selena Gomez's nose" or "I need Victoria's Secret model abs!" When we are bombarded by advertisements and so many TVs (or Netflix), we are continually facing unrealistic beauty standards.

How to Do

Remember that almost everything you see in magazines and advertisements is edited! Even campaigns without photoshopping are not "natural." The entire team consists of makeup artists, hairdressers, wardrobe designers, and lighting experts. Are there any ordinary people in the group dedicated to making them look perfect? Comparing yourself to others will not help. The less we associate ourselves with others, the more we focus on our love for ourselves, the better.

Trigger 3: Addicted to Social Media

In a word: FOMO! It's fun to see photos without our friends hanging out, and may put us in a downward spiral. FOMO is not only related to our friends. Compared to people who always post travel photos or brag about their huge engagement rings, this makes us feel that our lives are inadequate.

Even though our friends may not be celebrities, ordinary people can edit their faces in the posted pictures! Enter, Facetune. The application allows you to slide the appearance to edit the appearance with just a few taps. It isn't easy to know what is true and what is not.

How to Do

Remember, social media is a fantasy. People's social media feeds are usually selected pictures and videos. We will only post photos from the days when we looked the best and when we were "the best on Instagram." A few years ago, I deleted Snapchat after experiencing some incredibly frustrating stories (so many FOMO) and have never looked back. For now, I strongly recommend removing the social media platform if it makes you unhappy.

If it doesn't serve you, just let it go. Does Facebook fight overheat you? Do you find yourself forcing yourself to follow your ex-husband on every social platform that exists? It's time to take a break. Delete the problematic application for at least a few days and then see how you feel.

Trigger 4: Explain Online Communication

"What does this text message mean?!" The number of text messages I send or receive is sad. In face-to-face communication, it is usually easier to explain what someone means when talking to us due to voice and social prompts.

When we communicate electronically (whether it's with a friend via a mobile phone or an email with the boss), these don't exist, and it's hard to figure out what they say. Usually, we jump to the worst case. We must also deal with the lack of communication of explanations. The pressure that the unanswered text can guarantee is unprecedented.

How to Do

Don't be afraid to ask for clarification. Point out obvious problems-it's embarrassing! Sometimes, this can help you relieve some discomfort and confrontation immediately. You can say: "Hey, I know this is embarrassing, but I think this kind of news is used as. Sometimes it is difficult to interpret these things in words."

Also, remember that the idea of jumping to the worst-case scenario will not help you at all. Take a step back and breathe. In the grand plan, this is just a piece of news.

How Anxiety Causes Irrational Thoughts

Catastrophic or irrational thinking plays a typical role in the occurrence and severity of anxiety. It is not uncommon for anxious people to worry that threats or incidents will be overestimated. Usually, this kind of thinking and feeling like the event will go hand in hand with the "end of the world"-thinking that if the event does happen, they will not cope.

Sometimes this combination can be summarized as irrational thought, in which logic is negated by things that are considered unlikely or impossible. For some people, irrational thoughts first cause anxiety. For others, their anxiety seems to have led to the development of irrational beliefs. Many combine the two.

About Anxiety and Irrational Thinking

Many people with anxiety disorders have severe problems with anxiety, and irrational thinking-many people know that this kind of thinking is irrational. However, they still have difficulty persuading themselves to get a more logical and rational response.

These helpless thoughts may lead to the development of anxiety. The cognitive perspective of anxiety states that certain types of irrational thoughts (e.g., evaluation, interpretation of events, catastrophic thoughts (worst case and overestimation of danger), and other logically irrational thoughts may cause difficulties in coping and developmental symptoms of anxiety.

Also, people who are experiencing these thoughts may not even realize it. They may have only experienced emotional and physical reactions and need to determine the thought and why it happened. This is one of the causes why cognitive behavioral therapy (CBT) is so useful.

It is also controversial that anxiety can produce one's irrational thoughts. When a person is on the edge of suffering an anxiety attack, the chance of experiencing irrational thoughts may increase.

Anxious Thoughts May Be Behavioral and Genetic

Anxiety is a disease involving physical and emotional consequences. It is caused by (and caused) feeling, just like things are out of control, worrying about all kinds of problems that may not exist and worrying about something more than helping.

Anxiety has many different types of irrational thoughts. Examples of how these irrational thoughts may manifest include:

- Health fears-"My heart is beating fast-I may be having a heart attack!"

- General worries-"I don't have a letter from my mother. I hope her heart doesn't give up."

- Social issues-"If I go to a party, I will embarrass myself and become an abandoned person."

- The conclusion is incorrect-"I touched the doorknob. I will get sick!"

- Phobia-"That spider might kill me!"

Of course, most ideas are much more subtle than this. For example, common health fears may convince yourself that you may have a severe illness, such as multiple sclerosis, based on some mild symptoms. This is an example of catastrophic thinking. Another example may be worrying. When you wear a specific type of shoes, people will judge you, which will impact your life. This is an example of mind reading. Suppose you know what others are thinking. Any thoughts are inconsistent with reality and go beyond what is usually believed because this situation can be described as "irrational thoughts." The challenge comes from how reasonable the ideas at the time seemed.

The origin of these ideas is difficult to understand. It is commonly believed that they are a combination of genetic and environmental factors.

How to Deal with Interpersonal Anxiety

Relationships with others are vital to our physical and mental health. They can bring great joy and support to some people, but they can cause anxiety and cause a lot of distress for others.

What Is Relationship Anxiety?

Relationship anxiety and relationship-based anxiety refers to anxiety arising from intimate relationships. It is not a recognized, diagnosable disease, so there is no guideline on how to treat it, but, according to reports, it is a common problem that is expected to affect one in five people.

There are some reasons why someone may be anxious about their relationship. They may be afraid of being abandoned or rejected or worry that their feelings will not be rewarded. Some people may fear that their partner will be unfaithful or that the relationship will not last. Others may worry about having sex with their partner or committing to another person and miss other life choices.

Anxiety and Dating

Anxiety is especially common when starting a relationship or dating. Before the connection is fully established, it is difficult to tolerate the other person's feeling uncertain or the relationship's state. Many people are afraid of others' judgment or rejection so that the anxiety they produce will affect their dating performance, such as strong self-awareness and difficulty in making eye contact or maintaining a dialogue with others. This fear may be so great in some people that even though they want to build relationships with people, they avoid dating altogether.

Anxiety and Sex

Anxiety can affect sex and intimacy. For many reasons, anxiety can affect our libido or sexual desire, and it can physically make sex difficult or impossible. This can cause further anxiety or create a negative cycle. When we feel anxious, worried thoughts and tension can make it difficult for them to relax, to enjoy sex or show enough to maintain close relationships with others.

Sex-related fears, such as fear of appearance, performance, or vulnerability to others, can also make it very difficult for some people to have sex and physical contact and cause others to avoid this behavior entirely.

Why We Are Anxious About Relationships

The tendency to feel worried about relationships is usually due to the attachment patterns we experience with our parents and caregivers if we are young. These factors will affect our understanding of needs and meet their needs. If we experience an anxious attachment pattern, we are more likely to experience higher relationship anxiety levels.

Low self-esteem and long-term negative views of oneself can also lead to anxiety in love. If you think you are not good enough, or no one else offers so much in your relationship, then you might think that this is what your partner thinks of you.

Signs of Relationship Anxiety

It is normal for most people to feel a certain degree of anxiety or worry that their relationship is normal, but for others, this situation is more intense and lasting. The following are signs that you may be encountering relationship anxiety:

1. You often worry about what you mean to your partner, what your partner does when you are away, and whether your relationship will develop.

2. You are worried that if you have not heard the other person's voice for a long time, your feelings about your partner will change.

3. You don't distribute the situation proportionally, and it is easy to feel hurt or angry on minor issues.

4. You do not trust your partner, and you should be alert to signs that they are unfaithful, dishonest, or will leave you.

5. When considering your relationship, you will often experience anxiety symptoms such as nervousness, sweating, and difficulty concentrating.

6. You often check your partner, such as checking their emails or text messages, to find their latest news.

7. You often ask your partner to feel at ease about how they feel about you.

8. You will do your best to please your partner at the cost of your own needs.

9. If you are with your partner, you will not express your thoughts or opinions, nor will you feel that you can be yourself.

10. You make criticisms or requests and controls to partners.

11. You are estranged from your partner, far away or on alert, making some parts of yourself inaccessible to your partner.

12. You are stubborn and always want to be with your partner.

13. You are unwilling to establish a serious relationship with people or keep in touch with your partner at all because you are worried that such a partner will not work and will be hurt, disappointed, or betrayed.

14. You can test how your partner feels about you, for example, by pushing them away to see how much they will fight for you (which is then seen as a sign of how they feel).

15. You broke the relationship, such as secretly meeting with the "ex" to gain more control.

How Interpersonal Anxiety Affects You and Your Interpersonal Relationship

If you don't address your interpersonal anxiety, you may find that your anxiety becomes more frequent. In the long run, and this can lead to further anxiety, despair, and depression. Relationship anxiety can also affect your partner and relationship. This may cause you to keep a distance from your partner or even terminate the relationship altogether. It can also work through confrontation and control or passive and needy.

Our actions affect how others feel and therefore react to us. In some cases, interpersonal anxiety can produce a self-fulfilling prophecy, in which the behavior manifested by fear itself will lead to the negative consequences of fear.

If anxiety about your relationship is excessive, affecting your relationship or affecting your quality of life, then it may be time to do something about it.

Why Is Trust Important in A Relationship?

Five main reasons why trust is essential in relationships are as follows:

Trust Reassuring

When you believe that your partner loves you no matter what, you can rest assured that the relationship will continue to exist even if there is a dispute or fight. You know that your relationship is more potent than differences.

Trust Helps to Heal Injuries

When you are hurt by misunderstandings, different expectations, or unmet needs, trust enables you to heal and forgive.

Can't Live Without Trust

Trust is the foundation of relationships and the key to love. When you trust your partner, you can rest assured that they will not leave during difficult times. This is the key to love, to build and grow.

Trust Helps Overcome Obstacles

When you trust your partner, you will know that you are their top priority. They take your best interest to heart. When disagreements or challenges may arise in your relationship, you know that you can overcome problems together.

Trust Helps You Provide Space for Partners

When you trust your partner, giving you time or space to do things without yourself will not feel insecure. You don't doubt who he spends time with.

What Does Trust in A Relationship Look Like?

Here are some signs that you have trust in your relationship:

- **Open dialogue:** Both of you are willing to relax and share your secrets and fears.

- **Both are each other's priorities:** you both put each other's needs and interests first. You express concern and consideration for each other.

- **Maintain eye contact:** If you can look into each other's eyes while talking, it means you two have nothing to hide.

- **Actively listen:** If you both listen attentively, it means to love, care, and respect.

- **Physical intimacy:** It is made up of small things rather than sex, which shows the firmness of this combination-a of the gentle kiss, holding hands, or hugging.

- **Acknowledge your mistakes:** You should be honest about your mistakes and not use excuses or explanations to cover up your mistakes.

- **Get along with family and friends:** If you both like to get along with each other's family and friends, then it means that you both have good intentions.

- **Comfort and confidence:** If you are both true selves to each other, then it shows that you trust each other.

- **Effectively resolve conflicts:** If both parties can resolve their differences positively, this shows that your relationship is strong.

How to Control Negative Thinking in Relationships?

Negative thinking patterns can make life difficult because they can put you between right and wrong. Negative thinking usually hinders what you want. It makes you feel empty, unsatisfied, and upset.

When your glass is half empty, it is almost impossible to see the benefits, potential, or glimmer of hope and life lessons for every experience. In a relationship, this mentality makes it difficult for you or your partner to satisfy. For example, if your partner feels that they cannot please you and enhance your happiness, they may feel inferior, helpless, unappreciative, etc. If you feel that your partner will never do good enough things, the relationship is conflicted, tense, and likely to resent resentment. Unfortunately, this dynamic can quickly become a negative vicious circle.

The energy you put into the world will radiate back to you, so when you focus on the negatives, this is the relationship you will see and get. Although you may unconsciously or consciously form negative beliefs to protect yourself from harm or disappointment, when you want to maintain a healthy, loving relationship, now is the time to make valuable changes. I know that it might be easier to assume that a new relationship does not work (especially if you have been heartbroken) rather than hopeful, but isn't this one of the goals of satisfying a couple's ideals and success? If you answer "yes," then this is an opportunity to transform your negative ideas into a more realistic and positive attitude.

This is how to do it:

1. Honestly evaluate your beliefs about yourself, the world, relationships, and expectations of love. Do you operate based on ideas like "Nothing is effective for me," "Men (or women) always hurt me," or "The world is an ugly place"? If your thoughts sound like some of the above examples, then you are engaged in negative thinking.

2. Control your negative thoughts. Let us take "Nothing works for me" as an example; it makes people feel heavy, sure, and lasting. Change this thinking mentally to create space for you to solve problems and appreciate everything beneficial to you.

Think about your experience and remind yourself that many times life is right for you. Try different positive thoughts and see if it feels right. Healthier alternative ideas include: "I am willing to accept positive experiences in life and love." or "I am grateful for _____" or "I can handle my life."

3. Reconnect the brain. When negative thoughts or beliefs surface, confirm and transform them into one of the more positive thoughts you create. This is a significant change in your thinking, so it takes time, energy, and patience to imply that you want it to think in a new and healthier way. However, once you keep correcting it, you will notice that your negative thoughts will disappear, and healthier thoughts will appear. This is how you let go of the negative lens and see the world more optimistically and openly.

How Anxiety and Depression Affect Your Relationships

Anyone can be affected by depression or anxiety, even children. The American Anxiety and Depression Association found that generalized anxiety disorder affects 6.8 million people in the United States, or that number is much higher worldwide.

Depression is difficult to survive. These symptoms may affect your mental health, cause sadness and suicidal thoughts, and even have a physical impact on your life. Depression and anxiety increase stress, reduce energy, cause weight fluctuations, and cause insomnia, and this continues.

Living on your own is difficult, but depression and anxiety can also hurt your marriage.

The following are 4 ways your mental health affects your relationship and how marriage therapy can help.

General Dissatisfaction

Depression is an experimental experience. It may affect almost all aspects of your life and may even make you feel that you don't know who you are.

Feeling sad, helpless, or lonely every day is full of challenges for you and your partner. Falling in love with someone unhappy, challenging everyday life is full of challenges.

Life is a roller coaster full of ups and downs, but a good life should be full of ups and downs. By seeking marital therapy for depression and consulting a doctor, you can control your anxiety and regain control of your life.

Your Sex Life Suffers

The close relationship with your spouse is significant to the success of the marriage.

Intimacy is the key to connecting you, body, mind, and soul. Studies have shown that couples who have active and healthy sex lives release oxytocin in their bodies. This magical hormone is responsible for establishing connections, increasing trust, and reducing stress. Oxytocin also contributes to the emotional intimacy between partners.

Unfortunately, the study shows that depression (or taking antidepressants) can significantly impact relationships, quality of life, and mental health. It can also influence a person's sex life.

Depression has been shown to reduce libido, reduce sexual excitement, delay or reduce the ability to orgasm, and cause erectile problems.

When your sex life is affected, the rest of your relationship will also be affected.

Husbands and wives may be less intimate, loving, or trusting each other. This may also make a partner feel unimportant and may induce a divorce.

No Inspiration in Life

When you are depressed, you may feel almost unmotivated and unmotivated to do almost anything. This feeling of listlessness can make it hard for you to socialize, keep working, or find any joy in a hobby you previously liked.

Of course, these will affect your social life and your husband's or wife's financial situation.

If you suffer from anxiety or depression, sometimes just getting up in the morning and brushing your teeth may feel accomplished. It is essential to celebrate the small steps taken when suffering from depression or anxiety.

It is not easy for you to do what others cannot do.

At the same time, and it is equally important to take positive measures to improve your mental health.

Marriage therapy with your spouse (and taking an online marriage course) can help you deepen your understanding of the disease. It can also help your partner learn how to do things around you, avoid triggers, and empathize with how you feel.

Spouse Feels Helpless

Your spouse loves you. He and she hope to provide you with the best service in all aspects. When you feel anxious or depressed, your partner will do everything to make you feel better.

But depression is not like the common cold. Your spouse can't let your chicken soup and cold break out within a few days. Improving and managing your mental health is a lifelong journey. It requires constant attention.

Your mental health is your personal journey. Sometimes, no matter what you do, and your partner will not cheer you on. This fact will make your partner feel frustrated, helpless, and frustrated throughout the relationship.

Important Signs of Insecure Attachment

It is essential to understand this phenomenon when young children are not securely attached. In the interaction where the child is not firmly attached, the balance between "attachment behavior" and "exploratory behavior" is missing. Let's study the various insecure attachment styles, learn more about them, and then learn how to cure them.

Unsafe Accessory Sign

Attachment researchers have found that some children have no attachment to their parents but have the following three signs of "unsafe attachment":

Dismissive attachment signs (also called avoidance signs), focused attachment signs (also called ambiguities), and fear attachment signs (also called chaotic).

Dismissive Accessories

After the parents left, the child looked independent and confident, but it was not the case-their heart rate and cortisol levels were as high as the first child. However, when the mother came back, the child continued to play with toys. He or she did not seek assurances and did not seem to expect the parents to provide assurances. Their heart rate and cortisol levels are still high. When the parents stretched out their hands, the children dismissed the parents.

Busy Attachment

After the parents leave, the child will panic. Sometimes they have to take them back to their parents quickly because children with these signs of attachment are very painful without their parents. When the parents return, the child ran to the parents and held on tightly without letting go. Usually, children cannot be comforted; they just cry and weep. The parents did not seem to calm the child down. Their heart rate and cortisol levels are still high. When the parents try to let them go, they will resist and insist on being detained.

Fearful Attachment

These children are not sure what to do. Although contemptuous and attentive children have consistent strategies (avoid or hug), they have an inconsistent combination of seeking and fearing their parents. When the parents returned to the room, these children had been observed approaching and retreating. Some people shed tears in the middle of the room when they first sat down, lay down, or curled up. Their parents seem to be both a source of reassurance and a source of fear-both exist simultaneously.

These parents usually have depression, drug use, anger problems, or other reasons for inconsistent behavior. These children no longer know what will happen, but they urgently need to be relieved.

How to Overcome the Fear of Abandonment?

Many of us grew up on abandonment issues, which can have serious long-term effects on our adult relationships. For example, you may often feel paranoid about your partner's possible departure from you. Or, you may avoid romance altogether because you are too scared not to get hurt. Similar problems also arise in friendships, and you may find yourself hiding your true self to avoid rejection. All these experiences mean that the abandonment problem played a role in reducing your self-esteem. Therefore, when your confidence level is low, you will make it challenging to realize your full potential.

So, what if you are afraid of being abandoned? Fortunately, this is not something you have to accept; you can heal and move on. We will explore what fear of abandonment usually involves, explore adult abandonment signs, and explore five practical strategies to solve this common problem.

What Is the Fear of Being Abandoned?

In short, worrying about being abandoned is that you feel anxious about being abandoned by others, even those who seem reliable, who may agree to stick to you.

In a few cases, this fear comes from the losses suffered during childhood. Anything that creates an insecure or hostile family environment can prevent you from growing with a strong sense of self-worth. For example, you may have to deal with the death of your parents, siblings, or other relatives at a young age, or you may suffer from divorce.

In other cases, fear of abandonment is related to being neglected or inconsistent love in childhood. For example, if your parents suppress your emotional self-expression, make fun of you, bring you to an incredibly high standard, or rely on your "parents" (rather than making you a child), you may feel the fear of giving up as an adult Love relationship.

Fear of Signs of Abandonment

The fear of abandonment symptoms varies from person to person but may include the following:

- High levels of generalized anxiety

- Inferiority

- Depression/low mood

- Constantly feeling criticized

- Go back to the previous experience of abandonment

- Panic attack

- Feel unable to control my life

- Put yourself down

- loneliness

- Self-medication or drinking

- Obsessed with abandonment scene

- Attract people who seem to refuse

- Feel uncomfortable in social situations

A range of other mental health problems can also cause these symptoms, but the more you know about them, the more likely you will benefit from overcoming the abandonment problem.

Three Ways to Overcome the Fear of Being Abandoned

If you are struggling with abandonment, it is best to see a doctor. You can discuss the technique of giving up therapy with your counselor, and sometimes you may need to prescribe drugs to help you solve potential problems. It may also be necessary to solve some concurrent diseases (such as depression) simultaneously.

However, no matter what your doctor recommends, you can try other strategies at home to deal with your anxiety of being abandoned by your loved ones. Consider the following five methods. You can start with any step, but you may benefit from trying all these steps.

Determine Your Fear

Healing the problem of abandonment is about figuring out the nature of the things that scare you.

To start abandonment recovery, ask yourself what you think and feel about rejection. What is the worst-case scenario that you tend to imagine?

Apart from fear, when you think of being abandoned, what other emotions do you have in your heart? When you start to realize the possibility of abandonment, how do you feel (about yourself and others)? As you research your thoughts and feelings on the subject, you may find it helpful to keep a diary.

Simultaneously, learning how to overcome abandonment in childhood has a lot to do with what you experienced if you were young. When you had to guess, when would you think the abandonment problem started? Since then, how do you see the impact of a particular event (or series of events)?

Stop Generalization

When it comes to dating, people who do have abandonment issues can help them with their work. You may search it difficult to trust others, push them away when they begin to get close, or feel that the world is ending when the relationship is not harmonious.

You may also unconsciously think that your previous abandonment will repeat itself, and no matter what you do, you are bound to be abandoned. This can lead to avoiding relationships or accidentally destroying them from within.

To stop generalizing, you required to make these fundamental beliefs clear. Write down what your most pessimistic self tends to believe in people and relationships. Next, conduct a critical study of these beliefs and write down arguments against them.

For example, "People always lie," becomes "My mother caused me severe harm when lying to me, but people can be honest and honest." Try to turn affirmative statements into repeated affirmations.

Build A Network of Friends

When you are afraid of being abandoned, you may be attracted to focus on a relationship, especially a romantic relationship. You can break this habit by putting more energy into your friendship and actively building more relationships. This means that no matter what, you will not be abandoned. You will always have someone you can talk to, spend time with, and feel good.

When you consistently support and care for the people around you, it becomes much easier to deal with abandonment in a relationship. They will remind you that good interpersonal relationships exist and assure you that if you need to solve broken interpersonal relationships, you will be helped and nurtured.

When you find it challenging to make new friends, try joining a new club or take a series of courses to learn new skills. Also, look back at the old friendships that have passed over time to see anything worth looking back at.

How to Stop Overthinking About Interpersonal Relationships?

The best way to stop overthinking is not to feel understanding! Unfortunately, it is difficult to solve this problem entirely by yourself. In my experience, and the most effective way to stop overthinking is to share your fears with others and let them completely satisfy you.

The first two steps are constructive preparations for this. Getting rid of the vicious thought cycle and knowing it can help you express yourself more clearly.

In turn, this will make it very easy for the person who is speaking to get your chance! It can be beneficial to share with others why you are overthinking.

Because it can help you break out of your model and see things in a new way. Merely expressing your thoughts and speaking out their simple actions can make things more transparent. Also, having to deal with all fears and doubts on their own usually makes them stronger.

Sharing your worries with others can take away their power. Gabriel and I share all our fears and doubts. We went a long way, had a long conversation, discussed all the terrible ideas. It is best to be able to directly share questions and concerns about your relationship with your partner. He can deal with your fears and assure you.

We were unable to do this. There was a time in our relationship when we couldn't talk without arguing. But we communicated or found a way to listen to each other truly. Put your fears and doubts there, and let someone accept them will make you feel less lonely and overwhelmed.

It may also be helpful and reassuring to get an outsider's perspective on your problem. Overthinking relationships can be a big problem. It will make you doubt everything and cause a lot of emotional distress.

In my interpersonal relationship, the 3 steps I will use are:

1. Understand that overthinking is the result of fear

2. Get in touch with your feelings and figure out your anxiety.

3. Discuss your interests with someone you can trust to reassure yourself and understand

Effects of Anxiety on Relationships and How to Stop It

There is a lot of information about how anxiety affects our health (mentally, emotionally, and physically). Have you considered that anxiety may have an impact on the health of your relationship?

Anxiety can lead to a period of panic, fear, or overwhelming and general anxiety and tension. It can take over your thoughts and penetrate many areas of your life.

If you are feeling stressed about your relationship, anxiety may be at work. Does your anxiety (or partner) put your relationships at risk?

This is how and why anxiety can disrupt relationships and how to stop them.

Anxiety Destroys Trust and Connection

Anxiety can lead to fear or worry, making you less aware of your real needs at a given moment. It can also reduce your understanding of your partner's needs. If you are worried about what might happen, it isn't easy to notice what is happening. If you feel overwhelmed, your partner may think that you are not present.

So, train your brain to live in the present. If you find that fear or worry causes your thinking to deviate from the current facts, please stop and think about what you know (rather than what you don't know). Calm down before acting. You can take purposeful steps to build trust in your partners. When you feel worried, you can share it publicly; when you usually shrink or attack out of fear, consciously contact your partner (physically or verbally).

Anxiety Can Crush Your True Voice, Cause Panic, Or Delay

People who are prone to anxiety may not be able to express their true feelings. It can also be challenging to maintain reasonable boundaries by seeking the attention or space needed.

Because you feel anxious and uncomfortable, subconsciously, you can try to postpone the experience. On the other hand, anxiety may make you think you must take a break when, in fact, a short break may be beneficial.

If you do not express your true feelings or needs, anxiety will become more intense. Also, if you don't control it, your emotions may eventually get out of control. You may become overwhelmed and defensive.

So please acknowledge your feelings as early as possible. Feelings or worries do not necessarily become disasters. Be kind to your partner, so you don't procrastinate or panic. Please find time for yourself to unravel some of the thoughts or fears circulating in your mind. They are consuming your time and energy.

Anxiety Makes You Act Selfishly

Because anxiety is an overactive fear response, people who experience anxiety may sometimes focus too much on their worries or problems.

Your worries and fears may put unnecessary pressure on your relationship. You may feel that you need to worry about protecting yourself in the relationship, but this may make you lose compassion and vulnerability to your partner.

If your partner is anxious, you may also build resentment and react selfishly. Our attitudes and opinions are contagious. It is especially challenging to control the stress level when the partner is anxious, depressed, or defensive.

So, pay attention to your needs, not your fears. When you find yourself becoming frightened or defensive, take a moment to consider your sympathy for yourself and your partner. Ask you to get the support of being loved and understood. Feel sorry for the anxiety and make you self-attractive.

Unhealthy anxiety levels make you almost always feel the emotional "rock" in your stomach.

Anxiety Is the Opposite of Acceptance

The healthy form of worry tells you, "something is not right"; it comes by quickly pulling your heart or making your stomach feel tight. This signal can help you take action, for example, when you scream for bad treatment.

Unhealthy anxiety levels make you almost always feel the emotional "rock" in your stomach. Anxiety can cause you to reject things that are not dangerous and avoid things that might benefit you.

It will also prevent you from taking healthy actions to change the life that hurts you because it can make you feel hopeless or trapped.

So, it is uncomfortable to practice. You don't need to ignore or indulge in uncomfortable thoughts. If possible, please take constructive action. Sometimes your partner needs your relationship with him or her, and sometimes you need to offer the same gift to yourself. You can give your presence to your partner with soft eyes or soft hands and present yourself beside yourself with a calm breath.

Anxiety Takes Away Your Joy

To experience happiness requires a sense of security or freedom. Anxiety makes us feel scared or limited. Likewise, a stress-trained brain and body may have difficulty enjoying sex and intimacy. Negative thoughts and fears affect a person's ability to exist in interpersonal relationships and make joy disappear instantly. So don't take it too seriously. You can use a sense of humor to overcome anxiety. Remember to joke with your partner. Joy physically heals or comforts your brain in a way that is vital to healthy relationships.

64. Conflict in Relationships

Understanding Emotions Is Important for Your Relationships

Each of us experiences millions of emotions in relationships, and these emotions produce brain chemicals that change our feelings. Sometimes we (hopefully in most cases) are in a positive state of mind, while at other times, we can remain neutral and even feel negatively about our partners and ourselves.

Trusting your lover with your feelings is part of building a good relationship. Trust is created when you share something private (maybe you are anxious about something at work), and your partner is a supporter. It also gives you greater power to deal with any problems.

However, if your partner disappoints you or does not support you, then you may choose to reduce communication when sharing your feelings now and in the future. This is a harmful dynamic in any relationship or needs to be resolved to prevent damage or conflict.

When a conflict does occur, take a look at how you speak. Certain words may cause conflicts, so both of you need to be cautious and avoid saying offensive words or causing adverse reactions or shutting up both of you. When you know that certain words or phrases can make your partner feel uncomfortable and cause conflicts, avoid saying them or learn to speak from the heart rather than from angry places.

It may make things very difficult if you are angry or angry, and it is difficult to trust the angry person. If emotional discomfort occurs frequently, then your relationship will not develop. If you can no longer find a harmonious relationship, this relationship will slowly deteriorate. It's as simple as promising to be kinder to the people who share your life with. If you express your promise aloud, I promise it will make a difference. Please look at each other and feel your connection when you do.

One way to fulfill this new promise is to make sure that you treat your partner better than everyone else in your life (including other family members). This is not to say that you are abusing others, but ensuring that your partner feels special from time to time. That is all, by doing this, your love will grow a little bit every day. Developing together is a good habit; it will only make you feel more intimate.

Another tool for building an intimate relationship is to confirm when your partner does something that you think is good, attractive, or special. Verifying your partner will strengthen your bond and bring you closer to each other. We cannot build relationships in a vacuum. If you want to create the happiness that both parties deserve, then both of you need to show how much you care. Give it a try and let your positive emotions be your guide.

How to Communicate in Relationships

Most people have never learned how to communicate. Without this skill, one will lose intimacy. Partners cannot express their opinions and listen to others' voices, and they cannot achieve intimacy. By developing your communication skills, you or your partner will establish and maintain a loving and respectful relationship within two people who love each other.

The Purpose of Communication in The Relationship

One of the main problems in communication is that most couples have a fundamental misunderstanding about the purpose of communication. Most methods are to talk to partners as a debate, in which everyone presents an expected version of the reality that is happening between the two partners.

This method's error lies in the false assumption that either party can enter the conversation with an accurate perception of reality. This is impossible because neither person has the necessary information to determine what truth is, namely: what is happening between them.

One of the purposes of communication is to decide what reality is. Communication includes the collaboration of two people as they share and check all their perceptions, feelings, and thoughts to understand precisely what is happening.

Collaborative Communication

Everyone knows that communication is just a matter of talking or listening. But, most of us mistakenly believe that the problem of communication is simple. We don't realize that communication involves specific skills that can be learned and developed in ourselves and that we can talk and listen to relatives, rather than innate abilities.

- Step 1: Have a conversation with your partner

- Step 2: Talk to your partner

- Step 3: Listen to your partner

- Step 4: Confirm reality with your partner

Step 1: Have A Conversation with Your Partner

Rule #1 to follow when talking with your partner: Disarm unilaterally. In other words, give up the right demand! You will not participate in battles that must be won.

This is not to say that you will have to compromise or yield. This is not to say that you will not be angry, frustrated, or offended. You are entitled to all thoughts and feelings.

Only consider that your partner may have something to say, which is worth listening to and considering. Dialogue is not a battlefield where you must prove yourself right; it is not a battle that you must win.

Step 2: Talk to Your Partner

When conducting a conversation, there is only one reality that one can be sure of: you can know your thoughts, feelings, and opinions. You have no choice: what other people think, feel or think, or even the reality of what happened between the two of you.

The only conversation you and your partner need to have is for them to determine their thoughts, feelings, and opinions. However, talking about yourself in person is usually more challenging than you think.

Step 3: Listen to Your Partner

When having a conversation, you don't know much about your partner's real thoughts and feelings. You might think that you are doing this because you recognize the expression he/she always gets when he/she is hurt. Otherwise, you might even have exchanged some intense remarks. However, until you listen to your partner, you know almost nothing.

Listening is a skill that needs to be learned and developed. Just because we hear it does not mean we are listening. Only when we listen unconditionally to understand the person we are talking to can we truly know that person.

Step 4: Confirm Reality with Your Partner

When your partner really listens to your topic, both of you may have a deeper understanding of your experiences and feelings. Likewise, when your partner talks with you in person and really listens, you two are likely to have a deeper understanding of your partner's experiences and feelings.

This kind of insight and understanding, along with the empathy and compassion that comes with it, helps to clarify the many confusions between couples. A deeper understanding of each other eliminated many misunderstandings, misunderstandings, and misunderstandings that caused this confusion. All that remains is a clear understanding of the reality of oneself and the relationship.

At this point in the conversation, you and your partner may want to review what you know about yourself and each other and your relationship with you. By discussing what you have learned, you can identify personal issues and reactions that may cause trouble for each other. You will now know what to look out for to avoid risk in the future. If you have a problem with each other, you can recognize what is happening and deal with it more quickly.

Basic Communication Skills

We have provided a long list of specific communication skills. Then, we categorized the types of communication skills more intensively.

But today, we will reduce all these skills into 4 basic categories.

When people discuss learning a language, you may have heard of these essential communication skills categories. These are the 4 areas you must learn and excel in to be considered fully proficient in a language. And they can also help us consider improving communication skills in general.

Speaking

While we mention necessary communication skills, most people think of speaking first. There are multiple skills in this essential category. They range from having an extensive vocabulary to effectively using voice tones to using descriptions and stories to enhance your expression.

For convenience, we can also classify non-verbal and non-written expressions as oral expressions. In this category, some may even have the ability to express themselves through music or dance. In general, this category includes anything related to expressing yourself in other ways than written words or images.

Writing

This category will include all written and oral communication skills. Therefore, consider written letters, signs, stories, plays, scripts, novels, etc. But it also consists of any form of graphics. Logos, icons, drawings, pictures, etc. can help us express ourselves in a way that does not involve talking.

Understand/Listening

Several people refer to this category in different ways. Yet the most commonly used names are "understanding" and "listening." In any case, people refer to the ability to understand the non-written communication of others.

This includes understanding the meaning of the words they speak and considering how their nonverbal communication and personal and social characteristics clarify the meaning.

Reading

This is the ability to make any form of written communication meaningful. It includes not only identifying words but also extracting their meanings to gain understanding. It can also appreciate and analyze graphic artworks, such as those mentioned under the "writing" category.

When you consider conducting communication skills activities to improve your abilities, you may want to look at these four categories and evaluate each category's advantages and disadvantages. This will give you a framework to understand where your skills are most developed and where you can use more work.

These categories are also useful when teaching other people to communicate. As a learner, it helps to have a small and focused mode of thinking about future tasks. The broader communication skills and list of communication skills presented at the beginning of this article can also facilitate more in-depth research. However, the necessary communication skills category provides a broader overview through which the entire communication activity can be organized as a whole.

Side Effects of Bad Communication

While I was a kid, I used to play a game called disconnection. In this game, you form a circle, and one person thinks of a message they want to send in the circle. They whispered this information to the person next to them. Then, that person passes the message to the next person, and so on.

When the last person receives the original message, the original message always seems to be changing!

Communication is a two-way road. First, one person thinks of transferring to another person. Then another person is receiving the message. At both ends of the transmission, failures may occur.

How did the word elephant become a wheelbarrow in this elementary school game? Likewise, what you are saying will be misunderstood.

Communication is the lifeblood of your organization. Just like your body, bad things happen when blood stops flowing through your body.

If we want others to know us, we must communicate clearly. Lack of good communication can lead to:

Frustration

While your expectations are not met, you will feel frustrated. If you do not communicate the required information, you may not receive it.

How can I require my wife to bring me a bottle of Dr. Pepper if I don't tell me exactly what I want?

Lack of Understanding

If the communication is not clear, it cannot be understood. Understanding is the focus of information transmission.

Did you pass it? For the answer to be yes, and the person must already know you.

Understanding occurs when the people you communicate with can use your information.

I misunderstood the driving route before, which led me to the wrong place, but I will do more in the following content.

Anxiety

If you can't understand the communication, you will have anxiety.

When I misunderstood the driving route for a meeting in a city I was not familiar with, it caused some anxiety! I went to the wrong place, time is running out, and I will be late soon-due to a simple misunderstanding, all this anxiety.

If I spend a few minutes reviewing the route before leaving, I will understand where I am going.

Broken Relationship

When communication breaks, the relationship of the people trying to communicate also breaks. Misunderstanding can be regarded as an attack, or something is done deliberately or for deceptive purposes.

Usually, this is wrong, but bad communication exacerbates this type of relationship breakdown.

Production Loss

Any time you have to reinterpret because you didn't communicate the first time correctly, it's a waste of time to re-talk or re-do anything.

When you take the time to communicate, spend some time with the people you share with. Let me repeat what I said above. Communication is the lifeblood of your organization. Communication is the basis of your relationship with people, allowing you to build trust, productivity, and influence. Taking time to communicate clearly will never waste time.

65. Therapy and Treatment for Anxiety

Tips to Overcome Performance Anxiety

You can also play some psychological tricks to help you reduce anxiety. These include:

1. Focus on the friendliest face in the audience.

2. Smile when you can, it can help you relax.

3. Make yourself look good. When you look good, you feel good.

These techniques should help reduce performance anxiety. However, if not, please consult a counselor or therapist who has been treated for anxiety disorders. You may benefit from more in-depth treatments, such as cognitive-behavioral therapy, to help overcome performance anxiety. Also, anxious people sometimes use beta-blockers (such as propranolol) to lower their heart rate and block the effects of adrenaline.

Facing fear and learning ways to reduce and manage it can help others. Not only does it make you feel good about yourself, but you may also find yourself becoming more confident.

Tips to Help Reduce Anxiety During Exercise

Relax. You deserve it, and it's right for you, and it takes less time than you think.

You don't need a spa weekend or retreat. Each of these stress-relieving techniques can take you to OMG in less than 15 minutes.

Meditation

Exercising for a few minutes a day can relieve anxiety. Dr. Robbie Maller Hartman, a Chicago health and wellness coach psychologist, said: "Research shows that daily meditation may change the brain's neural pathways and make you more vulnerable to stress."

This is very simple. Sitting on the floor with his hands straight. Close your eyes. Focus on reciting positive mantras aloud or silently, such as "I feel peaceful" or "I love myself." Place one hand on the abdomen and synchronize the spell with the breath. Let any distracting thoughts float like clouds.

Take A Deep Breath

Rest for 5 minutes and concentrate on breathing. Sit upright, close your eyes, and place your hands on your abdomen. Slowly inhale from the nose, feeling the breath start from the abdomen and continue to the top of the head. When you exhale through your mouth, reverse this process.

Psychologist Dr. Judith Tutin said: "Deep breathing counteracts the effects of stress by lowering heart rate and lowering blood pressure." She is a certified life coach in Rome, Georgia.

Be Presence

Tutin said: "Spend 5 minutes and focus only on one conscious behavior." Please pay attention to the feeling of air on your face when walking and the feeling of your feet on the ground. Enjoy the texture and taste of every bite.

When you spend time focusing on your senses now, you should feel less nervous.

Reach Out

Your social network is one of the best tools for dealing with stress. Talk to others-preferably face to face, or at least on the phone. Share what is happening. While maintaining a strong connection, you can gain a new perspective.

Adapt to Your Body

Scan your body carefully to understand how stress affects it every day. Lie on your back, and sit on the floor with your feet. Start from the toes and go all the way to the scalp, paying attention to how the body feels.

Tutin said: "Just pay attention to where you will feel tight or loose, without trying to make any changes." In 1 to 2 minutes, imagine that every deep breath flow to that body part. When you move the focus to the body, repeat the process, and pay close attention to each body part's sensation.

Unzip

Wrap warm plastic wrap around your neck or shoulders for 10 minutes. Close your eyes or relax your face, neck, upper chest, and back muscles. Remove the wrapper and massage the tension with a tennis ball or foam roller.

"Place the ball between your back or the wall. Lean over to score the ball and maintain gentle pressure for up to 15 seconds. Then move the ball to another position and apply pressure," Columbus Ohio State University Wexner Medical Center Said Kathy Benninger, nurse practitioner and assistant professor of

Laugh Out Loud

Laughing cannot only reduce the mental burden. It reduces the body's stress hormone cortisol and strengthens brain chemicals called endorphins, thereby improving mood. Lighten up your mood by tuning in your favorite sitcoms or videos, reading comics, or chatting with people who make you smile.

Tuning

Research has shown that listening to soothing music can lower blood pressure, heart rate, and anxiety. Benninger said: "Create a playlist of songs or natural sounds (ocean, bubbling creeks, birdsong) and focus your attention on the different melodies, instruments, or singers in the music." You can also pass Swing out more happy tunes or sing on top of your lungs to emit steam!

Take Action

You don't need to run around to get high scores for runners. All forms of exercise, including yoga or walking, can help the brain release feel-good chemicals and allow your body to practice coping with stress, thereby relieving depression and anxiety. You can walk quickly around the block, take a few steps up and down the stairs, or do some stretching exercises such as shaking your head and shrugging your shoulders.

Thanksgiving

Keep one or more gratitude diaries (one by the bed, one in your wallet, and one at work) to help you recognize all the good things in life.

Joni Emmerling, a health coach in Greenville, North Carolina, said: "Thank you for your blessings, you can eliminate negative thoughts and worries."

Use these diaries to experience good experiences, such as a child's smile, a sunny day, and good health. Don't forget to celebrate achievements, such as mastering a new task or hobby at work.

If you start to feel stressed, take a few minutes to go through your notes to remind yourself what is essential.

Natural Treatments for Anxiety

Anxiety is a normal part of life. This is a byproduct of living in an often-chaotic world. Anxiety is not all bad. It makes you aware of the danger, and motivates you to stay organized and prepared, and helps you calculate risk. However, when anxiety becomes a daily struggle, it is time to take action and then snowball. Unchecked anxiety can significantly affect your quality of life. Control yourself by trying the following ideas.

Stay Active

Regular exercise is good for physical or emotional health. Regular exercise can reduce anxiety for some people, just like medication. This is not only a short-term solution; you may feel less anxiety after a few hours of exercise.

Don't Drink Alcohol

Alcohol is a natural tranquilizer. Drinking a glass of wine or a glass of whiskey when you are nervous may make you feel calm at first. But once the buzz is over, anxiety may have revenge. When you rely on alcohol to relieve anxiety instead of treating the root cause of the problem, you may develop alcohol dependence.

Stop Smoking

Smokers often smoke during periods of stress. However, like drinking alcohol, smoking during stressful times is a quick solution, and anxiety may increase over time. Research Trusted Source shows that the earlier you start smoking in your life, the higher your risk of developing anxiety disorders in the future. Studies have also shown that nicotine and other chemicals in cigarette smoke can alter brain pathways related to anxiety.

Caffeine

When you have a chronic anxiety disorder, then caffeine is not your friend. Caffeine can cause nervousness and restlessness, which is not a good thing if you are in a hurry. Studies have shown that caffeine may cause or exacerbate anxiety disorders. It may also cause panic attacks in patients with panic disorder. In a few people, eliminating caffeine may significantly improve anxiety symptoms.

Go to Sleep

Insomnia is a common symptom of anxiety. Make sleep a priority by:

- Sleep only when tired at night

- Not lying in bed reading and watching TV.

- Do not use your phone, tablet, or computer in bed.

- If you can't fall asleep, don't throw and turn over the bed; get up and go to another room until you sleep.

- Avoid caffeine, large meals, and nicotine before bed.

- Keep the room cool

- Write down your problems before going to bed.

- Sleep at the same time every night

Meditate

The central purpose of meditation is to remove chaotic thoughts from your thoughts and replace them with the moment's calm and mindfulness. Meditation is known for relieving stress or anxiety. Research by John Hopkins University (John Hopkins) shows that sitting still for 30 minutes a day can alleviate specific anxiety symptoms and have an anti-depressant effect.

Healthy Diet

Low blood sugar, dehydration, or chemicals in processed foods (such as artificial flavors, artificial colors, and preservatives) can cause mood changes in some people. A high-sugar diet may also affect temperament. If anxiety increases after eating, check your eating habits. Stay hydrated, eliminate processed foods, and eat healthy, rich in complex carbohydrates, fruits and vegetables, and lean protein.

Practice Deep Breathing

Shallow, rapid breathing is common in anxiety disorders. It may cause rapid heartbeat, dizziness or lightheadedness, and even cause panic attacks. Deep breathing exercises (deep breathing, the deliberate process of deep breathing) can help restore normal breathing and reduce anxiety.

Try Aromatherapy

Aromatherapy uses essential aromatic oils to promote health. These oils can be directly inhaled or added to a warm water bath or diffuser. Research shows that aromatherapy:

- Help you relax

- Help you fall asleep

- Enhance mood

- Lower heart rate or blood pressure

Some essential oils used to relieve anxiety are:

- Bergamot

- Lavender

- Sage

- Grapefruit

- Ylang

Drinking Chamomile Tea Cup

 Chamomile tea is a common home remedy that calms nervous nerves and promotes sleep. A 2009 study from a trusted source showed that chamomile might also be a powerful ally against generalized anxiety disorder. The study found that people who took German chamomile capsules (220 mg up to five times a day) had a more considerable reduction in their scores on tests measuring anxiety symptoms than placebo.

Medication Treatments for Anxiety

Medications for anxiety disorders are usually safe and effective. However, finding the best medicine for you usually takes time and patience.

The first-line treatment for anxiety disorders is usually cognitive behavioral therapy or CBT. This is a complete, efficient, and long-lasting treatment. Some people find that excessive levels of anxiety prevent them from taking full advantage of this treatment. In this case, the drug may allow full participation in CBT. Those who cannot obtain CBT or do not respond well to CBT may also benefit from medication.

Things to Consider

If you have severe insomnia (usually related to a generalized anxiety disorder or GAD), please discuss medications with your doctor. People with GAD typically suffer from repetition and excessive worry. They usually focus on the day's activities, such as forgotten places, what went wrong, what needs to be done tomorrow, etc. People with this condition describe it as irrational difficulty, and they often have difficulty falling asleep. Improving sleep can reduce symptoms of anxiety and depression, which can usually be achieved through medication.

Depression often complicates chronic anxiety. Don't ignore sad mood, tears, low self-esteem, feelings of inner or despair, and other depression symptoms. Medication usually helps to reduce symptoms of anxiety and symptoms of depression. Most drugs used to treat anxiety are derived from antidepressants, so these two diseases can be effectively treated.

Make A Decision

While you and your doctor have decided on medication as a treatment option, you have many options. Work with your doctor to search for the right medicine for you. With patience and perseverance, you will find a treatment that helps relieve anxiety symptoms.

How Much Time Shall I Take Antidepressants?

A standard clinical treatment for depression is a drug called an antidepressant. Antidepressants come in many forms, but they all work by affecting certain neurochemicals in the brain, such as serotonin and norepinephrine. A psychiatrist usually prescribes antidepressants, but they can also be prescribed by a family doctor or general practitioner to treat depression.

Various types of antidepressants include selective serotonin reuptake inhibitors (SSRIs), serotonin-norepinephrine reuptake inhibitors (SNRIs), and norepinephrine (norepinephrine) reuptake inhibitors, atypical antidepressants, tricyclic antidepressants (TCAs), and monoamine oxidase inhibitors (MAO). Different types of antidepressants take different time before you start to feel the effects of antidepressants.

The most commonly used modern antidepressants include SSRI (such as Prozac, Lexapro, Celexa, and Paxil) and SNRI (such as Pristiq, Cymbalta, and Effexor). Although some people claim that some people may start to feel depressed within two weeks after taking certain antidepressants, most people will not begin to experience this drug's full positive effects until 6 to 8 weeks after starting to take it.

In addition to reducing depression from antidepressants, people usually experience the side effects of antidepressants first. But these side effects are varying from person to person and from medication to medication; the most common side effects of antidepressants are:

- Decreased libido or no libido at all

- Dry mouth-your mouth feels dry, and you can't produce as much saliva as usual

- Mild to moderate nausea

- Insomnia-unable to fall asleep or having difficulty falling asleep

- Increased anxiety or restlessness

- Lethargy

- Weight gain

- Constipation or diarrhea

- Headache

- Increased sweating

- Tremor or dizziness

When you experience any of the above side effects while taking antidepressants, you don't need to worry too much, but you should still tell your psychiatrist or doctor. Once the body adjusts to the medication, some side effects may disappear on their own. Other drugs may not, or it may be resolved by changing the drug dose or taking drugs.

Antidepressants are not for everyone. Sometimes, the first antidepressant prescribed by your doctor may not work for you (because no 50% of people try antidepressants). Don't be frustrated; accept that you may need to try another drug, or your doctor may suggest that you need a higher dose. If you still do not feel any positive effects of the medicine after 6 to 8 weeks, please discuss with your doctor how to adjust the treatment.

Older antidepressants-MAOI and tricyclic antidepressants-take the same amount of time for most people; it takes 2 to 6 weeks. Most people will begin to feel the benefits within 3 to 4 weeks. It is unclear why antidepressants take longer to work than other types of psychiatric drugs.

Ways to Attract Good Energy

As the day progresses, we send energy to the world, and then we receive power back. Our mind, body, and spirit are composed of energy, which vibrates and is perceived by others. These vibrations resonate within us and affect our energy storage.

This is why we feel warm, calm, and cheerful when some people are present, but we feel cold, anxious, and melancholy around others. We bring this energy to us, and it affects all the other people we touch and us. Good energy can increase our happiness, eliminate anxiety, and improve communication-bad energy, leading to disharmony, conflict, or resentment. And your goal should be to attract good energy or reject bad energy.

Although you can do this by raising your energy level and adapting yourself to positive vibrations, it is simpler than you think. Starting with these four daily buttons, adjust your internal vibration, and begin to feel the way positive energy flows to you.

Pay Attention to The Energy You Emit

When you want to release negative energy, you don't expect to attract good energy. Think about how others will resonate with you. Do you exude a feeling of peace, calm, and happiness? Or are you more frustrated and doomed?

Negative energy is bound to affect your relationships. This may be subtle, but your attitude towards others will usually be reflected in you. What kind of impression do you leave?

If you seem to attract other people naturally and someone is looking for your company, you will probably be doing a good job of emitting positive energy. If people avoid you and avoid your help, you will be trapped in a lower negative vibration. Focus on being positive.

Change Your Mind

Negative thinking can be challenging to stop. It's easy to get yourself into pessimism or maintain a cold attitude. However, if you want to attract good things, you must let positive people guide you, not negative people. As the Dalai Lama said: "See the positive side, potential and make efforts." Actively work hard to change your thinking from negative to positive.

For example, you can rewrite the idea of "I am having difficulty adapting to this new situation" as "I know I will face challenges in this new situation, but I am capable of suggesting solutions to the problem, and I know that I Will adapt to these changes." Don't let yourself be addicted to pessimistic thinking. Stop looking for bad news or exaggerating negative news. Replace negative thoughts with positive yet realistic statements to motivate you to take action.

Eliminate Negative Effects

Negative resonance can destroy your happiness and cause your happiness and satisfaction to drain. These adverse effects may be people, places, or things that are bad for your life. Some people in your life may be harmful to your overall happiness. Maybe their constant criticism has disappointed you, or you may find that you have developed their bad habits.

Eliminate these adverse effects and start creating the life you want. Look for adverse effects in life. You may be able to avoid or delete some of them altogether. This is a reliable way to eliminate this effect. Those permanent fixtures can limit your contact with them and mentally strengthen yourself before encountering them.

Expand Your Circle

Just as you are trying to limit adverse effects, make sure you start to spend time on positive results. Serve yourself with active and successful people who support and care. Keep in touch with those who give them positive energy and make sure you nurture and protect these relationships.

Please bring your good energy into your circle and help build positive synergy and permeate it throughout the team. Look for someone who can tell you the truth and always be honest with you, but never disappoint you out of malice or desire.

What Is Cognitive Behavioral Therapy, Or How Does It Work?

Cognitive behavior therapy (CBT) is a psychotherapy that focuses on changing dysfunctional emotions, behaviors, and thoughts by asking and eradicating negative or irrational beliefs. CBT is considered a "solution-oriented" form of talk therapy, and its ideas and concepts influence behavior. In some cases, the feeling of distress may distort people's perception of reality. CBT aims to identify harmful thoughts, assess whether they are an accurate depiction of fact, and, if not, use strategies to challenge and overcome them.

CBT was founded in the 1960s by psychiatrist Aaron Beck, who was disappointed with Freud's psychoanalytic methods and explored more empirical therapy forms. CBT also originated from the brainchild of psychologist Albert Ellis, "Rational Emotional Behavior Therapy" (REBT).

CBT is suitable for people of all ages, including children, teenagers, and adults. More and more evidence shows that CBT can solve various diseases, such as major depression, anxiety, post-traumatic stress disorder, eating disorders, obsessive-compulsive disorder, etc. Among practitioners and insurance companies, CBT is the preferred treatment. Although there is no set schedule, it can be useful for a short period, usually 5 to 20 sessions. Research shows that in addition to face-to-face treatment courses, CBT can also be effectively provided online.

How Does CBT Work?

Contrary to children's activities, CBT pays attention to current situations and emotions in real-time. The clinician performing CBT may learn about family history to have a better understanding of the whole person but will not spend too much time on past events. The point is that a person is telling himself something that may cause anxiety or distraction. Then encourage a person to solve rational problems and challenge irrational beliefs, contemplation, or catastrophic behavior. For example, a person who is unhappy with singles will be encouraged to take specific measures and question any inappropriate denial or unprovoked premises ("I will always be alone") imposed on this current fact.

What Is Interpersonal Therapy, Or How It Works?

Interpersonal Psychotherapy (IPT) is a time-limited, focused, evidence-based method of treating mood disorders. The main goal of IPT is to improve the quality of customer relationships and social functions to help alleviate their troubles. IPT provides strategies to solve problems in four key areas.

First, it solves the shortcomings of interpersonal communication, including social isolation or participation in unhappy relationships. Second, if the onset of distress is related to a loved one (whether it is a recent or past death), it can help the patient resolve unresolved grief. Third, IPT can help resolve difficult life transitions, such as retirement, divorce, or moving to another city. Fourth, IPT is recommended to deal with interpersonal disputes caused by conflicting expectations between partners, family members, close friends, or colleagues.

When Using It

IPT was initially used to treat major depression. It can also be effectively used to treat eating disorders, perinatal depression, drug and alcohol addiction, mood disorders, and other mood disorders (including bipolar disorder). IPT differs from other traditional psychodynamic methods in that it examines current rather than past relationships and recognizes but ignores internal conflicts.

This approach is different from cognitive and behavioral therapy because the unsuitable thoughts and behaviors it deals with are related to interpersonal relationships. IPT aims to change the relationship pattern, not the associated depression symptoms, and address relationship difficulties that may exacerbate these symptoms. Compared with cognitive-behavioral methods, IPT is less instructive-focusing on the patient's designated target area without paying attention to their personality traits.

How It Works

IPT is a time-based treatment method for significant depression developed 20 years ago and has gained popularity in recent years. Practitioners believe that changes in the social environment are critical factors in depression and persistent depression. IPT was initially developed for adults and has now been modified to be used in adolescents and elderly patients. IPT first appeared as a part of research on the efficacy of antidepressants and is comparable in terms of drug efficacy.

What Is Psychodynamic Therapy and How It Work?

Psychodynamic therapy is related to psychoanalytic treatment in that it is an in-depth form of talk therapy based on psychoanalytic theories and principles. However, psychodynamic therapy pays less attention to the relationship between the patient and the therapist because it also focuses on the relationship between the patient and the outside world. In terms of frequency and number of treatment sessions, psychodynamic therapy is usually shorter than psychoanalytic therapy, yet this is not always the case.

When Using It

Psychodynamic therapy is mainly used to treat depression and other serious mental illnesses, especially for those who have lost their lives and have difficulty establishing or maintaining relationships. Studies have found that other effective psychodynamic therapy applications include addiction, social anxiety, and eating disorders. How It Works

The theories or techniques that distinguish psychodynamic therapy from other therapies include recognizing, understanding, expressing, or overcoming negative and contradictory feelings and repressed emotions to improve the interpersonal and the relationship of patients. This includes helping patients understand how suppressed early emotions affect current decisions, behaviors, and relationships. The purpose of psychodynamic therapy is to help those who understand and understand the roots of their social difficulties but cannot overcome them alone. Through in-depth exploration and analysis of early experiences and emotions, patients learn to analyze and solve current problems and change current relationships.

How People Self-Medicate

Drug abuse is a common form of self-medication, and people with mental illness often rely on this drug to cope with their emotional distress. The theory of self-absorption addiction was proposed in 1985 by Edward J. Khantzian, a psychiatry professor at Harvard Medical School. It describes how people use alcohol and other drugs to cope with emotional dysfunction. Trends, for example, and a range of mental illnesses, including anxiety and depression.

First of all, self-medication can temporarily relieve discomfort, pain, and pain. However, in the long run, alcohol or drugs are not an effective way to solve the problem. While people use "solutions" such as alcohol or drugs to cope, they become increasingly unable to deal with negative emotions and stressful situations independently. Some people will fall into a cycle of self-destruction. They rely on alcohol and drugs to make them feel better, leading to dependence on substances or behaviors and exacerbating mental health symptoms.

Although drugs or alcohol are the most common substances used for self-medication, self-medication can take many forms:

1. Food: Overeating, using food to comfort themselves or turning to food to reduce emotions, coping with stress, or suppressing uncomfortable emotions will eventually fall into a cycle of hopelessness and bad eating habits, which may end making them feel worse. For example, people with depression may crave carbohydrates or high-sugar foods because they increase the level of serotonin and a brain chemical that improves mood.

Eating these comfort foods may cause weight gain and increase the risk of health conditions such as heart disease and diabetes.

2. Alcohol can temporarily relieve symptoms of anxiety or depression, but it should be taken regularly. It may cause alcohol dependence, chronic health problems, and a series of adverse consequences. Alcoholism is often a coping mechanism for people with many different mental health conditions, including depression, anxiety, post-traumatic stress disorder (PTSD), and trauma. Alcoholism is usually one of the most dangerous coping mechanisms because it increases the risk of suicide and exacerbates mental illness symptoms.

3. Patients with depression, hypomania, and ADHD often use cocaine and amphetamines, and other stimulants to relieve the troubles related to these mental health conditions. The use of stimulants can cause addiction, exacerbate anxiety and depression, damage the body's cardiovascular system, and increase the risk of sudden heart failure, stroke, and death.

4. Cannabis is the most widely used substance among people who have a mental illness such as depression. Small doses of marijuana can effectively treat patients with depression. However, too much may still be harmful, leading to worsening depression and anxiety symptoms and producing psychotic symptoms at high doses.

5. Opioids or prescription opioids, such as codeine, oxycodone, fentanyl, heroin, and methadone, are often used by people suffering from affective and anxiety disorders, bipolar disorder, panic disorder, and major depression. I treat. The abuse of opioids can aggravate symptoms of mental illness and increase the chance of a combined drug use disorder.

66. Anxiety in Love: Relationship for Couples

What Does a Healthy Relationship Mean?

Healthy relationships are a necessary part of a healthy and successful life. Interpersonal relationships enrich our lives and increase our lives' joy, but we all know that no relationship is perfect.

What Is A Healthy Relationship?

A strong relationship is full of happiness, joy, and (most importantly) love. People are asked to establish positive relationships with others and constantly strengthen themselves, but unfortunately, this is not always the case. Sometimes, we allow the wrong people into our lives, our relationship with them is not positive, healthy, or uncultivated, and in most cases, the relationship is not fruitful.

A healthy relationship seems to have several characteristics:

Friendship

After establishing a healthy relationship, you will regard your partner as your best friend. You can tell him or her anything that bothers you. Both of you have come up with ideas for solving problems that affect your partner or relationship. A partner who acts as a friend and has a deep friendship has staying power. They love each other, and they sincerely like their best friends. They like to hang out, have picnics, watch movies together, and do things together.

Effective Communication

When you can express your feelings openly and avoid covering up hurt or anger, your relationship is healthy. Both of you can usually handle various situations more efficiently without wasting time.

Healthy interpersonal relationships have a good and effective communication structure. An unhealthy relationship has a bad communication structure between partners.

While you and your partner speak the same language emotionally, physically, and intellectually, this indicates that you are in a healthy relationship-which means you should be able to effectively communicate your needs, desires, sadness, and expectations. When needed, no partner should be timid, shy, or afraid to declare themselves.

Trust and Reliability

Trust is an essential element in a relationship because, without trust, there can be no healthy relationship. When determining whether a relationship is healthy, trust is the most important factor. You must be able to trust or rely on your partner, and your partner must also be able to trust and rely on you.

Both of you should give each other reasons and trust each other.

Reliability is the definition of a healthy relationship. Couples in a relationship want to rely on and depend on each other. If a partner in a relationship can do what they say and then say what they do, then understanding their words and actions means something to the other partner, it will create trust and trust. Atmosphere. Couples dependent on each other can breathe a sigh of relief to know that their partner has withdrawn.

Therefore, to build trust and reliability in the relationship, please do not keep each other secret, do not deceive each other, and in most cases, will do what you say, and saying what you do does not guarantee that you know you cannot achieve it.

Supportive

If your partner supports your personal life outside of the relationship, it can clearly show that you are healthy. In a healthy relationship, you or your partner must support each other's goals and life ambitions.

Interpersonal relationships require continuous work and require you and your partner to have the willingness and ability to cooperate, help each other achieve their goals, generate ideas together, and, most importantly, love each other. Your partner should provide advice, work, support, and help to achieve your desired goals and your goals in life.

In a healthy relationship, your partner will admit your identity. He and she accept and support your lifestyle, friends, and family, and most importantly, he fully supports your goals and aspirations.

You Fight and Forgive Each Other's Faults

In a healthy relationship, conflicts, or disagreements, and fights will not disrupt the transaction. Just because you disagree and argue with your partner does not mean it is time to break up and move on. On the contrary, conflict is seen as an opportunity to learn more about each other and grow together in love and harmony.

Always remember that closer to you, the person you love, and the person who loves you are more likely to hurt you because he (she) is closer to you than anyone else. No one is perfect, including you. When you know and understand this fact, you should easily understand each other's mistakes and differences. Forgiveness and forgetting mean letting go of offense and harm; don't keep sniffing against them.

Types of Romantic Relationships

We are all in love. You know what love is, don't you? You feel honored when someone becomes the object of your attention, thoughts, commitment, affection, and passionate fantasies. But let us put aside all knowledge about love at once and learn from famous philosophers and psychologists.

We will consider Yale University psychologist Robert J. Sternberg's views on romantic relationships in the book "The Triangle of Love," published in 1985. Canadian psychologist John Allen Lee (story in the book "The Color of Love" published in 1973).

We will consider seven romantic relationships and how they define love and affect the person who falls in love.

Sternberg determined that all relationships are based on three main factors. The combination of two of these three further led to seven or even eight other types of romantic relationships. These will be briefly explained below:

Intimacy

Intimacy, you can establish friendship and familiarity with a person, and eventually like that person and establish a connection with that person. Here, you will develop a sense of intimacy, a sense of connection, and a strong emotional bond with another person.

Enthusiasm

Starting from the liking or intimacy stage, you can feel emptiness with the individual, thereby bringing yourself into the passion stage, where obsession and sexual attraction become the center.

Committed To

Then comes the third stage of the commitment, where both parties decide to stick to each other between plans and details to maintain a beautiful relationship forever.

Fatal Love

The combination of passion and commitment will produce fatal love. When you have sex with someone you want to get married, you have affectionate love, and you don't have to know that person well based on friendship.

Romantic Love

This love is born in a place full of passion and intimacy. Here, the two people are sexually intimate because they are romantic friends, but there is no promise of a formal relationship. Love is maintained with sex and close friendship without planning to get married or anything like that.

Compassionate Love

This love is driven by intimacy and commitment, but not by sexual intimacy. Here, people become very close to friends and even devote themselves to establishing a lifelong relationship, but there is no sex. This kind of compassionate love is usually observed in long-term friends who promise each other without any sexual attraction.

Perfect Love

This love is full of passion, intimacy, and dedication. With perfect love, partners will not tire of themselves and enjoy great sex and physical affection for many years. They are committed to keeping the relationship functioning at all costs throughout their lives.

All romantic relationships take one or more of the listed relationship types, which define love for the individuals involved.

How to Better Understand Your Partner

All of us want to be seen, heard, or understood. We especially hope that our partners can help with this. We need our partners to say, yes, I am listening. Yes, I get it. Yes, I understand your pain. Sorry, it hurts, I am here. We required our partners to be interested in what is happening inside us and care about them.

Hope to be seen, heard, and understood is the basic human need.

The most common complaint therapist at LCSW, Rebecca Wong, has a relationship that her clients hear because they don't feel that way about their partners, even if this relationship is for healthy relationships. It is vital and vital. "The feeling of seeing, hearing, and understanding will lead to deeper intimacy and relationship development." She said, without this, we would feel rejected, just like we are okay, and over time, it will destroy our relationship.

It is generally (inaccurate) that knowing our partners means that we must agree with them. But as Mr. Huang said, "You can disagree." On the contrary, understanding means fully and attentively listening to our partners. This means absorbing their words. This means saying to your partner: "I think I know you. But let me check: what do you mean..." This means sticking to the process "until your partner does not need to clarify their point of view further because they know that you can understand. Even if you disagree, you can do it."

Wong shares below suggestions on how to "acquire" and better understand our partners.

Be Fully Present

Wong, founder of Contextless, a research-based practice, says you don't need to do anything when your partner is speaking. You don't need to try to solve the problem or improve the situation. "Your only role is to be the other half and let your partner share their personal experiences with them."

First, Understand

Wong said: "First understand, then understand." When listening to your partner, try not to express your response. This will only prevent you from understanding their speech deeply and hinder your true understanding. "If your partner feels understood, they will naturally become curious about your thoughts and feelings, and you will have the chance to share your opinions."

Avoid Complaining and Defense

Wong said: "[Defense and complaint] is a harmful relationship model that prevents you from truly establishing an intimate relationship." She said that when someone criticizes and complains, they will unintentionally put the other person in a defensive state. It tells your partner, "It's not me; It's you."

"So, the trick here is to take some responsibility, even a small iota, an unpleasant tidbit-'I understand what you mean, I did say... I need...'" The pair told you your partner's condition is also very helpful. Feel and what you need.

The Importance of Face-To-Face Communication

In today's digital age, and the importance of face-to-face communication seems to be gradually disappearing because people can communicate almost all day without interacting with others. People rely heavily on the convenience of email, text messaging, and social media.

Although there is no denying the importance of these platforms and how they have changed communication methods, it is important to balance these online interactions with face-to-face communication.

Digital Dilemma

One problem with digital communication forms is that they are often impersonal. Also, trying to make your digital communications look more friendly or personalized may be misunderstood or considered unprofessional.

Poor communication is one of the causes of inefficiency and workplace conflict. Many of these problems can be attributed to the various ways of digital communication and interpretation.

Face-To-Face Advantage

Nonverbal Prompt

You can judge someone's interest in what you're talking about by reading someone's body language. When you are in a meeting, and your colleagues are fiddling with their pens or checking their watches, you must:

1. Adjust the pitch of the sound or

2. Use more exciting language to attract their attention.

Similarly, if colleagues and partners are positively nodding and smiling, it is clear that they will interact with you and your information.

Effectiveness

Face-to-face communication and face-to-face meetings can increase efficiency. Instead of spending a whole day sending emails back and forth, you can hash all the item details at once. These meetings can also increase creativity because the overall energy will be higher to brainstorm and solve many problems at once.

Face-to-face communication can also be more effective for those who may have difficulty communicating in writing.

Everyone has their unique skills, and some people become more fluent and clearer through oral communication.

Personal Style

For those dealing with external customers and stakeholders, increasing the "personal style" of face-to-face communication is even more important. A sense of community is accompanied by the ability to interact and socialize. This laid the foundation for trust and, ultimately, a better working relationship.

Although face-to-face communication is not always an option due to long distances or conflicting schedules, you must not forget it completely. Whenever possible, please take some time to meet face-to-face with your colleagues and enjoy the benefits.

Stay Calm and Listen

We all feel upset and frustrated from time to time. This is a normal part of life. But what happens when anxiety or anger takes over, and you cannot calm down? Being able to keep yourself calm and listen at this moment is often easier said than done.

Therefore, when you feel anxious or angry, several familiar strategies can help you. Here are some useful and actionable techniques you can try next time you need to calm down and listen.

Breathing

"Breathing is the number one or most effective technique for quickly reducing anger and anxiety," When you are anxious or angry, and you tend to breathe quickly, shallowly. Xiaoxia said that this sends a message to your brain, which forms a positive feedback loop, enhancing your fight or escape response. This is why deep breathing for long periods can interrupt the circulation and help you calm down and listen.

There are more breathing techniques to help you calm down and listen. One is the three-part breath. The three-part breath requires you to take a deep breath and then fully exhale while paying attention to your body.

After adapting to deep breathing, you can change the ratio of inhalation to exhalation to 1:2 (slow down the inhalation rate so that it is twice the time of inhalation). Practice these techniques calmly, so you know what to do when you are anxious.

Admit That You Are Anxious or Angry

Let yourself say that you are anxious or angry. When you mark your feelings and let yourself express them, the anxiety and anger you experience may decrease.

Challenge Your Ideas

Part of the reason for anxiety or anger is that irrational thoughts do not necessarily make sense. These thoughts are usually the "worst-case." You may find yourself stuck in a "what if" cycle, causing you to spoil many things in your life.

When you encounter one of these ideas, stop and ask yourself the following questions:

- Is this possible?

- Is this a rational idea?

- Has this ever happened to me?

- What is the worst possible scenario? Can I handle it?

After answering the questions, it's time to rethink. Instead of "I can't cross that bridge. What if an earthquake occurs and you fall into the water?" Tell yourself: "Every day someone walks over that bridge, but it never falls into the water."

Release Anxiety or Anger

Xiaoxia suggests exercising to release emotional energy. "Go for a walk or run. [engage in] some physical activity [release] serotonin to help you calm down, listen, or feel better."

Although you should avoid physical activities that include anger, such as rushing to walls or screaming.

Doherty explained: "It turns out that doing so can increase the feeling of anger because it can enhance mood because anger will make you feel good in the end."

Imagine Yourself Calm

This technique requires you to practice the breathing technique you have learned. After taking a deep breath, close your eyes, and imagine yourself remaining calm and listening. See your body relax and imagine yourself remaining calm and listening to cope with stress or anxiety.

By creating a mental impression of keeping calm and listening, you can re-reference the image when you are anxious.

How Much Time Should A Couple Be Together?

How much healthy time do you spend with your date? We all know that those who seem to get involved in a new relationship first and spend 24/7 time with a new partner, but this sometimes comes at the expense of other relationships. At the same time, others feel that they must fight for a new partner's schedule.

Where is the balance? How much time do you spend healthy with a large number of other people?

If 100% time is too much and zero time is too little, we find the most effective time. Finding balance is often harder than people think: people are often forced to spend time with new and exciting people. They long for the opportunity to be in front of each other and miss each other when they are away. This time is very healthy and necessary for establishing interpersonal relationships and weaving the two lives together.

Work and life need often impose realistic limits on the time new couples spend together. From unexpected work obligations on weekends to sudden business travel needs, if another partner expects another level of availability, one partner's career goals and ambitions can pressure the relationship.

Newlyweds must also spend time with the time normally used for friends and family when people are in a relationship, their availability of existing relationships changes. For example, research has shown that women who spend more time with their lovers increase faster, and their time with their best friends decreases faster. When friends complain that they will never see you again, and your family wants to know where you have been, the tricky nature of finding balance becomes obvious.

Time spent alone is also important for individuals in building new relationships, although time spent alone is as effective as other needs. People benefit from time to reflect on their new relationships and devote time to activities they like to do. Self-care is equally important in the pressing relationship between one's work, the needs of family and friends, and the new relationship.

Of course, the goal is to find a balance, make the couple feel satisfied with the time together, maintain the friendship and family relationship with the outside world, move towards career goals, or give this relationship a chance to develop. There are many things to balance. Here are some tips to help you:

Acknowledge individual differences. People need different time with their partners. Classical attachment theory studies have shown that people who tend to be in love spend a lot of time in relationships with their partners. In contrast, people who tend to avoid them usually prioritize independence. Don't expect your partner to reflect your needs.

Sign in with your new partner. The most reliable way to see if you have invested enough time in the relationship is to ask. Knowing what your new partner needs and establishing a rhythm of interdependence is very effective for both parties.

Listen to your friends. Friends are not only supporting systems. Their view of your relationship predicts the success of your relationship. When establishing a new relationship, find a way to keep in touch with your friends. Incorporating new partners into your group of friends is a great way to keep in touch with friends, while at the same time providing a new environment for your relationship to grow and develop.

Keep "Appointment Night" on the calendar. If work and other obligations take over the schedule, find ways to maintain close relationships and priorities may make a difference. In these times of increasing work pressure, you expect your partners to be free and bargain by seeing forward to a special night or weekend.

Recognize the ebb and flow. When a new relationship develops into a firm relationship, the ebb or flow of different life stressors will translate into an ebb or flow of how much energy the couple can give to the relationship at any given point in time. As interpersonal relationships become the center of personal life, it is becoming more important to seize the opportunity to spend a good time with them while providing each partner with the space they need to become their partners' best.

Jealousy in Marriage: Causes and Worries

Is your spouse unreasonably jealous? Or is it someone in your marriage who feels jealous when your spouse focuses on other people or interests? Who can show such behavior? Jealousy of marriage is a poisonous emotion; when this emotion spreads too far, it will destroy the marriage.

However, if you have media influence and curiosity and are healthy in a jealous relationship, you may be affected, as shown in a movie or TV series.

Contrary to what the media portrays in romantic movies, jealousy is not the same as love. Jealousy stems from insecurity. A jealous spouse does not feel "enough" for the partner. Their low self-esteem makes them see others as a threat to their relationship.

In turn, they try to control their partner by preventing any friendship or hobbies they have with the outside world. This is not healthy behavior and will eventually make the marriage doomed.

Jealousy starts from childhood. When we call it "same level competition," we will observe it at the same level. At this age, children compete for the attention of their parents. The feeling of jealousy begins when the child thinks that he has not received his unique love.

Most of the time, as children grow up and gain healthy self-esteem, this misconception will disappear.

But sometimes, this phenomenon still exists, and the green-eyed monster continues to grow, eventually turning into a romantic relationship when the person starts dating.

Therefore, before studying how to stop jealousy and overcome jealousy in marriage, let us understand what causes jealousy and insecurity in marriage.

What Is the Basis of Jealousy?

The problem of jealousy begins with low self-esteem. Jealous people have no innate sense of worth. A jealous spouse may have unrealistic expectations of marriage. They may have grown up in the fantasy of marriage, thinking that married life is just like what they look in magazines and movies.

They might think that "abandoning everyone else" also includes friendship and hobbies. Their expectations of what a relationship is are not realistic. They do not understand that each spouse must have its external interests to be good for the marriage.

Jealous spouses have a sense of ownership and possessiveness towards their partners and refuse to allow their partners to be free agents. They worry that this freedom will make them find "better people."

Causes of Jealousy in Marriage

There can be many reasons for being jealous of relationships. The feeling of jealousy may arise due to certain situations, but if it is not properly resolved at the right time, it may continue to occur in other situations.

One of the key reasons for jealousy is unresolved childhood problems. The jealous spouse may have solved the problem of competition at the same level. This kind of competition is even possible in groups of friends or peers.

In addition to childhood problems, their previous experience in unfaithful or dishonest relationships was also bad.

They believe that by being vigilant (jealous), the situation can be prevented from happening again. On the contrary, it caused insecurity in marriage.

They did not realize that this unreasonable behavior would be harmful to the relationship and drive out their spouse, becoming a self-fulfilling prophecy. The sickness of jealousy creates a situation that the sick person tries to avoid.

Pathological Jealousy

A very small amount of jealousy in marriage is healthy; most people say that when their partners talk about an old love or maintain innocent friendships with members of the opposite sex, they feel jealous.

But excessive jealousy and insecurity in marriage are abnormal and may even lead to dangerous behaviors. For example, OJ Simpson is a jealous husband, and Oscar Pistorius is a jealous lover. . Fortunately, this type of pathological jealousy is rare.

A jealous spouse is not only jealous of the partner's friendship. The objects of jealousy during the marriage may be working hours or indulging in weekend hobbies or sports. In any case, the jealous person has no control over the situation and therefore feels threatened.

Yes, this is unreasonable. This is very harmful because the spouse can hardly assure the jealous partner that there is no threat "there."

How Jealousy Destroys Relationships

There are too many jealousy and trust issues in marriage, even the best wedding, because it permeates all aspects of the relationship. Jealous partners demand that we continue to ensure that the threat imagined is not a real threat.

Jealous partners may take dishonest actions, such as installing a keylogger on their spouse's keyboard, hacking their email accounts, browsing their phones and reading text messages, or following them to see where they "really" went.

They may destroy their partner's friends, family, or colleagues. These behaviors have no place in healthy relationships. A spouse who is not jealous finds himself in a constant state of defense and must consider all measures taken when not with his spouse.

Is Jealousy Unknowable?

Dealing with jealousy in marriage requires a lot of time and energy. However, you can take appropriate measures to eliminate and eliminate the deep roots of jealousy.

So, how to deal with jealousy in marriage?

There are several steps you can take to prevent jealousy from interfering with your marriage. The first step is to communicate. You can try to make yourself full of trust in your relationship and make your spouse feel comfortable with the problems that are bothering them.

Also, if you feel that you have contributed to jealousy in your marriage, you must try every possible way to suppress your emotions. If your wedding is threatened, it is worth consulting to eliminate the source of jealousy.

Typical areas where a therapist will provide you with services include:

- Realize that jealousy hurts your marriage

- Admit that the act of jealousy is not based on any facts that occurred in the marriage

- Give up the need to control your spouse.

- Stop all spying and surveillance.

- Rebuild your sense of self-worth through self-care and therapeutic exercises, aiming to teach you to be safe, loved, and worthy

Whether you suffer from unusual jealousy in your marriage or your spouse, we suggest you seek help when you want to save your marriage.

Even if you think that marriage is no longer helpful, it is best to receive treatment to check and eliminate the source of this bad behavior. Any relationship you may have in the future can be a healthy relationship.

How to Deal with Conflict in Marriage

Conflict in marriage is inevitable, and it will cause damage or discovery-we choose what will happen. If we fight for marriage, discovery means learning new ideas, methods, and solutions.

Conflict is not a problem. The question is how we deal with conflicts. DEAL is a problem-solving tool, representing:

1. Don't bait.

2. Explain the impact of the behavior or express your needs and expectations.

3. Ask questions to entice your spouse to have a conversation to increase understanding.

4. Let go of the need to manage spouse's behavior to manage yourself.

Let's explain each part of the process in more detail.

Don't Bait

The motivation for conflict is usually to make another person serve his purposes, regardless of the other person's impact. That is manipulation.

Everyone has hot buttons-things that push him or her to the edge. When someone presses a button, he or she usually reacts instead of reacting. The difference is that response is a purposeful and thoughtful process. The speaker usually regrets when he leaves his lips.

Use purposeful communication to establish dialogue, not debate. Pause and consider the best answer, because words can create peace or inspire strength, which will bring two people into conflict further and stay away from the agreement.

Explain the Impact of Behavior and Express Your Expectations

This step can help your spouse understand the impact of their behavior. If the dialogue has become a fierce game, it also helps to alleviate the situation. Describe your spouse's behavior and its impact on you. Then express your expectations as the conversation progresses.

For example, if your spouse speaks out the main points out loud, overwhelming you and dispelling your concerns, it is important to respond appropriately. The conversation started as follows: "Not only does making a purchase ignore the agreement we reached, but I also feel disregarded. This is a question of trust. We need to discuss this. I say you to speak respectfully without shouting."

Once you have explained the impact and determined your expectations for continuing the conversation, you can move on.

Ask Questions to Attract Your Spouse to A Conversation

Ask your spouse yes or no questions-"Do you remember our topic about saving money? Do you promise to do it?"-Not a good corkscrew. It tends to eliminate discussions without inviting dialogue.

Rather, use open-ended questions that begin with "how" and "what." These questions draw your partner into the discussion. They welcome dialogue, and this is where discovery comes into play. When you invite your husband's or wife's thoughts and thoughts and then listen carefully, you may find a successful way to solve a problem that you haven't considered.

Let Go of The Need to Control the Behavior of Your Spouse and Manage Your Behavior

Please keep the following rules in mind: This conversation is not about me controlling you. I'm here to control myself. Even if you never said it, don't forget. Your hands are full of the ability to manage your behavior. If you remember this principle, you can readjust the tone and direction of the conversation.

If your spouse has trouble controlling his emotions during a conflict, you may want to do this for him or her. Remember, your first task is to let your spouse understand how his or her behavior affects you. It's best to do it in a conveyable attitude; I'm here to provide you with useful information about me and its impact on me. And I'm sure if you know how this makes me feel, then you would never want me to experience it. This method brings the benefit of doubts to your spouse, reduces detectable crime, and promotes the relationship between the husband and wife.

Marriage is a continuous work. We can never say: "Then, here we are." Sharp tools make work possible. So next time there is dust in your home, please deal with it!

Relationship Maintenance Advice for Healthy Couples

How to make a healthy couple has become the subject of many studies, writing, and theorizing. In her years of experience as a therapist, Dr. Ellen Wachtel has come up with seven qualities that she believes are the kind of relationship that all of us strive for or hope to build.

Designed to Make Your Partner Feel Good About Themselves

It is not the partner's responsibility to build another person's low self-esteem or lack of self-worth. Nevertheless, those with general healthy self-awareness still need to engage in behaviors that can promote each other.

Remember, you often criticize your partner, and the goal is to actively strengthen and sincerely praise you may go a long way. Criticism is likely to disappear often, but this should not be the main form of feedback you provide or receive.

Do What You Like Together

Wachtel said that "date nights" are usually advice for struggling couples, but the pressure and obligation to force them together each week can make entertainment fun.

Instead of a mandatory date night, try to come up with things you like to do together and do more.

Around Healthy Competition That Can Be Said to Be "Yes"

In most cases, healthy couples get along well. No two people will agree 100%, but people who match each other usually agree on daily activities and larger or longer-term plans. Wachtel suggests that couples want to say "yes" to each other's ideas as much as possible.

Of course, this does not implement in situations where a partner feels insecure or seems to have crossed the border, but moving to consent ability in an appropriate and safe area can positively impact the relationship.

Communicate Your Love in Person

As the relationship matures, emotions may avoid physical contact, especially if a betrayal or other life event has caused the couple to separate.

Wachtel recommends starting on a small scale and proceeding in secret for those who may need to break the ice. When you walk past your partner, place your hand on your partner's arm or back, or promise to kiss them in the morning or night before going to bed.

Mutual Authentication

Safety is a key part of a healthy relationship, and emotional safety is a key part of feeling safe. And practice listening to your partner when they are in distress, without succumbing to the urge to repair, solve, or evaluate things.

No feeling is invalid, so even if you disagree with your partner's point of view, you can always say: "I hear your voice" or "I can understand why you feel this way" or "I can tell you the truth. It's hard to "for you" when they are upset. Unconditionally verifying your partner will let them know that you are a safe ally and stand by them. This can-do wonder while it comes to establishing a safe relationship.

67. Increase Couple's Intimacy

How to Improving Emotional Intimacy with Your Partner

Emotional intimacy is essential to our happiness and the health of our relationships. Stress, changes, schedule, physical distance, mental focus, ebb, and flow of life... Too many things can cause us to wake up in the morning and be alienated from another close person.

If we regard intimacy as a special connection, we will realize that even the "good" things that happen in life can decrease intimacy. After all, "good" changes or personal accomplishments often include substantial investments in activities that do not necessarily include our partners. For example, getting promoted at work or helping friends during difficult times.

If you think you and your partner can use intimacy, here are four great ideas to improve the connection that needs to be updated or just some of the connections that TLC needs.

Get Time to Do Things That Are Meaningful to Both of You

Of course, date night is essential. However, if it is a ceremonial activity in which you go out and sit in a booth confronting each other, checking emails on the phone, or discussing the latest ridiculous things your 13-year-old is trying to escape at school, then you won't deepen Your connection.

Deeply connected activities allow you to focus on each other and focus on your relationship. Get a scenic drive to get ice cream, clean the bathtub together, or take a cooking class. There is no greater path to spread the usual stress sources in a better environment, like a restaurant, than to spread stress sources on the kitchen table when establishing intimacy.

Curious

Usually, because we put a lot of energy into our opinions' correctness, we are no longer curious about why another person feels about a particular issue. Appreciating where an intimate partner comes from-without feeling threatened, why they would beat your partner-is a powerful means of building empathy, and compassion is a deep intimacy. Trying to get to know another person does not mean you agree with them. However, even in the case of differences of opinion, it does show deep concern.

Available in New or Different Ways

To infuse intimacy into your relationship immediately, decide to provide services to your partner in a way that is not normally used. Not because you should and because you "owe" them, but because you can. Agree to take care of the trivial things that you usually protest/avoid, surprise them; be willing to accompany them to do things you would normally ignore; or surprise them with things they care about...make a favorite meal or watch them Favorite movie, and you can't stand while hugging. Surprise generosity is a great sense of intimacy.

Make A "Good" List

It is easy to focus on each other's defects, and there will always be many defects. Try to sit down alone or with your partner, build gratitude or a "good" list, and describe the things you appreciate and/or appreciate your partner in as much detail as possible. Even if you do it yourself, it will help you refocus on the point of contact that initially attracted you, regardless of all the troubles we inevitably encounter during the intimacy process.

Intellectual Intimacy Improves Romantic Communication

The intellectual intimacy shares your thoughts and skills. Intellectual intimacy can be your hopes and dreams, fears, and experiences. When your partner shares their inner identity and establishes an intellectual connection with you, they will trust you with their secrets. They removed the shield that protected their heart.

Many people can have romantic relationships that include sex without the need to be intellectually respectable, like one-night stands or causality. A good example of intimacy is when couples have the same hobbies, occupations, passions, or augmentation: fishing, bonding, cooking, or controlled substance augmentation. Therefore, successful relationships include a certain degree of intellectual (good or bad) intimacy. Through intellectual intimacy, a couple becomes friends and establishes a connection outside of the physical or sexual relationship.

Here are five attributes that increase intellectual intimacy:

Attitude

There is an old saying: "Attitude determines altitude." People are usually attracted to and connected with others who have the same attitude as them. When you have a positive attitude or desire, you will be attracted by a positive attitude. When you are a negative person, you will be attracted to those with negative attitudes.

Interesting

You found each other interesting and intellectually exciting. Do you have the same degree in the same field? Do you have a common hobby? Every love song begins with a story. Every business starts with an idea. Will always arouse interest in every romantic relationship.

Fun

People keep in touch with other people who like to talk to and spend time with. One person's concept of entertainment may not be another person's concept, but to enjoy each other's company, you both have some activities. The reason why people feel restrained in finding someone for fun and hanging out with them is that there are so many negative emotions in the world.

Support-You

Two may be under a lot of pressure at work and share experiences that others do not understand? According to Priceonomics and U.S. Census statistics, agricultural workers, teachers, doctors, police officers, truck drivers, military personnel, and lawyers have high marriage rates in their professions.

Loyalty and Values

some couples have bonds in loyalty and moral values. For example, missionaries marry each other because they often find themselves in countries/regions they are not familiar with, but their careers are the same. Some couples will not date and marry outside of their religion or culture. No one wants to build an intellectual bond with someone they think they cannot trust. Therefore, loyalty is on everyone's list.

What is Physical Intimacy?

Physical intimacy usually includes the emotional and sexual activities between two people and the reactions, thoughts, and emotions involved in these activities.

Intimacy includes a variety of behaviors. From holding it in hand to having sex all day long, it has everything. It includes extensive physical contact, such as:

- Foreplay or non-erotic sexual activity

- Take a bath together

- Swimming together

- Please

- Touch each other's body

- Sexual intercourse

- Afterglow (for example, tender words exchanged later sexual activity)

Potential Barriers to Physical Intimacy

Physical intimacy is sometimes hard to develop, and sometimes obstacles may occur:

- One of the main obstacles is that most people have limited attention to behavior in this area. Normally, people tend to focus on sexual intercourse as if it is an expression of uniqueness or sexual feelings for another person. Having sex too quickly is one of many women's main complaints about their physical intimacy with their partners.

- When people ignore their worries about the timeliness of specific activities or behaviors, another obstacle to comfortably expressing intimacy arises. Ignored worries produce sexual barriers, hindrances, and rejections. One source of worry may be fear related to physical intimacy.

Fears that may be related to intimacy:

- One kind of fear is the fear of being moved. Some people are not used to being touched, being caressed, and comfortable with tactile stimulation.

- There may be a fear of breaking taboos. In many cultures, there are many taboos related to physical intimacy. Even if a person is married, it is usually difficult to eliminate the influence of certain taboos that they lived before marriage.

- Some people worry about losing control of themselves and giving up their body enjoyment. Physical intimacy often involves giving up control-letting go, and for someone afraid of losing control, this can be an anxious situation.

- Many people worry about getting pregnant due to physical intimacy. Although contraceptive information or birth control techniques are readily available, people still worry about pregnancy, possibly due to information or myths about children or adolescence. These fears interfere with the comfort of physical intimacy.

- People are worried about sexually transmitted diseases (STDs), which in many cases, is a real fear, especially if any partner has sex with other partners and if any of them has not practiced safe sex skills.

- Companions, family members, or in some cases, the church will feel inward or condemned.

- For many people, an intimate relationship is a novel experience. For a person who establishes an intimate relationship with others, there are many new things to experience. If a person is worried about a novel experience, the novel experience's fear will create barriers to interpersonal intimacy.

Ways to Overcome Physical Intimacy Barriers

- One of the very important things a person can do is operate at their rate (that is, at a rate they feel comfortable with).

- When "No" is your correct answer, it is important to allow yourself to agree to say "No"; on the contrary, when "Yes" is the correct answer, allow yourself to say "Yes" or be willing to accept his responsibility for the consequences of these decisions and actions. When these yes or no answers come from one's values, the comfort of physical intimacy increases.

- Be aware of your fears and possible reasons for fear of physical intimacy. Once the fear is recognized, it can be dealt with.

68. Stop Overthinking

What Is Overthinking?

Excessive thinking is just as the name suggests; it means thinking too much. Overthinking is thinking about the same ideas repeatedly, analyzing the simplest situation or event, until all the sense of proportion is gone. An overthinking brain cannot convert these thoughts into actions or positive results, creating a sense of stress and anxiety.

Signs of Overthinking

When you are more aware of your tendency to overthink, you can take steps to change. But first, you must realize that overthinking does more harm than good.

Sometimes people think that their overthinking can prevent adverse events from happening. They believe that if they are not worried enough or reorganize the past, they will encounter more problems. However, this study is very clear-overthinking is not good for you and does not help prevent or solve problems.

Here are ten signs that you are a super thinker:

1. I recalled the embarrassing moments repeatedly.

2. It's very hard for me to fall asleep because it feels like my brain can't shut down.

3. I ask myself a lot of "if..." questions.

4. I spend a lot of time thinking about the hidden meaning of what people say or what happened.

5. I reorganized the dialogue with the person in my heart and thought about all the things I wish I had said or never said.

6. I keep repeating the same mistakes.

7. When someone says or does something in a way that I don't like, I keep repeating it in my mind.

8. Sometimes I don't know what's happening around me because I'm obsessed with what happened in the past and worried about what might happen in the future.

9. I spend a lot of time worrying about things beyond my control.

10. I can't get rid of my troubles.

Types of Overthinking

Overthinking is a thought process that is too complicated and leads to a waste of time, risk due to inaction, and poor-quality decisions. The following are common patterns of overthinking.

- **Abstract**

Far from the reality of feasible abstraction.

- **Complex**

Without filtering and weigh the importance.

- **Avoid**

Use the decision-making process as an excuse to avoid things you don't want to do.

- **Cold Logic**

Use logic to make decisions that require emotion.

- **Intuition**

Ignore what you already know.

- **Premature Decision**

Waste time and resources are thinking about decisions that have not yet been made.

- **Irrelevant Decision**

Make decisions that you don't need to make at all. For example, consider the unlikely future situation.

- **Create Problems**

See the problem where it doesn't exist.

- **Ignore Speed**

A situation where quick and mediocre decisions are more valuable than slow decisions optimize decision making.

- **Over-Optimized**

Adjust minor details and ignore the overall situation.

- **Ambiguity Aversion**

Inadequate to decide due to a lack of information.

- **Lack of Principles**

Establish basic principles to guide decision-making, and problem-solving tends to make them more efficient.

- **Analysis Paralysis**

The analysis is the process of breaking things down into their constituent parts. This is a basic thought process that may help, but it also unnecessarily complicates decision-making.

- **Big Idea**

Create huge solutions to solve small problems.

How Overthinking Affects Mental and Physical Health

Overthinking is not a medical term in itself, but research shows that this habit can have a real impact on our happiness. Often, overthinking involves negative effects-reorganizing the past, indulging in bad experiences, or worrying about the future.

Ashley Carroll, a psychologist at Parkland Memorial Hospital, said that it might roll into larger, more extreme negative thoughts when reflecting on certain ideas. Carroll says that when overthinking starts to affect daily life, it becomes a problem.

Carroll said: "When it wreaks havoc on our lives or damages our daily operations, for example, if you cannot fall asleep at night because you cannot reject these ideas, it will affect your daily operations." "If This affects your appetite, so if you lose your mind, you begin to isolate yourself from others..."

Carroll said that reflecting on the worst situation and outcome can be a misleading form of self-protection.

She said: "For some people, this may be as a defense mechanism." "'So I will automatically assume that everyone is not worthy of trust, so that I will not be close to anyone, so I protect Lost myself."

Excessive thinking can also affect your health, Carroll said. She said that some of her negative thoughts and anxiety sufferers have also experienced headaches, body pains, and stomach problems. Overthinking is also usually associated with mental health problems, such as depression, anxiety, post-traumatic stress, and borderline personality disorder.

To get rid of the habit, Carroll said, a good first step is to pay attention to the cause of your overthinking. It may stem from past trauma or something in life that is currently causing stress. Once you have identified these triggers, Carroll said, you can start looking for ways to overcome these triggers.

She said: "Whenever patients enter this cycle of repeated thinking, I always encourage controlled breathing exercises."

"It can help them shift their attention to breathing and calm the central nervous system. Like a diary, [Activities] can help them express and process their thoughts in their minds. Therefore, any mindfulness activity that truly focuses on the present moment can free you from thoughts about the past or the future."

The Difference Between Overthinking and Anxiety

People often use the terms "overthinking" and "anxiety" interchangeably, but they are very different mental states. Although both are related to general feelings of worry and apprehension, how we experience them is very different, and so is their impact on our emotional and mental health.

10 Differences Between Overthinking and Anxiety

We Tend to Overthink in Mind and Anxiety in The Body

Overthinking tends to focus more attention on the brain's thoughts, while anxiety is more visceral because we can feel it throughout the body.

Overthinking Is Often Specific, While Anxiety Is More Diffuse

We have considered arriving at the airport on time (a specific threat), but we are anxious about traveling, which is a vague and more general problem.

Too Much Verbal Thinking, While Anxiety Includes Verbal Thinking and Mental Images

This difference is significant because emotional images related to anxiety (such as emotional images related to overthinking) trigger a much greater cardiovascular response than emotional oral thoughts. This is another cause of anxiety throughout our bodies.

Excessive Thinking Usually Triggers the Ability to Solve Problems, But Anxiety Does Not

Overthinking makes us think about solutions and strategies to solve a given situation. Anxiety is more like a hamster wheel. It makes us spin, but it doesn't make us get an effective solution. Indeed, the dispersion of anxiety makes it difficult to solve the problem.

Excessive Thinking Can Cause Mild Emotional Distress, And Anxiety Can Cause Severe Emotional Distress

Compared with overthinking, anxiety is a more powerful and, therefore, destructive and problematic mental state.

Overthinking Is Caused by Worries That Are More Realistic Than Anxiety

If you are worried about being fired because you didn't do a good job on a project, you worry. If you are worried about being fired because your boss did not ask about your child's piano recital, you will feel anxious.

Overthinking Is Often Controllable, While Anxiety Is Much Less

By solving problems and using thinking strategies to address our overthinking reasons, we can greatly reduce this situation. We have much less control over anxiety, because "getting out of trouble" is much more difficult.

Overthinking Is Often Temporary, But Anxiety Will Persist

Once the problem of our overthinking is solved, our overthinking will disappear and disappear. Anxiety may last for a long time and may even shift from one focus to another (for example, we feel anxious about work, health, children, etc.) For a week.

Excessive Thinking Will Not Affect Our Professional and Personal Functions; What About Anxiety

No one spends a lot of time sitting down and pondering whether their teenagers will perform well in exams. But anxiety can make us feel uneasy, uncomfortable, and unable to concentrate, so that we may indeed feel troubled by work.

Overthinking Is Considered A Normative Mental State, While Anxiety Is Not

At certain intensities and duration, anxiety is considered a true mental disorder and requires psychotherapy and/or medication.

Stress and Depression

Stress is good for you. It keeps you alert, motivated, and ready for danger. As anyone facing a work deadline or participating in a sport knows, stress mobilizes the body to respond, thereby improving performance. However, excessive stress or long-term stress may cause severe depression in susceptible people.

"Like e-mail and e-mail spam, a little stress is a good thing, but too much is a bad thing; you required to shut down and restart," the head of neuro-stress endocrine immunology and behavior at the National Medical Association of America Researcher Esther Sternberg, MD, said.

Even positive events such as getting married or starting a new job can be stressful and lead to severe depression. However, about 10% of people suffer from depression without triggering stressful events.

Stress Depression Connection

Stress, whether is a chronic disease (such as caring for parents with Alzheimer's disease) or an acute disease (such as unemployment or the death of a loved one). It can cause susceptible people to fall into a severe state of depression. Both types of stress can cause the body's stress response mechanism to be overactive.

Constant or chronic stress, in particular, can cause hormones such as cortisol, the "stress hormone," to rise and reduce serotonin and other neurotransmitters (including dopamine) in the brain, the latter being associated with depression. When these chemical systems work properly, they regulate biological processes such as sleep, appetite, energy, and libido, allowing the expression of normal emotions and emotions.

After experiencing a difficult situation, if the stress response cannot be turned off and reset, it may lead to depression in susceptible people.

No one in life can escape the stress associated with events, such as the death of a loved one, unemployment, divorce, natural disasters (such as earthquakes), or a sharp drop in your 401(k). If you are looking for work for a long time, layoffs-an acute stressor-can lead to chronic stress.

Loss of any kind is the main risk factor for depression. Grief is considered a normal, healthy loss response, but if it lasts too long, it can lead to depression. Serious illnesses, including depression itself, are considered long-term stressors.

How to Stop Negative Thinking?

Overcoming negative thoughts is one of the main problems you may encounter when applying the law of attraction. After all, even if you are using all these amazing new tools to help you think positively or look forward to a brighter future, you are still struggling with helpless restrictive beliefs early in your life. Many of these beliefs will spread endlessly and start to destroy your impression of a good life.

Fortunately, there are many practical things you can do to help you stop negative thinking. These are the five most effective ways to stop negative thinking.

4 Techniques to Stop Negative Thinking

Thought Stop

When you find negative thoughts or images start to enter your mind, try to say, "Stop!" To yourself. If you are alone, you can try to say it out loud, but it can also be very effective when you say it in your head.

If you want, you can use a stronger language than "Stop" (for example, "Get out of my head!" or even more colorful). For those who will not be moved by words, images may be more powerful. A classic example is a bright red stop sign; when you start to have intrusive thoughts, you will see it in your mind.

There are more direct ways to stop thinking. For example, you can try the old strategy of splashing water on your face or change your mind's direction. Some people like to count down from 100 to 1.

For Sure

It can be used in two different ways. First, they may be deployed in the same way as thought suppression techniques. In other words, when you feel that negative thoughts are coming, you might say affirmative.

For example, when you are trying to use the Law of Attraction to find new partners and find that you think you are not worthy of love, then you can say, "I am a valuable and lovely person, and I will find a good relationship." "

Secondly, however, saying affirmative words every day will start to reshape your thoughts, even when you are already in a good mood, they become powerful tools. Design your affirmations carefully and try to make eye contact with yourself in the mirror as you recite.

Strengthen the Border

While you have been thinking negatively for a long time, you may think that it is unrealistic to expect yourself to change your approach suddenly. In this case, even positive attitudes and thought suppression methods seem only to postpone negative thoughts.

If it sounds familiar, you may need to spend at least a few weeks strengthening the boundaries of negative thinking. The idea here is that you choose a fixed, limited period to make your thoughts negative and promise to forcibly stop or oppose them at other times of the week.

When you are assured that you will have time to consider these ideas, you may find that they do not seem to be that powerful and do not have the potential to dominate your thoughts.

Also, many people find that they don't even think of anything when arranging their time to think negatively, which helps them break the rules.

Writing and Destruction

If your negative thoughts are associated with specific strong emotions (such as fear, anger, or jealousy), try to exclude them all in writing. Use pen and paper to express all the suppressed negative emotions truly. Then, you can choose a way to destroy this article to show your determination to move on. For example, you can tear it apart, crush it into balls, burn it, or apply it on it.

For those who are unwilling to express themselves in words, artistic creations will have a similar impact. For example, you can carve a negative representation, paint it, and then destroy it (or change its shape).

This technique aims to obtain a certain physical representation of negativity so that you can eliminate it in a satisfactory symbolic way.

How to Stop Overthinking?

End rehashing repeated guessing and catastrophic predictions are easier than harder to do. But with consistent practice, you can limit negative ways of thinking:

Be Aware That You Think Too Much

Consciousness is the first step to prevent overthinking. Start paying attention to your way of thinking. When you find yourself replaying events repeatedly or worrying about things you can't control, make sure that your thoughts won't help.

Challenge Your Ideas

You are easily confused by negative thoughts. Before you conclude that calling in sick will cause you to be fired, or forgetting the deadline will cause you to become homeless, and acknowledge that your thoughts may have been exaggerated. Learn to recognize or replace thinking errors before driving you into madness.

Focus on Proactive Problem Solving

Focusing on your problem does not help, but finding a solution is helpful. Question yourself what steps you can take to learn from your mistakes or avoid problems in the future. Instead of asking why and what happened, ask yourself what you can do.

Arrange Reflection Time

Solving the problem for a long time does not affect, but brief thinking will help. For example, thinking about how to do different things or recognizing potential pitfalls of planning can help you do better in the future. And incorporate 20 minutes of "thinking time" into your daily plan. During this time, let yourself worry, meditate, or think carefully about whatever you want. Then, when the time comes, switch to more productive products. When you find yourself thinking too much outside the planned time, remind yourself to think again later.

Practice Mindfulness

When you live in the present, yesterday's hash table or tomorrow's worry is impossible. Committed to the present and becoming more understanding now. Mindfulness requires practice like any other skill, but over time it can reduce overthinking.

Change Channel

Telling yourself to stop thinking can backfire. The more you want to avoid thinking from entering your brain, the more likely it is to keep appearing. Being busy with an activity is the best way to change the channel. Exercise, have a conversation on a completely different topic or work on a project that will distract your thoughts from many negative thoughts.

Ways to Reduce Stress in The Workplace

Stress is one of the difficult obstacles for employees to participate in the modern workplace. Research estimates that stress causes US companies to lose approximately $300 billion a year, and the workplace has been recognized as the number one source of stress for American workers.

Workload, lack of job safety, and human problems increase employees' burden and reduce their satisfaction. The negative impact of stress is so great that the World Health Organization has declared it a worldwide epidemic.

Although many people try to construct stress reduction strategies that cover all aspects, recent research shows no "one size fits all" approach.

In the workplace, the adaptability of employees to the environment should be the primary focus. If matched properly, employees are likely to relax. Improper fit will increase stress and pressure.

As managers and companies, we need to check our employees and the environment created for them. We need to ensure that the office we provide meets our employees' definition of "no stress," not just what we think it looks like.

We have a wide range of ideas that can be used to reduce stress in the workplace, but please tailor it to your job. Put these ideas into practice; remember that the best strategy starts with the leader's example.

Encourage Health in The Workplace

Exercise and healthy living are some of the best weapons against workplace stress. Exercise frees employees' energy from work pressure and focuses on the task at hand. It also improves mood by increasing the production of endorphins (feel-good neurotransmitters in the brain).

- Encourage employees to take a walk during lunch break.

- Subsidized gym membership

- Bring a yoga instructor to the office every month.

- Hold a ladder competition in a team for people with fitness trackers.

- Provide healthy snacks in the office

When employees think you are looking for your health, they feel precious! A Peapod.com study reported that 66% of employees feel very happy when their boss regularly stores refrigerators and cabinets, and 83% of employees say that having healthy and fresh snack options is a great benefit. For employees, simple things like putting fresh fruit or a box of yogurt in the refrigerator are very long.

Transform the Habitat

A lot of pressure comes from the environment. Consider all aspects of office space and its impact (or no impact) on team health. Simple things, such as the quality of coffee or the next partition's height, can affect employee engagement.

Update the office with an optimistic color scheme, other plants, or new silverware. If there is enough space, consider adding a ping pong table or foosball table to free employees from stress within a few minutes. Any change that increases employee enjoyment will make them feel less stressed.

Allow Flexible Time and Remote Work

You hire employees because you are confident in their ability to do their jobs promptly, so ask them to prove it. Your office should not be like a cell, but like a convenient place to get work done. Let your workers know that their work is determined by their quality and timeliness, not by their working hours.

Allow your employees to work remotely and provide flexibility for start and end times. This freedom is essential for improving office morale, and the policy shows employees that you trust them enough to prevent them from being a nanny.

Encourage Social Activities

Employees spend a lot of time together, or the more comfortable they are, the less stress they feel. With the understanding between colleagues, expectations and communication barriers are broken, which facilitates future communication.

Provide On-Site or Remote Consultation

Many companies have also begun to provide consulting services to help employees relieve stress. In a recent study, almost half of workers believe they need help in learning how to deal with work stress. Whether in the office and outside the office, this strategy can help employees prepare for the upcoming pressures in a group setting or a separate situation.

Recognize Your Employees

Employees like to be praised for their outstanding work, and recognition of their success will greatly increase their engagement. Every employee has a different personality, so keep in mind when considering how and when to recognize it. Some employees like to make calls during meetings or compliment in company-wide emails, while more reserved employees prefer business cards on their desks or personal thanks.

No matter what you choose to admit, your employees will appreciate your awareness of your success and want to share it with others. This makes them happier and more comfortable, thereby reducing stress levels.

Exercise and Nutrition

Why Exercise?

Regular exercise benefits are improved posture, self-esteem, weight management, increased energy levels, increased muscle and bone strength, and reduced risk of heart disease.

How Much Exercise?

- Adults should take at least 150 minutes of moderate to vigorous exercise every week.

- Everyone can do some form of exercise. Although better and better, everything is important. Becoming more active is easier than you think!

Supplement Low-Fat, High-Carbohydrate Foods

- The body's preferred fuel is carbohydrates because they are easily converted into glucose, and cells immediately use it as energy. Carbohydrates can also be stored in the form of glycogen for later use by your cells.

- I was eating low-fat, high-carbohydrate foods (such as biscuits) or low-fat fruit yogurt an hour before exercise will increase the fuel the body needs for this exercise.

- The best carbohydrate foods are brown rice, grains, whole wheat bread, carrots, and other starchy vegetables and fruits.

- If you exercise for more than 30 minutes or eat low-fat, high-carbohydrate foods (such as apples or low-fat muffins) within 15 minutes after exercise or after exercise, it will help replenish the muscle sugar consumed during exercise original. Exercise.

How Much Protein?

- Although many active people believe that protein in foods such as meat, chicken, eggs, or fish is not an important fuel for exercise.

- Although long-distance runners and weightlifters may need more protein than recreational athletes, most of us get enough protein by eating regular foods and various foods.

Take Vitamin C And E

- Many studies have shown that being active produces free radical-harmful particles that can damage cells and genetic material (DNA).

- Eating foods rich in antioxidants, such as vitamins C and E, may be important.

- Foods rich in these nutrients include strawberries, oranges, kiwi, olive oil, wheat germ, and nuts.

Eat Iron-Rich Foods

Studies have found that runners, especially female runners, may have low iron. This may be due to the low absorption of iron, the choice of eating less meat, the high iron content, the restriction of calories, and the continuous beating on the feet' soles, which leads to blood breakdown.

It is important to eat iron-rich foods, such as dried fruits, grains, and meat.

Replenish Yourself!

Water is an essential nutrient and part of a good exercise plan.

- Half an hour before exercise, use a glass of water or diluted fruit juice to hydrate yourself.

- During physical exercise, drink ½ to ¾ cup every 15 to 20 minutes.

- Within 30 minutes after exercise, drink plenty of water to replenish the water lost due to sweat.

Healthy Sleeping Habits

Your actions may have a major impact on your sleep and may cause insomnia. During the day, especially before going to bed, your behavior may make it difficult to fall asleep, stay asleep, or fall asleep.

Your daily activities-diet, medication, schedule, and choices at night-can seriously affect your sleep quality. In some cases, even minor adjustments may mean that sleep is different from restless nights.

The term "sleep hygiene" refers to a series of habits and habits that can improve falling asleep and maintaining the ability to fall asleep. Board-certified sleep doctors recommend following a series of common-sense healthy sleep habits to promote better sleep.

These healthy sleeping habits are the basis of cognitive-behavioral therapy, which is the most effective long-term treatment for insomnia patients. CBT-I can help you resolve harmful thoughts and behaviors that prevent you from falling asleep. It also includes techniques for stress reduction, and relaxation, or sleep plan management.

Sleep experts recommend that you follow the healthy sleep habits highlighted in this article. When you have trouble falling asleep or want to improve your sleep, try following these sleep hygiene tips. If your sleep problem persists, AASM recommends that you seek help from the sleep team at an AASM-approved sleep center.

Quick Sleep Reminder

Follow these few tips to establish healthy sleep habits:

- Maintain a consistent sleep schedule. Get up at the same time every day, even on weekends or holidays.

- Set a bedtime early enough so that you have at least seven hours of sleep.

- Don't go to bed unless you are sleepy.

- When you still do not fall asleep after 20 minutes, get up.

- Establish a relaxing bedtime ceremony.

- Use the bed only for sleep.

- Make your bedroom quiet and relaxing. Keep the room at a comfortable or cool temperature.

- Limit exposure at night.

- Don't eat big meals before going to bed. If you are hungry at night, eat light, healthy snacks.

- Exercise regularly and maintain a healthy diet.

- Avoid caffeine in the afternoon or evening.

- Avoid drinking alcohol before going to bed.

- Reduce the amount of water that you drink before going to bed.

69. Determining What is Important to You

What Is Positive Thinking?

Positive thinking or optimism is the practice of focusing on the product in any given situation. It will have the main impact on your physical and mental health.

This does not mean that you will ignore reality or belittle the problem. This means that you approach the good and bad of life to expect that your life will be better.

The Benefits of Positive Thinking

Many researchers have looked at the role of optimism and positive thinking in mental and physical health. There is not always a priority: mentality or these benefits. But staying optimistic does not have any adverse effects.

Some physical benefits may include:

- Longer life

- Lower chance of heart attack

- Healthy body

- Higher resistance to diseases such as the common cold

- Lower blood pressure

- Better stress management

- Better pain tolerance

Spiritual benefits may include:

- More creativity

- Higher problem-solving skills

- Clearer thinking

- Better mood

- Better coping skills

- Reduce depression

People in one research were exposed to the flu and the common cold. People with optimistic prospects are less likely to get sick and have fewer symptoms.

In another study, optimistic women were less likely to die from cancer, heart disease, stroke, respiratory disease, and infection.

In research of people over the age of 50, those who had more positive aging ideas lived longer. They also have less stress-related inflammation, which suggests that there may be a connection between their thinking and health.

Optimistic people may be healthier because they have greater hopes for the future. But the researchers considered this, and the result still holds.

Benefits of Decluttering Your Workspace

Sometimes there is chaos everywhere, but this can have a detrimental effect on your productivity.

An established workspace is more than just a beautiful area. It will also have an effect that benefits you psychologically. In other words, learning how to organize a desk or cubicle at work can make you feel good.

Improve Impression

If your boss often sees chaos in your workplace, he or she may be against you. The boss or manager may think you don't care about the job. When you are a sales representative, your sales manager may be worried that your desk will give the impression they are trying to establish a relationship with the client, client, or business. You feel more motivated when people with power in the company are satisfied with your company's presence.

Improved Comfort

You might try to put an important file on your desk at some point, but you can't find space to put it on a messy workstation, which seems to be shrinking around. You may start to feel closed at your desk. Keeping your workspace tidy can make your work more comfortable. More open space or a more comfortable environment can increase productivity. Consider the difficulty of completing a task when you are uncomfortable and apply it to this situation.

Confidence

A messy desk may also mean that you have lost something at some point. Maybe your manager comes to find important documents. When you look for it, you cannot see the item. Even if the file is finally restored, you may not feel good in front of the manager. When you can easily produce the materials you need without a wander around the table looking for them, you can be more confident in your work. Knowing that you leave a better impression on the manager can further increase your confidence.

Strengthen Immunity

If your desk has been professionally cleaned for a while, you may leave bacteria on the surface left by a sick colleague. If you keep finding yourself feeling uncomfortable, you might blame others in the office. However, it may be that your desk is causing the weakening of the immune system. People who work in major cities such as Detroit or Baltimore may have weaker immune systems than those who work in the suburbs. There is no reason to cheer for that fire.

Cleaning up debris and wiping the table with some disinfectant can help you minimize the risk of illness.

How do We learn to Be More Decisive?

Yes-the good news is that decision-making is a skill you can practice. Like any other skill, some people know how to be decisive more naturally than others. If you find procrastination, over-analysis, or yielding to others when deciding, you need to take some steps-start with your mentality.

Overcome Fear

This is a secret: if you want to know how to be more decisive, you may shrink from fear. No matter how small, any decision implies some change, which can lead to major changes in our lives, and the lives of those we care about. This fear of change can swallow you and cause devastating effects, paralyzing you when you need decisiveness most. How do you break this negative pattern? Willing to change rather than afraid to change. Acknowledge that life itself is always changing or that you can control your life by making decisions (even if uncertain).

Stop Over-Analysis

You are not alone-no one will always be completely sure of everything. Those who have discovered how to be a decisive person are as uncertain or nervous as you. They are just willing to make a choice. Maybe the decision they made was wrong. So? They can learn from wrong decisions and usually learn quickly. A bad decision leads to a better decision, and no decision leads to stagnation. Nothing will get better. The situation may not worsen, but you will certainly not sit where you are and do nothing to improve your situation. Over time, the inability to make a choice is a choice in itself.

Real leadership comes from the ability to make decisions, even if you are not sure whether the decision is correct. If you want to lead work, life, or anywhere in your life, you must be prepared and decisive even if you don't know the right path. Therefore, please stop thinking and start practicing decisively!

Search A Mentor to Show You How to Be More Attractive

Often, what prevents us from making a decision is that we feel that we do not have all the information we need. One thing that can help you stop over-analysis and prepare to decide is to collect this information. Don't ask questions, cross channels, and seek different opinions. The more information you have, and the more prepared you will be for all the results.

The best leaders seek continuous improvement, including decision-making skills. The instructor is always here to answer your questions, help you get all the information and experience collected, and shape it into valuable skills that can be used in the future. For those who need to learn how to be more decisive, finding a mentor is a must.

Visualize the Results

Visualization is often used to set and achieve goals, and the same concepts can be applied when learning how to become more decisive. Double-check every option you have, and then visualize what might happen to each option. Don't just consider negative results, but consider positive and neutral results. Make a list of "pros or cons" for each option. This strategy not only helps you make the final decision, but it limits your thinking to make decisions faster in the future.

How to Break Bad Habits?

Everyone has habits, and they are inherently right. Some of these features are very useful-maybe you set up your clothes to work the night before and automatically turn off the lights when you leave the room.

But other habits, such as biting your nails, and drinking caffeine too late in the day, or napping too much sleep, may not be beneficial.

Breaking bad habits can be difficult, especially if you have been engaged in them for a long time. But first, understanding how habits are formed can simplify this process. There are some ways to eliminate bad habits.

Replace with Another Habit

If you replace unwanted behaviors with new behaviors instead of simply blocking unwanted behaviors, you may be more likely to break the habit.

Suppose you want to stop eating sweets when you are hungry at work. If you want to avoid eating sweets, you may get used to it again when you can't stand hunger. However, the crisper with Tupperware dried fruits and nuts placed next to your desk will provide you with another snack option.

When you repeat new behaviors, you will follow new habits. Ultimately, after reaping the rewards from your new habit (more energy and less sugar after the breakdown), the urge to continue this behavior may exceed the desire to pursue the old habit.

Leave A Reminder

Using stickers, sticky notes, and other visual reminders wherever a habitual behavior occurs can help you rethink the behavior that triggered you.

Here are some ideas:

- Do you want to eliminate the habit of drinking soda at every meal? Try to leave some small stickers on the refrigerator; you will see when you get the jar.

- Want to remember to turn off the lights when you leave the room? Leave a note on the light switch or door.

- Want to start saving keys in a designated location so that you don't lose them often? First, leave a dish for your key. You will see it when you return home.

You can also use your smartphone for reminders. Set the alarm and add a touching note for yourself, such as "It's time to turn off the TV! :)" or "Walk after dinner-remember how it feels!"

Change the Environment

The surrounding environment can sometimes have a major impact on your habits.

Maybe you are trying to get rid of the habit of always ordering takeout because it will cost you too much money. However, every time you enter the kitchen, there is a to-do menu hanging on the refrigerator. You can try to replace the menu with a printout of your favorite simple recipe.

Other examples include:

- Leave diaries, books, or hobby items (sketches, crafts, or games) on the coffee table to encourage you and pick them up instead of scrolling through social media.

- Spend 10 or 15 minutes clean up the room every night to encourage you to stay tidy

- Change your morning walk time to work not to bring tempting, overpriced lattes through the cafe.

Remember, the people around you are also part of your environment. Consider spending time with people who help you build habits or do not support you in breaking them.

How to Stop Worrying and Focus on Achieving Goals?

The key to remember is that you need to focus on achieving your goals, not just "get rid of troubles."

Getting rid of troubles is a challenging task. We cannot tame our thoughts in a way that is not at all worried. Humans worry; this is a fact. Just imagine that getting rid of worries will put pressure on yourself. If this is your goal, then you will start to worry! In this way, you are not only worried about the struggles and pressures of life, but the worrying situation makes the situation more complicated! Double worries...

Therefore, to avoid these worries, you will distract yourself and achieve goals you don't seem to worry about. But you will not move towards your real goal.

Choose avoidance because you may not want to worry... As a result, the release will increase exponentially until you distract yourself.

Your first step can be to practice willingness. What to say to me: I want to achieve my goals, and I am willing to accept that I will encounter many worries and fears in the process.

Or change "I want to do some work for my goal now, but I am worried..." to "I want to do some work for my goal now, I am worried."

You will find that worry is natural... if we accept it will be there... then this does not prevent us from moving forward! Then over time, it may disappear because we have not given it any power.

Also, you can try to separate yourself from worry. When you hear a worrying thought, pay attention, grab it and say to yourself: "Ah, just worry" or "Thank you for the worrying brain," and move on towards your goal! Bring your worries, and when it realizes that it cannot control you, it will stop clinging to it!

What Is Goal Setting?

Goal setting is a powerful motivation, and its value has been recognized in clinical and real environments for more than 35 years.

The "objectives" defined by Latham & Locke (2002, p.705) are "for example, the goal or purpose of an action that usually achieves a certain proficiency level within a specified period." They are the level of competence we hope to achieve and create a useful Perspective to evaluate current performance.

Goal setting is our process of achieving these goals. Locke (2019) said that the importance of the goal-setting process could not be ignored, "Everyone's life depends on the process of choosing the goal to pursue; if you remain passive, you will not thrive like a human being."

The goal-setting study is based on the premise that conscious goals affect actions (Ryan, 1970), and intended human behavior is purposeful and regulated by personal goals. In short, we must decide what is right for our welfare and set goals to achieve it.

Why do few people do better at work than others? The goal-setting theory explores motivation issues from a first-level perspective. Its focus is to explain individual differences in task performance immediately. According to Ryan, if individuals are equal in ability and knowledge, then the cause must be motivation.

The study states that the simplest and most direct explanation of why some people's performance is better than others is due to different performance goals, which means setting and adjusting goals will significantly affect performance.

Set Specific Goals

A success goal is a specific goal that contains an action plan that outlines how you will achieve the goal and a performance indicator that tells you whether you are successful.

This is the goal-setting formula to ensure you set a specific goal:

"I will pass (target + performance indicator) (specific action)."

The performance indicator in a goal is usually a date or length of time. Still, it can be an objective criterion that can be used to determine whether you have completed a specific goal you set.

Suppose your goal is to lose weight. Examples of specific goals that help you achieve this goal are:

"If I run on a treadmill for half an hour every six days, I will lose 10 pounds in two months."

Set Attainable Goals

Working towards the goal can make you have a sense of purpose, and reaching the destination can enhance your self-confidence. However, many people make a significant mistake: setting unrealistic goals that you cannot achieve. Rather than feeling satisfied and fulfilled, it is better to say that you will become worse than before.

Suppose you had a physical examination recently, and the doctor said that if you exercise and lose some weight, you will be healthier, so you decide to lose 25 pounds (11.3 kg) in four weeks. You think you can do this by exercising for 90 minutes a day and strictly following a 1,000-calorie diet. However, when you are too tired to exercise, eat more than your calorie intake, or do not lose weight, you will feel defeated.

It is unrealistic to expect you to exercise for an hour a day if you have never exercised. For most people, eating 1,000 calories is not enough, so the diet is entirely understandable. Most doctors recommend that you lose no greater than 4 to 6 pounds (1.8 to 2.7 kg) per month. You are not a loser-you fail to achieve your goals because it is unrealistic.

How do you understand that you have set a more reasonable goal? One way is to use a technology called SMART:

- Be specific - as precise as possible. Your goal should be "exercise 30 minutes a day," not "exercise."

- Measurable - propose a way to measure your success. "Playing the guitar better" is impossible to measure. "Discover how to play a new song every week."

- Achievable - If you cannot achieve your goal, then you have to be prepared for failure. If you only have a $50 checking account left after paying your bills, you cannot achieve "$100 monthly savings."

- Reality - Your goals can make you stretch yourself, but not necessarily easy. "No more coffee" may be less realistic than "only coffee every week."

- Timely - Set an exact time frame to achieve the goal. If there is no deadline, you may not have the motivation to push yourself.

Our relationships with others usually play an essential role in our happiness. When one of your goals is to improve and strengthen relationships, consider the importance of forgiveness. We will discuss it next.

70. Practicing Positive Mindfulness Meditation for Anxiety

What Is Mindfulness?

Mindfulness is human beings' ability to fully demonstrate their raw ability to understand where we are and what we are doing without overreacting or overwhelmed by things around us.

Mindfulness is a quality that everyone already possesses. This is not something you have to remember; you just need to learn how to use it.

Types of Mindfulness Practice

Mindfulness is innate and can be cultivated through mature techniques. Here are some examples:

1. Sitting, walking, standing, and moving meditation (you can also lie down, but it often leads to falling asleep);

2. A short pause allows us to integrate into our daily life;

3. Combine meditation practice with other activities (such as yoga or exercise).

Benefits of Mindfulness Practice

If we meditate, it is not helpful to stick to the benefits, but practice, but there are benefits, or no one will do it.

When we maintain mindfulness, we will reduce stress by observing our thoughts, improving performance, gaining insight and awareness, and paying more attention to others' happiness.

Mindfulness meditation provides us with a time in life where we can stop our judgment and release our natural curiosity about the operation of the mind, and treat ourselves and others with a warm and friendly attitude.

How to Reduce Anxiety

Feelings of anxiety (an inexplicable sense of restlessness, fear, fear of impending doom) can be very unpleasant. Whether anxiety manifests as stomach upset, heart, nervous tension that discolors everything, or even panic attacks, discomfort, and distress are incredibly challenging.

Here, we are not talking about general daily anxiety, but clinical anxiety, which will go all out and sometimes debilitating. According to the American Anxiety and Depression Association, anxiety is classified as a disease, which is "continuous excessive worry" individuals may lose their rational insights, and "even if there is no obvious reason for worry, they may expect the worst situation."

Chronic or severe symptoms may be a sign of generalized anxiety disorder (GAD), affecting nearly 40 million adults in the United States. According to the WHO, 1 in 13 globally. Fortunately, as doctors and healthcare professionals determine the best treatment options for you, there are effective therapies and medications.

No matter what size you are in, natural remedies are worth considering, either alone or as a supplement to traditional therapies (although if you get professional care, please consult your doctor first). Some lifestyle changes can help relieve long-term anxiety, such as regular meditation practice, physical exercise, spending time outdoors, or some food exchanges. Other techniques, such as deep breathing and distraction, can provide natural anxiety relief when your brain emits SOS.

With the right skills or lifestyle changes, we can better regulate our emotions and train our brains to look at life with a more balanced and less fearful perspective.

The following are ways to relieve anxiety naturally and consciously:

- Take a deep breath

- Go for a walk

- Try a mini-meditation from the headspace.

- Drink some herbs, chamomile, or green tea

- Distract oneself

How to Change Your Lifestyle?

One of the important things that therapy taught me is that changing your way of thinking can change your life. Based on our learning, observation, and inherited knowledge, we have grown into a deep-rooted thinking mode. Some are more positive, such as "helping others feel good." But some may be more frustrating, such as "I must succeed, or I am not worth it."

These thought patterns are the actual neural connections in our brains, and they are strengthened over time. So, changing them is not easy. This is like retraining muscles. It takes time and energy, but when you do, men are worth it!

Step 1: Identity Thinking Patterns

The first step in changing the way of thinking in your life is to start to recognize it. Often, we think in a certain way without even knowing. First of all, confirm the moment when these thought patterns began. For example, I recently realized the pressure I was under to do everything correctly. When I feel stressed all day, I notice these moments and learn that this thinking process usually causes them. It's even as simple as getting the right route in the grocery store. I feel slightly anxious and realize that it stems from the idea that I cannot do anything wrong.

However, instead of being ashamed of my thoughts, I tried to admit them. I will notice when they are there. I will not attempt to change them immediately, but it is important to proceed to the next step by confirming them. This also makes me feel less anxious. Naming the thoughts or emotions that occurred in my mind can alleviate some of the anxiety associated with that thought.

Step 2: Know Its Source

It is very important to understand precisely what these thinking patterns mean, where to learn them, and their true beliefs. Once we have studied them, we will realize how illogical or impractical this way of thinking is. This may be the most beneficial for the therapist, but you can certainly do it yourself or with a friend.

What you required to do is continue to ask yourself some questions, such as "Why are you doing this?", "And what do other people in your life think?" "And who taught you this way of thinking directly and indirectly?" "What is your earliest memory of this way?" "What will happen if you don't think like this?" etc. Similar questions can help you fully understand yourself. And once you understand better why you want to think in a certain way, you can change that way of thinking more easily.

Step 3: Create an Alternative Response

Once you take the time to think about the source of these thought patterns (which may take hours or even years), the next step is to create alternative responses. Try to come up with something you can say to replace the thought process you are trying to change. For example, under the tremendous pressure that I put on myself, another option I thought of was: "You don't have to be perfect." When I can hear those old thought patterns, I will repeat myself. It may sound simple, yet as long as you come up with an alternative answer that can speak to you, it can help.

Step 4: Practice and Patience

According to my arrangement, it seems that you only need to complete three steps, and then you can solve it. Well, that is not very effective. It takes time or effort to change the way of thinking. This is very similar to muscle memory-training muscles is like training the brain. So be patient. Allow yourself to stay in step 1 long enough, or repeat step 1 when you are eager to hear the alternative answer. And, if you gradually realize that your alternative answer is invalid, let yourself explore another option. Give yourself time and space to change this way of thinking as needed.

71. Tips and Techniques to Use to Practice Mindfulness - Practice Regularly

Declutter Your Environment

The term health covers your physical and mental state, and the surrounding environment has a significant impact on your mental health. If you walk into a room where the room is disorganized, disorganized, and stressed, we will undoubtedly feel the effect.

A recent study in the New Journal of Neuroscience found that placing multiple stimuli in front of you can cause these stimuli to compete for your attention, which means you will find yourself distracted.

Therefore, it is not easy to throw paper scraps into the trash can or fill the box in the corner. And this is a journey of self-discovery, an opportunity to learn how to "live" before and what changes to make to improve the environment. Think carefully about what you need and want, and what can be recycled or sorted.

"A neat space is a neat mind."

The mess is not just physical; it can also be digital-like, having too many files on your computer and too many open tabs on Internet Explorer. This chaotic digital format can affect your productivity and ability to focus on a task.

The decision to organize and organize your life not only empowers you but can have a substantial positive impact on your health, leading to more mindfulness, less stress and anxiety, a better quality of life, and better concentration. You can start to curb the habit of accumulating unnecessary debris.

How to master clutter:

Make a list - start with the simplest or most important place and write down all the areas that need to be "organized."

Check weekly/monthly - whether it's a closet or a computer; make sure you spend time every week/month to check your "needs" and remove all unnecessary things.

Issue a "clear workbench policy" - We have developed a "clear workbench policy" at the Stress Management Association to ensure that our environment is stress-free and that we can always maintain clear thinking.

Why A Shorter Meditation Is the Best Way to Start?

If you want to increase your focus? Want to be inspired by creativity? Or is it just to reduce stress and relax? Meditation is there for help. Since ancient times, it has been its mission to restore health.

But Is Longer or Shorter Time More Beneficial?

Most people will say that prolonged contemplation will better help you get out of silence. Indeed, you can benefit a lot from long meetings. However, there are three reasons why a short session is a good start. Check out now.

Short Meditation Works-Research Confirmed

Yes, research shows that short meditation is useful. "Study published in the journal Psychological Science found that a short meditation practice of about 15 minutes can help you make better decisions.

Another study published in the journal Psychological Neuroendocrinology argued that 25 minutes of meditation could already reduce stress levels for three consecutive days.

Finally, the American Medical Association Journal published an 8-week meditation program involving 3,515 participants and conducted a study. It shows evidence of improvement in anxiety and depression after sitting for about 30 minutes a day.

Shorter Meditations Can Help You Stick to Your Habits

In the long run, how to stick to your meditation plan? A brief meditation fascinated me.

If you tell yourself that I only sit for 10 minutes because 10 minutes is not important, then you have won. The idea of not having a big plan or investing a lot of time encourages us to start. Then, when you are ready, you can naturally sit longer.

Trust me; sometimes you will be surprised how long you can sit!

Brief Meditation-The Relationship Between Focus and Frequency and Time

Why is shorter or longer timeless important? Just because concentration will bring the most significant benefit. A shorter meditation focused on meditation may be more powerful than a more extended meditation concentrates on meditation.

When I transitioned from "normal consciousness" to "contemplative consciousness," I found myself very focused on the first minute of meditation. The difference between the two is pronounced, and it has brought me many benefits.

"Don't worry about how many minutes, hours, or years you should sit, but make the most of each practice time. It's all about quality, not quantity".

What Is Anger Management?

Anger management refers to the process. It can help people identify the source of stress. People learn some steps to help them stay calm in anger management. They can then respond to the tension with a constructive and positive attitude.

The primary purpose of anger management is to help a person reduce anger. It reduces the emotional and physical stimulation that irritation may cause. It is usually impossible to avoid all the people and circumstances that cause anger.

But a person may learn to control the reaction and respond in a socially appropriate way. In this process, the support of mental health professionals may be helpful.

Explore the Source of Anger

Many different events can make people angry. These may include:

- Internal events, such as perceived failure, injustice, or frustration

- External events, and such as loss of property or privileges, teasing or humiliation

Anger can lead to external behavior. These may include oral arguments and tantrums. Anger can also lead to internalized behavior. Internalizing actions may consist of increased symptoms of anger or depression. People may show anger through aggression. Aggression is the biological function of anger. This is an evolutionary response that helps prepare people to resist threats. Vulgar expression of anger may indicate a more serious mental health or emotional problem. People who receive anger management therapy will learn skills that slow down their response to irritation. This can help them discover the cause of the feeling. The root of anger may be buried in emotional trauma, addiction, sadness, or other problems. But the natural tendency may be to seek temporary relief in bondage. This can mask the real cause of anger. If this is your case, working with a therapist may help.

How Anger Management Works

Anger management therapy provides a clear set of recovery guidelines. It gives a controllable platform for people receiving treatment to release their emotions. And at the same time, it aims to achieve a constructive response, not a destructive response. Encourage people in treatment to study the causes of anger. They try to be aware of their emotions at each arousal level. People learn how to use these signs as a map to control anger.

During treatment, people can gain insights into how their bodies react to past and future events. They do this by determining the emotional response to a specific situation.

The therapist also helps people notice angry reactions, which may be a defense mechanism for other problems. These problems may be depression, anxiety, or other mental health problems.

Anger management therapy can usually help people with anger problems. It can also help people who make up their social networks. Uncontrollable anger can lead to harmful mental and physical conditions. Anger management helps reduce and control anger. This makes people less stressed. And it can also reduce the risk of severe health problems. These may include heart disease and high blood pressure.

Although the purpose of anger management therapy is to teach people how to check triggers. It can also help people adjust their perceptions of the situation. Successful anger management therapy provides a healthy way for people to express anger and depression. Some techniques used in anger management therapy include:

- Impulse Control

- Self-Conscious

- Meditation

- Frustration Management

- Breathing Technique

- Relaxation Strategy

Anger management therapy can be done one-on-one or in small groups. The class solves specific types of anger problems. These may include interpersonal issues, parenting, youth, and work-related anger or anger. Sometimes people are ordered by the court to attend anger management classes. This may be the result of domestic or legal issues.

Treatment can be continued. Those interested in anger management can also take retreats or online courses. Most anger management courses include homework and exercises. These reinforce the techniques learned in treatment. They also allow the treated person to practice new skills in real life.

Pay Attention to Your Mindful Eating Habits

Healthy eating is more than just the food you eat. It will remember your eating habits, take time to eat, and notice when you feel hungry and full.

Pay Attention to The Benefits of Eating Habits

Paying attention to eating habits means being aware of:

- How do you eat?

- Why do you eat?

- What did you eat?

- While eating?

- Where do you eat?

- How much do you eat?

Attention can help you:

- Make healthier choices

- Make positive changes to daily eating behavior

- Pay more attention to the food and eating habits you eat

- Build awareness in your daily dietary decisions

- Reconnect the eating experience by enhancing awareness of:

- Feelings

- Thought

- Mood

- Manner

How to Pay Attention to Eating Habits?

Use these ideas to help you pay attention to eating habits.

Create A Healthy Eating Environment

You're eating environment will change according to your life, study, work, and entertainment places. Focus on eating and eating environment.

No matter where you are, you should try to change your surroundings so that healthy choices are simple choices.

Use Your Senses

Paying attention to the food you eat will encourage you to pay attention to the aroma, texture, flavor, and taste of the food. Use these senses to pay attention to your likes and dislikes. This can help you connect you're eating experience with others and become more aware of the food you eat.

72. Relationship Between Emotions and Empathy

What Is Emotional Intelligence?

Emotional intelligence leads to the ability to recognize and manage your own emotions and the emotions of others.

Generally speaking, emotional intelligence includes at least three skills:

- Emotional awareness, or the ability to recognize or name one's emotions

- The ability to use these emotions and apply them to tasks such as thinking and problem solving

- The ability to deal with emotions, including regulating one's emotions when necessary and helping others to do the same

There is no validated psychological test or scale for emotional intelligence and no psychological test or scale for general intelligence factor "g." Many people believe that emotional intelligence is not an actual construction but a way of describing other names' interpersonal skills.

Despite this criticism, the concept of emotional intelligence (sometimes called emotional intelligence) is widely accepted. In recent years, few employers have even incorporated dynamic intelligence tests into their application and interview processes. The theory is that people with high emotional intelligence will become better leaders or colleagues.

Although some studies have found a link between emotional intelligence and job performance, many other classes do not correlate. Without a scientifically useful scale, it is difficult to measure or predict EQ at work or at home truly.

What Does Emotional Intelligence Mean?

An EQ person is highly aware of his emotional state, even negative emotions (frustration, sadness, or more subtle things), and can recognize and manage them. Such people particularly like the feelings experienced by others. Understandably, sensitivity to emotional signals in one's own internal and social environment makes a person a better friend, parent, leader, or romantic partner. Fortunately, these skills can be honed.

Tips for Emotional Intelligence

Performing these three steps consistently is a challenge... and ask the question: What skills can I practice to complete this process more effectively? We have developed a set of eight specific, learnable skills to make the process work appropriately through our research and experience.

Here are some ideas for getting started. First, remember that this is a loop. We may not have perfect consciousness or cannot determine the right choice, but it will become easier as we continue this process!

Knowing Yourself

- Everyone is present all the time. Who are you, not only obvious but also hidden in the background?

- Remember, emotion is data. They are chemical signals that help us deal with threats and opportunities.

Choose Yourself

When the situation starts to heat up, please "press the pause button." Hold your breath. Drink some water and say, "Let me think about it." There are very few situations that require an immediate response.

Remember, you have many choices. Sometimes it isn't easy to see these. You can change your mind, have new feelings, and try further actions. You may not have a "perfect solution," but it is indeed possible!

To Yourself

There are always more stories. When people do nasty things or say hurtful things, please be curious: what is going on?

Your choice is important. The way you respond affects others and affects you-so you affect the future. What effect do you want to produce?

What Is the Importance of Emotional Intelligence?

The term "emotional intelligence" first proposed by psychologists Mayer and Salovey (1990) refers to a person's ability to accurately and effectively perceive, process, regulate the inner emotional information of himself and others, and use it to guide his thoughts and knowledge. Act and influence the actions of others.

Emotional intelligence can lead us to a full and happy life by providing a framework through which intelligence standards are applied to emotional responses and understanding that these responses may be logically consistent or inconsistent with specific emotional beliefs.

With the development of the workplace, research institutions also support individuals with higher EI (from interns to managers) to make them more capable of uniting in the team, coping with changes, and managing pressure more effectively to be more Pursue goals effectively. Business goals.

Goleman (1995) recognizes the five different skills that constitute the critical characteristics of EI and suggests that, unlike human intelligence quotient (IQ), these classification skills can be learned in the absence and improved under existing conditions.

Therefore, EI is relatively fixed with its cousins, not IQ, but a dynamic aspect of psychology, and includes behavioral characteristics. These characteristics can produce significant benefits through hard work, personal happiness, and happiness to the professional background.

Emotional Intelligence in The Family

There is nothing like family. Our close ties to blood and marriage are expected to become our closest allies and our most significant source of love and support. However, our interactions with family members are often full of misunderstandings and resentments, quarrels, and scolding. The people we should know and know best ultimately feel like rivals or strangers.

Family is the source of our first and strongest emotional memory, and it is also the place where they continue to appear. This is why emotional intelligence (EQ) succeeds when other efforts to resolve family harmony fail. Active awareness and compassion (the ability to perceive, accept, and permanently adapt to ourselves and others) tell us how to respond to each other's needs.

Emotional intelligence is compelling in the family because it allows you to control your relationships with parents, children, siblings, in-laws, and extended families. When you know how you feel, you will not be manipulated by others' emotions, nor can you attribute family conflicts to everyone else. Therefore, most of the techniques to improve intimacy are centered on communicating your feelings with family and friends, while intimacy is centered on feelings.

Without this emotional intimacy, family contact will become a burden because no one would be willing to spend so much time with strangers. If you want your family to know and accept each other lovingly, you must start with your emotional honesty and openness. When you do this, the advice provided below has changed from knowledgeable reasonable advice to an efficient way to bring the family closer together. The following ten tips will bring you closer to your family and emotional intelligence.

5 High Emotional Intelligence Skills to Improve Family Relationships

1. If you wish to take care of anyone else, please take care of your health. The more time your family requires, the more exercise is needed. Maybe you and your family can find a way to exercise together.

2. Listen, if you want to hear. Lack of communication is the largest complaint in most families. The answer is, "Why don't they listen to me?" It may just be, "You don't listen to them."

3. Teach personal choices. Manage your emotions by making all feelings possible, but not all behaviors. A role model that respects and encourages others' feelings and rights but clearly shows that we can choose how to deal with our own emotions.

4. Teach generosity through acceptance and giving. Giving and receiving are part of the same continuum of love. If we do not provide, we will find it difficult to accept; we will have nothing to give if we cannot get it. This is why dedicating selflessness to the extreme does not help others.

5. Take responsibility for the content of your silent communication. Regardless of age, young children are particularly sensitive to nonverbal cues. Voice, posture (body language), or facial expressions convey our feelings better than our words. We must listen to our tone and look at ourselves in pictures and mirrors to assess our emotional consistency. Gritting your teeth will not make people feel love, but will be confused.

Emotional Intelligence

When scientific thought was first codified, the thought of rational intelligence came from the Enlightenment. An important principle of the early "natural philosophers" was the idea of rational objectivity—individuals should strive to look at the world not as they wish, but as it is. Although this idea sounds reasonable on the surface and has played a massive role in science and technology, it may also distract believers from intuition, tact, and even emotions to find solutions to common problems.

Rational intelligence focuses on "hard facts" and strict logical reasoning, leading to futile "lose-lose" scenarios. Although this idea is useful for building systems, the solution is usually found in an emotional intelligence toolkit once it is up and running.

What can we say about emotional intelligence? Gardner's classification provides some insights:

Interpersonal intelligence - discover and respond to the emotions, motivations, and desires of others.

Interpersonal intelligence - self-awareness and consistency with values, beliefs, and thoughts.

Combining these concepts provides an excellent overview of emotional intelligence and its relationship to business leadership. Without the guiding influence of rational intellect, emotional intelligence may become very subjective in ways that are not conducive to business goals. However, the proper use and use of it is essential to promote internal collaboration and external alliances.

EQ In the Workplace: The Key to Communication

In its most refined form, emotional intelligence provides the necessary empathy to understand the opinions of others fully, even when they contradict the opinions of others. Research shows that women who traditionally score higher on emotional intelligence tests tend to be more collaborative and inclusive leadership styles than men. Emotional intelligence is practiced by people of any gender and can provide many services to modern workplaces and stakeholders in all functions:

- By understanding the motivations of others, it can help leaders motivate and inspire good work.

- It brings more participants and helps avoid the many pitfalls of collective thinking.

- It enables leaders to be aware of opportunities that others may not realize and take action.

- It assists in the identification and resolution of conflicts in a fair and just manner.

- It can generate higher morale and help others discover their professional potential.

Like rational intelligence, emotional intelligence can also be cultivated through hard work and study. The first step in developing greater emotional intelligence is usually to strengthen your introspective ability. Knowing your thought process, emotions, and prejudices can help you make more comprehensive decisions. Exercising emotional intelligence often requires a person to act confidently, get rid of concerns about the state, and question or bypass knee reactions.

What Is Self-Awareness?

The definition of self-awareness is a clear understanding of one's character, including strengths, weaknesses, thoughts, beliefs, motivations, and emotions. Self-awareness allows you to understand other people, how they perceive you, your attitude, and current reactions to them. We may soon assume that we are self-aware, but this is not a skill measured in the binary form of "get" or "not get" (on/off) options. A specific range of awareness will help. When you have ever had a car accident, you may experience everything that happened in slow motion and notice the details of your thought process and events. This is a state of increased consciousness. With practice, we can learn to participate in these enhanced states and see new choices and opportunities for interpretation in our thoughts, emotions, and dialogue. Consciously creates opportunities to change behavior and beliefs.

A simple and quick assessment of self-awareness might be:

- Basic - Be aware of your thoughts when you have them.

- Intermediate - understand your current thoughts and emotions about your ideas.

- High - able to focus on your emotions and physical state in a relaxed way, thereby changing your thought process.

Perhaps you are at a higher level of self-awareness in a relaxed state. Still, under stress, you may shift to a moderate or primary level of self-awareness—even our position on the frequency spectrum changes based on other factors of the day.

What Is Empathy?

Empathy relates to the ability to understand others' feelings emotionally, see things from the perspective of others, and imagine yourself in your place. In essence, this is putting yourself in someone else's position and feeling what they must feel.

If you see another person suffering, you may be able to imagine yourself in the other person's position immediately and feel sympathy for what they are going through.

People usually adapt well to their feelings and emotions, but it may be more challenging to get into others' minds. It can be saying that the ability of empathy allows people to "walk a mile in other people's shoes." It enables people to understand the emotions of others.

It seems entirely incomprehensible for many people to see another person reacting in distress, even indifferent or even hostile. However, this is true for some people's reactions. This fact clearly shows that compassion is not necessarily a general response to the suffering of others.

Signs of Empathy

There are signs that you tend to be a considerate person:

- You are perfect at really listening to what others are saying.

- People often tell you their problems.

- You are good at understanding how others feel.

- You usually think about how other people feel.

- Others ask you for advice.

- You often feel overwhelmed by tragic events.

- You try to help the suffering person.

- You are good at telling people when they are dishonest.

- In social situations, you sometimes feel exhausted or overwhelmed.

- You care about others very much.

- You find it so difficult to set boundaries in your relationship with others.

Having great empathy will make you pay attention to the happiness and well-being of others. However, this also means that sometimes you will always feel overwhelmed, exhausted, or even over-excited by thinking about other people's emotions.

73. Improve Your Communication and Social Skills

What Are Social Skills?

Social skills are used every day to communicate with others in various ways, including verbal, nonverbal, written, and visual methods. Social skills are also called interpersonal or soft skills.

Language skills involve oral language, and non-verbal communication includes body language, facial expressions, and eye contact. Whenever you interact with others, you use social skills in a certain way. Strong social skills can help you build or maintain professional and personally successful relationships.

Why Social Skills Are Important

Social skills are very important because they can help you communicate more effectively, thereby establishing, maintaining, and developing relationships with colleagues, customers, and new contacts. Regardless of your position, industry, or experience level, these skills are important to maintain and improve.

There are many benefits to your career by developing social skills to invest in relationships, including:

- Get ideas, information, technology, and opinions from people in different professional fields.

- Provide your own opinions for the benefit of others

- Complete tasks and collaborate with others to achieve common goals

- Provide mutual support for difficult or difficult to navigate situations

- Expand your network to understand and seek new opportunities

- Get feedback and recommendations from people who can personally prove your job, skills, and qualities (you can do the same for them)

- Make the workplace more enjoyable.

It is also important to demonstrate your social skills during the recruitment process. Establishing work and relationships with others effectively is an important quality that employers seek among applicants. It can indicate whether you are suitable for their company culture.

To show social skills in your cover letter, please give an example of how long you have worked with others to accomplish a goal that brings success to the team or organization. In your resume, list specific, measurable achievements, and then you can elaborate on how to use social skills to achieve your goals during the interview.

Basic Rules of Ground Communication

Pay attention to the verbal or nonverbal communication of others. Ask others how they feel or what they are thinking, rather than making assumptions. If you are not sure, please repeat what you think the other person said. Pause for a while, then think about what to say before speaking. Make eye contact. Avoid side conversations. Turn off the phone.

Speak Directly, Honestly, And Concisely

Share your ideas. Speak for yourself. Communicate agreements or disagreements. Don't think that others know how you feel or what you are thinking: tell them. If needed, ask for help to clarify what you have to say speak loudly.

Tell the Truth About Yourself

Attention, sincere, and true. Synchronize mind and body, and stay here and now. State your feelings and beliefs.

Let Everyone Have A Chance to Speak

Wait for the host to approve. Allow other people to speak without disturbing them. Work with the host so that everyone has a chance to speak. No one can lead the conversation. If you are worried that you forgot to say something, please write it down.

Assuming kindness

If you don't understand, please clarify. Confirm the feelings expressed by others. Don't attribute it to the motives of others.

Mutual Respect

Respect others. Avoid judging, accusing, or patronizing others. Avoid irony and other forms of emotional coercion and clearly explain your disagreement with an idea. Talk about this when you disagree or criticize instead of focusing on the individual.

Respect the Group

Use the basic rules of caring communication. Follow the time agreement. Respect the host. Avoid arguing or participating in other destructive behaviors. Resolve personal conflicts, not in groups.

How to Deal with Difficult People

We all have such difficult people in our lives that make us crazy! They are annoying, frustrating, and exhausting, but I have some ways to help you cope with them.

Here are few thoughts on how to deal with people in difficulties in life:

Identify 4 Types

There are four different types of people in difficulty. Think about the person in your life or figure out which category they belong to:

- Downers are also known as negative Nancy or Debbie Downers. They always have something to say. They complain, criticize, and judge. They are almost impossible to please.

- The better dunes are also called omniscient, upper, or show off. They like to try to impress you, name them, and compare them.

- Passive is also called push-ups, yes people, and weak people. They are not very helpful to the conversation or the people around them and let others work hard.

- Tanks are also called explosive, very few, or bossy. They want their way and will do their best.

Don't Try to Change Them

When we meet a difficult person or a person in our family or circle of friends, and our instinct is to try to change them. We tried to encourage Downers to become more active, Passives stood up, Tank calmed down, Better Thanks became humbler. This will never work! If you try to change someone, they will resent you, dig their heels, and get worse.

Try to Understand Them

The way to disengage people in difficulty is to try to understand where they come from. I tried to find their value language. Values are what someone values most. Decide what they decide. For some people, it's money. For others, it is power or knowledge. This not only helped me understand them, but also helped them relax their minds and become more open. For example, sometimes Tanks want to explain their point of view. If you let them talk to you, you might help them avoid a breakdown or try to control the situation.

Don't Make Them Poisonous

Some difficult people may be toxic. Toxic people may be negatively aggressive, mean, or harmful. Therefore, if you have to deal with them, you can understand their source and keep your distance. The toxic relationship is unhealthy. Consequently, you need to create a buffer zone by surrounding yourself with good friends, reducing the meeting with them, and, if you must be with them, you need to complete it in the shortest time.

74. Public Speaking

What Is Public Speaking?

This is a live demonstration in front of the audience. Public speaking can cover a wide variety of topics. The primary purpose of the speech may be to educate, entertain, or influence the audience. Usually, visual aids in electronic slides are used to supplement the voice and make the audience more interested.

The presentation of a public speech is different from an online indication because the online exhibition can be viewed and listened to at the viewer's convenience. In contrast, public speech is usually limited to a specific time or place. Online presentations typically consist of a slide show of the speaker or pre-recorded video (including recordings of live public speeches).

Since public speeches are conducted in front of a live audience, speakers need to consider some unique factors. We will discuss these in the short term, but first, let's take a quick look at public speaking history.

Public Speaking Myths

We discuss five main myths below.

Myth 1: To Be A Good Speaker, You Must Be "Natural."

Reality: Anyone can be an excellent public speaker. Tom Monaghan, the founder of Domino's Pizza, was the owner of the Detroit Tigers. He was born with strong operating skills and set the industry standard for record-breaking pizza making. But he will freeze in front of the crowd and join Toastmasters to help him shine in front of a large audience.

Myth 2: Experienced Speakers Will Not Be Nervous

Reality: According to Mark Twain, there are two kinds of speakers globally: 1) nervous people and 2) liars. The trick to overcoming nerves is to know that you are in control.

Billionaire investor Warren Buffett (Warren Buffett) said before overcoming the fear he used to throw up before speeches. Buffett started speaking in front of small groups until he became more comfortable, and he is now one of the coveted speakers in the world.

Myth 3: Introverts Are Not Good Public Speakers

Reality: If you are quiet, shy, or introverted, you can be as good as any outgoing social colleague in a public speech. Susan Cain is a self-styled introvert and the author of the New York Times bestseller "Quiet: And the Power of Introverts in a World That Can't Stop Talking" she wants to let herself talk about her in front of a large number of people. Book, so she joined the local Toastmasters club. "Participating in the club gives me the ability to get used to public speaking in a safe way," Cain said.

Myth 4: Remember the Best Speech

Reality: Perform a speech in front of an audience. The speech will provide you with valuable feedback, but don't remember. Patricia Fripp, the award-winning keynote speaker, warned: "You should not remember your entire speech, but your opening remarks, points, and conclusions. Then, rehearse enough so that you can "forget it."

Myth 5: When Speaking, You Must Stop Behind the Podium

Reality: The best speeches or TED talks are usually based on actions. When it fits your presentation, walking around and using gestures can make your speech easy. Former NBA player Mark Eaton, a Utah Jazz center, was often constrained by his tall 7-foot-4 frame till he learned how to use gestures and movements in speeches. "I realized that I had to learn how to get rid of this sense of self and learn how to be satisfied with who I am," said Eaton, who joined Toastmasters and is now a professional speaker.

How to Start A Speech?

That was a terrible moment. You have just been invited to the stage, the audience remains silent, waiting for you to open their mouths, now it's your turn.

How do you say how do you start your speech with strength and confidence instead of the usual "Erm...thank you so much for inviting me here..."

The simple fact is... From the beginning of your speech, the audience will judge you. And it may sound harsh, but it is true. Therefore, it is best to start speaking with certainty and confidence and quickly establish contact with the audience to be eager to hear what you have to say next.

There are many ways to start a speech, but they are not limited to the words you use. Creating a good first impression is not just your beginning.

- Prepare to be yourself!

- First word

- Tell your story

- Try different methods

- Reconnect with yourself

How to End A Speech?

These are three effective ways to end a speech. Each item can ensure that your speech ends forcefully, rather than endlessly to ensure forgetting.

You need to summarize the most important points and then end the selection:

- Strong offer

- A challenge

- Call back

To figure out which way to use and ask yourself what you want others to do or feel after listening to your speech. E.g.;

- Do you need to motivate them to work so harder?

- Do you need them to join the cause you want to promote?

- Do you need them to remember a person and his unique qualities?

The ending you choose should support the overall purpose of your presentation.

Let's take a look at three different scenes that show every way to end the speech.

How to End A Speech with A Strong Offer?

The purpose of your presentation is to inspire people to join your business. Specifically, you want their signatures to appear on the petition lobby to make changes, and you have everything ready so that they can sign as soon as they stop speaking.

You have summarized the main points and want to make a statement to prompt the audience to take action.

Borrowing words from a respected and respected leader can align your career with the cause they are fighting for, thus fusing the past with the present.

How to End A Speech with A Challenge

The purpose of your presentation is to motivate your sales team. You have introduced the main points, including the introduction of incentives-holidays for the best sales performance in the next three weeks. You have summarized the main points and reached the closing sentence. Ultimately, it is a challenge.

How to End A Speech with A Callback?

The purpose of your speech is to commemorate a dear friend who passed away. You have briefly reviewed the main points of the speech and hope to leave an intoxicating and convincing impression on the audience.

In the early days of the speech, you told a poignant story. It's you to return or call back.

75. Using Body Language When Public Speaking

What Is Body Language and Its Importance in Public Speaking?

Body language is part of nonverbal communication. It is a combination of movement, gesture, and posture. This includes the way the speaker speaks, moves, and views the stage. Body language is part of the message that the speaker wants to convey.

Many people think that body language is just your posture on stage. So, this is a big part of it, but there is more. Body language shows your confidence. The correct stage attitude will give you a breath of authority, which can support your story.

The Importance of The Body Language in Public Speaking

Why is body language important? You can say that body language errors can make your speech almost unsuccessful. It would help if you had other talents to make up for bad body language.

Some examples of bad body language include: turning your eyes back to the audience, walking around, or hiding behind a table. Gestures can also adversely affect your speech. Gestures are too aggressive; playing drums or even biting nails are bad examples.

However, even if you perform well at work, improving your body language can greatly affect you. Especially on the way, the audience will hear you. This may make a difference between a good conversation and persuading people. This is why everyone must pay attention to.

The Art of Reading People

Several people seem to be born with social wisdom. But for most of us, this is something that develops or develops slowly over time.

If your parents instructed you not to cry when you were young or tend to say "good" when doing anything else, you might be less perceptual than your family members who figure out how they felt during dinner. Psychologist Dr. David Caruso said that he is the co-founder of EI Skills Group, a company based in Connecticut dedicated to training people's emotional intelligence. (There are some exceptions: for example, it may be difficult for people with autism to detect subtle differences.) Your daily activities can also affect your social intelligence. If you spend more time using glue on the screen, it will be less likely to understand other people's social cues accurately, or even at first. Last year, a study published in "Computer of Human Behavior" found that sixth-grade students went to outdoor training camps to give up their smartphones, iPads, and TV turkeys for only five days, and their readers' emotions were better than those of sixth-grade students in the same grade Much better. I did not go to the camp to give up the school of digital equipment.

Now, for the benefit. First of all, social intelligence plays a pivotal role in your health. Few studies have shown that people who are socially connected are happier, have lower blood pressure, are less susceptible to colds, and even live longer than isolated people. Social knowledge may also be just the secret of professional success. According to a 2014 research in the Journal of Organizational Behavior, employees who are good at reading emotions and using other skills such as social skills tend to earn higher incomes. The co-author of the study, Dr. Yongmei Liu, an associate professor at the Illinois State University School of Business, said: "People with emotional intelligence are also more likely to become team leaders and show greater leadership effectiveness.

Social intelligence skills can be used for face-to-face interactions (for example, a grumpy teller who wins a bank) and virtual interactions (for example, sending emails to sensitive colleagues). Here are some emotional detective skills that can make all encounters more rewarding and successful.

Relaxed Body Language

A relaxed body usually has no tension. Muscles relax. Movement is not fixed, and the person generally seems happy or irrelevant.

Relaxed Body

Trunk

The torso may sag slightly to one side (but cannot be held still due to irregular tension). The shoulders can also be balanced, and the shoulders above the pelvis should be balanced. Although it may curl in a quiet position, it will not curl in fear.

The shoulders are not taut and usually hang loosely.

Breathe

Breathing is steady and slow. This may make the sound lower than usual.

Color

The skin color is usually normal, neither turning red due to anger or embarrassment nor turning white due to fear. There are no abnormal patches, such as on the neck or cheeks.

Relax Limbs

Relax your limbs and hang. They don't twitch, and they rarely cross each other unless it is for comfort.

Arms

The tension arm is tough and can fit tightly to the body. They may move suddenly and intermittently. A relaxed arm can hang loosely or move smoothly.

If the arms cross each other, their hands will loosen. Of course, any crossover may indicate some tension. Folding arms may be very comfortable.

Hand

When we feel anxious, we often touch ourselves with our hands, squeeze ourselves, or express tension in other ways.

A relaxed hand will loosen or be used to enhance what we are saying. They are usually open and may shape ideas in the air. The gestures are open and gentle, not sudden or tense.

Legs

Sitting legs may sit gently on the floor or throw them away at random. They may listen to music in time with the tap of their toes. They may cross, but they will not entangle each other.

Please note that the legs may be a special sign of hidden tension when a person controls the upper body and arms. When they sit at the dining table, what you see may relax, but the legs may tighten and wrap.

Relaxed Head

There is the main mark on a relaxed face.

Mouth

The person may smile gently or broadly without any signs of a grimace. Otherwise, the mouth will be relatively still.

When speaking, the mouth is opened moderately, neither moving nor moving. The sound sounds relaxed, with no unusually high pitches and no sudden pitch or speed changes.

Eye

Smile with your mouth, especially in the small wrinkles on the side of the eyes.

A relaxed gaze will look directly at the other person without staring and will hardly blink. The eyes are usually dry. Eyebrows are stable or may move with speech. They do not frown.

Somewhere Else

Other muscles of the face usually relax. The forehead is the main indicator, and the lines only appear with a soft expression. The sides of the face will not be pulled back.

When the head moves, it will speak smoothly and maintain other expressions promptly.

76. How to Communicate Through the Face

Talking to Yourself Is Perfectly Normal

Are you talking to yourself? We mean to express it out loud, not just under your breath or on your head-almost everyone does it.

This habit usually starts in childhood and can easily become second nature. Even if you find that there is nothing wrong with talking to yourself (and you shouldn't!), you may want to know what other people think, especially when you often think aloud at work or in the grocery store.

If you are worried that this habit is a bit strange, you can relax. Even if you do this often, it is normal to speak to yourself. When you want to be better at talking to yourself, you can avoid doing so in certain situations. And we have provided some tips that can help you.

Why Is This Not A Bad Thing

In addition to being completely accustomed, private or self-directed speech (the scientific term for talking to yourself) can benefit you in many ways.

It Can Help You Find Things

You have just completed an impressive shopping list. Congratulations on memorizing everything you need next week or so, and you can set off to the store. But did you leave the list? You searched around in the house and murmured, "shopping list, shopping list."

Of course, your list cannot be responded to. But according to a 2012 study, saying aloud the name of the content you are looking for can make it easier to find it than simply thinking about the product.

The author recommends this because hearing the product name will remind your brain of what you want. This can help you visualize and notice it more easily.

It Can Help You Stay Focused

Recall the last time you did something difficult. Even if the description clearly shows that this is a two-person job, maybe you built the bed yourself. Or maybe you have to undertake the extremely technical task of repairing your computer.

You may feel frustrated by some exclamation marks (or even foul language). You may also talk about the most difficult part and even think of your progress when you want to give up. In the end, you are successful, and it may be helpful to talk to yourself.

Explaining the process out loud to yourself can help you see the solution and solve the problem because it helps you focus on each step.

Asking yourself some questions, even simple or rhetorical questions-"What would happen if I put this part here?" can also help you focus on the task at hand.

How to Relax Facial Muscles?

Our facial expressions reflect our emotions, and they often do so without our knowledge. Although this can help us communicate, it also means that our faces tend to carry the signs and pressures of our inner emotional life. Fortunately, there are several ways to help relax these important muscles, from whole-body methods (which minimize systemic stress) to specific facial exercises (which can help you release tension).

Use Relaxation Techniques

Take A Break and Pay Attention to The Jaw Muscles

The best way to prevent tension is first to learn how to avoid clenching your jaw muscles. You may find that in some cases, you clenched your teeth or had facial discomfort. Please pay attention to the impact of these activities or moments on you, pay attention to them, and then stop straining your face and jaw.

- Bad habits are hard to break. Be patient, but persevere.

Change Your Resting Posture to Minimize Tension

If you are sitting at your desk or working on a job while driving, do you find that your jaw is clenched? Reduce the tension on the face or jaw by changing the static position of the mouth. And place your tongue on the top of your mouth and let your jaw hang down. Breathe deeply through your nose often.

- Many people will tighten their jaws without realizing they are doing it.

Practice Progressive Muscle Relaxation to Calm the Facial Muscles

Choose a quiet place where you can sit or lie down. Take a deep breath, concentrate first, raise your eyebrows as much as possible to tighten the muscles of your forehead. Then relax. Next, try to frown. Then relax. From there, move to your eyes. Squeeze them, then release them. Traverse the rest of the facial muscles and relax each group tightly. Take at least a little time every day to focus on the muscles of the face, neck, and other parts so that you can get rid of the tension, which can cause pain or discomfort.

- By concentrating on specific parts of your face or body, gradual relaxation can enhance your awareness of physical stress and help you eliminate it.

- Extend its benefits by moving from the face, head, and neck to the entire body.

Ways to Stop Being Afraid of Others' Judgment

People do their best to avoid the possibility of being negatively evaluated by others. They avoid telling others what they want to tell them. They will not yell out in class or work meetings. They avoid telling their lover their true wishes. They do not ask for a raise. They will not tell the new dates where they want to eat.

This fear of judgment is associated with the desire to be liked by everyone.

Although this is impossible, this is a failed game, which prevents people from experiencing and expressing their true selves without restriction.

Let's face it; humans are always judging others (good/bad or like/dislike), and there are many nuances between the two. With the arrival of new information, human thoughts are re-evaluated: this is a continuous process.

Instead of doing anything, you don't have to say anything about your preferences but work overtime to try to shape people's lives so that they don't judge you. You can accept this process instead.

Here are four ways to let people live without fear of judgment:

Never Ending

The reality is that the human brain has limited data reserves. Although we may judge, these judgments have little meaning and cannot occupy a permanent place in our memory bank. Therefore, when someone makes a judgment on you, it is likely that the judge will make them unconscious after a moment or a few days. We build an understanding of people, not based on small mistakes or frustrations we observe, but on the big things they do or say, how they interact with us, and the patterns established overtime—kind of mode.

The Judgment Is Inevitable

Don't try to control the judgment of others. Asking others not to judge us has become part of the spirit of our age. Consider some popular statements such as "no judgment" and "this is a non-judgment zone." All of this is to no avail: you cannot control the thoughts of others. Maybe they will not express their judgment, but this does not mean that they can stop the physical brain process.

Alternatively, try to explain the context of what you feel so that the people you are open to understand and sympathize with you. Compassion is the stone of judgment. When it exists, judgment is not great because people can imagine themselves feeling the same.

Let Them Judge!

Only allow a judgment to release intimacy. In any case, don't stop yourself from becoming open or vulnerable or sharing things that are not good for you but important. As I mentioned in the book "5 Steps to Building Self-Esteem", if you find yourself shrinking from being afraid of judgments, please ask yourself: "What kind of judgments would I be afraid of because of my openness? "And "What is this? I am worried that it will happen if they make a special judgment on me?"

Once you have identified the fear, try to reassure yourself or find a way to resolve the fear (if it does). Remind yourself that when people risk judgment, intimacy and intimacy will deepen. If this kind of openness does not happen, it does not necessarily mean that you did something wrong. Still, it may mean that the person you associate with is not capable of establishing emotional intimacy.

Pay Attention to Your Judgment

There is no better way than judging yourself and others less to care less about others' judgments. Of course, judgment is inevitable, but please pay attention to using your own words to talk about people and things in life.

Change the focus of your judgment: ask yourself, what is the influence of this person on you, you want to avoid or realize in the future, instead of "making her bad" or "he is a loser." For example, "She never keeps her promise to me." Or, "He tells me he is working hard, but I always end up disappointed." From the good and bad characteristics of those in life to be healthy and healthy for your Unhealthy things.

77. Conclusion

When anxiety becomes a third member in a relationship, suffering appears. The style of communication changes, discussions, irritability, and even emotional coldness appear. It is necessary to be attentive to the indicators. However, how anxiety affects our environment's relationships will always depend on the extent to which the person is located.

We can all suffer stress at a certain time, feel more anxious than normal on a few specific days. Some unknowingly drag a generalized anxiety disorder or other disorders in which anxiety is present for years.

Anxiety affects the quality of our relationships and can do so in many ways. Each case is unique, and every experience is exceptional, but there are always some repeated patterns. Some people take many years to receive a diagnosis, which causes them to build, for example, effective relationships where unhappiness is always breathed.

In other cases, the couple itself is aware that something is happening. There is a sudden change in behavior, communication, and even health or lifestyle. In these latter situations, it is easier to identify the problem, and it is also a moment when the greatest possible support is needed.

In conclusion, as we can see, anxiety affects the quality of our relationships. The same is true of other conditions, such as depression or any other type of mental illness. In these circumstances, the most necessary in all cases is understanding, closeness, and stainless support to convince the affected person to seek specialized help. The key to communication and relationships is awareness. What is this strange word? You have to be aware of what?

I'm going to ask you a question. Did you ever get to be able to explain because Dude seemed weird to you that day? Or when, at a job interview, Caio didn't give you a chance?

That's probably because you said one thing with words while your body said another. Yes, because the body can betray emotions. Which, if you don't understand from the interlocutor, interprets them in its way, and it's usually never the correct meaning.

Like a flu vaccine, knowing how to communicate and listen effectively perform a preventative function against these problems. And they solve the relationship difficulties. In open dialogue, I believe a lot in communication effectiveness in knowing how to choose the right words, both towards the person and the specific situation.

For this reason, I have designed a pre-training course that aims to provide useful guidance on how to best use your communication tool. I titled it "Not only communicate to express strength, charisma, and personality."

Thus, thanks to our communication style's mastery, knowing how to identify the right words concerning the situation allows us to create good and effective interpersonal relationships. It is effective communication that allows us always to be masters of ourselves and situations. It is always an effective communication that gives us the charisma and the strength to manage aggressive people, those who put us in difficulty, those who make us feel wrong and anxious.

Part 4

MINDFULNESS MEDITATION FOR ANXIETY

78. Introduction

When we experience stress and anxiety, it is often merely worrying over the past or fears that we are having about the future. The best way to overcome these constant fears is to be mindful in the present moment to keep your thoughts grounded in reality. In this meditation, we will help you stay aware of focusing on what matters the most—healing.

You cannot heal if your thoughts and emotions are glued to some period that is out of your control. You cannot change the past, so guilt and remorse are only going to keep you stuck in a different dimension. In this meditation, you will learn precisely what it means to stay in the present moment to start the healing process.

Meditation For Self-Healing Mindfulness

For this meditation, you will want to be in a completely comfortable place. It is preferred that you do this meditation when you can fall asleep afterward, but that's also not entirely necessary. Doing this outside where you can take a nap with nature would also be an excellent way to feel this meditation's beneficial effects fully.

This will be a visualization exercise that will help take your mind to a calm and relaxed place. You will remove any thoughts that keep you glued to some period you cannot change. To feel the benefit of this meditation, focus on your breathing, and keep a clear mind.

Anytime that thought starts to travel into your mind, gently push it away. You do not have to force them out of your mind. You do not have to block out negative thoughts and punish yourself for having them. Simply let them drift in and out like a car passing you by. There is no need to latch onto these thoughts, and you don't need to shove them to a corner of your brain. Let them come into your mind and push them out as soon as they do.

Keep every part of your body relaxed and let your eyes gently close—no need to hold them closed tightly to the point that you are straining yourself. Let your eyelids gently stay shut. We are going to count down from twenty. When we reach one, you will be into the meditation. Let your mind become wholly black and continue to feel the air come in and out of your body.

Respire In For Five And Out For Five.

Your mind is entirely blank. You do not see anything at all.

In your mind, you start to see a small bright dot. The dot continues to grow bigger and bigger until you discover that you are engulfed in sunlight.

You look around and discover that lush, green trees surround you. Each thing that you see around you is a reminder that you are a part of nature. All of these various aspects are part of a living ecosystem in which you are also operating.

As you look in front of you, you see a little trail between some of the trees. You take a step forward and begin to walk around. You can feel like the dirt and the leaves crunch beneath your feet. There's a light breeze, but nothing that is keeping you too chilled at this moment. You can see bits of the sky above you. Bright blue is beaming through the break of the leaves. You continue to walk forward and see in front of you that there are multiple paths.

Now, many individuals have already walked down this path themselves before. You are not concerned with what has happened over the past or the potentials of the future. You are wholly grounded in the present moment and only focused on this at the time being. Breathe in this good energy and breathe out anything that has been keeping you trapped in a place you do not have control over. All that you have experienced leading up to this moment has brought you to be the exact person you are. Even if you are not happy with who this person is at the present moment, there will be one day where everything makes sense. You will be able to look back on your past and know that each struggle was just another step towards making you the individual you are. Not everything has been easy for you until this point, but it has been a learning experience that teaches you something greater about yourself. Breathe in now as you begin to accept the things that have happened in your past. Breathe out as you are letting go of any of the emotions that you have experienced. You continue to walk towards more trees, and you think about how nature is so incredible. You are a part of all of these living things. No matter what these trees and flowers and other little plants might experience, they continue to live on. Nobody is tending to them.

These plants don't have a gardener who comes and makes sure that they are free from any diseases or root rot. Nobody is watering them and nurturing them. They're able to take care of themselves on their own because they are a part of a more extensive system. Bugs help keep them pollinated, and plants around them will also aid in how they grow. Animals might come and feast on them, and they soak up as much sun and rain as they possibly can.

This is a reminder of the powerful ability that all living things have to carry on, no matter the circumstances. Your body will always be there and provide you with the nourishment and fulfillment needed to make sure that you are as healthy as possible. No matter what you give to your body, whether it is something healthy, or a type of junk food, you will be able to take the most important and beneficial aspects of this using your body. Everything that exists inside of you is something that happens on its own. You don't have to voice your body how to process and break down food. It naturally does this all. All of this is a reminder that you are a part of a more excellent living organism. This earth is flowing around so freely and gently, as it should be. You continue to walk forward, and you notice that there is a little pond. You walk up to it and see that there are some small fish swimming around at the bottom. These fish could be a source of food.

These fish could be somebody else's family. These fish are their living organisms, and they are merely existing. They swim against the current, and they look for food on the top of the surface. No matter what they might experience, their main focus will always be on continuing to live. It is a powerful reminder that when you feel lost, you can always rest assured that your intention and purpose is to carry on living, breathing simply.

Breathe in as you notice the site and breathe out as you let go of any sort of thoughts that are keeping you glued somewhere else. It is okay to think and plan for the future. And we all have moments where we reflect on the past. The issue comes when you obsess over these things. If you are only thinking in different periods, other than what is occurring now, you will not give your full energy to the everyday items surrounding you. Breathe in the excitement over staying mindful and productive at this moment. Breathe out any desire to remain stuck in a different time.

You look down and notice the fish. You could grab any one of them that you wanted. This pond isn't that large and not that deep. You would probably be able to pick one up as long as you gave it a few tries.

This is something within your power, and you have a choice. You choose not to and instead let these fish continue swimming on. There's no point in taking one of these fish from the pond. Sure, you might be able to use it for food then, but you don't need that. You simply continue to watch as these fish float around. You don't scare them away, and you don't try to move them. They're simply there. This is how we need to start to treat our thoughts. Our thoughts can sometimes just be like fish swimming around in a fishbowl. The views will always be there. They won't go away. The thing is, you don't have to feed these fish. You don't have to pick them up. You don't have to move them around. You don't have to kill them. You don't have to do anything. You can simply let them continue to swim around and around. Your thoughts do not have to be given attention. These thoughts can come into your mind, but you don't have to be afraid and push them out negatively. Instead, you can simply focus on yourself and create a positive and healthy mindset. When you have negative thoughts, remember that they can simply swim away like fish. Breathe in and out, in and out.

You sit after the pond and close your eyes once again. You dip your toes down into the cold water. Even though it is a fall day, it is not freezing just yet, and instead, the water reminds you of the last little bit of summer that's left. Breathe in and out, in and out. You close your eyes and lay back against a thick layer of leaves on the ground. You feel completely comfortable, at peace and ease. Breathe in and out, in and out.

You close your eyes, and everything starts to fade away once again. All is becoming black, and there are no thoughts left that are traveling through your mind.

This is a safe and relaxing place that you can travel back to anytime that it is needed. You are entirely at ease, and peace is seeping out of every last one of your pores. You have no thoughts that are keeping you stuck in a hostile place now. You cannot heal unless you are relaxed and free from the fears that have been holding you back for so long.

Continue to feel yourself relax. You are sinking deeper and deeper and further and further into the couch.

There isn't a single thing that is keeping you held back at this moment. You are entirely relaxed and at ease. We are going to count down from twenty once again.

79. Defining Meditation

Meditation is a skill that is acquired through dedicated training of the mind and practice. Meditation is compared to fitness and exercise about body training and

overall wellness. The training includes claims to train the attention or to achieve a calmness or a forgiving mood. The dictionary defines meditation as the deep thinking of something or focusing one's mind for some time on one specific thing without losing focus. Meditation is also defined as the artistic nature of giving attention to one thing or engaging in mental exercise to heighten spiritual awareness and understanding.

According to psychology, meditation is highly characteristic of its role in getting beyond the reflective discursive thinking beyond the logical mind achieving a deeper, more devout, and more relaxed state. It brings forth general mental well-being like calmness, clarity, and concentration. On the other hand, meditation is also viewed as a practice that self regulates the body and mind, affecting mental events. Other psychologists define meditation as a stylized mental technique practiced in repetition to attain a subjective experience that in mind describing it will be having a very restful, silent, blissful, and highly heightened alertness state of mind.

Hence, meditation is believed to be the acquisition of peace and quietness against every day, stressing life and opening doors to the deepest and divine parts of our lives. Meditation helps to train in awareness, thus getting a healthy sense of perspective by observing your thoughts and feelings without being judgmental and understanding them with time.

Having mentioned that meditation is a skill that means meditation has to be learned, it is reasonable to look at reflection like muscle exercise, which one has not done before. Therefore, for the muscle exercise to work and be comfortable with the body system, one will need to do a lot of practice. To get to a level of comfort, understanding, and doing the right thing, one must have a teacher or a trainer who will guide and help one do the exercise in knowledge. Learning from a knowledgeable person is critical in getting it right and concerns within a specific time.

They knew the art and the skill of meditation and are willing to pass the knowledge to those interested. As such, it is necessary to take advantage of such people and learn more about meditation.

Meditation is a practice that is not always as easy as it may seem. Those who have done it for long will say how, when meditating, there are times when they will lose focus, and the mind will wander and consequently cause them to forget to follow the breath.

They say the way the mind loses focus and begins to wonder is just part of the memorable experience they are creating. The critical role of meditation is consistency and willingness. Meditation, in other words, is termed as one of those things where the journey is what is more important than the destination. Meditation puts more value on the trip, the practice, the commitment, and dedication to achieve a peaceful state of mind.

During meditation, it might take time before your mind gets comfortable with the whole exercise. Chances that setbacks will be present are very high, but the good news is that those setbacks are part of the meditation process. It needs a lot of practice, and just the fact that you are creating time for training and learning is very important in the journey of meditation. One primary invariant ingredient in meditation is the meditator's crucial need to sustain their attention through the concentration or the mindfulness of the whole process. With the retention of engagement, achieving the skillful nature o meditation can be attained.

More often than not, we are controlled and dominated by our thoughts or feelings. Under normal circumstances, we believe we are precisely what those thoughts and feelings say we are. For example, when we have ideas that this is a sad situation, we somehow reflect the sadness on our faces, and in the long run, we feel anxious and stressed. The same applies to the feeling of joy and happiness. We focus on something as being good, then the sense of satisfaction is reflected on our faces as laughter or a smile. Meditation picks us up by letting us be, giving us a positive experience without any interference of our state of being. Meditation is then concluded to be the natural state of nature, and that is why more than often, it is thought that we can read an individual's thoughts by looking at their faces, which is a clear reflection of what is their minds or what they are experiencing at that exact moment.

Meditation is made up of different techniques that we shall expand on each other than in the teachings. The meditative methods, processes, or devices are then how we create an intimate personal ambiance, which is the facilitation force that disconnects the body and the mind and allows one to be. Of great importance is setting aside time from practicing the meditation techniques and finding which method would work well in an everyday life practice context without affecting your work schedule, leisure, and interaction with people at different levels.

80. Origin And History Of Meditation

Some meanings define the concept of 'meditation.' For this reason, it can be so perplexing for those that attempt to engage with it and achieve its goals. The purest description of its meaning is that it is the way, or the journey, by which a person is led internally to a state of being consisting of calm awareness and keen intuition. Therefore, it is more accurate to understand meditation as a tool to help reach an ultimate objective, rather than an end in itself.

It is typical for the chanting of repetitious words or phrases, or a commitment to focus entirely on some external image, to be used in meditative practices as a means to assist a practitioner in their attempts to transcend the chaos of ordinary thought. These practices are usually deeply immersed in particular cultural traditions, and it can be argued that they constitute several principles that aren't relevant to modern society. It is often argued that certain aspects of these traditions restrict them from merely scratching the surface in terms of spiritual experience, leaving the deepest current needs undiscovered and unresolved.

Of course, it can give some relief from the relentless compulsions and distractions of uncontrolled thought and emotion, and traditional meditation techniques can provide this relief. But a genuine transcendence of mental chaos comes from some analysis of our thoughts' content so that psychological considerations can be incorporated into our practice, rather than teaching yourself to ignore thoughts and thus push what could be more troubling content into the unconscious mind. Many complexes, neuroses, and problems may be present in the average person's mind, and the only way these can indeed be addressed is by listening to the thoughts they cause. Don't be conned into thinking that one can achieve a transcendental, detached existence by simply conditioning oneself to avoid or ignore ideas; psychology teaches us that doing so will bury those thoughts in places where they will continue to pull on our minds and bodies.

To be liberated from their hold over us, we must learn to understand them for what they are, a consequence of emotional and psychological needs and desires at every level of our being.

There is a constructive, healthy way of thinking. Its opposing, destructive alternative, and the real purpose of meditation must bring a practitioner to a profound understanding of that distinction between thought patterns.

Exploring The Subconscious Mind

Through its inherent comprehension of the distinction between healthy and unhealthy thinking, a healthy mind will be enabled to entertain thought as the origin of inspired inner direction and creativity. Thus, with the correct application of meditating with purpose, our practice encourages the capacity to possess a mind of the utmost discernment, to be able to make clear and accurate decisions as to which thought patterns are worthy of support and which need to be eliminated from the mind as they arise.

Furthermore, it must be understood that any form of meditation that purports to achieve quick results is likely to be a relatively superficial practice—reaching the depth of knowledge that we uphold as the ultimate objective of meditation takes time and discipline. A meditation practice that is exceptionally challenging and slow to progress in the early stages is the type that will eventually lead to more profound results if a practitioner can persevere with it. There are no shortcuts in meditation, and any techniques that purport to offer them will never take you to the purest of conclusions.

The truth is, it is far easier to merely ignore the observation of thought content than it is to confront it directly. Once you have learned, through a meditative practice, some techniques for not engaging with thoughts, you will find it becomes increasingly easy to do so; proponents of meditation with purpose will say that this practice method will never lead to the pure objective of self-renewal. They will state that to achieve a calm and centered state of existence, one must be prepared to direct their practice towards integrating the promotion of healthy thinking into their meditation, reserving the ability to not engage with thoughts only for when malicious thought processes arise.

Learning to connect with and understand the subconscious mind takes time and dedication. In subconscious thought processes, we can find all the forces and desires that play upon our conscious mind and motivate us to feel and act in how we do. Facing this dimension of the mind forces us to confront our imperfections and inadequacies by examining the thoughts that affect us from a level beneath our conscious awareness.

These thoughts are alive but mostly undetected until they find a way to surface in emotion or desire that directs our conscious thoughts and actions.

Individual research groups have devised a method of identifying or detecting latent, subconscious thought derivations using a device similar to the polygraph machine used in lie-detecting tests. The person undergoing the test is encouraged to look into their past to discover memories that instigate a significant emotional response, identified by the 'biofeedback machine' registering the changes those emotions cause in certain body functions. Through this method, a person can discover unacknowledged past feelings that have been buried in the subconscious, providing the opportunity to explore them and draw conclusions about what effect they have on the subject's present thoughts and actions.

Once you are made increasingly conscious of powerful emotional affecters that have long been buried in the subconscious, you can work on purging your mind of the response patterns they have long exerted on your thought processes. Through this realization, the researchers believe, you can liberate yourself entirely of such dormant influences on your life, enabling you to truly move towards the tranquility of mind that is the objective of meditative practice.

The Missing Link: Prevention

However, the one thing that would appear to be lacking in this research is developing a non-emotional capacity related to the discovery of dormant thoughts to ensure the destructive thought patterns won't resurface in the future. It is here that meditation comes into its own; as the phase of discovering sources of mental chaos and trauma is complete, so begins the process of preparing the mind for its inevitable future encounters with similar emotional programming taking place. Through meditation, we can conquer the mental chaos that already exists and condition the mind to prevent similar disorders from future experiences.

Through personal, private meditation, a person can perform this 'self-audit' on their mind. Additionally, one can also take the necessary steps to be prepared for future experiences that could lead to new subconscious thoughts, causing problems. This does not mean that the person becomes cold and emotionless to the point that they cannot experience the highs and lows of a rich and varied life.

It means, preferably, that the thoughts and emotions are monitored and assessed by a higher awareness, strengthened continuously by dedication to daily meditation practice. By slowing and considering the onset of emotional reactions, the practitioner begins to gain a profound comprehension of the fact that he or she has the opportunity to choose between interpretations of all experiences. One can choose to react emotionally and thereby allow a foundation for negative thinking. One can withhold decisive emotional judgments in favor of dispassionate observation of other people's fallibility without allowing it to consume their mind.

It is a great power to control your emotional responses, which brings a person to higher consciousness to experience life before a block from their awareness and understanding. The doors of perception and creativity become fully open, allowing the ultimate seizure of opportunities and knowledge of situations, and thus the ability to fulfill the true extent of one's potential. A person's inner reality will flourish under these circumstances.

In Summary...

The buried, negative, traumatic memories seep into your being and obstruct the path of proper growth as a person. To overcome this, one must identify and unlock those deep-rooted emotional thought triggers from the unconscious, process them, and then train the mind to avoid taking on similar destructive baggage in the future. This takes time and dedication but can set a person on the right path towards fulfilling their potential as a human being.

Meditation is an active practice. It should not be contemplated an end in itself; it is merely a tool for a person to achieve their personal and spiritual development goals, eventually allowing them to reach a state of love, light, and peaceful awareness and intuition.

Meditation, as a practice, can be defined in several ways; it can be to engage in deep contemplation or reflection, or it can be a mental exercise to heighten one's spiritual awareness. It is sometimes associated with Buddhism or Hinduism, while many consider it a purely secular activity. Contemplative practices are also prominent in Judeo-Christian culture, wherein significant figures have been known to 'meditate' as a form of reflecting on some lessons learned.

The suggestion is that meditation should not be considered to be a process of merely emptying the mind of thoughts altogether. Instead, it should be a practice of consciously discerning between harmful or beneficial thoughts and processing/expelling the negative to fill the mind and spirit with all that is good and positive. This can bring about a real feeling of release during meditative practice, where you no longer have to exert such effort to cleanse yourself of thought altogether.

81. What Is Mindfulness Meditation?

When you enter mindfulness meditation, you become like a mountain. You are surrounded by movement and changes, but you remain just as still and strong. Your thoughts would then be like clouds that float over you. They are there, but you do not interact with them; they merely pass you by until they fade away into the distance.

Mindfulness meditation in the formal sense can be practiced daily, but you need to set aside a specific time, just like exercise and eating. However, unlike the first two, you do not have to change into a different set of clothes or prep some ingredients to practice. You can start anywhere and anytime.

How To Apply The Right Meditation Posture?

It is crucial to make specific that you follow proper posture while being still for several minutes. Here are the steps on how to properly position yourself for meditation.

Sitting On A Chair

Sitting still for a certain period requires good posture not only for health but also for comfort. Slouching, after all, is the surest way to cause long term damage to your spinal cord. Here are some tips on how to improve your sitting posture for meditation:

- Make sure to sit on a chair that will enable you to put your feet flat on the ground. If the chair is too small or high, you would be better off sitting on the floor.

- If you have a slouching problem, you can place wooden blocks or old magazines beneath the two back legs of your chair to allow it to tilt forward slightly. This slight tilt will compel you to maintain a straight back to keep balance.

- Visualize that you have a string pulling your stomach forward until your spine is naturally straight without any feeling of strain. Allow your head to lift naturally until all the discs in your spine are naturally aligned.

- You may place your hands on your knees. They can be facing downwards, upwards, or to the side. You can also spot a cushion on your lap and place your hands on top if you feel the tension on your shoulders.

Sitting On The Floor

The more traditional and formal sitting practice for meditation is on a cushion on the floor. There are two basic postures for that: the kneeling posture and the Burmese posture. It is greatest to invest in a good quality meditation stool with a flat cushion (called a zafu) on top so that it can absorb the pressure of your weight instead of the back of your legs.

To properly do the kneeling posture, here are some tips:

- Always shake and stretch your legs and rotate your ankles before you go to the kneeling posture. This will minimize feelings of tension or strain.

- Prepare the kneeling stool and cushion on the floor, then carefully sit back down on it. Shift your weight until it is evenly distributed.

- Gently straighten your back and place your hands on your knees or lap.

To do the Burmese posture, here are the steps:

- Do some stretching exercises for the legs to prepare them for the position.

- Layout a mat or blanket on the floor. Over it, place a firm, flat cushion on which you will be sitting.

- Carefully lower yourself over the cushion into a sitting position. Try to let your knees touch the floor; if they do not, you may need to add more pillows until they do.

- Let your left heel touch or be as close to your right inner thigh as possible. Let your right leg be in front of your left leg with its heel directed at the lower left leg. You do not have to position this correctly, so adjust according to what is comfortable and stable for you.

- Gently allow your back to become straight, but with your shoulders relaxed. You may then place your hands on your knees or a cushion on your lap.

Aside from following proper posture, it is essential to make sure to meditate during the times when you are not hungry or too full. Otherwise, you will be too distracted or sleepy.

That said, let us move on to one of the most fundamental mindfulness meditations, mindful breathing.

Mindful Breathing Meditation

Mindful breathing meditation is the core of all mindfulness meditation exercises. The first thing you usually do to enter the state of mindfulness before you proceed with walking mindfulness, eating mindfulness, and other mindfulness exercises.

Beginners are highly encouraged to practice every day for at least two weeks so that they could get into the habit of meditation.

If you do not want to get lost in time or be worried about how long you are meditating, you can set a timer on your phone or alarm clock to signal you when to come out of the meditation. It is best to select a gentle tone on the alarm instead of a ringing one, as you would want the reminder to be peaceful rather than a disturbance. You can start with 10 minutes if you like.

Here Are The Steps To Mindful Breathing Meditation:

Step 1: Get yourself into a comfortable sitting posture, be it in a chair or on the floor. Give yourself time to become stable and comfortable.

Step 2: When you are ready, announce to yourself and the universe that you will focus on the present moment. You may start by saying out loud, "I am in the present moment. I am ready to meditate." Invite an attitude of kindness, curiosity, and acceptance.

Step 3: Shift your focus towards your nostrils. Notice the feeling of your natural breath as you inhale through your nostrils. Then, trace the sensation of the breath as it flows down through your windpipe into your lungs, causing your belly to expand.

Notice how it flows out of your stomach, causing it to deflate and then go back up through your windpipe and nostrils. Continue to focus on this sensation for as long as you like.

Be careful not to change how you are breathing as your purpose here is not to judge how you are doing it. Instead, it is a mere observance of your natural breath, the core of your present moment.

Step 4: As you continue to focus on your breath, you may soon notice your mind wandering off. This is entirely normal and should not cause you to worry. All you need to do when you see this happening is to draw your focus back towards your nostrils.

Each time you start to entertain thoughts unrelated to the sensation of breath, call to mind the word "thinking..." You can also make it more specific, such as "worrying..." or "planning..." or "ruminating..." After the thought floats away, ground yourself back towards your breath.

Once you hear the timer go off, you can either gently come out of the meditation but bring the state of mindfulness with you throughout the rest of your day. Some like to shift their focus from their breath towards their surroundings after mindful breathing meditation. They focus on the colors, textures, shapes, sounds they hear, etc. This enables them to become more in tune with the present moment than ever.

Guided Meditation

Mindfulness meditation practices may be problematic at first. This will allow you to build a meditation habit with less than 10 minutes a day.

Try practicing mindful breathing meditation right now. If you don't have much time or can't sit down, pause, and take a few breaths in and out. Focus on your breath.

Mindfulness Exercise

Mindful Breathing

You can try short meditation and mindful breathing anywhere. You don't have to be sitting down to try it.

To start to focus on breathing in through your nose and focus on the air going in at your nostrils, just focus on this point. Then breathe out through your mouth, focus on the air just as it leaves your lips.

Count 1 when you breathe in and 2 when you breathe out. Keep counting until 10.

As I breathe in, my mind becomes calm.

As I breathe out, my mind becomes clear.

Let go of thoughts, worries, and things you need to do and just focus on your breathing. You don't have to do this for very long, but if you found it helpful, you can try for longer or do it a few times during the day as you feel you need to calm your mind a bit.

82. Basics Of Mindfulness Meditation

Have you ever been so topped off with considerations that you can't focus on whatsoever? We have wholly been there, and once you think about the number of musings a person has a day that is slanted toward pessimism, there's a little marvel. The Buddhists take into account care in their lives since they follow a code, which implies that they should carry on in explicit manners that incorporate focus and doing things the correct way.

For the following few minutes, simply sit and do whatever you usually do, but instead of ignoring thoughts, take a look at them and see where they take you. If they take you into situations that have already happened, then you are thinking about the past. If they take you into worrying about the future, then you are placing your mind in the future. Mindfulness takes both of these out of the equation because the past has happened, and nothing you can do can change it, and the end hasn't happened yet. Thus, empty those thoughts and be here now. For a minute, close your eyes and spend your senses to think about the environment you are in. What can you smell? What can you taste? What do you feel? The idea of mindfulness is to make each moment of your life count as a new experience, rather than wasting the moment by spending it either in the past or the future. Some believe that multitasking is the order of the day in their lives, but the fact is that the brain parts that deal with logical thinking can't multitask. You may be able to jump quickly from one task to another when this becomes a habit, but the brain won't be processing more than one study at a time, and that's why it's able to respond so quickly when changes occur.

During learning care, you might be approached to attempt various things. For instance, you might be closed to focus on relaxing. Many individuals don't understand the noteworthiness of this undertaking. The subject's integrity is that most of us don't utilize the lung limit we have because we don't have to remain alive. Be that as it may, when you inhale accurately, you improve what's happening in your body and frameworks. For example, the intelligent sensory system can accomplish its work all the more effectively. This framework sends blood to muscles and permits you to be dynamic.

It's a similar framework that manages warmth and cold and its human view. There is such a wide range of occupations done by the body that isn't possible accurately, while breathing is shallow. Hence, the main thing you are instructed is to be in the breath or focus on relaxing. When you do something like yoga, breathing comes into it since it causes you the most extreme adaptability for the moves you are urged to do during a yoga meeting.

Other things you notice when you are mindful are all the things that touch your senses.

- Sight

- Taste

- Touch

- Hearing

- Smell

You might have the option to hear the fowls singing outside, or taste that last taste of espresso that you had, or contact the left of a plant or even observe spider webs framing on the shrubberies toward the beginning of the day dew. You are aware existing apart from everything else you are in. When you are careful, you notice everything occurring around you and can remain without demolishing it with a superfluous idea.

We are not accustomed to the quiet of the mind. In fact, in this day and age, what happens is that we are continually being interrupted by alerts, by noises around us, by advertising, and all manner of things that we think are normal. But, if you can cut out the background noise and get back to feeling silent, you will find that stress will diminish, and your heartbeat will be slower. You will be more conscious of yourself and your relationship with your body and thus learn to live a very peaceful existence even though you cannot imagine this at this point.

One of the most incredible things about this is the peace that it brings you, but in the early stages, it will take a while to get out of the habit of noise – both from external sources and from the thoughts that you allow to rumble through your mind. The whole basis of mindfulness is to let go and stop judging people and things so that negative thoughts are kept to a minimum, and you are more comfortable with the thought processes that are going on in your mind – and thus become less stressed by them. It is a recognized fact now by doctors and scientists that this helps you improve your state of mental health and assist you in staving off the effects of aging and remaining mentally active for longer. Mindfulness takes part of its roots from meditation, but bearing in mind the lives people live in this day and age, it goes further than that it takes you back to when your senses were used more, and your intuition was sharper. The relationship that you strike up between your mind and your body helps you to stay well and to fight off stress as and when it happens. Does this mean that you avoid your problems? Of course not, but you learn to become stronger to see these problems as stepping stones toward something more important than hurdles that give you stress. The compassion that you gain during mindfulness practice means that you are better armed to deal with events in your life that may otherwise cause stress.

Think about it for a moment. There are instances in your life when life is indeed difficult. How do you think that an overloaded mind can deal with this? It gets to the point where you can no longer hear your thoughts, you have no clarity of vision, and are unable to deal with problems because they become too much of a weight for you to be able to cope with. When you practice mindfulness, you start at the basics and learn to breathe, learn to relax, and learn to empty all of the garbage accumulated in your mind. You may say that you have always been a person who worries, but nothing stops you from changing. Once you procure into a habit of using mindfulness, you find that your mind can deal with things that you may have thought impossible in the past.

There are different kinds of mindfulness too. Let's look at ways in which you can practice mindfulness:

- While doing breathing exercises
- While eating
- While walking
- While bathing
- While enjoying the company of friends
- While reflecting on the day
- While trying to go to Sleep

- While getting up

It is not about the singularity. It's about peace inside you, and that, in turn, will attract those people who are also positive in their approach to life, so your social life can improve with very little input at all. You are more conscious of the people nearby you and more compassionate in your dealings with others. You are kinder to yourself and use all of the human resources available to face life with the right attitude. That's what mindfulness is all about, and in a nutshell, it's called "being in the moment" and being able to use all of your senses to make the most of that moment.

So how can mindfulness help you with the above activities? It's simple. If you are doing breathing exercises, you feed your body with the right amount of oxygen, but you are also helping your body receive the right amount of oxygen, which will relax the body and make it feel fresh. You are also adding clarity to your thoughts so that you can tackle the more difficult things that come into your day without as much confusion and difficulty. As far as Sleep goes, this is a crucial element in your life because it's when the body can heal itself. When rousing up to a new day, you will feel less tired and more capable of facing whatever the world throws at you.

Mindfulness is based upon simplicity. It means simplifying your life to the extent that your head is uncluttered. Think of mindfulness as decluttering the mind and thus changing your whole approach and attitude toward life.

You will find that relationships will improve because you take more time to listen, and your mind is slow enough to enjoy relationships instead of always seeing them negatively. The compassion you gain toward other people through mindfulness helps you drop the concept of criticism and adopt compassion and understanding. Thus you are not as judgmental, and this makes you a more pleasant person to be with. We are all too rapid to disparage and judge others. Still, mindfulness puts judgment into its rightful place, and you begin to cherish your friendships and be more attentive to people who need you or even people who shower you with their love that may otherwise be taken for granted.

The relaxation and breathing exercises are essential before you go headlong into mindfulness meditation. These help to prepare you, so don't think that there are shortcuts.

There are no shortcuts to becoming the best person you can be, but you will undoubtedly see a difference you emerge at the end of the day. There are also exercises in mindfulness on its own, which can help you become a more positive person and make the most of the experiences you have in your life. As for inner strength, you will find that through the use of mindfulness meditation, but you will also find that your intuition is better honed and that you will begin to enjoy all of the human senses that you were born with, instead of taking them for granted and forget what they are there for.

83. How To Practice Meditation?

If, like most people, you get upset and annoyed with yourself for feeling disturbed, edgy, or panicky, and you try to resist these feelings in response to your frustrations, you will soon realize that you are only strengthening these negative emotions and making them worse than they already are. Instead of resisting your feelings, you should allow yourself to feel the way you are feeling. Learning to accept this will help a great deal, and it will eventually settle down and pass.

Here are three fundamental and brief mindfulness techniques that you can apply to help you find a release from worry, anxiety, and a panic attack before it escalates.

Anchoring

One of the best ways to quiet yourself down is to ground yourself. Yes, ground yourself. In other words, anchor yourself. You can achieve this by channeling the totality of your thoughts and attention into the lower half of your body.

1.   To begin, focus your attention on your feet. Concentrate on how they feel inside your socks or shoes. Pay attention to the hardness of the ground against them.

2.   Now that you have a complete focus on your feet, allow that focus to move from your lower legs and gradually through your upper legs. Savor the sensation. How does it feel? Dense or feathery? Toasty or chilly? Excited or paralyzed?

3.   To conclude the process, feel yourself inhale, exhale, and relax as you continue the breathing process.

This is an extraordinary method of anchoring yourself. You can practice something at any time, having your eyes open or closed, in a seated position, or even while moving around. It is easy: anchor yourself and then breathes.

Breath Counting

The mind is always busy, recounting stories, translating our experience by filling in missing snippets of information, and afterward ruminating over the actions it has created, whether they are true or false.

This method can either be utilized in conjunction with anchoring or used alone.

1.   The first step is anchoring. Count up to "6" as you inhale deeply. After that time, you breathe in.

2.   Then count up to "10" as you exhale.

This strategy impacts protracting both the in-breath and the out-breath, thereby slowing down your breathing. It additionally lengthens the out-breath more than the in-breath, driving you to discharge more carbon dioxide, slowing your pulse, calming you down, and re-establishing emotional equilibrium.

If you can't manage to count because you feel panicked, then as you breathe in, say to yourself, "in," and as you breathe out, say, "out," ultimately endeavoring to extend the out-breath. Repeat the process for at least one minute, or you can go for whatever length of time that you require.

Finger Inhalation

Finger inhalation is another adaptation of breath counting.

1.   Bring one of your hands in front of you with the palm facing towards you.

2.   Follow up the outside length of your thumb with the index finger of your other hand while you inhale. Pause at the highest point of your thumb and then trace it down the other side while you exhale. That is one breath.

3.   Follow up the side of the behind finger while you inhale. Pause at the top and, afterward, trace down the other side of that finger while you exhale. That's two breaths.

4.   Continue tracing along with each finger as you count every breath. Move back up the last finger after getting to the end of the finger and repeat the process in reverse.

This exercise is precious when a lot is going on around you, and you find it difficult to close your eyes and focus inwards. It gives you something visual to focus on, something kinesthetic to do with your hands, and it also helps you focus on counting and breathing. This is an effortless procedure to teach young people and children.

Doodling

Doodling is an incredible tool to activate your celestial creative self. When combined with the power of the mandala, it can help you access profound parts of your brain.

1.   Draw a dot at the center of your canvas or paper. This dot represents the seed of an idea you want to expand on and get innovative with. Everything creative started on a raw basis. It's like a big bang.

2.   After, you develop your idea and creativity by drawing four lines out from the dot, each line pointing toward north, south, east, and west, respectively.

3.   Continue expanding your idea by drawing the subsequently four lines out from the dot, which will look like lines extending NE, SE, SW, and NW.

4.   Draw a petal on each line. The petals represent your personal, creative development.

5.   Draw a heart in the middle of each petal and a circle around the lines.

6.   Then, again, draw a heart in between every two petals

7.   Now, draw a circle around the entire center. This speaks to advance creativity and growth within the rings you have made with the networks and connections you have framed.

8.   Draw a point that connects each line with the round and then draw eight dots on the circle. This depicts co-creation within your connections and networks and embedding seeds of progress along the way.

9.   Draw the image for the lotus petal, joining each dot.

10.   Inside each lotus petal, sketch any preferred symbol (the symbol must be similar).

Sketch a character representing something significant to you, such as a flower, a musical note, or maybe a football inside the lotus flower; what you doodle does not matter. Make a doodle of anything that comes to your mind. That is your mandala!

There is no restriction on how big or how much you draw, so you can keep expanding out and including details. Bear in mind, however, that it will not be perfect, but it will be lovely!

Coloring

This is similar to doodling.

- Keep it simple. Start with an empty page and a pencil.

- Start with a shape that you find easy to draw—for example, a circle. Remember to keep it simple.

- Draw shape after shape, and trust your gut. Perhaps create a bunch of circles together.

- If you feel there ought to be a few lines, go ahead. Make those lines. Go crazy.

- Authorize yourself to put anything on the page. You can fill the page as far as possible or stop when you have a craving for halting. Simply stay with it until you feel done.

- Go on with your day feeling invigorated. The simple act of drawing on a page can do wonders.

These mindfulness techniques are not new. Many psychologists and counselors have utilized them for years. We can all benefit from these techniques, and that they are useful for everyday experiences is a relative discovery. Try them and notice what happens.

84. Benefits Of Mindfulness Meditation

The ubiquity of meditation is expanding as more individuals find their advantages.

Meditation is a routine procedure of preparing your brain to center and divert your musings.

You can use it to manufacture awareness of yourself and your natural components. Various people think of it as a way to deal with decline pressure and make the center.

People also use the preparation to make different worthwhile affinities and conclusions, such as a positive perspective and outlook, patience, hearty rest plans, and even extended torture flexibility.

Benefits Of Meditation.

1. Decreases Stress

Stress decline is one of the most broadly perceived reasons people endeavor reflection.

One examination, including more than 3,500 adults, indicated that it fulfills its reputation for stress decline.

Consistently, mental and physical weight cause extended degrees of the weight hormone cortisol. This creates a significant part of the dangerous effects of value, for instance, the appearance of irritation propelling engineered materials called cytokines.

These effects can disturb rest, advance misery and anxiety, increase circulatory strain, and add to shortcoming and obscure thinking.

In an eight-week study, a thought style called "care reflection" decreased the bothering response achieved by pressure.

Another examination in very nearly 1,300 adults showed that thought might decrease pressure. Strikingly, this effect was most grounded in individuals with vast degrees of weight.

The examination has demonstrated that reflection may improve the results of weight-related conditions, including bad tempered gut problems, post-ghastly weight, and fibromyalgia.

Overview:

Various styles of consideration can help decline pressure. Thought can similarly reduce appearances in people with pressure initiated infirmities.

2. Controls Anxiety

Less weight implies less pressure.

For example, an eight-week examination of care reflection helped individuals decline their anxiety.

Like manner, it diminished the results of disquiet, for example, fears, social pressure, unsteady contemplations, and the top dire practices and attacks of nervousness.

Another assessment found 18 volunteers three years after they had completed an eight-week reflection program. Most volunteers had continued practicing joint reflection and kept up lower anxiety levels as time goes on.

A more significant report in 2,466 members additionally demonstrated that a wide range of contemplation systems might decrease uneasiness levels.

For instance, yoga has been appeared to assist individuals with decreasing uneasiness. This is likely because of advantages from both contemplative practice and physical movement.

Reflection may likewise help control work-related uneasiness in high-pressure workplaces. One examination found that a contemplation program diminished nervousness in a gathering of medical attendants.

Synopsis:

Ongoing reflection decreases tension and uneasiness related to psychological well-being issues like social nervousness, fears, and fanatical enthusiastic practices.

3. Advances Emotional Health

A few contemplation types can likewise prompt a developed mental self-portrait and progressively uplifting point of view.

Two investigations of care contemplation discovered diminished sadness in further than 4,600 developed-ups.

One assessment followed 18 volunteers as they practiced reflection for over three years. The evaluation found that individuals who experienced a prolonged stretch decrease in trouble.

Red hot engineered blends called cytokines released in light of pressure can impact the attitude, provoking hopelessness. A recall of a couple of examinations proposes reflection may decrease despair by reducing these blazing artificial materials.

Another controlled examination took a gander at electrical development between the cerebrums of people who practiced consideration reflection and the brains of others who didn't.

The people who reflected exhibited quantifiable changes in development in zones related to positive thinking and great confidence.

Rundown:

A few types of reflection can improve discouragement and make a progressively uplifting point of view. Research shows that keeping up a progressing propensity for contemplation may help you keep up these advantages long haul.

4. Develops Self-Awareness

A couple of examination types may help you develop a more grounded cognizance of yourself, helping you form into your best self.

For example, self-demand reflection explicitly hopes to assist you with working up a more noticeable perception of yourself and how you relate to everybody around you.

Various structures educate you to see thoughts that may be pernicious or absurd. The idea is that as you increment more unmistakable awareness of your thought penchants, you can guide them toward progressively valuable models.

An examination of 21 women fighting chest dangerous development found that their certainty improved more than those who got social assistance gatherings when they partook in a yoga program.

In another examination, 40 senior individuals who took a consideration reflection program experienced decreased melancholy assumptions, diverged from a benchmark bunch put on hold on the overview for the program.

Also, association with consideration may grow dynamically inventive basic reasoning.

Abstract:

Self-demand and related styles of thought can empower you "to know yourself." This can be an early phase for turning out other complimentary upgrades.

5. Broadens Attention Span

Focused thought consideration takes after weight lifting for your ability to center. It helps increase the quality and steadiness of your thought.

For instance, an assessment took a gander at the impacts of an eight-week care reflection course and thought it improved people's capacity to reorient and keep up their idea.

A similar report exhibited that human resource workers who ordinarily practiced consideration thought stayed focused on additional endeavors.

Moreover, these workers recalled their tasks' nuances better than their colleagues who didn't practice consideration.

One overview surmised that reflection might even chat models in the cerebrum that add to mind-wandering, focusing, and lacking thought.

Regardless, contemplating for a short period may benefit you. One examination found that four days of practicing consideration may be adequate to construct the capacity to center.

Summation:

A couple of sorts of examinations may build your ability to redirect and care for thought. As pitiful as four days of reflection may affect.

6. May Reduce Age-Related Memory Loss

Updates in thought and clarity of thinking may help keep your mind energetic.

Kirtan Kriya examines a mantra or melody with the fingers' tedious development to focus on contemplations. It enriched individuals' ability to perform memory tasks in various examinations mature enough related to memory disaster.

Besides, a report of 12 assessments found that various reflection styles extended thought, memory, and mental energy in more prepared volunteers.

Despite doing combating standard age-related memory setback, reflection can at any rate midway improve memory in patients with dementia. It can help control with centering and improve adjusting in those pondering family members with dementia.

Overview:

The improved focus you can increment through legal consideration may fabricate memory and mental clarity. These favorable circumstances can help fight age-related memory incidents and dementia.

7. Can Generate Kindness

A couple of kinds of consideration may particularly fabricate positive suppositions and exercises toward yourself and others.

Metta, such an examination in any case called loving care reflection, begins with making kind thoughts and assumptions toward yourself.

Through preparing, people sort out some way to grow this care and exculpation distantly, first to buddies, by then, associates, and last, foes.

Examinations of this kind of reflection have demonstrated its ability to extend social orders' compassion for themselves and others.

One examination of 100 adults erratically given out to a program that included valuing care consideration found that these favorable circumstances were divide subordinate.

The more effort people put into Metta's examination, the more sure feelings they experienced.

Another get-together of studies exhibited that people's valuable feelings through Metta's appearance could improve social anxiety, decrease marriage battle, and help shock the board.

These points of interest in like manner appear to the total after some time with the demonstration of worshiping thoughtfulness consideration.

Abstract:

Metta, or worshiping generosity reflection, demonstrates making positive assessments, first toward yourself, and a short time after others. Metta grows motivation, compassion, and sympathetic direct toward others.

8. May Help Fight Addictions

The mental request you can make through reflection may help you with breaking conditions by growing your watchfulness and cognizance of addictive practice triggers.

The examination has exhibited that reflection may help people sort out some way to redirect their thought, increase their goal, control their sentiments and main impetuses, and appreciate the causes behind their addictive practices.

One examination told 19 substantial recovering consumers the best way to think found that individuals who got the arrangement improved at controlling their desires and aching for related weight.

Consideration may, in like manner, help you with controlling food desires. A report of 14 assessments found consideration reflection helped individuals decline enthusiastic and insatiably expending food.

Summary:

Reflection makes mental request and assurance and can assist you with avoiding triggers for bothersome main impetuses. This can help you with recovering from impulse, get more slender, and redirect other bothersome inclinations.

9. Improves Sleep

Just about an enormous part of the general population will fight with a lack of Sleep sooner or after.

One assessment considered two consideration based reflection programs by subjectively designating individuals to one of two social affairs. One social occasion practiced review, while the other didn't.

Individuals who thought fell asleep sooner and remained oblivious longer appeared differently about the people who didn't ruminate.

Getting skilled in the examination may help you control or redirect the hustling or "runaway" thoughts that routinely lead to a resting issue.

Besides, it can help extricate up your body, releasing weight and setting you in a

Overview:

A collection of reflection systems can help you loosen up and control the "runaway" insights that can interfere with rest. This can contract the time it takes to fall asleep and increase rest quality.

10. Assists Control With Tormenting

Your impression of distress is related to your viewpoint, and it might be brought up in horrendous conditions.

One assessment used viable MRI methodologies to watch mind activity as individuals experienced a challenging lift. A couple of individuals had encountered four days of care reflection getting ready, while others had not.

The considering patients showed extended activity in the cerebrum natural surroundings known to control torture. They, in like manner, point by pointless affectability to suffering.

In all of these circumstances, meditators and non-meditators experienced comparative explanations behind torture. However, meditators showed a more specific ability to adjust to suffering and even shared a diminished impression of agony.

Framework:

Consideration can diminish the perspective on distress in the cerebrum. This may help treat steady anguish when used as an improvement to clinical thought or dynamic recuperation.

11. Can Decrease Blood Pressure

Reflection can, in like manner, improve physical prosperity by reducing tension on the heart.

After some time, hypertension creates the heart work all the more sincerely to siphon blood, provoking disgraceful heart work.

Hypertension also adds to atherosclerosis or narrowing the corridors, prompting coronary episodes and strokes.

This was increasingly compelling among more established volunteers and the individuals who had more severe hypertension before the investigation.

An audit reasoned that few sorts of reflection created comparable upgrades in circulatory strain.

85. Mindfulness Meditation Into Your Life

A widespread misconception is that the only way to exercise mindfulness meditation is to sit down comfortably, close your eyes, and focus for a period. There are several ways you can weave mindfulness into your busy schedule, both at home and at work. Here are several ways to integrate mindfulness into your everyday life.

Start Your Day Mindfully

Here is an example of a mindful morning routine. Feel open to making changes according to your lifestyle, preferences, and responsibilities.

5.30 am: Wake up naturally. Before, you needed an alarm clock, but now you have a fixed bedtime, so you wake up on time too. You twitch your day with a smile and a few mindful breaths as you prepare to get up.

5.31 am: You practice a short morning stretch, a few mindful yoga poses, and then prepare a cup of tea. You hear the sound of the boiling water and see the steam rising. You start to reflect on all the aspects of your life you are grateful for; you enjoy the soothing sound of hot water filling your mug with lemon and ginger tea.

5.45 am: You sit down on the chair facing your garden or spend a few minutes enjoying the view towards the sky while sipping your tea. Then practice mindfulness exercise for 10 minutes.

6.00 am: You wake your kids and tell them to get ready for school. You reminisce how thankful you are to have such lovely children.

7.00 am: You have breakfast with your family. Before starting, ask your entire family to take three mindful breaths together.

7.30 am: You all leave the house together. You have enough time to go to your office, mindfully.

Traveling Mindfully

Here is how to travel mindfully:

Start Your Journey With Mindfulness

By training using mindfulness practice, you set the tone for your day. Drive a little slower than you are recycled to and allocate more of your brain's resources to driving with mindful awareness. Expect delays and traffic when going. This way, if you have a smooth journey to work, you can be pleasantly surprised rather than upset and angry.

Turn Off Your Phone

Studies show that chatting on the phone while driving is as dangerous as drunk driving. Be mindful of your surroundings and see driving as an opportunity to practice mindfulness. End driving mindfully. When you reach your office, finish with another little mindful exercise, such as mindfulness of your body, mindfulness of the sounds, or mindfulness of breath.

Mindfulness At Work

When working, pause between work and practice a short mindfulness exercise. Set periodic alarms on your phone to remind you to take a break and occasionally practice mindfulness. You can custom an app or a diary to remind yourself to take breaks and practice. Look for creative ways to incorporate mindfulness meditation into your work.

Mindful Coffee Breaks

Your coffee break is an excellent opportunity to practice mindful breathing. Follow these tips when taking a break:

To enjoy conscious drinking, reserve time for your break

Be cautious when preparing your drink: notice the sound of the boiling water, watch the steam, listen to the sound of water filling your cup, and smell the aroma.

Take a seat, switch off any potential distractions, and concentrate on your drink. Choose a spot where you are unlikely to be disturbed.

Take mindful breaths. Feel your breath as it goes in and out of your body; feel your body and the cup in your hands.

Take a sip of your coffee. Feel the warm coffee entering your mouth and slowly going down your throat. Continue holding the cup, smell the aroma, and watch the steam rising from it.

Do not rush or finish hurriedly. Take your time and ignore the temptation to rush.

Express your gratitude when you have finished your coffee and show appreciation for this opportunity to practice mindfulness exercise.

Develop A Mindful Evening Routine: How To

The following is a list of everyday evening activities and ways to make them more mindful after a busy day at the office:

Watching TV

If you have developed a habit of watching TV in the evening after work, start a journal for your TV habits. Writing down your TV habits will help you manage your time more mindfully.

Cooking

Cooking offers you an excellent opportunity to practice mindfulness. Try to connect with your senses as you cook.

Eating

When eating, focus, and appreciate every element of your dinner. Use your five senses to enhance the eating experience.

Exercising

Exercising or playing sports offers you another great opportunity to practice mindfulness. Any hobby or activity can also be mindful.

Sleeping

Studies suggest that mindfulness can help you sleep better. If you wrestle with falling asleep, try a mindfulness exercise when you are in bed. Mindfulness is very restful; thus, it should help you quickly fall asleep

How To Be Mindful In Your Digital Life

One of the most effective ways to spend your day mindfully in this information or digital age is having downtime. Unlike computers, you need frequent breaks and rest to work effectively; otherwise, your attentional resources deplete rapidly, as do your enthusiasm, intelligence, and energy levels. The following are a few ways to create digital downtime:

Take Short Breaks

If your work requires continuous computer work, then take a few minutes to break every half hour or so. Taking frequent breaks, walking around, and having conscious breaths are all good for your body and mind.

Avoid Screens A Few Hours Before Bedtime

After a busy office day, take a break from computers and gadgets. Spend time socializing, participating in sport, or doing a spot of mindfulness-awareness.

Occasional Breaks

Take a break from technology every week. The aim is to spend at least one day without using any computer or Smartphone. During this time, avoid logging onto social media or checking email, and do something more natural and energizing.

Take A Vacation

If it is possible, take a few weeks' holidays once a year. During your holiday, avoid spending time on computers, smartphones, TV, or iPads. You will be astounded at how clear your mind can become after a great technology-free holiday.

Communicating Mindfully

Mindful communication focuses on bringing a greater level of conscious awareness and reflection on how you communicate with others.

Benefits Of Communicating Mindfully

Mindful communication gives importance to face-to-face communication, which offers an array of services such as:

Personal Touch

When you meet a supplier, a customer, or a colleague in person, the interaction is not similar to other communication modes.

The in-person discussion can lead to constructive conversations, insights, and better ideas.

Non-Verbal Communication

Face-to-face meetings allow you to pick up all sorts of clues from a person's body language, clues you will not get through other communication forms, but very important in communication.

A split-second pause when you mention a new deal or idea may tell you that the other person is unenthusiastic about it. With this additional information, you can make better decisions. Teams work better together. Studies show that teams working face-to-face tend to make fewer errors and have reported improved performance and teamwork.

Mindful Emailing

These tips will help you email more productively and mindfully.

Use a notebook and write down whom you plan to send emails to today and a few brief essential points regarding those emails.

Then, write those emails first and check new emails after. Forecasting will only take a couple of minutes, but it can save you hours reading and answering emails that are not important.

Fix a time for checking and answering emails, unless your primary role is dealing with emails. Before you send an email to someone, take three mindful breaths. Doing this will help you become more conscious, give you time to reflect on what you have just written, and help you stay focused.

See your emails from the receiver's perspective. After taking three mindful breaths, visualize how the other person will feel when they receive and read your email. You may decide your email needs minor editing, or you may even give them a video call instead.

Develop the habit of sending at least one positive email every day: Concentrating on the good things in life helps counteract your brain's natural negativity bias and makes you and your recipient feel better. Thank your boss for their help with the critical report yesterday, praise a new employee for settling into the team so quickly, or congratulate your colleague for her sales presentation.

Control your emails and not let emails control you: Avoid replying to every email that lands in your inbox and only respond to essential emails.

Practice your favorite mindfulness meditation before and after emailing to help you achieve greater focus.

Phoning Mindfully

Practice this mindfulness exercise the following time you make a phone call:

Before calling, take a few moments to be mindful. Feel your breath and practice a short mindful pause. Write down the purposes of the conversation you are about to make. This will take only a few seconds. When creating a phone call, stand up, and walk to move your body. During the conversation, listen more than you speak. If the conversation makes you feel angry or anxious– feel the emotions with your breathing, notice the feeling in your body, talk from your wise mind rather than react spontaneously to your feelings, and say things you may regret afterward.

Do not prolong the conversation- end the call when you need to. Doing a short mindful exercise is the key to aware of phoning.

How To Engage Social Media Mindfully

Social channels, such as Facebook, LinkedIn, Twitter, and Instagram, has changed how we operate. Here are a few tips for using social mindfully:

See your business-related social media undertaking as a part of your working day. When spending time with your family, off it.

Use apps to manage your social media more efficiently and check and update your social media accounts at set times.

Be friendly, and do not see people as just another number. If they have a question or a comment, respond in kind. Try to make genuine connections rather than superficial and insincere contacts. Seek to help others, give more than you receive. If anyone needs help regarding an important matter, see if you can help.

86. Better Manage Your Interpersonal Interactions

Principles Of A Minimalist Approach To Doing Relationships

1. Less Is More.

In his Nicomachean Ethics, Aristotle talked about how most of our relationships are based on utility and convenience and are empty of any value. However, when we hold on to one or two valuable relationships, we emphasize those relationships that contribute to our overall well-being. When you can focus on a few excellent connections, you'll enjoy your life a lot more because you'll worry less about what others think of you and think more about how you can live a happier life.

2. Let Go Of Toxic Relationships.

The second thing that you must do is eliminate every toxic relationship that negatively influences your life. One example of this type of connection is when a person sucks all the energy out of your life and plays the needy victim. Victims play the role of the victimizer, and they zap you of your needed resources. Eventually, they will take every trace of life from you if you are not careful. Victimizers can also become the center of our lives. And when that happens, you cannot do what you want to do because you have to take care of a very needy person. Instead of holding on to this toxic relationship, you should try to get rid of it as soon as possible. Indeed, it will be difficult for you to relinquish your hold on this relationship because you may have empowered a lot of time and energy into it. Still, it will be better to get rid of it sooner rather than subsequently.

3. Be True To Other People.

In today's world, an authentic man or woman is to be exalted. Being real is something that people in society need to do to live better lives. Being a con artist and lying to others is easy, manipulative, and evil, but our world is filled with such people. It harms your image, and it can also hurt your soul. One of the most extraordinary things you can do for yourself and others is to be true to yourself and other people.

This way produces less stress and enables you to live a life that will bring you greater happiness in the end. If you want to be the right leader or manager, authenticity is increasingly important because people glance up to you and trust you to do your job the right way. If you don't do that, they may look elsewhere for work. The basic principle that should underlie all of this is to never compromise on regulations in your life.

4. Live Your Life About The Here And Now.

Humans tend to look to the distant past and hold unforgiveness feelings or think endlessly about the future. Both of these methods are not at all productive. We must keep our eyes focused on present circumstances, and this applies to our relationships. There is no better way to help a friend than to be for them here and now. Your friends need you now. Your wife or husband needs you now, and your kids need you now. Don't waste too much of your time surfing the web, working, or doing other things. Instead, you should prize the relationships that you have at this moment and not compromise on them for anything.

5. Get Rid Of Unreasonable Expectations Of Others.

Another thing you need to do is release the burdensome expectations you have of other people. This is an essential part of your friendship or love relationship. When you maintain clear and reasonable expectations for your relationship, you will experience a smoother and more manageable relationship with whomever. Many people have unreasonable expectations of their spouse, significant other, or friend. This will only lead to heartbreak and friction in the relationship. Breakups and divorce can be the worst result of these expectations. Therefore, it is crucial to maintain good relationships with others while getting rid of other people's unreasonable expectations.

6. Connect With Your Friend Or Partner Deeply.

In relationships, you must go deep rather than seeking more. When you get to know someone deeply, it will require a significant investment of time and energy. Most of our relationships will be based on a superficial level, and they will disappear when the person goes out of our life. It could be that the person moves away from us or work situation changes. In real relationships with others, permanence should be a vital marker of the relationship. Do you spend most of your time talking to your friend about sports, Netflix, or something else superficial, or do you spend more time talking about more profound and more philosophical things? It is worth verdict out more about how you can spend more time on the more profound things of life than dwelling on the useless and meaningless things that don't matter. Going deep will help you to have deeper connections with people.

7. Focus On Shared Experiences.

Applying time with friends, family, or other people in our lives allows us to have shared experiences that will last a lifetime. When you make the most of these times together, you can create unforgettable memories. Such recollections will stay in your psyche and heart for quite a while. These recollections are a higher priority than the material stuff we obtain. They will guide us toward something more profound within us that we can share.

8. Deliberateness.

Having deliberateness is an essential part of making great connections. When you are deliberate about your various relationships, you can have smoother and more compelling correspondence, which will enable your contacts to get off the ground in a superior manner. Discover a reason for investing energy with your companion or accomplice, and you will find that the time spent will help get you in the ideal spot. Purposefulness will improve your fellowships, love connections, and family connections.

9. Love Your Neighbor.

The best approach to seek after an essential relationship with someone else is through affection. This isn't the sort of suggestive love that we are acclimated with considering. Instead, it is an idea of human love that applies generally. It is adoration for a sibling or neighbor that characterizes how an individual can carry on with a more meaningful life. Love ought to pervade your associations with others. It likewise makes things much prettier and less chaotic because what characterizes your relationship is what you can give to the relationship instead of what you can acquire from it. This makes it a less upsetting sort of relationship.

10. Seek After Relationships With Passion.

One last point is that we have to seek after our associations with enthusiasm. We ought not to make do with not as much as greatness. Seeking after connections require devotion and duty.

Numerous individuals don't care to assign things since they are apprehensive or excessively occupied. In any case, you can position out from the group and focus on a relationship, regardless of whether that is with a companion or noteworthy other, and that can be a fabulous thing for your life. Discover something that you can never really up to your life by partnering with delightful individuals who will help you not far off to achieve in your life.

87. How To Start And Continue A Good Meditation Practice?

How To Get Started With Meditation?

Rehearsing contemplation is one of the essential things that everybody must educate as a significant aspect of their lives. Everybody wants to sit for quite a long time together and impersonate the sages and the profound masters in any case, which is undoubtedly incomprehensible. Contemplation would not stop by wishing; instead, one needs to rehearse it routinely with no explanation.

However, correctly like exercise and hitting rec centers is conceivable just by making up the psyches effectively and with all-out commitment, reflection is additionally unequivocally a similar way. Dhyana requires more responsibility than the everyday activities, as it is fundamental to sit for quite a while, at any rate, with no interruption.

With reliable readiness, one would have the option to spend more than a few hours ruminating without any problem. Be that as it may, it requests to turn into a custom; now and again, you may need to drag yourselves. However, the aphorism is to prop up regardless. With 1,000,000 motivations to prevent you from rehearsing contemplation, you should make a point to have just one reason, 'Constant devotion' and responsibility.

Through this article, you would have the option to discover approaches to rapidly enlist yourselves into the most excellent and peaceful craft that can assist you with finding the enhanced you, "Reflection."

1.   Read Through The Different Forms Of Meditation

There are numerous types of strict foundations where one can rapidly become more acquainted with different contemplation types. Perusing the various types of intercession and seeing each school's way of thinking would, without a doubt, explain the sort that is reasonable for you.

2.   List Down A Few Meditation Procedures That Interest You.

When you are finished perusing and understanding the various types of contemplation methods, it is fundamental to list the best ones. Break them down altogether by experiencing diaries, sites, and different materials, lastly picking the best one. When you follow this technique, you would have the option to get into rehearsing reflection rapidly.

3.   Start Devoting Time Listening To People On Meditation

There are a few recordings and sound documents that are accessible online on contemplation. Tuning in to these records can assist you with getting a handle on more subtleties on reflection. Likewise, generally on these recordings, you would have the option to tune in to individuals rehearsing reflection for quite a while. In specific recordings and sound documents, you may listen legitimately to the contemplation Gurus themselves, attempting to clarify the ideas of thought most extensively. With this, you would grow more enthusiasm for reflection and gradually become acclimated to the training meetings.

4.   Call A Spiritual Center And Take Part In A Group Meditation.

There are many reflection places that you can discover around your premises. You could decide to visit any of these premises and partake in the gathering occasions. A large portion of the reflection places direct contemplation camps and a one-day contemplation presentation course at amateur levels on special days and events. Visiting during those days can assist you with studying thinking and get yourself accepted to it.

5.   Get Instated To One Of The Meditation Courses.

When you visit the contemplation habitats, you can decide to converse with the administration or the volunteers and rundown the various sorts of reflection directed. Peruse the handout altogether, and afterward, you can pick the thinking you need to join up with. A large portion of these reflection courses would be for a day or two, and selecting yourself in these courses would help you gradually build up an enthusiasm for contemplation. This can likewise assist you with beginning sitting in one spot without getting diverted.

6.   Get Some Like-Minded Friends.

Likewise, it is fundamental to be encircled by similar individuals when you begin engaging in reflection when you invest energy with individuals slanted towards contemplation, your enthusiasm towards a similar increment bit by bit.

7.   Get Some Journals And Spend Time In Gathering Knowledge.

You could also decide to put resources into a couple of reflection diaries composed by extraordinary creators. Becoming more acquainted with their encounters with contemplation can assist you with building up an enthusiasm for reflection. A few writers would likewise write a bit by bit methodology that must be followed for each kind of contemplation. Perusing every one of these focuses can assist you with getting accepted into reflection quickly rapidly.

8.   Start Practicing Slowly

It is fundamental to begin gradually and stay consistent during the training meetings. A few people get overpowered with the sentiment of daze and wind up exaggerating the contemplation meetings. By doing this, they would rapidly wind up stopping on contemplation. This is one of the most significant things to recall when you need to get into reflection.

9.   Be Consistent

There are days when you would feel depleted. On such days, maneuvering yourselves into the reflection corridor is required. On the off fortuitous that you let go of that one meeting recklessly, you could always be unable to re-visit your reflection practice again. Thus, remaining predictable regardless of the emotional episodes is obligatory. Even though you don't perform undeniable reflection nowadays, you could decide to sit and close your eyes or even sit unobtrusively in one spot.

10.   Stay Flexible

Consistently isn't Sunday; moreover, it may turn out to be incredibly challenging to fix your psyches to a tight timetable with regards to reflection. Sticking to the timeline would be conceivable by those with more astonishing long periods of involvement with consideration.

Subsequently, when you are starting to rehearse reflection at the apprentice level, it is fundamental to stay adaptable. At whatever point you discover the time, you should figure out how to rehearse quietness. Independent of the spot or time, you should start contemplation. You don't need to consider timings; instead, it is compulsory to draw all your energy and center towards the reflection corridor.

11. Get A Companion

Contemplation is simply the best when you practice without anyone else. On the off chance that you think that it's repetitive to sit relaxed all alone, getting a partner may be of great assistance. There are similarly invested individuals rehearsing reflection together, the dissemination of positive energy in and around the room, and you would be more. This would make your reflection practice meetings pleasant. This is probably the least difficult because you could take a stab when intending to get into the reflection unexpectedly.

12. Music Can Help Too

Many individuals experience the surge of contemplations when they plunk down to ponder if you knowledge something very similar. Music can be a great guide. Turing on the lovely and mitigating piece can assist you with centering better. Turn on the music and keep the volume incredibly low; as you progress, you can decide to kill the music and begin encountering the energy stream.

13. Practice, Practice, And Practice

If you settle on contemplation practice, it will end up being a delightful excursion. On the off chance that you must remain glad all the time with no concerns, the main route is by encountering the intensity of contemplation through reliable practice meetings. As you practice more, you would have the option to uncover the various parts of this delightful framework. Taking advantage of the more significant levels of cognizance would possibly be conceivable when you continue rehearsing. The specialty of reflection takes you to various domains, just with training.

14. Progress Into Advanced Levels

Gradually and consistently, you should begin advancing into cutting edge levels of contemplation. Until you, except if you make it a propensity, meditation could never turn out to be essential for your lives. As referenced before, reflection turns into your way of life just when you intentionally put forth an attempt towards it. Else, in contrast to some other propensities, you would rapidly drop out of it also.

15.   Start Teaching Different Techniques Of Meditation

When reflection turns into a vital aspect of your life, you might not want to pass up on even a solitary opportunity to play out your training. Assume you need to get committed to contemplation. Deciding to instruct reflection or turning into a mentor at any contemplation communities can be an incredible move to hoist yourself in the contemplation venture.

These are the essential things that everybody seeks to teach intervention as a significant aspect of their carries on with must follow. These things are incredibly easy to the unaided eyes, yet actualizing them can be tested on the off chance you aren't sufficiently centered.

Reflection gets fruitful just to advance into ending up as a fulfilled person. Contemplation can cause you to feel pleasured out slightly if you experience it all alone. Joining the focuses referenced above, advancing into different elements of Dhyana or meditation can get straightforward. We trust that this article would prove to be useful when you want to begin with a reflection.

88. Practical Exercises for Every Posture to Get Your Body Ready for Meditation

Before we proceed to the meditation proper, you should keep in mind some essential guidelines to observe how to meditate correctly. Let us discuss them one by one:

Proper Posture

When you meditate, you must observe the right posture. Now, there are many ways to meditate. You can meditate while lying, sitting, standing, or even while walking. However, there are detailed pros and cons to every posture. When you meditate in a lying down position, you can more easily relax. However, a common problem with this posture is that you can also easily fall asleep, which is a problem for many beginners. When you meditate in a standing position, although it will prevent you from falling asleep, it will be harder for you to focus since you will have to exert some physical effort to hold the position. Not to mention, this posture can be tiring after some time. The same reasons apply when you meditate while walking or doing something else. Now, as for the most recommended posture for meditation, it is the sitting position. This posture enjoys the benefits of being awake and focused and also not falling asleep. This is also the most recommended posture of many spiritual masters. Even the great Buddha achieved enlightenment while meditating in a sitting position. You can deliberate while sitting on a chair or even on the floor. If pondering on the floor or your bed, you might want to put a pillow below your tailbone to make you feel more comfortable.

Keep Your Spine Straight

Regardless of the meditation posture that you use, you should always keep your spine straight. This is very important when you meditate. You support the range straight to ensure the free flow of energy through the seven main chakras. Remember that your main chakras are located along your spinal cord. Keeping it directly, the energy flows freely and smoothly, which is also essential in awakening the kundalini. Now, a common mistake is to slouch during meditation.

Before you even attempt to meditate, be sure to teach yourself how to assume the proper posture.

In the beginning, you might discover it a bit difficult not to slouch, especially when you are in a sitting position. Do not be discouraged. With enough practice, your body will learn to adjust, and you will get good at it. Therefore, just keep on practicing.

Focus

When you meditate, you will be asked to focus on something. It can be a mere visualization exercise or a simple sound or object. Do not allow your mind to wander. Remember what your point of focus is in certain meditation practices and stick to it. If other thoughts arise in your mind, ignore them, and bring your focus back to the object of the meditation.

Now, the most common challenge when a person learns to meditate is known as the monkey mind. What is the monkey mind? It is a state of mind that is full of thoughts. Just like a monkey that jumps from one branch to another, so does the mental leap from one study to another. This is what is called a monkey mind. People who are just beginning to meditate will face this challenge. So, how do you deal with the monkey mind? There is only one way to overcome the monkey mind, and that is to continue practicing meditation. The more that you contemplate, the more you will be able to control and still your mind. There are no shortcuts except for continuous practice.

Relax

When you meditate, you should be as relaxed as possible. Allow your body to fall asleep and let your mind become free. Do not ponder that what you are doing is difficult. This will only put unnecessary strain and pressure on yourself, preventing you from reaching a higher state of consciousness. Just relax and place all your focus on your meditation practice. The more you put pressure on yourself, the more you will not free yourself from your physical body. Relax so you can become light. When you are light enough, then you will transcend into a higher state of consciousness. The key is to relax and let depart.

You Are Safe

Perhaps one thing that you should know is that the practice of meditation is safe.

Unfortunately, some people think that reflection can kill you or put you in danger. Well, as long as you do not meditate while driving or while crossing the street and similar circumstances, then rest assured that you are safe. In fact, according to experience to meditators and gurus, if ever your physical body is put in danger while you are in a state of meditation, such as if a fire breaks when you meditate, you will be instantly brought back to your physical body. Therefore, when you meditate, do not worry about your safety. This will only cause your energy and attention to be divided. Instead, put all your focus on your meditation practice.

It is recommended to teach you the essential guidelines when meditating since having too much information can tempt your mind to wander even more. It is now time for you to learn and finally experience what medication is genuinely all about. Remember that even if you do not notice any changes, do not be discouraged even in your state of mind. Regularly, you will get better and better at doing meditation. Continuous practice is critical. Let us now move on to the reflection proper.

Basic Meditation Practice

It is suitable for your first meditation to learn about the reflection on the breath or merely breathing meditation. This is probably the most basic meditation technique in the world. However, do not underestimate the power of this meditation. Many spiritual masters and even the great Buddha practiced this meditation for a long time. It is also not uncommon even for experienced monks to stick to this meditation for years. The power of this contemplation lies in its simplicity. The steps are as follows:

Assume a meditative posture. Just unwind, and do not think about anything. Now, focus on your breathing. Breathe in and out gently. In.... Off... do you realize just how sensitive life is? This in and out breathing cycle simply cannot be interrupted, or it would mean danger or even death. Appreciate the beauty of your breath. Breathe in and breathe out. Behold the gift of life. Now, put all of your focus on your breathing. Do not think about anything else, and just be mindful of your breathing. Relax and let go. Be one with your breath.

You can do this meditation technique for as long as you want. If you are just starting, you might want to do it for a few minutes.

However, it is also noteworthy that many experienced meditators do this medication for an extended period, even for hours. For now, just do whatever is comfortable for you. After all, it is not acceptable to rush your spiritual progress. Just be sure always to do your best and be committed to it. It is also worth noting that this simple meditation energizes and empowers all your chakras. This regular practice meditation will allow you to reach such a state of mind that you have never experienced before. By the time you finish doing this meditation, you will be in a peaceful and harmonious mindset.

Common Pitfalls

Let us now talk about common pitfalls or mistakes in meditation. It is suitable for you to be aware of these pitfalls so that you can avoid committing them. Still, it should be noted that many of these pitfalls are quite challenging to avoid, so do not be discouraged if you fall into them even though you have already been warned. Just continue to do your best and keep on practicing.

Thinking

You should understand that meditation is not about thinking, but it is more about doing. It is not about thinking of the present moment but about being in the present moment. When you meditate, do not feel. Just be.

Another common mistake is to think, "Am I doing it right?" while you are meditating. If you think about this, then you are doing it the wrong way. The time to ask yourself this kind of question should be after the meditation but not during the meditation properly. When you meditate, you should not allow yourself to be divided in any way.

Wrong Focus

It is correct that when you meditate, you usually have to focus on something. Unfortunately, some meditators focus on focusing instead of focusing on the point of an object in meditation. Okay, this might be confusing, but you need to understand this lesson. When you meditate, do not tell yourself, do not tell yourself that you need to focus on this or that. Instead, you have to do it. To focus entails an actual action and not a mere command. There is a variance between concentrating on your breathing and telling yourself that you should focus on breathing.

You should provide yourself some time to reflect on this and be sure that you understand it completely.

Scratching

When you meditate, you may sometimes feel like a part of your body may get itchy. Of course, the tendency would be to scratch it. The problem with this is that the mind will return its focus to the physical body. If you preserve on doing this, you will not reach a trance state or a deeper consciousness state. So, what should you do? Well, you just have to ignore it. Although it is normal to feel itchy while meditating, you must not let it bother or distract you. This might be quite difficult to do initially, but you have to resist it and get used to it. With enough practice, you will no longer be bothered by this itchy feeling. You will not even think about it. Remember to ignore it. The more that you think about it, the more distracting it will be. Once again, continuous practice is the key.

Not Enough Practice

Learning to meditate is just like learning a new skill. And, just like learning a new skill, it requires practice. Do not expect that you can do well if you only practice once a week. If you are serious about your spiritual development, you should prioritize meditating at least once every day. If you are opening, you can do even only five or ten minutes of meditation per day. However, as you improve and get used to it, you have to practice more. Continuous practice is essential. It is recommended that you arrange a timetable for when you will meditate and stick to that routine. This way, you can be evident that you make time for your meditation practice. Without continuous training, then you can't reach an adequate level of spiritual maturity.

89. Daily Meditation Exercises

It doesn't matter what meditation you choose to receive these benefits but continue to practice for at least 3 minutes HD rather than 30 minutes once a week. Don't beat yourself too hard if you end up skipping a day; simply start over where you stopped. Before starting any of your practices, make sure you do a few warm-up exercises. Usually, most kundalini meditations come with a few warm-up exercises, so your body is ready to receive its benefits.

1. Relax And Settle The Breath

Begin by finding a quiet place to settle and sit down. Keep your back straight and in a comfortable pose. Light a candle if you want to. Scratch your nose, adjust your legs, and then once you are done moving, take note of the state of your mind.

As soon as your breath is at a regular rhythm, and your mind focuses on every breath, start counting on every breath. When you breathe consciously, note how your diaphragm is moving and how your belly expands with every inhalation and flattens with every exhalation.

Compel stress to release by giving up and allowing your breath to move away from your body. Relax your neck, shoulders, or back consciously with every breath a little more. Don't worry about losing track of your counting. Just go back to the last number and continue this mindful breathing technique.

Take about 20-30 minutes to count breaths to 50.

2. Circular Breathing

Circular breathing is the term given for the practice of deep, gradual, and slow breathing through your nose from the abdomen. Both the inhale and exhale should be the same length. There should also be no pause between the breaths. Circular breathing for meditation, according to meditation practitioners, can help release negative energy or stress accumulated in the body. The method also suggests that it helps promote long-term health by increasing fresh oxygen to your blood, making it stiffer for viruses and bacteria to enter the body.

3. Shoulders And Breath: Key To Releasing Tension

Start by making yourself agreeable. Sit in a seat and permit your back to be straight, however not firm, with your feet on the ground. You can do this on the basis or a tangle on the off chance you feel more agreeable. You could likewise do this work on standing, or if you like, you can rests and have your head upheld. Your hands could be resting tenderly in your lap or even after you. Permit your eyes to close or to stay open with a delicate look.

Take a few long, slow, full breaths, and breathe in wholly and breathe out gradually. Take in smoothly through your nose and out through your nose or mouth. Feel your stomach develop a breath in and unwind and let go as you breathe out.

Start to relinquish commotions around you. Start to move your consideration from outside to inside yourself. If sounds in the room divert you, just notification this and take your concentration back to your relaxing.

At that point on this way out-breath, permit the legs to disintegrate in your brain. What's more, move to the sensations in your lower back and pelvis. Mellowing and delivering as you take in and out. Gradually move your consideration up to your mid-back and upper back. Become curious about the sensations here. You may get mindful of feelings in the muscle, temperature, or purposes of contact with furniture or the bed.

With each out-breath, you may relinquish the pressure you are conveying. And afterward, delicately move your concentration to your stomach and all the inner organs here. Maybe you notice the sentiment of garments, the cycle of absorption, or the gut rising or falling with every breath. If you notice feelings emerging about these regions, tenderly let these proceed to re-visitation of seeing sensations.

As you keep on breathing, carry your attention to the chest and heart locale, and simply notice your pulse. See how the chest ascends during the breath and how the chest falls during the breath out. Relinquish any decisions that may emerge. On the accompanying out-breath, move the concentration to your hands and fingertips. Check whether you can channel your breathing into and out of this region as though you inhale into and out from your hands. On the off chance that your psyche meanders, delicately take it back to the sensations in your grasp.

4. Worry Ruminations: Getting Unstuck

Unnecessarily worrying causes stress and tension. When it comes to our thoughts, we want to create a safe space for our thoughts and our emotions because it goes hand in hand. Instead of telling yourself that you would just empty your mind and be free from thoughts, we can instead get released from this scenario by going through a worry-free, acceptance-based meditation created to help us focus on making room for our thoughts and feelings - a worry-free zone.

This type of meditation focuses on your breath and the PMR, which is for progressive muscle relaxation. It allows you to tense and relaxes your muscles as you go through your meditation.

Allowing your thoughts and emotions, both positive and negative ones, to have a safe space in your mind and a judgment-free space will enable us to confront them and deal with them, eventually reducing these thoughts over time.

5. Notice And Stop Negative Thinking

Any thought we have is connected to our emotional side, and it also gives rise to physical sensations. It's all the same. Whenever you feel something negative like 'I'm a loser' or 'I don't think I'm good enough,' there are physical sensations in your body.

This practice can be used anytime you think negatively, whether during your meditation or in your day-to-day life. Throughout the exercise, take the time to accept an absolute sensation, image, or memory and see where it affects the mind and body.

Track down any thoughts you sometimes take for real, like, 'I'm not good enough,' 'I'd have to do it better,' 'I'm weak,' or 'I'm helpless.' Where do you feel these emotions present in your body, and how do you think it is a reality of yourself when you take this thought? Do you believe it in your heart, your gut, or your throat, or somewhere else entirely? How do you feel - happy, relaxed, tensed?

6. Sit With The Emotion To Decrease Worry

This therapeutic script is intended to deal with negative thinking. This self-talk may lead to distress and low self-esteem that is sometimes associated with negative thinking.

A calming hand will help you recognize feelings and thoughts related to rejection and disappointment and shift your negative thinking.

7. Feel The Fear To Reduce The Anxiety

Just sit down and place your feet flat on the floor with your hands and shoulders relaxed. Put your hands underneath the lower ribs near where your kidneys are located. Visualize them in your head.

Shut your eyes, smile, breathe into your belly, and imagine a dark blue light and peace in your kidneys and adrenal glands. Now slowly exhale by pushing your gut back in.

Repeat two more times.

8. Take A Mindful Walk

In our mindful walk, we want to begin, obviously, by walking at a natural pace. You can be wearing anything (high heels even), and you can be anywhere (make sure it's safe where you are). Continue walking at a natural pace. Following, place your hands to your side or even on your belly, behind your back, or to your sides - whichever is comfortable for you.

9. Distraction Challenge

This unwinding content is for defeating interruptions by managing a portion of the reasons for this conduct and expanding inspiration to control the things you plan for the day. Tune in to this unwinding sound to make a move inside after that 24 hours.

Start by finding an agreeable position and permitting your body to start to unwind.

10. Traffic Light Meditation

In traffic light meditation, we look at meditating when we are at stop signs, in a traffic jam or when you are stuck in the middle of the day at a red light. You may be controlling late for a meeting or to pick your child up from school. All you need to do is get going, but you're stuck. Now what?

- Look directly at the traffic light, giving particular focus to the red light.

- Allow your vision to soften its gaze. You can do this easily by remembering something you like or someone you love, or even your favorite ice cream flavor. You'll find that thinking about this automatically makes you feel better, and your vision softens.

- Allow your breathing to slow down and your shoulders to relax each time you breathe in and breathe out. It can make all the difference.

It's incredible how even a few minutes of mini-meditations at the most unlikely places can bring a considerable difference in handling the stress of a busy day. If you piece them together with other lots of 'few minutes', you will soon notice your stress melting away and your experience of life-changing.

90. How Can I Establish A Good Meditation Practice?

One effective way to consistently practice meditation is to create and plan out a practice that you can follow, according to your needs, daily schedule, routines, and timing.

The thing about meditation is that you need to be mindful of everything that you experience in your session. With mindful meditation, there is a goal and a purpose. It is to help you be conscious and mindful of everything you do.

Benefits Of Establishing A Meditation Practice

A foundation of your meditation session is necessary because, in many ways, when you set the stones to your practice, your brain will start moving toward making this practice happen. For example, if you decide to buy a new meditation mat, your mind will be reminded (or you will remember) that you purchased the mat, and you want to know the feeling of sitting on the mat and practicing.

Without A Firm Foundation, You Will Not Be Consistent

It won't be long before whatever you're doing eventually crumbles and falls because nothing supports it. That's just one way of describing how important it is to develop a sound meditation practice right from the beginning of the process.

It Helps You Create A Habit

But although meditation is beneficial for everyone, not everyone is currently putting it into practice. Some people are not practicing meditation at all. Why? Because it isn't a habit. Many of us lead hectic lives, so sometimes our plates seem too full to take on anything else. There will always be a reason not to start something, which is why it is entirely up to you to make time for it.

The motivation behind building up a contemplation practice is because you need to make reflection a propensity, an aspect of your day by day life, and something that you are eager to do each day without reconsidering or opposing it. You are in a hurry.

It Makes Your Practice Ingrained, Almost Second-Nature Activity In Your Life

Contemplating will turn out to be a lot of like brushing your teeth or showering, planning something to eat, and in any event, going on an everyday drive to work. Those propensities are so profoundly imbued in you that you do them with no exertion or a ton of thought put into it.

That is what builds up a reflection practice plan to accomplish for you at present, and it is something you have to set up as an establishment to make your training predictable.

Here is how you can start establishing a meditation practice for yourself.

- Start small. Start little from the outset by ruminating for brief periods, possibly 5-10 minutes per day, particularly if you're new at it. You can do anything for 5-10 minutes every day with no obstruction, and the time will pass before you even know it. When you perceive how simple that was, it keeps you roused to continue including onto that. By creating small, achievable goals, you begin building the habit of making meditation a part of your daily life.

- Use tools to help you. There is an app for just about everything these days, even meditation, so why not make the most of the tools you have to help you establish a successful daily practice? For example, a few applications, Headspace and Calm, can help you upgrade your reflection meetings, including clocks to surrounding sounds, to help set the state of mind. On the off possibility that it helps make your everyday practice more agreeable, why not? You are bound to adhere to something on the off chance that you like what you're doing.

- Use YouTube. Guided meditations that you like on YouTube can be a great tool, especially for beginners on this journey. It helps you stay on track and the right path. Some medications are given daily, whereas some are based on your goals, such as Meditation for Focus and Meditation for Sleep. Guided reflections make it a lot simpler for apprentices, particularly to begin getting into the progression of things and make you progress the correct way with your contemplation meetings, mainly when you're doing only it as a performance practice.

It would be good to know that you are heading in the right direction.

- Make space. This is critical. Making space in your home or anyplace you feel good is an imperative aspect of your training. A devoted space for your reflection meetings ought to be a protected and agreeable spot for you, and ideally calm. Consume that space with anything you need to make you feel better or something that makes you incline that you should be there for quite a while. You can fill it with cushions, pads, pictures that move you, incense or scented candles in case it aides, and anything that reduces your spirit and presents to you a conclusion of quiet. That will go far toward helping you make contemplation a consistency in your life if you have a space that you anticipate investing some energy in every day due to the solace and quiet that it envelopes you in.

- Make it a timetable. OK, so very few individuals like everyday practice and timetable. However, this is basic if you are beginning in contemplation rehearses. Make it a feature, pencil it into your timetable, or make a note of it on your timetable application on your phone. It might be fundamental for various things to keep during the day to eclipse your consideration meeting, which is why you need to purposefully make that chance to stop and think before the day finishes up. You understand you didn't get the chance to invest any energy ruminating whatsoever.

When Is A Good Time To Meditate?

The short answer to this is preferably at a quiet time and as long as this time works for you. You can choose to meditate in the morning, afternoon, evening, or even before you go to bed. That's the beauty of this practice; it is entirely up to what works best for you. Every individual is distinctive, and no two people will be doing things the same way with the same experience. Some people prefer to meditate in the morning because it sets the tone for the rest of the day, while some prefer to do it at night because it helps them unwind, calm down, and relax after a long and hectic day.

The most significant time of the day for you to meditate would be any time that you can consistently and realistically commit to it.

It can be in the morning, in the afternoon, in the evening, or at night; it doesn't matter. As long as you are getting it done, that is the only thing that matters, even for just 10 minutes a day. A short meditation session is better than nothing at all.

When I'm Meditating, Is There A Specific Posture I Need To Follow?

No, there isn't because everyone is different again, and some people may prefer one posture, while someone else may prefer another. That is okay. The posture you decide to go with should be the one that feels most comfortable and what you are happy with. If sitting in a chair works better for you, go ahead and do that. If you prefer to sit cross-legged on a mat, that's alright. If you prefer to lie down, that's alright too. It is essential to do what is right for your body and what you feel most connected with, which will allow you to relax yet stay alert during your session at the same time.

Making Use Of Meditation Anchors

Even the most advanced meditation practitioners could use an anchor now and then. Our minds are such a versatile thing that sometimes it can get easily distracted and wander before becoming aware and bringing it back to focus again. This is why meditation anchors are helpful, especially if you are new to this practice. It will help you find the focus and concentration that you need during your meditation session. Even if you're an advanced practitioner, having an anchor will help you on the days when your mind may be struggling to grasp the concentration that it needs.

A meditation anchor will allow you to steady your mind and maintain focus on what you are doing. An anchor gives you a point to bring your mind back to whenever it deigns to wander off. An anchor gives you something to connect your mind as you strengthen and build on mindfulness, a practice that will eventually come with time.

A meditation anchor can be anything that you find useful and which helps you to maintain your focus. Some suggestions of what could be used as an anchor when you meditate include the following:

- Focusing on your breath as it moves in and out of your body

- What your body feels like with each deep breath you take

- Your chest as it ascends and falls slowly and rhythmically with each breath that moves in and out

- If you're using music or any ambient tones to help set the mood, you can focus on that and the way it makes you feel as you listen to the rhythm

- Physical sensations that slowly emerge as you progress throughout the meditation, for example, the way your hands feel or the way the muscles in your body feel

Are you starting to get the idea? Your anchor can be anything that you want it to be. It doesn't have to be specific to the list. It just has to be something that you can connect on, which your mind can focus on while you meditate. It helps you give you a purpose, especially when you're just starting. Otherwise, you could find yourself aimlessly sitting on the mat, wondering if you're doing it right or not being able to meditate at all.

This would be an excellent time to find an anchor that works best for you and helps you with your meditation practice. Being able to bring your thoughts back to your anchor when needed will be a great help in your four-week plan to achieve a deeper state of meditation.

Having a consistent anchor that is consistent would help, but if you ever feel that you want to choose or use something else as your anchor, go ahead and do it. If it helps you stay focused and works for you, your anchor can be anything you want it to be. Remember, it is all about finding what works best for you because meditation is such a personal experience, one that is entirely yours.

91. Frequently Asked Questions

Why do people do mindfulness meditation? The causes may not be clear to you at first, but it is worthwhile noting the scientific facts surrounding Mindfulness Meditation. Before we give you the step by step instructions, you need to know why it helps and who it helps.

How Meditation Helps With Depression Relief

Meditation is used to help depressed people because it focuses their attention on something other than negativity. When people are miserable, they tend to go over the same negative thoughts and go back to times when they have been hurt by life. Depression accumulates different emotional responses to stimuli, but not everyone reacts in the same way. There are forms of behavior that tend to push people toward depression. By learning to meditate and involve yourself in mindfulness, you discover ways to accept yourself and understand the workings of the inner mind better not to dwell on the negative.

Scientists who researched the brains of people who regularly meditated found more activity in areas of the brain that meant better efficiency in the memory and a much more peaceful demeanor. They were not prone to depression and certainly displayed a kind of oneness, which was not present in the scan of someone who did not meditate. They were calmer and more focused, which generally meant that they were more contented. There are obvious benefits for those who are depressed because their thought patterns are often negative and, as such, will encourage even more negative thought. If you take away those negative thoughts and replace them with breathing exercises such as when people meditate, it becomes easier for depressed people to find peace. This practice also lowers blood pressure and heart rate, which may be too high caused by depression.

While it may be more challenging for those suffering from depression, the benefits outweigh the inconvenience after a while. You start to learn to let go of negative thoughts and replace them with thoughts about the moment you are in. This helps you train your mind toward the positive, rather than grasping hold of the negative and believing there is no alternative. This is one reason why general practitioners recommend mindfulness meditation for people suffering from chronic or repeated depression as an alternative to traditional medicines.

In the United Kingdom, this has proven to be a popular choice and a successful one. The frontal cortex, responsible for well-being and happiness, shows decreased activity while someone is depressed. However, this is the area targeted by mindfulness meditation. Changes have been noted that are positive, which means that subjects are less prone to depression and more drawn toward seeking a positive nature.

How Meditation Helps With Anxiety Relief

Mindfulness meditation helps the sufferer to slow down in the breathing techniques used. This, in turn, stops the body from making too much oxygen and over-oxygenating the system. Half of the anxiety is due to panic and over-oxygenation, and breathing correctly can normalize this. You may have heard of people being asked to breathe into a paper bag when they feel anxious. This makes the stress less hard to cope with, and the anxiety lessens when you can look at the problems in question with a clear mind. Quite often, the pressure is a direct result of over-thinking things, and mindfulness helps you base your thoughts at the moment rather than holding onto them and trying to deal with things en-masse. When the mind is in overload, stresses occur. Thus, mindfulness slows down that process and allows an individual to be able to cope more effectively.

How Meditation Can Help With Pain

Pain management experts are using meditation to help patients to deal with chronic pain. It helps because it relaxes the body and mind and the concentration on the area of pain. When this is all that you focus on, then, of course, the problem comes before everything else. However, when you learn to meditate, you take your mind away from thinking about the pain while still being aware of it and not judging it in any way except that it may be a slight irritation. Gabriel Tan, a pain psychologist from Houston, said in a report on the pain that you cannot experience pain unless your thoughts are centered upon it. Therefore, giving the mind something else to concentrate on emphasizes the problem and makes it easier for people with painful conditions to get through those bad times when the pain seems unbearable. Studies from Switzerland back this up and say that meditation helps chronic sufferers of illnesses like fibromyalgia cope with pain and deal with the depression that comes with the disease. In fact, in a follow-through, three years after, those patients who had chosen to practice mindful meditation were still able to cope with their painful symptoms and found improvement in their state of mind. The only difference between treating mobile people and those who were less mobile was that it helped to teach lying down relaxation methods that lead to meditation, as this seemed to be easier on their bodies.

How Meditation Can Help With Stress

We know that stressed people suffer from increased blood pressure, quicker heartbeat, and exaggerated breathing. What this does inside the body is releasing a hormone called cortisol. Cortisol in small doses is reasonable, but when your system overloads, it has consequences. These include health threats and anxiety, depression, and even heart problems, and thus, meditation is used to calm down the breathing and regulate the production of this cortisol. In excess, it can make you feel very ill, which adds to the stress factor. Let me give you an example. A young woman worries because she feels pains in her chest. She is alone, and she is afraid. This makes her even more stressed. The body's answer to this stress is the release of cortisol. This adds to the stress, makes the heart beat faster, and makes the blood pressure even higher. Instead of helping her, it hinders her thought processes in that she will concentrate on the pain, logically trying to find a solution for it although thinking the worst. This kind of stress is expected in this day and age, but meditation does so much for you that it isn't merely a case of bringing down your blood pressure. It opens up avenues for creativity, as scientists have seen on practicing Buddhist monks' MRIs and your awareness of self. This awareness also helps you to understand what's going on in your body and be able to listen to it more effectively, thus cutting down the stress and the cortisol at the same time.

When a company asked its employees to take part in Meditation, and this was measured over some time, what they found was that stress was reduced by 28 percent, 20 percent of the employees suffered less pain and consequently needed less time off work, and 19 percent of the people involved found as a side effect to meditation that they got a good night's sleep. That's terrific news for those starting on the journey into reflection because it's not hard to do, but it can build all the difference in how you greet the world and how your body reacts to your lifestyle are living. Getting sufficient sleep is vital because this allows the natural healing processes of the body to function. Getting up and then meditating starts the day on a positive note and helps people who are easily stressed to reduce that stress to a minimum.

How Meditation Helps With Illness In General

When you meditate regularly, you are more in touch with how your body feels and are aware of changes that need you to introduce changes. The relationship between you and your inner self is improved, and you are unlikely to abuse your body, knowing that the habits you have been following are causing illness to occur. Drinking more water and exercising regularly are part of life, but the part that many neglect. However, when you meditate, you have a crystal clear idea of what your body needs to recuperate. You tend not to neglect yourself and understand that personal suffering is simply your body sending a message to your brain to help you to understand yourself better. People who are busy in their stressed lives and who do not meditate don't find the time to deal with small ailments and these then become long term ailments, whereas someone who meditates is instantly aware of little things and deals with them. The spiritual part of the equation is essential because people who practice mindfulness are aware of their senses and know that they are more than the sum of their discomfort. When the pain of illness is dealt with promptly, they suffer less, and it makes perfect sense to them that their feelings guide them to better look after themselves.

It is merely a question of getting in tune with your mind, and that's what the world today does not allow you to do. We are too busy in our lives, and people are starting to realize that you cannot judge your life by what you own, nor your success by what position you hold within a company. If your thoughts and feelings are muddled, then being wealthy or successful won't change that muddle, although meditation can.

How Meditation Helps With Concentration

In Liverpool, John Moore University studied the effects of meditation for a simple period of 20 minutes a day on students' concentration levels instead of those who did not perform meditation. During the 16 week study, in which 40 adults took part, tests were given that allowed the scientists to measure the level of concentration, and this clearly showed that those who meditated were better able and equipped to answer the questions asked of them.

Concentration is sharper and more focused when practicing mindfulness meditation regularly. Imagine the mind as a series of cardboard boxes.

Every time that the mind is drawn toward one of these boxes or another, it evokes emotions. These remain open in the sense that they do not practice meditation, while in those who do, the reason is more organized and less likely to succumb to forgetfulness. The focus is sharper as if the weight of those boxes of thoughts has been taken away, and the mind is left to concentrate on what is particularly important at that moment in time.

It's also worth noting that even small breathing exercises used at points during the day can help clarify the mind and the practitioner's perception.

How Meditation Helps Self-Acceptance

Mindfulness meditation allows you to spend more time exclusively with yourself, and you get to know yourself better than you would typically do. Friendliness and kindness are part of the picture, as well as empathy and understanding. When you have practiced mindfulness meditation, you have a better mental picture of who you are rather than who people say you are. The compassion that you feel from mindfulness meditation helps you accept yourself and be kinder to your person. Negative thoughts are not encouraged, but they are acknowledged. You can't hide them because they will happen, but students are taught how to deal with them and give them less importance.

92. How to Manage Stress with Meditation?

So what is stress? Stress is the body's way of responding to pressure that may be exerted physically or psychologically. Stress occurs when the body releases stress chemicals, usually adrenaline, into the blood to combat whatever force it is confronted with. Stress can be classified as follows:

- Survival stress. This is the stress that we face when confronted by dangerous situations where you feel that physical harm is imminent. It is here where we have a fight-and-flight response to fight stress.

- Internal stress. This is stress caused by worries over things that are out of your control. Put merely, and inner focus is self-imposed stress that can be avoided by not giving yourself so much pressure over things that are beyond you.

- Environmental stress. This is stress caused by factors in your surroundings, like noise. Stay away from ecological stress triggers, and you will have a happy life.

- Tiredness. This type of stress is caused by fatigue, which usually accumulates over a long period due to overworking.

Stress is an unavoidable part of life, and sooner or after, we experience it. We need to learn how to manage it, not to overwhelm us and take over our lives. Stress is not an entirely bad thing as it can enhance our alertness and concentration. However, in excess, it is very unhealthy.

Symptoms Of Stress

How do you know if you are stressed? The following are some signs that will let you know if you are stressed.

Cognitive Symptoms:

- Problems remembering things

- Low concentration

- High anxiety
- Constant worry

Emotional Symptoms:

- Being moody
- Highly irritable and angry
- Loneliness and reclusion
- Sadness

Physical Symptoms:

- Low libido
- Aches and pain
- High heart rate
- Dizziness

Behavioral symptoms:

- Eating disorders (bingeing or self-starving)
- Lack of Sleep
- Substance abuse
- Nervousness

Causes Of Stress

External Causes:

- Significant life changes (divorce, chronic illness, the death of a loved one)
- Work burden
- Financial problems
- Trauma

Internal Causes:

- Constant worry

- Negativity and pessimism

- Fear and anxiety

- Unrealistic expectations

Side Effects Of Stress

Stress can cause severe health and social problems if it is not dealt with immediately and well. Here are some of the side effects of stress:

- Mental disorders, like depression and anxiety

- Weight problems, such as obesity

- Problems with menstrual cycles

- Skin and hair problems (acne, hair loss, etc.)

- Sexual dysfunction

- Gastrointestinal problems, like ulcerative colitis

Meditation And Stress Management

Meditation has been proven as a stress reliever and is being embraced by many for relaxation. Stress relief needs both mental and physical relaxation, and meditation provides that. To understand why meditation is so helpful in reducing stress, we should know what it takes to relax:

- Deep breathing. Deep breathing is a quick and sure way of deflating pressure from your system. This is a simple technique with far-reaching positive consequences in keeping stress in check.

- Balancing the nervous system. For the body to function optimally, the nervous system must be at equilibrium. You must be at peace mentally. Stress destabilizes this balance, and the only way to stead your system is by relaxation. A state of profound serenity of the nervous system is the counter to stress.

- Yoga: Yoga is a series of steady movement and stationary poses combined with deep breathing. Yoga reduces stress and improves flexibility, strength, balance, and stamina if practiced regularly. Almost all yoga types are beneficial for stress and anxiety relief as they combine steady movement, deep breathing, and stretching. You may try the following types:

- Satyananda. This is an old-style yoga form that uses meditation, gentle poses, and deep relaxation. It is a model for those who want to start practicing for stress and anxiety relief.

- Hatha Yoga. This is also a gentle form that is ideal for you to ease your way into practice.

- Power Yoga. Power yoga is more advanced and is for those who are already familiar with the basics. It is more intense, and the focus is on fitness. This is ideal for those seeking relaxation and stimulation.

- Tai Chi. Tai Chi is a mellow form of meditation suited for everyone. It is especially suitable for the elderly recovering from injuries and illnesses common with those of advanced age. It is a series of slow body movements, emphasizing concentration, circulation of energy through the body, and relaxation while breathing.

To effectively deal with stress and anxiety through meditation, it is essential to practice whichever type of meditation you settle for. Make it part of your life. Practice it regularly until it becomes second nature. Here is what you need to do for a successful stress-relieving meditation experience:

1.   Get a quiet, serene place for your meditation exercise; this can be anywhere as long as it has no interference. It can be in your backyard, living room, in a park, etc.

2.   Assume a comfortable posture, whether seated, standing, or lying down. Start tuning your mind to the here and now: focus and concentrate.

3.   In the posture with eyes closed, take a slow deep breath and relax your body as you do this. Get into an inhaling and exhaling rhythm.

4.   Clear your mind of disrupting thoughts and concentrate on your meditation. Pay care to your breathing, and focus on that only as you relax.

5.   Channel your mind to happy thoughts of a comfortable place you have been, or concentrate on the present while listening to your breathing. Push out unwanted thoughts that may come your way.

6.   Keep your eyes closed, take deep breaths, and imagine your body relaxing. Keep doing this until you are entirely relaxed.

Imagine a life of reduced anxiety and stress. Isn't that what we all want? Whenever pressure is left to get out of control, depression sets in. Depression is a condition that is directly linked to the mismanagement of stress. Depression is an extreme form of stress. Let us understand what depression is and how meditation can help in its relief.

Fighting Depression Through Meditation

Depression is a disorder of a person's mood or emotions, causing sadness and loss of interest.

When one is faced with extreme emotions or feelings of hopelessness, anxiety, sadness, despair, or low self-esteem, they can be considered depressed. This type of depression is situational as it is triggered by circumstances that the person is dealing with. Clinically, depression is caused by a chemical imbalance in the brain, causing bipolar disorder and manic depression, generally referred to as organic depression. Stress hormones (cortisol and epinephrine) found in adrenaline has been proven responsible for organic depression.

Depression is usually exhibited or accompanied by the following symptoms:

- Loss of interest in hobbies and usual activities

- Reclusiveness

- Feelings of hopelessness and worthlessness

- Difficulty or lack of sleep

- Restlessness and fatigue

- Lower concentration

- Suicidal thoughts

Once in a whereas, we all face some form of mild depression. Unfortunately, some of us experience extreme forms of this condition that can overwhelm them, leading to significant mental deterioration, social self-exclusion, and even suicides.

Causes of Depression

Depression is caused by several factors or, in some instances, a combination of these factors. They are as follows:

- A chronic and long illness

- Some personality traits are more susceptible to depression (e.g., low self-esteem)

- Family history (those from families where some have suffered depression before are highly likely to be affected)

- Giving birth (some women get postnatal depression because of physical and emotional changes)

- Loneliness and drug abuse

- Chemical changes in the brain (clinical depression)

- Physical and emotional abuse

- Some medicines

- Conflicts

The good news is that depression can significantly be managed and even treated through meditation, as we shall learn herein.

How Does Meditation Help Deal With Depression?

When we think about how we can fight depression by meditative means, we need to understand both and know how they correlate. In both situational and organic definitions, we have seen that depression is a mental disorder caused by triggers that will destabilize the mental balance. Conversely, we have seen that meditation has been proven and used by many to reinstate this elusive balance.

All types of meditation have their foundations in the pursuit of a balanced mind where depression is not welcome. The many meditative techniques for mental focus and exercise are why meditation works to curb problems with depression. Meditation will teach you the techniques necessary for mental clarity and serenity with regular practice and adoption into your life. You will learn positive mental focusing on a healthy and calm mind.

When the mind is so balanced, one becomes more positive, happy, and optimistic. These attributes manifested as a result of meditative practice are what will keep you from getting depressed. The biggest secret of meditation is the ability to change one's thought process if embraced and practiced over time.

Changing the way we think to negate and effectively deal with negative situations and thought is the fundamental lesson of meditation. We need to take control of our minds to deal with our environment.

Bipolar and manic depressants can also gain a lot in management and even get cured of their condition through meditation. Using prescription medicine, the medical world recommends and uses reflection to treat these conditions, and it is working! Meditation is making these patients calmer by focusing their thoughts and mental energies positively. It trains them on how to control their mental emotions in circumstances that may exacerbate or trigger problems.

The ability to fight depression goes to the core of meditation's goals, elevating the mind to a level of self-regulation. Self-regulation leads to self-control, which spawns mental positivity, so a positive, happy mind cannot be depressed. Therefore, the psychological and physical exercises found in meditation are essential for defeating depression. A healthy reason, together with a fit, muscular body, is a balance that is not easily tipped by mental emotions.

Research has shown that meditation works to eliminate or control depression by boosting one's social behavior and emotional well-being, which can work very well for situational depression cases. Additionally, meditation has been proven to lower stress hormones released by the body responsible for depression. Adrenaline causes panic, which in turn causes depression if not checked or well managed. Meditative practices serve to calm a person down, thus regulating the production of these hormones.

Meditation will also train and help you detach yourself from emotional stress and still deal effectively with difficult situations to avoid the load of depression. In the following part, let us learn how to achieve the ultimate state of relaxation through meditation.

93. Meditation for Anxiety

Unfortunately, many individuals have to cope with stress and anxiety. While it's a natural reaction for our bodies, there is a way to control these feelings through mindfulness meditation. To begin, we'll start with a basic anxiety relief script to help get you started.

Basic Anxiety Relief Script

If you suffer from anxiety, realize that you're not alone in feeling this way. Anxiety is something that genuinely affects several different people. If you would similar to take a few moments to help relieve your anxiety by gaining control of your breath, find a comfortable position, and then we can begin our meditation.

Once you find a comfortable position, go ahead and begin to find your breath. Take a deep breath and exhale slowly. Gently take a few more breaths until you feel your heartbeat begin to slow down.

As you continue to focus on your breath, realize that anxiety is a natural reaction for your body. One of the best ways to help incapacitate natural anxiety is to relax. Once you relax, you'll be able to gain control over the automatic response your body is having and be able to fix your anxiety.

At this moment, you may have several symptoms of anxiety, whether you are shaking, are having worrying thoughts, your breathing is rapid, or maybe your muscles are just a bit tense. What's essential right now is that you realize that these things are happening. Before we can relax our bodies, we must relax our mind and gain control of the situation.

First, I want you to focus on your breath. Calm breathing is going to be the key to become relaxed. Go ahead and take a bottomless breath through your nose and exhale through your mouth. Good. Now, I need you to inhale deeply and exhale as if you are blowing a candle out on a birthday cake. As you exhale, be sure to release all of the air in your lungs.

On your following breath in, I want you to inhale and focus on slowing down the process of breathing, make it a calm rhythm. At this moment, you have the control to calm yourself.

As you continue breathing, realize that you are giving your body the oxygen it needs to relax.

The only job that you have at this moment is to create a comfortable environment for yourself. When we fight against anxiety, it only helps the feeling grow more vigorous. Once you face that you are feeling anxious, you'll be able to calm your thoughts and relieve anxiety all by yourself. Remember to keep breathing through this process. You will want to inhale slowly. Feel your heartbeat begin to slow down and become steady.

When you are ready, I would like you to repeat a couple of phrases after me.

At this moment, I am feeling very anxious, but I'm okay.

In a few moments, this feeling will pass, and I'm in no way harmed.

I'm safe even though I feel as though I am panicked. Soon I'll be calm even though at this moment I am feeling anxious.

I can get through this. I'm taking steps to make myself feel relaxed and comfortable while the anxiety passes.

I believe that I can make myself calmer and more relaxed. Soon this too shall pass.

As you focus on your breath, go ahead and give yourself some more calming messages. You can tell yourself whatever it is you need to know at this moment.

If you are undergoing a severe anxiety attack and your muscles are trembling, you may be able to shake the tension out of your muscles physically. I want you to imagine that you are shaking water off your hands as if you were drying them. Go ahead and shake your hands and allow your wrist to fly limp as you shake your hands back and forth gently. As you do this, go ahead and imagine the water drops flying off your fingertips. The water is your tension draining away from you and being shaken away. Once you feel you have shaken the tension from your hands and your wrist, take a moment to stop and see how your hands feel. With the tension gone, you should have a more relaxed feeling in your hands. Now, return your thoughts to your breathing and remind yourself that you are overcoming this feeling.

Exhale gently and remind yourself that you feel more and more relaxed with each breath you take.

Once you're breathing has evened out, I want to take a final moment to focus on your muscles. When we are anxious, they often become tense and painful and tired. I would like to take a minute now to help relax your muscles one at a time.

First, I would like you to drop your lower jaw. Go ahead and drop your jaw so that your teeth are no longer touching. Allow for your jaw to become relaxed and loose, and feel how much better your jaw feels when your teeth aren't clenched together.

Now, I would like you to go ahead and lower your shoulders. Allow them to drop away from your ear and allow your shoulders to relax and loosen. Move your shoulders gently forward in tiny circles and backward. Allow your shoulders to become limp as you help create distance between your shoulder blades and in between your ears.

Now, go ahead and carefully turn your head to the left and then back to the center and gently to the right. Return to center and gently tip your chin toward the ceiling and feel the stretch in the back of your neck. Now restore your head to a neutral position, straighten your back and feel how much more relaxed your muscles have become.

Before we finish our relaxation for anxiety script, go ahead and take a few more moments to move and relax; however, you need to help relieve your anxiety.

As you carry on with your day, there are four steps for you to remember to help cope with anxiety daily.

First, remember to breathe. When we experience anxiety, our first reaction is to begin to hyperventilate. If feelings of anxiety slip into your mind, remind yourself to inhale slowly and exhale fully. When you are in control of your breath, you are in control of your mind.

Second, remember to calm your thoughts. Of course, this is simpler said than done. However, the first step is being aware of your anxiety, and after that, you can take a deep breath and calm your thoughts down.

If needed, you can always move on to the third step and physically shake the tension out of your body.

It only takes a few moments to shake your hands and just imagine the tension dripping off of your hands like water.

And finally, remember to relax your muscles. If an anxiety attack comes on, take a deep breath, release your jaw release your shoulders, and remember that these feelings will pass. As long as you stay in handling your thoughts and body, you will overcome anything thrown at you.

94. Meditation for Deep Sleep

Before you continue with your day, I would like you to take a few more moments to bring awareness back to your breath. When you are ready, gently bring awareness back into the room, hear the noises surrounding you, touch the ground beneath you, take a deep breath, and carry on with your day with his new sense of peace. Over the afterward half an hour, we will help guide you into a deep, relaxing sleep. If you have been struggling to sleep because of things on your mind or the stresses you have been distributing throughout the day, this meditation will help you relax your mind and body to get the sleep you need.

Before we start, it's important to remember that it is okay if you are not asleep by the end of this meditation. People need varying times from night tonight, in which they can fall asleep. If you are still conscious at the end of this meditation, repeat the steps in your mind, and you will be capable of falling asleep at your own pace.

Start by making yourself friendly and comfortable. Get into a comfortable position in bed, ideally the kind of situation you would usually sleep in. You can close your eyes now if you want to, or you can keep them open. Whatever makes you feel comfortable.

Grab in a deep breath and then gently breathe out. Allow the air you are living in to flow through your body. Take in an added deep breath and as you breathe out, imagine that you are releasing any tension you may be feeling. Now just allow yourself to settle into the bed. Mentally register that this is the time to start switching off. You don't need to be thinking about anything or worrying about anything. This time is just about relaxing and getting sleep.

Spread your awareness through your entire body. Sign if you are holding any tension anywhere. Throughout this meditation, you will gradually release these feelings of uncertainty so you can settle down into a relaxing sleep.

Take in another deep breath. Now exhale slowly. As you gulp in, imagine that the air you are breathing is bringing feelings of rejuvenation and relaxation. And then, as you breathe out, you live away from any tension or intrusive emotions you may be feeling.

As you sink deeper into the meditation and closer to falling asleep, you might have thoughts coming to mind. They could be about things you need to do tomorrow or things that happened today. Some of these thoughts might start to generate toxic emotions or negative thoughts in your mind. Remember that now is time to let those thoughts drift away gently. You do not need them at this time. This is a time standoffish just for you to relax. Sleep is a precious thing, and you deserve to be able to enjoy it without any difficulties.

Just offer yourself a moment to allow these feelings to pass. Allow your mind to clear. Permit yourself to have this peaceful time just for yourself. Tell yourself that you deserve to have a quiet night's sleep, and you do not need to be kept away by instructive thoughts or negative emotions. You deserve to have a peaceful night's sleep. Suppose you can imagine those thoughts and feelings floating away, like a small white cloud in a beautiful blue sky. Just picture them floating further and further away until they have entirely disappeared. As you do this, just focus on your mind on the natural rhythm of your breathing.

Turn your devotion to how your body feels. Have you been able to notice any tension? This tension could have been manifested in your mind by stress or feelings of anxiety. Just take a moment to take in any feelings of uncertainty you may have, no matter where they are in your body.

Now that you have noticed the tension areas, try and focus on one place for a moment. Fully take in how it feels. Now, as you bring in another refreshing breath, imagine that the air is moving to the area of tension. Imagine that it is gently soothing the room, almost like a gentle wave of warm water washing over the place. As you exhale slowly, imagine that the air is now carrying the tension out of your body and into the air. Leaving your body with more room to feel warm and relaxed.

This may not necessarily work the first time you do this. It is entirely normal for there still to be a little lingering tension. Simply repeat the process. Breathing in soothing air. And then living away from the pressure. Keep undertaking this until your entire body feels warm and relaxed. Utterly free of tension. Able to embrace the feeling of relaxation.

Scan your body again. Fully take in the relaxing feeling you feel in your body. Let the calmness wash over you thoroughly. Every time you exhale, letting out that little bit more tension. Every single breath is bringing you closer and closer to a peaceful sleep.

Now, we are going to count down from ten to one slowly. With each passing number, you will feel more and more relaxed. Moving closer and closer to the peaceful night's sleep that you both need and deserve.

Ten. Focus on number ten. Then move your attention to your breathing. Bringing in air. The feeling as the air comes in through your nose and your mouth. The rise of your chest and your stomach. And then breathing out. Feeling the relaxation spread through your body as your chest muscles and ribs relax. Becoming more and more relaxed with each breath.

Nine. Sinking deeper into relaxation now. Falling deeper and deeper into the bed. Your entire body is feeling heavy. All the tension was slowly leaving your body every time you exhale.

Eight. Embracing this feeling of being totally at peace. Breathing in. And then breathing out. Breathing away all the tension. Living away from the negative feeling. All you feel now is the relaxation in your body and happy, positive thoughts.

Seven. Focus on number seven. Then move your attention back to your body. The tingling feelings through your legs and your arms as they become more massive. Closer to a relaxing and recharging sleep.

Six. Drifting deeper and deeper into calmness now. The sensations of sleep starting to wash over you. You feel totally at peace. Completely centered. Fully embracing this serenity.

Five. Focus on number five. Fully experience the calm and positive feelings entering your empty mind. You don't need to think about what happened today. You don't need to think about tomorrow. All you require to do is focus on the feelings of relaxation that you have at this moment.

Four. Your body and mind are one. The connection between them growing more robust as they relax together. Completely calm and centered.

Three. Fully appreciate this wonderful feeling. You have been able to create this feeling through the power of your mind. Just by giving yourself this break, you have opened the door to a peaceful and relaxing sleep.

Two. Focus on number two as you slowly start to drift away. Your mind is now just drifting aimlessly. Your entire body is feeling like it is floating down a gentle lake.

One. Focus on the number one now as you feel completely at peace. Just allowing yourself to drift off into a gentle sleep.

If you are still awake, that is okay. It is perfectly normal to be always awake. All you need to do is repeat the counting, this time going up from one to ten. With each passing number, fully embrace the feelings of relaxation running through your mind and your body. Keep counting until you find your mind can't concentrate on them anymore as you drift off to a peaceful sleep.

Fully immerse yourself in this feeling of blissful relaxation now as you slowly drift off. Taking with your feelings of happiness and positivity about yourself and waiting for you when tomorrow comes.

95. Meditation for Stress Relief

Once again, any form of meditation will help you relax and relieve some stress, as meditation forces the body to slow down and become calm, and the mind quiets and pushes away all unneeded thoughts, including the ones that stress us out. Still, some techniques are better at relieving stress than others, especially in the long run, when it comes to more profound stress than that caused by daily life. One of the best things about regularly practicing meditation is that, with time, you will build up a resistance, and it will take a lot more before you get stressed out.

The most effective technique for stress is metta meditation. It teaches love and compassion and is especially useful if the source of your stress is other people. While practicing metta meditation, focus on the people who are causing the most stress in your life. Use your mantras and send them your love and compassion. Metta meditation will take a while to work fully, but with enough time and practice, your meditation will help you accept these people and their ways, and in turn, their actions and personalities won't stress you out so much anymore.

Mindfulness meditation also works great for stress relief, as it forces you to focus on the present and leave your stress and anxiety behind. During mindfulness meditation, your subconscious mind isn't dwelling on all the things that because you stress. The more you practice mindfulness, the less you'll worry about your everyday life. Of course, there are different types of mindfulness, and some have been created to be especially useful for stress relief.

A long, luxurious bath is one of the best ways to meditate using mindfulness. Added to the simple act of meditating, you have the warm water that will relax your body's muscles and ease tension. It's also one of the few meditations where you don't have to worry about posture and position. Simply get in the tub, let your body relax, and take in the incredible sensations. Slow down your breathing, let yourself fall into a meditative trance, and focus on the beautiful, relaxing feel of the warm water. To give yourself an even more comfortable experience, you can add a scented bubble bath, bath salts, or essential oils. You can also use candlelight and soothing music to create a relaxed atmosphere. Simply focus on all the sensations and let your troubles flow out of you. By the time you get out of the tub, you should feel relaxed and tranquil.

This technique is especially suited for when you've had an unusually long and stressful day or when you have a lot of tension built up inside your body.

Listening to music or using aromatherapy are great ways to meditate for stress relief. Even if you aren't actively contemplating, the right music and incense can soothe your subconscious and help you feel relaxed.

Mantras are also great for stress relief, and there are hundreds to choose from to find what works best. Mantras that usually work best are things like 'I am fine,' 'I'm at peace,' 'I am calm,' 'What will happen, will happen,' etc. Suppose you want to use a Sanskrit mantra. In that case, you can use a mantra-like an om mani padme hum, which helps develop compassion and love and works excellent with mindfulness, or om ram Tamaya Namaha, which helps get rid of negative energy and stress and is believed to bring pure thoughts.

If you want to use a mudra, the earth's sign is the one to go with. This Mudra helps you connect to the planet, stay grounded, and find balance in your life. With harmony and a sense of security and strength, your stress will automatically melt away. For this mudra, bend your pinky and ring finger and touch their tips to the tip of your thumb. Stretch out the other two fingers while keeping them pressed together.

Chocolate Meditation

This may seem a tiny far fetched, but no, chocolate meditation is a real thing. This is a form of eating mindfully, in which the purpose is to focus on the taste of the food you're eating, which will help you enjoy it a whole new level. Chocolate is explicitly used for stress relief because the subconscious mind automatically associates it with feelings of comfort and relaxation, and eating chocolate always makes us feel better. Even the aroma of chocolate has a calming effect on the mind.

Chocolate meditation works by involving the senses in your meditation and mind, and regular practice can have a long-lasting effect on your stress levels. As the name implies, you'll need a piece of chocolate. Ideally, you should be using dark chocolate with a high cocoa content, but you can use any type of chocolate you like eating. It may seem like a bad idea to meditate with chocolate every day, but you only need one or two bite-sized pieces. Incidentally, many people use this form of meditation to help them eat less chocolate than usual.

If you don't like chocolate or are allergic, you can use nuts, dried fruits, other types of candy, or any food you want to treat yourself with.

1.   Begin by relaxing your body and meditating on your breathing. A seated position works best for this. Make sure your chocolate is close by before you start meditating.

2.   Once you feel entirely relaxed, bring a piece of chocolate close to your face. Take a deep breath and effort on the aroma of the chocolate. Take a good look at it and notice the deep, rich color and the smoothness of your chocolate.

3.   Shot a small bite and let it rest on your tongue for a bit. Focus not only on the taste but on the texture as well. Feel how soft and smooth the chocolate becomes as it melts in your mouth. Note the sense of warmness and joy that flows over you as you swallow the chocolate.

4.   Keep replicating these last two steps until you've eaten all your chocolate. After that, you can either continue meditating using any other technique you like, or you can finish off your meditation and go on with your day.

5.   As you go within your day, keep going back to the experience you've had with your chocolate and remember wonderful aroma, taste, and texture. The memory of your chocolate meditation should be enough to help you calm down and feel less stressed.

Walking Meditation

This is another form of mindfulness meditation that's exceptionally great for stress relief. This technique is as simple as taking a walk outside and has the added benefit of giving you some exercise and fresh air. Walking meditation is useful because it helps you put physical distance between you and your worries and mental and emotional space. This technique also forces you to set aside time for yourself.

To practice walking meditation, you'll need to find a park, beach, forest, or safe neighborhood where you'll feel safe and comfortable to walk by yourself. You'll also have to make sure your shoes are suitable for walking, and your clothes are comfortable. The suggested length of your walk is thirty minutes, but you can make it shorter or longer, depending on what you want and how much time you have available.

You may want to set the alarm for yourself on your phone, and if your surroundings are too noisy, you can use earphones to listen to a guided meditation or soothing music.

1. Make sure you won't be interrupted on your walk, and your phone is switched to silent so you won't be bothered by calls and messages. Start your meditation practice by walking at a pace you're comfortable with. Most people prefer walking relatively slowly, so they can concentrate better, but you're welcome to speed it up if that works better for you.

2. As you walk, start to focus on the movement of your body. Feel the earth beneath you with every step you take, the wind in your eyes, and the swing of your arms as you walk.

3. You can start focusing on your breathing and even try to synchronize your breathing and footsteps. Try taking two steps every time you inhale and another two every time you exhale. If you get distracted by thoughts of all your problems or things that tend to stress you out, or if your mind begins to wander, simply acknowledge the views or take note of where your mind is going and refocus yourself.

4. If you're not heading towards a specific destination, or you haven't planned a route that brings you back to where you started, you'll have to turn around and walk back at some point. When your time is up, or you've reached the end of your walk, end your meditation by letting your mind slip out of the meditative trance. Walking a little quicker for a few steps is an excellent way to help you get that done.

When To Meditate To Relieve Stress

Once again, there are no rules to when and where to meditate to relieve stress, other than trying to keep a regular meditation schedule with daily practice. If you live or work in a very stressful environment, you may have to meditate regularly when the stress starts getting to you. A five-minute meditation is a great technique to work in a quick meditation session whenever you feel like the pressure is getting too much.

96. Meditation to Control Your Thoughts

Our emotional traps are sometimes the things that make or break our day. We succumb to overthinking about what could go wrong or about what someone said or what someone thinks about us. Before we know it, we suddenly have that feeling of panic creeping up inside of us. We get sweaty, we have a hard time breathing, our pulse races, and we feel like getting choked. Does this happen to you?

We all experience these sensations in life, especially when we want something to happen so badly to our favor.

At the point when you overthink, this prompts nervousness assaults, just as fits of anxiety. Since you have envisioned your mind's situation is excessively phenomenal or excessively extraordinary until you can't conquer it, you begin to get stressed that you can't control it.

Taking Back Your Control On Thoughts

According to Dr. Catherine Pittman, a clinical psychologist and professor at Saint Mary's College Psychology department, people with high overthinking levels are because of pathological reasons. She says that the average person does overthink and that overthinking is rooted in the feeling of uncertainty.

To scientists, there is no apparent reason as to why the process of overthinking happens. However, they agree that overthinking engages the same parts of the brain that triggers fear and anxiety. According to Pittman, the cerebral cortex in the human brain is the center of all thinking. It is a logical part of the brain related to memories. It also helps us think about and also anticipates things.

But the danger lies when you start obsessing about something, and it triggers the amygdala's attention. Amygdala's attention is the brain's emotional system, and through research, scientists have found it to include fear and, yes, anxiety.

When we experience fear, anxiety, or panic, the amygdala is why our heart pounds, our muscles tense up, and it makes us feel uneasy.

The more you worry about something, the more you train your brain to overthink and, eventually, the more you activate the amygdala. It is a vicious cycle, no doubt, and you end up putting yourself at risk of getting anxiety disorders.

Understanding Panic Attacks And Its Stress Responses

What Are Panic Attacks?

Panic attacks are a type of anxiety disorder. Researchers have not found specific causes of panic disorders. Still, some say that it is a combination of environmental and biological factors. These factors can be stressful life events, traumatic childhood, family history, drug, alcohol abuse, and environmental factors.

According to Dr. Barbara Rothbaum, a psychiatry director and professor at the Trauma and Anxiety Recovery Program at the Emory University School of Medicine, Atlanta, people can feel anxious for various reasons, including work and family-related issues. Anxiety can also stem from making an important decision or waiting for an important decision and taking a big exam.

Someone who suffers from panic attacks reacts to even moderate pressures with an exaggerated physical reaction. It is a full-blown adrenaline, fight-or-flight response that takes place. It can severely hamper a person's daily activities and, also, their overall quality of life.

Not only that, but you will also explore meditation and how it can help you calm yourself and be more relaxed.

While self-help is excellent because taking that first step to identify a problem you have and wanting to do something about it is excellent if you ever feel like you need more help and guidance, speaking to a therapist or a counselor is the best way forward.

Fight Or Flight Response

As humans, we have this response called the fight or flight tendency, a reality honed in prehistory. Scientifically, it is a mode that our minds put us in when faced with what our body considers life-threatening or dangerous. This response is also referred to as an acute stress response. It shares the same reactions or feelings, such as shaking, anxiety, and fear, which occurs when our body prepares for a possible emergency. The term fight or flight started going around sometime in the 1920s. The alternative to this type of response is the relaxation response that the body has. This is known as the time the body allots for recovering from the time the distress call was rung. It is the body's way of normalizing its functions. This happens between 20 to 60 minutes after the perceived threat disappears.

Motivations Behind This Response

This phenomenon features basic instincts at work. It tackles stress and restores the body's state of calm. This type of response evolved from our ancestors' crude means of living, where they had to act on survival instincts to keep them alive. For example, prehistoric cave dwellers were in constant danger of animals. One minute, they might be lighting a fire, and the next minute, there's a stampede coming their way full of mammoths. The human design then kicks in. We have a maximum surge of energy and strength to respond to the threat by removing ourselves from danger and increasing our chances of survival quickly.

This Instinct Coupled With Panic Disorder

To some researchers, the association between these two stress reactions has been a product of the time. The fight or flight phenomenon seeped into modern-day society in different forms, and one is panic disorder. This can be something like being afraid of large or small spaces or being in situations that are shady or no-easy-escape route.

So that takes place when this reaction has been activated? Numerous physiological changes have been acknowledged by researchers that happen when the flight-or-fight response takes place. It is believed that these changes are prompted by the sympathetic nervous system that, at the moment, saw it necessary to discharge loads of stress hormones into our body. When this happens, it causes a quick and instant physical reaction to prepare the body's muscles for its flight mode to seek safety or fight mode if deemed necessary or unavoidable.

Some of the changes that take place during this process include:

- Having a tunnel vision
- Sweating

- Expansion of the blood vessels to the muscles

- Enlargement of pupils

- Auditory exclusion

- Constriction of blood vessels to other areas of the body

- Amplified heart rate and quick breathing

These changes occur instantly. In case you find yourself in mortal danger, you can expect to feel of these physical occurrences happening to your body. However, suppose you suddenly feel like this when you're quietly having dinner or even grocery shopping. In that case, this is something to be looked into. A large part of the stress experienced by modern-day culture is very much linked to the so-called psychosocial stress. Still, if you do get physical stress occurring all the time, it could be harmful to one's overall well-being and health.

How Fear Is Reinforced When There Is No Danger

When a person experiences a panic attack, the body's system is triggered without any visible signs of danger. It is the lack of or the absence of risk that greatly magnifies fear linked to panic attacks. If there is an identifiable danger, we see it, and we understand the symptoms associated with it, and then we wear the threat but not the signs.

If there is no danger, but a person begins to sweat, the breathing and heart rate become rapid, the sense of sight or hearing diminishes, and a person begins to fear the symptoms and even believes that they are life-threatening. Your body is telling you to get ready physically and that you are in grave danger, but what about the psychological aspects of dangers you cannot see? Experiencing these thoughts do not get you out of danger; they also strengthen and reinforce your association with fear, and it is not based on the actual threat.

Practicing Relaxation Daily

Relaxation can be anything, but it is a state where you feel at peace and calm, and you can manage your day-to-day life. It can be difficult to relax when you have a busy life, but practicing it even in small ways can help you manage anxiety and stress.

Improve Mental Health With Relaxation

Stress and other mental health symptoms, such as schizophrenia, depression, and anxiety, are reduced when we relax and make plenty of relaxation habits and techniques throughout the day. Apart from that, we also experience many other benefits that are not immediately seen, which are:

- Lowering blood pressure

- Lowered breathing rate

- Lowered heart rate

- Mood improvements and better concentration

- Less anger and frustration

- Confidence boost

- Ability to rationally solve problems

97. Meditation for Body

Body scan meditation helps reduce stress by making you aware of how your body feels instead of paying attention to stressful thoughts. When you feel stressed out, your body also feels those effects, and it starts to show signs of stress through pain in your back, stomach, or tensed shoulders. You may even experience neck ache, mainly if you have been concentrating on difficult things, which strained you somehow. You may just have aching bones because you are cold or worn out in general, but a body scan can help you feel much better.

By practicing body scan meditation, you distract your mind from the stressful thoughts by paying attention to those parts of the body that feel stressed. As a result, you become mindful of your body and forget the thoughts that bring you stress. Thus, you feel relaxed, and your stress levels are significantly reduced.

Here is a step-by-step guide on how you can perform this meditation technique.

How To Perform Body Scan Meditation

The first step is to find a quiet place to perform this meditation technique, which is similar to the other techniques that I have mentioned earlier. Once you are in a quiet place with no distractions, then follow the steps mentioned below:

- Lie on your back on the floor in a position that makes you feel comfortable. Make sure that your posture doesn't make you uncomfortable. If lying on the floor hurts, then you can lie on a mattress or bed instead; there is no hard and fast rule that you have to lie on the floor.

The aim here for you is to feel comfortable. You can slide a pillow under your back if you feel uneasy, or you can lie on your side: right or left-whichever makes you feel relaxed. The preferred position is on your back, using only one pillow to support your head so that your airways are clear.

- As soon as you settle, take a deep breath to calm your racing mind. Sometimes, it may take you longer than just one deep breath, depending on how your day went.

If that's the case, keep breathing deeply until you feel a sense of calmness in your mind. A great way to calm your racing mind is to focus on the breath as you take it. If it helps you, use the counting that you used before – 8 for the breath intake through the nostrils and 10 for the exhale. You can even see if you are breathing deeply enough by placing a hand on your upper abdomen and feeling it going up when you breathe in and down when you exhale.

- Once your mind is calm, bring your attention to your body. Feel every sensation in it. Start with the tingling feeling in your toes and feet. Once you feel it, slowly shift your attention from your feet to other parts of your body.

Feel the tension in each part as you move up from your toes to your head.

Feel the tension in your legs' muscles and the sensations in your belly or the tension in your shoulders and back, depending on where you feel the most stress and pain. Feel the strain in your head, and your eyelids hurt as you open and close them.

Note: In the process of examining every sensation in your body, your mind will try to distract you by bringing in different thoughts. If that happens, bring your focus back to your body and start again from the toes and slowly move up to the head and try again to feel the tension on each part. If it helps you at all, I find that being conscious of that area of the body, followed by tensing the area and then purposely relaxing it helps a lot. As you relax that part of the body, feel the weight as the body relaxes.

- Do this exercise for 15-20 minutes at the start and then slowly increase the time you get good at it. Remember that your mind is your #1 enemy, as it keeps distracting you from bringing in countless thoughts that only end up causing stress and anxiety. However, you have to fight it (which is a continuous struggle); with time and patience, everything can be achieved.

- Body scan meditation is hard compared to the other techniques that I have mentioned before. If done correctly, it is a great technique, as it can significantly help you relieve stress and anxiety almost instantly. It also helps lower your blood pressure and bring your heartbeat down, so remember to get up slowly from the exercise and relax for a moment before going into your everyday activities again.

So far, you have learned three of the most effective meditation techniques to reduce stress and anxiety. To get better results, it is essential to enhance their effectiveness.

98. Managing Panic Attacks Using Mindfulness

Often, when anxiety is at a very high-level, you can experience a panic attack. Just to clarify, if you are somebody who is having multiple panic attacks frequently, you could have a panic disorder, which is classified as its type of anxiety disorder. People who suffer from GAD can also have panic attacks as a symptom, but they will not be diagnosed with panic disorder if it is not as severe or frequent.

Panic attacks are described as having 'attacks' of anxiety that are recurring and debilitating. Panic disorders are defined as:

- Recurring and unexpected panic attacks

- Worrying for over a month about an impending panic attack right after you just had a panic attack

- Constant worry regarding the effects and consequences of a panic attack

- Experiencing behavior changes that are significant and linked to panic attacks (e.g., avoiding exercise because the heart rate will increase)

Symptoms Of Panic Attacks

Usually, when someone is experiencing a panic attack, they become overwhelmed by many physical symptoms. A panic attack's peak is usually 10 minutes and could last up to 30 minutes and can leave you exhausted and exhausted afterward. Panic attacks can happen multiple times a day (likely a sign of a panic disorder) or only a few times a year. Panic attacks can even happen when someone is asleep, which causes them to wake up during it. Most people have experienced at least one panic attack in their lives. This does not mean you have a panic disorder; it simply means you had a panic attack. Here are the common symptoms of a panic attack:

- Trembling or shaking

- The accelerated heart rate of the feeling of your heart 'racing.'

- Excessive perspiration

- Shortness of breath

- Chest pains

- Sensations of heat or chills

- Numbing or tingling sensations

- Feeling scared

- Feeling like you are 'losing control.'

- Choking sensations

- Feeling like you are 'going crazy.'

- Fear of dying

- Feeling light-headed, faint, or dizzy

- Dissociation (a sense of detachment from yourself or surroundings)

In some instances, individuals have reported that when they go through a panic attack, they experience 'dissociation.' This is an experience where you feel like the world around you is not real. This symptom is linked with the extreme physiological changes that are happening to your body during a panic attack.

Panic attacks tend to peak at the 10-minute mark, and the symptoms will lessen in intensity after that. They will not often last over an hour in duration, and they average around 20 - 30 minutes total. A lot of people wonder if panic attacks are nasty for their hearts. Although it is not proven that if you have panic attacks, you will 100% develop heart disease - some studies have associated the frequency and intensity of panic attacks with a higher risk of heart disease at old age. A recent study compared individuals who had panic disorders to individuals who didn't. Those who have panic disorders are 36% more likely of heart attacks and 47% more likely to have heart disease.

A primary symptom that people feel during panic attacks is the feeling of death. Although panic attacks come with a whole host of unpleasant bodily symptoms and sensations, you cannot die from a panic attack.

There are many causes for panic attacks, the main one being anxiety. Besides, people who suffered from a traumatic childhood upbringing like abuse tend to be more likely to experience panic attacks after in life. Individuals with parents of relatives diagnosed with anxiety are much more likely to develop a disorder involving panic attacks.

How You Can Stop A Panic Attack Using Mindfulness

When you feel that a panic attack is about to happen, follow this step of instructions below to help manage it.

1.   Make A Plan Before Any Panic Attacks Happen.

Regardless of what plan you have made for yourself, have one ready to go is the most important. View the plan you have made for yourself as a list of directions for you to follow when you anticipate that an attack is approaching. Your plan may involve getting yourself away from the environment you are in, laying down, then calling your family as a means of distraction for yourself from the panic to bring yourself back down. By getting yourself out of that current situation, you can then start the plan as outlined below:

2.   Employ Your Deep Breathing Methods Regularly.

Since feeling short of breath is one of the recurring symptoms of panic attacks, practicing deep breathing can help alleviate it. Having shortness of breath is also one of the main contributors to franticness and lack of control. Make sure you acknowledge this fact and attribute it to being a symptom of this panic attack, reminding yourself that it is likely not due to a medical condition, nor is it permanent. Subsequent, take one deep breath to inhale for at least 3-4 seconds. Hold it for a second and then release it for another four seconds. Continue to repeat this method until your breath becomes steady. Paying attention to counting to four when breathing will prevent hyperventilation and distract other symptoms from occurring.

3.   Practice Muscle Relaxation.

If you have a panic attack, you will likely feel as if you have no control over your physical self. Using techniques for relaxing your muscles helps you regain control over your body to some degree.

Muscle relaxing is a technique that is very useful to help alleviate symptoms of anxiety and panic disorders. The first step is to start clenching your fists and holding the clench for 10 seconds. When you count to 10, loosen your clench all the way and relax the hand. Then, try this practice in the same way with your feet, then begin to move further up the body by tightening and loosening every part of the muscle. This includes the abdomen, buttocks, legs, back muscles, arms, fists, face, neck, and upper back.

4.   Choose A Mantra And Repeat It Regularly.

This technique often sounds a little cheesy or awkward, but it is a great coping technique specific to panic disorders. Saying a positive phrase repeatedly while having a panic attack is an excellent way to center yourself back in the moment. Try repeating simple phrases like "This is just a temporary feeling." or "I am okay, I will be okay." or "I'm not going to die, I just need to focus on my breathing."

5.   Focus On An Object Near You.

This technique begins by picking an object that is in the area you are in. Take note of everything you notice about this specific object. For example, focus on the color, size, or any patterns that this object may have. Think about where you have seen other objects like this or what other objects look similar to this. You may either try it in your head, or you can say it out loud as if you are talking to someone. This technique helps you bring your attention away from the feelings of a panic attack and into your surroundings. By refocusing your attention, you should be able to decrease the severity of the panic attack.

99. Meditation for Compassion

Common meanings for the word compassion include definitions such as 'suffering alongside others' or 'feeling pity for others.' Take a moment to consider what compassion means to you.

If you can, listen to this daily over the week. Record any observations and thoughts in your journal. You could do this early in the day or at night before you go to sleep. Just do it at a time that suits you. You might think, why should I practice compassion and kindness to help with anxiety and stress?

In many Asian languages, the words for 'mind' and 'heart' are interchangeable. So we can read 'mindfulness' as 'heartfulness.' The core attitude is compassion for everybody and everything.

In looking at what drives peoples' behavior, Dr. Jud Brewer has studied the effects of kindness.1. In a nutshell, he has looked at how behavior triggers the reward centers in the brain. So, for example, a person might associate eating cake with parties, happy feelings, and all the short-lived, feel-good chemicals that might come from the sugar-rush. He has seen how being kind also triggers pleasant sensations. So the associations we build up by being kind become positive.

The exciting thing is that it is not just the person in receipt of the kind act but also the giver. The more we practice being genuinely kind, the better we feel. Such acts give us a sense of connectedness with others. We feel less alone, less anxious, and fearful. Feeling more connected with others is a sign that mindfulness is working in our lives.

Settle yourself into a comfortable lying or sitting position with a straight spine. Close your eyes and bring your awareness to the breath. Just observe the breath. Be aware of how fast or slow you are breathing. Take notice of how deeply you are breathing. Deepen the breath. Be conscious of the abdomen inflating and, without undue exertion, bring the breath right the way down into the lower belly. As you exhale, consciously slow the breath down, breathing out through the nose. As you do so, feel any tension slipping away from your shoulders. Relax the jaw by dropping the jaw slightly.

On the following out-breath, relax the chest and abdomen.

Feel a sense of looseness in the whole torso, head, and neck. Breathe in deeply and, as you breathe out, focus on releasing any tension in the arms and hands. Relax the fingers, allowing them to go limp with a natural curl of the fingers inwards towards the palms. Now bring the attention to the buttocks, hips, and thighs. As you breathe out, allow this area to relax. Have a sense of being grounded in this part of the body as you sit or lie. Feel a sense of heaviness here that helps this area sink more deeply into the surface supporting you.

Bring your attention down your legs into the feet. Notice any sensations around the feet. Or notice any lack of sensation around the feet.

Sit for a few moments, aware of the entire body as you lie or sit.

After a few moments, bring your attention back to the area around the chest. Focus on the heart. Keep your focus on the heart and chest area as you breathe gently, deeply, and steadily. Put your right hand over your heart and breathe into it. Perhaps you are aware of the beating of the heart. Sit with the breath for a few moments.

Bring to mind the thought all humans and sentient beings have a heart. A heart and mind that feels all the range of emotions you feel. Have a sense of gentleness and compassion for yourself. Focus on your own heart, and as you continue to breathe in and out, breathe in the word 'kindness' and breathe out 'compassion.'

Direct this kindness and compassion towards yourself. Then, after a few breaths, consider the people in the room or dwelling you are in. Direct the kindness and compassion towards them. Continue in this way, considering people in your local community, even people you don't know. Include all living beings as you wish. Radiate your focus out to include all people in your town or city. Then all people in your country and so on. Eventually, moving your consciousness out to include everyone on the continent you live on and then the whole globe. If you lose focus, just bring the attention back to the breath and the heart area.

Sit with this focus for a few moments. Breathing in: 'kindness' and breathing out: 'compassion.'

Now let the breath settle into its usual pattern. Just notice how you feel. Do this without judgment.

After a few moments, deepen the breath. Stretch your arms up and allow for a refreshing stretch.

Stand up slowly and carry on with your activities with an attitude of kindness and compassion for all beings.

1. What Is Compassion And How Can It Help Me?

We might think we would intuitively know what we mean by compassion and kindness. However, a few years back, an item on the news caught my attention. Compassion is now a taught subject on the university curriculum for student nurses. It surprised me that this should be a skill that needed to be taught. Indeed, anyone who was interested in being a nurse and helping others would be a naturally compassionate person? I was wrong in my thinking.

Anyone who has raised children or worked with them in a professional capacity has most likely seen how young children can be kind and sweet, but children need to learn to be compassionate. Activities and games that encourage these attributes are now on most schools' Personal Social and Emotional Health curricula.

Often as adults, we can get so caught up in the rush and pressure of life and lose connection with the heart's quietness that prompts us to be compassionate and kind towards others and ourselves. We can get so entangled in the daily grind of making a living, paying bills, meeting deadlines, and keeping the wheels of our lives, turning that making time to be compassionate seems almost irrelevant. So sometimes we need to remind ourselves to be kind. Compassion doesn't just happen.

This is where mindfulness is so beneficial. By looking at our own lives and those with a genuine spirit of kindness and compassion, we see and connect with what is in front of us. When we are distracted by worries, concerns, and negative feelings, we won't have this sense of connection or awareness.

If we are not mindful, we can drift into indifference and being judgemental. Then harshness can creep in. This hard attitude fosters many unhealthy and unhelpful behaviors towards ourselves and others. We might get locked into our sense of suffering, closing ourselves in a prison of victimhood, unable to help ourselves or anyone else. We might feel a sour attitude towards the success of others and gravitate towards unpleasant news and complaints. We become reactive and angry.

Research carried out at the University of Michigan by Sarah Konrath has shown how we are becoming less compassionate as a society .1. She has examined studies that were made between 1979 and 2009 of 13,000 college students. Konrath discovered that self-reported concern for others' welfare was steadily declining, particularly from the early 1990s. Alarmingly rates of compassion are at their lowest levels for thirty years and are continuing to decline. Interestingly, these figures appear to correlate with an increase in stress and anxiety levels, as I noted before.

Research has shown that meditation stimulates the brain's areas responsible for a sense of social affiliation rather than the areas responsible for recognizing and empathizing with others' suffering 2. This is significant because studies have shown that when this 'suffering connection' part of the brain is activated, genuine compassion is short-lived and is quickly replaced with compassion fatigue. However, by connecting with others in a social and empathetic way, we can sustain compassion and active concern. So meditation helps us to become more compassionate and sustain compassion in the longer term.

Practicing compassion helps us to identify with others and lifts us out of isolation and a sense of lonely suffering. We realize that suffering, to a greater or lesser extent, is part of the human condition. As we identify strongly with others, we feel more of a sense of being in this together. This sense of identity and togetherness is important. As human beings, we are hard-wired to feel part of the tribe. It is an ancient and deep-rooted alarm system that goes off when we feel isolated or on edge. By feeling part of humanity, we feel connected and bonded with others. If we practice compassion with an open heart, we will feel the benefits of belonging, a feeling of peace, and calm and enhanced self-esteem. Hopefully, our acts of kindness and compassion will help others, so it is a win-win situation.

Dr. David Hamilton looked at how being kind is right for our hearts. Being kind releases another hormone called oxytocin, the 'hug drug.' Oxytocin is the hormone that helps us feel connected to others. Besides this positive effect, this also helps to strengthen our heart health. When the hormone is released, the heart's blood vessels dilate (open up), easing heart muscle stress.

When practicing compassion, it is worth bearing in mind that we genuinely aim to enhance others' lives when we are considerate or of service. We are not seeking approval or validation from others.

This might be a pleasant side-effect, but try to be motivated by a sense of doing your best for someone else. Your worth as a person does not depend on the opinion or validation of others. Work on building up your opinion of yourself. You can hold yourself in high regard as someone kind, compassionate, and considerate of others. The other person need not show you gratitude or appreciation. Some people might not even notice, and as your practice grows, you could be randomly kind in anonymous ways.

No one else will know, but the important thing here is that you know.

2. How Do I Develop Kindness And Compassion?

Compassion is best practiced daily, and not just reserved for those we love, pity, or naturally feel moved to be compassionate towards. Compassion is an unconditional practice. Even with very challenging people, we can understand that those in the most pain often try to inflict the most pain on others.

If you struggle with developing compassion or have difficulties in showing compassion for certain people, that is understandable. The important thing is that you are becoming aware of any difficulties you might have with practicing compassion. You might just want to meditate and reflect on what compassion means to you for now and notice how you react towards others in pain, discomfort, or difficulties. Perhaps you feel nothing. Perhaps you feel distaste or irritation. Just notice these reactions without judging yourself.

100. Meditation to Control Your Anger

There's nothing wrong with getting angry, or even furious when the situation warrants it. Anger inspires us to defend ourselves and correct injustice. However, too much anger takes its toll on your mind, body, and relationships.

If you have an anger problem, mindfulness practice will help you learn how to spot the warning signs that your anger is spinning out of control.

Anger Doesn't Always Come From The Outside

The commonsense view is that external events trigger anger. For example, if you think you lost your job for no reason other than your boss dislikes you, you may be angry. If someone cuts you off in traffic, you may feel mad.

However, anger can also stem from a loss of joy. Psychologist Stephen Dansiger, who specializes in anger management, points out that no mood state is permanent. It's unrealistic to expect that we can be happy or relaxed all the time. Unfortunately, some people find this hard to accept, and their disappointment may manifest itself as frustration or anger. Dansiger notes that these individuals feel a sense of loss when feelings of contentment or joy pass, especially if they have a generally unhappy disposition, which manifests as irritability.

So, How Does Mindfulness Help?

Mindfulness helps you check in with your body, detect the early signs of anger, and respond to the situation in a way that doesn't harm you or others.

Mindfulness Exercise: How Angry Are You?

If you know or accused you of an anger management problem, start by checking in with yourself every two to three hours. All you must do is set aside a couple of minutes to tune into your mind and body.

Ask yourself the following questions:

1) On a gage of 1-10, with 10 signifying an extreme level of anger, how angry am I right now?

2) How does my body feel?

3) What emotions am I feeling right now?

4) What thoughts are going through my head?

This practice helps you detach from your emotions, which makes it easier to remain calm. Remember, anger itself isn't the problem; it's when we start identifying with our anger that we run into trouble.

Mindfulness Exercise: RAIN

This practice, developed by teacher Michele McDonald, can be used to handle any difficult emotions. It is especially useful for taming anger.

RAIN stands for Recognize, Allow, Investigate, and Nurture.

1) Recognize: Begin by permitting yourself to feel your anger. Label it. If you are alone, speak aloud. Tell yourself, "I am angry." Scan your body; do you notice any sensations that signal anger? For example, is your breathing shallow? Have you curled your hands into fists?

2) Allow: Hold your anger. Let it just be there. Don't try to reason it away. Whatever your thoughts and feelings, accept them exactly as they are. If you can sit with your anger, you'll learn that it doesn't have to overwhelm you.

3) Investigate: Only after you've recognized and felt your anger could you explore what triggered it. Take an attitude of gentle curiosity; there's no need to beat yourself up for being angry. Ask what happened immediately before you feel the fury bubble up inside you.

You don't have to make psychological breakthroughs every time you do the RAIN exercise, but you'll start noticing your anger patterns over time. For example, you might notice that you are quick to get angry when you think someone has failed to respect your authority.

Discovering your triggers gives you an advantage. Depending on the situation, you might be able to avoid triggers, but you will need to learn how to work with them in most cases.

This may mean challenging your assumptions (e.g., "Everyone should respect my authority at all times, and if they don't, it's terrible!") or working on your emotional intelligence (e.g., learning to be more patient towards others.)

4) Nurture: Anger is often a sign that your needs are going unmet. For instance, suppose you are angry because your mother doesn't seem interested when you tell her about the problems you are having in your marriage. Your anger may stem from the fact that she isn't offering the kind of nurturing parental love that you want and need.

However angry you may be, you deserve self-compassion, not condemnation. You also need to learn how to nurture yourself when others cannot provide you with love and support. Self-care is an essential part of the RAIN exercise. Have a bath or shower, do some exercise, mindfully eat your favorite food, or do something else that makes you feel good. Congratulate yourself on taking responsibility for your feelings.

Any Progress Is Great!

If you frequently get angry, cut yourself some slack when you do these exercises. Your anger won't disappear immediately. You'll probably still feel frustrated, even when the most intense emotions have passed. That's OK. Getting angry is a learned behavior, and changing an old habit is difficult. You deserve lots of praise for trying a new approach.

Get Mindful About Your Thought Patterns

Mindfulness gives you the space to play detective, which can help understand your anger patterns. The next time you get angry, watch your thoughts. Remember, you don't have to argue with them or wish them away. Reframe them; instead of making your life difficult, try to see your thoughts as clues to your anger patterns.

Do you notice any of the following thoughts pop up when you get angry?

Blaming: Do you shift responsibility onto other people? For instance, do you catch yourself saying things like "It's her fault" or "He always makes me mad"?

The truth is that no one can "create" you mad. You have a choice. You can respond to a situation mindfully and mindfully handle your anger. You do not have to identify with your anger.

Over-generalizing: Do you use words like "never" or "always"? For example, do you say things like "You never listen to what I have to say" or "You always try to bring me down"?

These statements are rarely accurate, and they only escalate the tension between you and someone else. Be mindful of the language you use. If you have difficulty with someone else's behavior, identify exactly how they are triggering your anger.

Using "should": Do you feel as though people should act somewhat towards you at all times? Do you think they always have to act reasonably, include you in their activities, and value your opinion?

Although this would be nice, it just isn't how the world works. "Shoulding" will keep you miserable and trapped by your unrealistic expectations.

Mind-reading: Do you assume that you "just know" what someone else is thinking? Do you catch yourself thinking things like "I know that he gets angry with me" or "I know that she doesn't think I'm up to the job"?

Unless someone tells us exactly what they're thinking, it's dangerous to assume that we know what's going through their minds. Assumptions can lead to unnecessary arguments and misunderstandings.

Don't beat yourself up if you notice yourself blaming, over-generalizing, "shoulding," or mind-reading. Everyone falls into these traps sometimes. The trick is to spot your thinking errors and realize that you don't have to identify with them. Instead, you can choose to use tools like RAIN to respond more healthily.

Grudges, Past Hurts, & Releasing Anger

So far, we've looked at how you can use mindfulness to deal with angry outbursts and isolated events that make you see red. But what about grudges and long-term grievances? It's worth addressing old hurts because they can cause needless pain for decades if left to fester.

Mindfulness Practice: Using Mindful Visualization To Release Anger

This exercise helps you let go of simmering resentment. You can use it as a tool for forgiveness or only as a way of releasing frustration and rage when your anger flares up.

1) Find a quiet dwelling where you will be undisturbed for several minutes.

2) Close your eyes and imagine a peaceful scene, preferably outdoors. You could choose a meadow, a forest, or a beach.

3) When an angry thought pops up, imagine encasing it inside a large pink bubble. Visualize the thought inside the bubble. Feel a sense of liberation as you realize that it can't harm you.

4) Picture the bubble floating off into the sky until it is out of sight.

Be Willing To See Change In Other People

Living in the present helps you make a fresh start in your relationships because you can see someone as they are now, not as a shadowy figure who hurt you in the past. People can and do change.

Sometimes, someone will suddenly develop an interest in personal development, often after a significant transition like an illness or milestone birthday. Others change gradually over time. They might mellow with age or slowly shift their priorities and goals.

Either way, try to stay open to the possibility of reconciliation. This doesn't mean you have to pardon and forget. Neither does it mean you should rekindle a relationship with someone who has abused or mistreated you. In some cases, it's best to cut all contact forever. On the other hand, if your objection is relatively minor and a lot of time has passed, why not try casting your assumptions aside?

When To Seek Help

These exercises can go a long way to resolving pathological anger, but they are no substitute for professional help. If your anger is disrupting your relationships or career, it's best to make an appointment with a doctor or therapist as quickly as possible. Most mental health professionals are happy to use mindfulness as part of a treatment plan, so you'll be able to combine these practices with other interventions.

Summary

- Anger is not an intrinsically evil emotion, but too much can harm you and those around you.

- Mindfulness practices can help you identify anger in your body, accept it, and release it.

- Identifying your anger patterns can help you overcome thinking errors.

- Staying mindful can help you appreciate the positive change in other people.

You can use mindfulness when working with a mental health professional who specializes in anger management.

101. Additional Forms of Meditation

Various meditation techniques can be used by anyone at any time and virtually in any place. These techniques can help center your thoughts, thereby eliminating the veritable monkey mind that otherwise has our thoughts random and scattered. Alternatively, specific meditation techniques can reduce stress, depression, anger, and any other extreme emotional condition that would create or increase the physical suffering you experience. While there are almost countless meditation available variations, they all fall into three necessary forms—concentrative, open awareness, and mindfulness. When practiced daily or reasonably regularly, these three meditation techniques have been shown to improve a person's health both in terms of physical well-being and mental well-being. These techniques can require some practice before you can get the full benefits they have to offer. However, they are quite simple and straightforward. Therefore, if you can set aside the time each day, and you have a relatively quiet place where you can practice, then you can put any or all of these techniques to use in your life.

Concentrative Meditation

Concentrative meditation is perhaps the form that most people envision when they hear the word 'meditation.' The main characteristic of this form is that the practitioner focuses on a single item, thereby eliminating all other thoughts from their mind. In this scenario, a person sits in a comfortable position, usually cross-legged, and they focus on a single object. This object can be just about anything imaginable; however, the objects most commonly used include candles, plants, colors, water features, and crystals. As the practitioner sits in their comfortable spot, they will observe their object of choice, allowing that object to fill their mind. One by one, they let go of any thoughts that are currently in their minds until, eventually, the only thing that they are thinking about is the object they are observing. Usually, this process takes from 10 minutes to 20 minutes, depending on the time the practitioner has available and the amount of practice they have in meditating. It is advised that a beginner practice this form of meditation in 10-minute durations, as longer durations can cause the practitioner's mind to begin to wander.

As the individual becomes proficient, they can extend the length of each session accordingly. The basic technique of this meditation is as results:

- Find a resting place where you can be undisturbed for at least ten minutes.

- Find a comfortable place to sit. It is usually recommended that you sit on the floor, so be sure to bring a pillow, mat, or some similar item that will make the floor more comfortable to sit on. If you cannot convene on the floor for physical reasons, you can sit in a chair or on a sofa. The main thing is not to allow yourself to drift off to sleep if you have to sit on a sofa!

- Place the object you have chosen as your focal point in front of you. It is ideal if you have a table to set it on, creating a natural line of sight.

- Begin to breathe deeply, concentrating on your breathing's depth and regularity until you feel physically relaxed and mentally calm.

- Start to focus on your meditation object, forcing your mind to fixate on the object and let go of any other thought or emotion you are experiencing.

- Remain focused on your object, maintaining a deep, steady breathing rhythm. Whenever a thought or emotion pops up unrelated to your object, simply increase your focus on the object and allow that thought or emotion to fade away.

In addition to visual objects, sounds can be used in concentrative meditation. This is where the form of meditation, known as Transcendental Meditation, comes into play. Transcendental Meditation is where a person sits in a comfortable position, just as already described, and chants a mantra. This mantra can be as meek as a single sound or word or as complicated as a whole thought or sentence. In the case of a single word or sound, the objective is for the practitioner to become fixated entirely on the sound, much the same way they would be with an object in the past example. One of the advantages of using sound instead of using an object is the vibration that the sound produces. Many traditions teach that vibration can purify a person's energy, bringing it to a higher or better frequency.

Different sounds can be used to obtain different results, and this is where it is beneficial to have a teacher or guide to refer to. A trained meditation expert will be able to advise you on which sound would benefit you the most. Variables such as mood, body type, personality type, and other similar considerations can make certain sounds more effective than others. Full-sentence mantras can be used to create a focused thought process, similar to that created by a visual object. Using an affirmation as a mantra will help focus your mind on what you want to achieve the most, thereby establishing the right thinking, speech, and even the right action. The steps of this meditation are as follows:

- Choose a quiet place where you can be alone for the period of your meditation practice.

- Find a comfortable domicile to sit, preferably on the floor. Again, be sure to bring a mat or pillow to prevent discomfort while sitting. Additionally, a chair or other seating area can be used if necessary.

- Begin to breathe deeply, focusing on the length and regularity of your breathing. Once your breathing is relaxed and natural, and your body and mind are also relaxed, you can recite your mantra.

- Recite your mantra in a way that is relaxed and consistent with your breathing. Be sure to be calm in reciting your mantra as you want the words' sound to be soothing.

- Focus on your mantra until all other thoughts and emotions are gone from your mind. Whenever a thought comes into your mind, increase your concentration on the sound of your mantra until it fades away again.

Open Awareness Meditation

Another form of meditation that is very effective is what is called Open Awareness Meditation. The goal of this form is virtually the opposite of the goal of Concentrative Meditation. While the practitioner of Concentrative Meditation focuses on an object until that object is the only thing that occupies their mind, the practitioner of Open Awareness Meditation strives to not focus on any single thing.

Instead, Open Awareness Meditation encourages the practitioner to allow their mind to freely roam from one thing to another, never fixating on one object or situation for more than a few seconds. This form of meditation aims to instill the practitioner with a sense of detachment from their surrounding environment. If Concentrative Meditation is about taking a few steps closer to physical reality, Open Awareness is about taking several steps back. Since attachment to things is considered a significant cause of suffering, then Open Awareness Meditation can be highly beneficial in eliminating suffering by training the practitioner to become mentally and emotionally detached from their surroundings.

At first, this form of meditation may seem a bit hard to understand. After all, how can letting your mind wander from one thing to another ever be a good thing? The truth is that many people perform this type of meditation daily without ever realizing what they are doing. Whenever you sit outside when you go to a restaurant and watch the people walking by while you eat, you perform Open Awareness Meditation. People watching, crowd watching, and any other practice that allows a person to observe things from a detached perspective is nothing less than a form of Open Awareness Meditation. Therefore, if people-watching is something that you have already done in the past, then this is a form of meditation that will come easily and naturally. The steps of Open Awareness Meditation are as follows:

- Find a place where you can securely watch an active environment for the specified amount of time. Like with Concentrative Meditation, a period between 10-20 minutes is ideal.

- Sit in a comfortable position. Unlike Concentrative Meditation, a chair or other conventional seating arrangement is ideal for this form.

- Begin to breathe deeply and regularly. Focus on your breathing until it becomes relaxed and natural. You should also maintain this focus until your body and mind feel more relaxed.

- Begin to observe your surroundings. If you are sitting outside a café, you can begin to watch the people walking by. Purposely observe a single person for about 5-10 seconds, and then turn your attention to someone else.

- Recap this step for the duration of your time. People-watching outside is an ideal environment for this meditation as most of the people won't be in your ground of view for more than a few seconds.

- It is essential to focus on the person, taking in one or two details, before moving on to the succeeding. If you don't take in any details, your mind will begin to wander, and the exercise will produce no results.

- If you are paying attention to stops walking, be sure not to fixate on them for longer than the 5-10 second span. If you fixate on a person or event, then you become attached to that thing. Therefore, it is critical to continually shift your attention from one person or event to another.

Another environment where Open Awareness Meditation can be performed easily is in a social event, such as a concert, a play, or a sporting event. While you will not inevitably be able to leave after the 10-20 minutes that you meditate, that is not a problem. In this situation, you will simply take your attention away from the event itself and begin to observe other elements around you. If you are at a sporting event, you can begin to notice the field on which the game is being played. Observe the grass's color, the lines on the field, and even the goalposts, or whatever other equipment or fixtures there are. Subsequently, you can observe other spectators, much like you would observe people walking by at a café. As you begin to become aware of the other people around you, your mind will become detached from the event itself. This is a beautiful way to practice detachment, especially if the event is something you are particularly interested in. After all, being able to take your concentration off of a vital soccer match is no small feat! Simple steps to follow for this technique are as follows:

- Assuming you are at a match or event, begin to pay attention to your breathing. Begin to take in deep, regular breaths, and focus on your breathing until your breaths are relaxed and natural.

- Stay focused on your breathing until your mind and body also feel more relaxed.

- Once you have achieved relaxed breathing, begin to look around at the people around you. Ignore the event itself. Instead, pay attention to those who are paying attention to the event.

In this way, you go from being an observer to observing the observers themselves. This is the basic principle of being in a constant state of detachment.

- Shift your attention from one person or object to another every 5-10 seconds. Be sure to note details of each thing you observe before moving on to them afterward.

102. Meditation for Weight Loss

What Makes You Gain Body Weight: Meditations And Daily Habits

Negative emotions can lead to rapid weight gain and, in turn, causes bulimia. This is when someone starts to find comfort in food. They have a constant need to eat and cannot stop themselves from eating. As they eat, so does their weight increase. They may gain weight that they will not be able to lose if given a chance immediately.

Your third eye chakra is the sixth located between your eyebrows and up about 1-2 finger widths. The color indigo represents this chakra. Rarely will an imbalanced third eye chakra lead to weight gain, although an imbalanced third eye can indicate that you are experiencing imbalance elsewhere in your body? Symptoms of imbalance include nightmares, headaches, and struggling to see the entire truth of your life. One way this may translate to wellness could be in your inability to see your beauty and the reality that you are more than just your body, mightily, if you are struggling with body image issues and self-esteem.

How To Seized Mental Blocks To Lose Weight?

We are prisoners of our minds. Our mind, in turn, is responsible for the stock and healthy functioning of the body. Grounding our thought patterns with pessimism only returns negativity feelings, which eventually affect one's mental health. This is because the latter issue only contributes to mood and anxiety symptoms.

Yet, what is this phenomenon called "meditation"? Meditation is a practice that involves the application of various techniques such as breathing and mindfulness to achieve a calm mental state and train focus and attention. The practice's primary purpose is to help you observe your feelings and emotions without judgment with the benefit that you will get to understand them well. Therefore, meditation does not make you a holy person or a different person, but it can if you wish to take the path.

What is not meditation? Meditation is not a practice meant to make you high or zone out or even have bizarre experiences.

Many people carry this notion around with them. It would be a helpful idea to dispel some of these thoughts before getting yourself to start the practice lest you feel deceived. Meditation is an avenue to train your mind in awareness.

How The Mind Controls The Metabolism?

Know how different kinds of food make you feel. This is after you eat them. This statement mostly responds to questions like, which meal makes you tired or energized? Avoid food that makes you tired since they reduce the body's metabolism.

Many people will use hypnosis to change their cravings, improve their metabolism, and even help themselves acquire a taste for eating healthier foods. You may also use this to help encourage you to develop the motivation and energy to prepare healthier foods and eat them so that you are more likely to have these healthier options available for you. If cultivating the motivation to prepare and eat healthy foods has been problematic for you, this type of hypnosis focus can be incredibly helpful.

Using alternative methods for relaxing and nurturing your chakras is an excellent opportunity for you to improve your spiritual wellness further while also improving your physical wellness. Alternative methods are often known for improving your physical condition, meaning that things such as your hormones, digestive function, and metabolism will all be improved through maintaining your chakras.

In addition to directly impacting your well-being, healing your chakras can also help you on a spiritual level, directly affecting your subconscious and further improving your ability to integrate your healing benefits from hypnosis. Most often, those who incorporate both hypnosis and chakra wellbeing into their weight loss journeys experience a form of weight loss that is both rapid and long-lasting.

The Tools To Lower Your Body Weight: Meditate Your Food, Meditate Your Movement

When people get angry, get excited, get upset, they hunt for food. In other words, a person's mood determines their eating habits. Drugs that need to be used for treatment can increase appetite and consequently cause weight problems.

Gaining weight can result from inherited genes, control disorders centered on appetite and will, disorders of the digestive system, bowel laziness, irregular eating, and fast eating. The main problem of those who want to lose weight is the sensation of hunger. You may think that your stomach sends direct messages to you, and if you don't satisfy this body part, you could even collapse. Regardless of the causes, psychological or physical roots have settled into the subconscious and become a habit. But a personalized diet and exercise program is not enough.

Fortunately, you can control this horrible inclination by controlling your mind. Subsequently, you can have your ideal shape.

Unhappy Marriage And Difficulty Losing Weight: Strategies And Meditation To Improve Metabolism

Dana is a pretty brunette and a successful person. She's a mother of two children, has a beautiful marriage, and enjoys a thriving career. But when I asked Dana what her percentage of belief for Weight Mastery's success was, her number was 27 percent.

"I will never believe I'll be a success at Weight Mastery because I have failed so many times. There is a big part of me that knows I am going to be a failure again," she told me.

I asked Dana, "Are there other times in your life when things didn't go the way you wanted, but the setback ultimately created a breakthrough of some sort?"

Dana said, "My husband and I went through a very rough patch in our marriage after the birth of our second child. Our son was born with special medical needs. I spent most of my time caring for and paying attention to him. It wasn't intentional, but my husband and I grew apart and often argued. My husband seemed jealous of the attention I was giving my son. It was a very dark time in which we both were struggling with whether we wanted to stay married."

"So, what happened?" I asked.

She said, "We decided to get some help, and things changed. Today our marriage is better than it ever was. We learned how to work together as a team. We also learned to have more empathy for each other and recognize how hard it is to parent a child with special needs.

Our family life is so much happier because we went through that challenging time and were forced to shift our thinking."

"Dana, can you see how that dark time was a part of your successful marriage story?" I asked.

Dana paused for a moment. You could read on her face the new perspective of her weight story forming in her mind. "So, you are saying that everything, all of my failures with my weight so far, is ultimately a part of my long-term Weight Mastery success story?"

I nodded. "At any time we want, we have the power to reframe the dark times that we have gone through during our weight struggle and reframe them from a different perspective as building blocks for our weight success story, allowing ourselves to believe with 100 percent that we can achieve weight mastery. So can you reframe your struggle and see it as part of your own successful Weight Mastery Journey, Dana?"

"Yes, I am now seeing that all of the diets I went on and all of the times I broke the diet and gained back the weight and all of the frustration I have felt with myself over the years has been preparing me to be finally figure things out for myself and release the weight once and for all." Dana smiled, "I feel like I have just released a 100-pound weight from my heart!"

"I am so relieved that no matter what happens on my journey, I will never fail again. I believe that 100 percent! 'Failure' is a word I have wiped from my mind for good." Dana C. (Released 70 pounds, maintaining for more than two years.)

The Mistakes To Lose Weight: Carbohydrates, Fats And Calories

Some restaurants use large portion sizes to give the illusion that they are giving you more for their money. Fast food restaurants and sit-down chains will advertise huge portions, boasting about burgers that are a quarter of a pound. This kind of "more for your money" mentality is present in all forms of capitalism, but it is dangerous in terms of food.

The larger the drink you get at the movies, the more money you save. Why get a medium when a large is only a quarter more? We think we're getting such a great deal for our money, but really, we just paid a small fee to get twice as many calories as we need.

The most addictive foods are filled with refined carbohydrates and added fat and sugar. When those foods are eaten, there is a significant increase in blood sugar, which signals your brain's pleasure centers, making you want even more.

The reason why fast food is so good is that it is completely loaded with sugar. Even though Whoppers and Big Macs are not considered sweets, they still have a ton of added sugar that makes them addictive.

Sweets like cake and ice cream are dangerous because of all the fat and sugar. If you are seriously addicted to sugar, you might also endure withdrawal symptoms when you don't get enough. Grumpiness, headaches, and other dangerous cravings are common symptoms of sugar addiction, so this individual issue must be addressed in a weight-loss journey as well. You have to consider all of your dependencies and addictions to develop a weight-loss plan that works.

Lose Weight Quickly And Easily 8: Change The Brain Before Changing The Body

The most important part of the DASH diet is to eat healthy, nutrient-dense foods. The second most important part is to eat those beautiful foods with the appropriate frequency for your body's needs. There's no denying that following the DASH diet principles, regardless of changes to your weight, will significantly impact your overall health and greatly benefit your blood pressure. However, when it comes to losing weight specifically, that extra bit of attention to portion sizes will allow you to enjoy the great diversity of foods available to you on the DASH eating plan while still putting you in a position to progress toward your weight-loss goals.

There are other benefits of using hypnosis for weight loss. The obvious big one is that you lose weight. That's the one people will notice. You'll start to shed those pounds, and you might lose more than you expected. It won't be significant, such as like fifty pounds or more, but if you want to help your body and allow yourself the benefits of controlling the cravings to lose weight, then this is perfect for you.

103. Sensory Clarity

In a way, our experience of life is nothing but the experience of our senses. Without our sensory contact with others, the world, and ourselves, we would be on the level of fungus or bacteria—existing, but without any experience of existing. Of course, conscious awareness is the key to knowing we exist, but what is it that we are consciously aware of 99.99999... percent of the time? Sensory experience. This is especially true if we include thinking and imagination as "internal senses" as internal analogs of seeing and hearing.

If our life experience is nothing but a sensory experience, what does it mean to increase sensory clarity? You'd think that enhancing the resolution on the central sense of aliveness would revolutionize your life, and you'd be right. It opens the door to a profound change in the depth of enjoyment and meaning we derive from existence. You could almost say in a metaphoric sense that increased sensory clarity gives you more life since each moment of life can be experienced at a "higher resolution."

Working with sensory clarity is the leading way, in my opinion, to boost the development of your insula. This is speculation, but the insula is concerned with feeling sensations in the body. The more you focus on those sensations' minute details, the more likely you build connectivity in the insula. And remember that the insula is extremely important in understanding how you feel and connecting with other people. The way I see it, reaching toward more sensory clarity builds the insula, and growing the insula enhances sensory clarity. This creates a powerful feedback loop and is an excellent example of using brain plasticity in your favor.

While the above only applies to body sensation, concentrating on gaining sensory clarity in the other senses probably does something similar in those domains. You cultivate your ability to connect deeply, ultimately, and in many different ways to the present moment. As I've mentioned, curiosity is one of the main ways to cultivate concentration. Combine this with openness and nonjudgment, and you've got a recipe for growing sensory clarity. You'll find yourself drawn in more and more deeply to the details of things. It's unavoidable.

The world of the senses in the world of the present moment. It's an embodied realm, outside the slick-but-shallow virtual world of the conceptual mind. Contacting your senses automatically begins to pull you out of your mental preoccupations and into what is happening right here and now. One of the significant profits is that you don't miss out on your own life. It's all too easy to be lost in the clouds while exquisite things are occurring right at your feet. We spend money on expensive food but are distracted at dinner and don't taste it. We buy beautiful objects but are quickly bored and ignore them. Under those conditions, what's the point of acquiring such things in the first place? Why take a vacation if you can't stop thinking about work concerns on the beach in paradise? Intentionally cultivating sensory clarity in meditation will help you with all of these issues. The senses are like an anchor into the present moment, and that is where all the action is. That's where your life is.

Stuck In A Good Place

As a meditation teacher, I often run into people who present me with the following problem: They have been bearing in mind for a long time, usually between five and fifteen years. When they first started practicing, they made a lot of progress and had significant insights. It changed their life, and they got a lot of benefit out of it. The practice helps them be more agreeable to other people, experience less anxiety, and be more focused at work. But for several years now, their practice has plateaued. They're dedicated and enjoy their practice but don't feel that they're still making progress or getting new insights.

This situation is called "getting stuck in a good place." They've gotten to a certain depth in their practice, but they don't know how to go any deeper. If the idea is to make the unconscious conscious, they've excavated down to a certain level but don't know how to dig any further. At least 95 percent of the period, the answer is straightforward: they need to learn to cultivate greater sensory clarity. Exploring smaller and subtler dimensions of sensation is the key to getting out of this rut.

Let me explain. Typically the initial instructions beginning meditators are given is to "meditate on body sensations." They are told to look at a few interesting aspects of these sensations. And that short instruction gets them all the benefit that I'm calling the "good place." But the reason they've become stuck is that the instructions can only take them so far. It's like their meditation engine has run out of fuel.

The growth in brain structure it took to get them to this point has worked its magic. But now they have adapted to this level of contact with sensation and aren't pushing to go any further. So the secret is to begin investigating more and more minute levels of detail in sensation. To increase the resolution of your senses.

This implies getting considerably more interested in the delicate subtleties of body sensations in the body's domain. There are a few different ways to chip away at developing this. For one, I've regularly seen that individuals will, in general, consider body sensations as being level two-dimensional. Yet, since the body is a three-dimensional item, body sensations are not commonly level but somewhat 3D. That implies they can have an unpredictable morphology, which is fascinating to investigate. They can take different shapes: circular, cubic, star-formed, conic, round and hollow, and so on. Genuine sensations are only here and there flawless mathematical solids, yet you can figure which one a specific sensation is nearest to. Three-dimensional sensations can have "sides." The top can feel unique about the base. The front can feel not the same as the back, etc. Dimensionality likewise implies that they have a surface zone; however, a volume and those various regions inside that volume can feel very extraordinary. For instance, a sensation may have a moderately nonpartisan, soft quality creation up most of its mass. However, coasting inside that mass of oats, there may be "raisins," in a manner of speaking. Little spots of extraordinary, pointy sensations. So this three-dimensionality of body sensation opens up endlessly more unpredictable and itemized opportunities for investigation. Also, the equivalent goes for passionate sensations.

Another part of body vibe that can expand your tactile clearness is that it isn't generally substantial or stable. Numerous sensations feel as though they are the equivalent, second to second. They don't appear to be changing or moving, particularly by any means. However, certain sensations are not all that consistent. They can be getting more grounded or more fragile, more significant, or littler. They can move around, from area to area, or modify their shape and 3D morphology. So as you're pondering a sensation, notice on the off chance that it, or any little some portion of it, is changing in any capacity. Perhaps the corner is pounding or beating. Perhaps it's marginally moving its middle to and fro a couple of millimeters. Possibly one side of it is growing out a piece and afterward flattening back. To cite the drifting head of Carl Sagan in a container, there are "billions and billions" of potential outcomes.

A third method to increment tactile lucidity is to research regions of the body you don't commonly examine. If you somehow managed to keep a rundown of body districts that you have reached in contemplation, you would find that there are a few spots that you never contact for reasons unknown. What about the upper sense of taste of your mouth? The back of your ear? Inside the line of the spine? Inside your joints? Take the way newer. Search out and find the way puts you have at no other time mulled over upon and welcome them on the web. Similarly, to help with clarifying sensation, this can have an amazingly staggering effect on your coordination feeling.

A fourth strategy for going further into the sensation is to go most likely as an intensifying instrument. Shouldn't something is said about vibes of the size of a grain of sand? Figuring out some approach to distinguish these littler and humbler sensations will uphold your material clearness. You, as a general rule, can't exaggerate this method for working.

A minor takeoff from this is trying to feel an ever-expanding number of simple sensations. It's possible to slow down out, just tendency impressions that are phenomenal or "uproarious." So get interested in arriving at vibes that are subtle or "light."

There is a fifth methodology that works contrastingly to help unmistakable clearness. Rather than expanding the objective, it works by making simple separations between kinds of sensations. For example, you can perceive exquisite and repulsive feelings, two head orders that give a lot of information into your experience. Notwithstanding, it's possible to get nerdier than that. Have a go at perceiving "surfaces" of sensation: smooth, horrendous, sharp, delicate, lopsided, goopy, shivery, stinging, and so forth.

On the other hand, note the differentiation between vibes that are moving and those that are still. Subcategorize those into impacts that are moving had right, up-down, forward-backward, or various headings. Perceive wave-like advancement from the broken turn of events. And so on, I recollect once spending a whole weeklong contemplation retreat reflecting on little, inconspicuous sensations in my skeletal structure. Although I'd been catching wind of the intensity of tactile clearness from Shinzen for quite a while, that was where I understood how astounding it is. Developing tactile clearness in all the faculties has advanced my contemplation practice a long way past anything I might have envisioned.

Furthermore, it's directed to positive life changes and a genuine feeling of prosperity that I can't resist the urge to need to offer to you. Set aside the effort to profoundly investigate your own tangible experience and find where you are alive, as though unexpectedly.

.

104. Awareness of Self And With Others

Everything We Experience Is Internal

Human experience exists 100% internally. Everything you have experienced has happened inside you, including your mental/emotional feelings and senses of sight, sound, smell, taste, and touch.

What you see: You are genuinely never experiencing the physical world. Point your finger at what you are looking at right now. Where is what you are seeing? If you say "where I am pointing," you are incorrect. Light is falling upon what you are looking at, which then reflects and enters your body through the lens of your eye, where it is projected as an inverted image on your retina. Your brain then interprets this image (and turns it in the correct position) and identifies what you are looking at based on stored memories of past experiences. What you are seeing is taking place within you. Depending on the material it is made of, different light waves are absorbed, and others reflected off, giving it an appearance of different colors when your brain interprets the frequency.

It is your past experiences (stored in a framework of memory and resulting beliefs), not the current object in front of you, that ultimately determines what you see. There is a hotly debated story about a native tribe that lived by the ocean who had never had visitors approach their land from the sea. A large ship was approaching the shore, and the natives could not see the ship until their leader, who had noticed unusual wave patterns and intently observed to see where they were coming from, became aware of the ship and alerted his tribe. He didn't know it was a "ship"—in fact, and there are many accounts of natives describing ships as floating houses or moving islands.

The story is debated because there is no historical recorded evidence. Many argue that although they could not understand what they were seeing (interpretation), they could still physically SEE the ship. This, however, isn't necessarily true. Have you ever been looking for something, such as your keys or an item in the refrigerator, and you cannot find it, and then you realize it was right in front of your face?

The truth is that, although we can usually see things that are "new" and not know what we are seeing, there are times when our references (beliefs) prevent us from seeing what is right in front of our faces. This is precisely why magicians can trick us so quickly.

Physical touch: If you pet a cat, you may think you are experiencing their fur or the vibration of their purr, but actually, you are experiencing the sensation in your hand that you are only able to feel because your brain is interpreting the vibration of friction between you and the cat. Even more interestingly, at an atomic level, it is technically impossible to touch anything. Quantum physicists have taught us that the atoms we are made of are mostly space (which is a mind-boggling point for another time), with a compact neutron at the center and protons and electrons orbiting around it. The most straightforward approach to explain it is that these particles operate much like magnets. Electrons are negatively charged, and protons are positively charged. There are many more electrons than protons, and therefore the electrons in atoms repel the electrons in other atoms, and so two atoms never touch—they simply hover close. This means the atoms in our hand never touch the atoms in the cat's fur.

Emotional experiences: External situations may stimulate you, but the source of your experience of it is within you. Whether you feel emotional pain or blissed out, the source of those emotions is chemicals produced within your own body. What you observe outside of you is interpreted by your brain, based on your beliefs and expectations. Then your brain responds by concluding that it triggers chemicals to be released and signals to be sent throughout your body, causing you to feel emotions and react to what you observe. So, it is not what happens in your life that makes you feel the way you do. It's the meaning you ascribe to the situation determined by your framework of understanding, your beliefs, and your interpretation. And finally, your brain responds, and you "feel" the effects of the chemicals that are released into your body and your body's response.

It sounds a bit weird. We know. But this is how it works. And it's good news because if your emotional and thought experiences are internally generated, this means you can create them intentionally. Your brain may automatically interpret what you take in from your senses and react physiologically, outside of your control. However, the thoughts you hold ABOUT what you take in through your senses, and the thoughts you think about that are NOT related to your immediate surroundings, and therefore the emotions you experience, ARE within your control.

Meditation: Self- Examination Meditation

Self- Investigation Meditation

Self-acknowledgment initially starts by acknowledging what we are not. Mindfulness enables us to intentionally react to our current circumstance, purposely make our contemplations and feelings, and identify with and comprehend others.

We're going, starting with a self-request contemplation that will investigate the response to the inquiry, "Who am I?"

- Get in an open to sitting position

- Take a couple of full breaths and permit yourself to get comfortable and get focused.

- Now concentrate on the inward sentiment of being you. Ask yourself, who am I? Envision this "I" is situated in the focal point of your temple. Ask yourself, how can it feel to be me? Permit any sentiments, regardless of whether they're physical or enthusiastic, to come into your mindfulness

- After sitting with the sentiment of being you for a couple of seconds, carry your regard for the substance of your current circumstance. For this aspect of the cycle, you may open your eyes. See what you find in the space around you. The articles, space, excellence, the blemish. State to yourself, "this isn't who I am." Followed by "Along these lines, who am I?" Just sit with whatever answer goes to your mindfulness as of now. Become mindful that as your outside climate or life circumstances change as often as possible, there is an "I." Ask, "Who am I?"

- Now, carry your thoughtfulness regarding your receptors. Notice what you hear, smell, feel, taste, or see. Envision your capacity to see was drastically debilitated. Notice that the change doesn't affect the "me" that is the soothsayer in your capacity to see. Ask, "Who am I?"

- Now close your eyes and carry your attention to your indispensable organs and real cycles.

Sense your heart pulsating, your absorption, and the intricacy of the human-machine that you are. Notice that whether your pulse is quick or moderate, your stomach is full or void, or your machine is working in the agreement or a condition or illness, there is an "I" that exists past everything. An "I" that encounters life in this body yet isn't merely the body. Ask, "Who am I?"

- Bring your attention to the considerations in your brain. You might be hearing the expressions of this activity in your brain, regardless of whether my voice or yours. You may have been encountering discontinuous arbitrary musings all through this activity. You may wind up pondering the sensations in your body identified with what you were simply considering. You might be hearing answers repeating in your psyche to the inquiry you posed, "Who am I?" Whatever contemplations might be in your brain now or at any second, notice words typically go with them. Here and there, these considerations move quickly, different occasions moderate.

- In some cases, they are positive, different occasions negative. Once in a while, they care about your character, your attributes, or who you think you are. On different occasions, they're about others or your sentiments or decisions. Now and again, they care about what's going on right now, and on different occasions, they are about recollections or the possibilities than on. However, more than anything, notice that paying little heed to the substance of your brain and musings, there is consistently an "I" who is there past the considerations and "I" that doesn't change contingent upon your contemplations. Ask, "Who am I?"

- At the start of this activity, you were approached to envision that this "I" existed at the focal point of your brow. In any case, you are a lot more extensive than this. In this way, ask yourself, "Where am I?" and just watch the musings or vibes that come as an answer. Feel that you occupy everything... the psychological space, the body, the faculties, and even your current circumstance... feel yourself filling your body and flooding into the space around you. Be with those things. However, realize that they are not what or what your identity is. What your identity is underneath, past, and more noteworthy than any of it. Feel the force and greatness of what your identity is.

Self-Compassion Exercise

Many people find it easy to have compassion for others. They recognize others' struggles, honor their needs, understand their concerns, and wish them well. But when it comes to how they view and treat themselves when they are experiencing similar life challenges, they do not extend that same kindness. It is usual for people to judge themselves harshly, put undue pressure on themselves, and negate their own needs. But by learning to practice self-compassion, you can improve your well-being, confidence, and resilience. You deserve to be honored and acknowledged for your struggles and to be treated with loving-kindness by yourself.

This simple self-compassion exercise will help remind you to acknowledge your pain and be kind to yourself. Any time you are feeling accentuated, overwhelmed, or in pain, use the following process.

- First, pause.

- Touch your heart with your hand or hug yourself.

- Take a few deep breaths.

- Acknowledge that you are suffering and treat yourself as you would a small child who was struggling.

- Offer yourself phrases of compassion, first by acknowledging your suffering. You can say, "This is painful," "I am suffering right now," or "This is difficult," or "Suffering is part of being human."

Then, finish the exercise with a final phrase that wishes yourself well. Here are several ideas—use whichever one fits the situation:

- May I hold me with compassion?

- May I love and accept me just as I am.

- May I experience peace?

- May I remember to treat me with love and kindness?

- May I open to my experience just as it is?

Then you can return to your daily activities while continuing to hold an attitude of self-compassion and acceptance throughout your day.

105. What You Must Know Before Practicing Mindfulness

Preparation

Preparation is vital in the whole practice of yoga and meditation. It determines the success or failure of the practice. So, what are you imaginary to do here?

1.   Dedicate Some Space And Time

The place you choose for your practice has to be calm, quiet, and soothing. You also want to pick a convenient time, which you are unlikely to be interrupted. If possible, you can create some space in your house that is rarely used. It should be peaceful and one that can encourage you to relax as you practice mindfulness and yoga. You should not use this space to do anything else apart from these spiritual practices. That way, when you rest down, your mind and body will instantly switch to calmness and be ready to begin the practice effortlessly.

2.   Ground Yourself

You also have to ground yourself, mostly just before you start your session. Grounding is a term that refers to calming your mind and being consciously aware of the present moment. It is generally divided into two categories:

- Connecting yourself with your body

- Connecting yourself to the earth, particularly before meditating (this means being aware of the force of gravity on your body-think of it as being grounded)

What to do to connect with the earth each time you are on the mat, ready to begin meditating.

Notice any imbalance of your body weight either front to back or left to right and try to correct that imbalance; if your body is tilted in one direction, you will feel like you are falling over.

After that, release any stiffness in your muscles to allow your body tissues to be soft and fold to the surface below them. Soft muscles are critical as they create a fuller base and bring the feeling of "being planted."

Then, make you are sitting upright comfortably and leisurely by releasing your psoas. This instruction is mostly used in yoga sessions. In meditation or yoga, the psoas is the deep muscle in the core that connects your torso to each leg.

Lastly, imagine roots growing deep down into the earth. At that moment, visualizing that creates some energetic connection with the earth.

Note:

In any practice of mindfulness and yoga, it is always essential to have tools that make it simpler. When you plop yourself on the cushion, it simply means that you might struggle to start meditating, and if you've already begun, you may have a problem continuing. When you, however, take a moment to ground yourself and prepare for the practice, your mind and body become primed. You thus struggle a lot less, and your practice goes on smoothly.

Create Contentment

Just before you start meditating, it is essential to create contentment in your body as much as you can. Ideally, you should make your bodily comfort a priority before you start your practice. You should also do what you can to avoid starting the session too full or too hungry, for instance. Also, try to dress in clothing that is easy on your body and put any electronic devices away. If possible, switch them off altogether because you want as few distractions as possible that separate you from the practice. Take a couple of moments before you start setting an intention for the practice. This could be something as simple as 'ease my anxiety' or 'stay present.' It doesn't matter what your purpose is-you can go back to it in your practice to keep yourself on track.

We've seen various kinds of meditation, and now it is essential to share some basic guidelines on how to prepare yourself for meditation properly. There is no hard and fast rule on what to do and not do or what to wear or not.

However, specific do's and don'ts will enhance your overall meditative experience and help you settle into this new practice comfortably if you take care of them. Let's begin.

Pick A Nice Spot

It is advisable to choose a clean, organized nook or room of your house and dedicate it entirely to meditation. You can place any object that calms you down there or lights a few scented candles to soothe your senses; for some people, a small miniature figurine of Buddha does the trick. You have the liberty to choose whatever you want or opt for nothing at all.

When you dedicate a place entirely to meditation and meditate there regularly, it soon turns into your meditation trigger. This means that every time you sit in that spot, you quickly enter a deep state of reflection and start to meditate.

However, this does not denote; you must always meditate in the same spot. You can meditate in a park, garden, in your car, kitchen, and anywhere you want. Starters should choose a nice, clean spot, and once you build enough focus, you can then easily meditate anywhere you like.

Choose A Time Of The Day You're Free

Meditation is crucial for you, but at the start, when you do it, you will find your thoughts wandering off to scores of other tasks. This distraction can ruin your focus and interest in the practice, which is why it is advised to meditate during a time of the day when you are free, even if it is just for 5 to 10 minutes. When you recognize you have nothing else to do, you will find yourself focusing better on the practice.

Wear Comfortable Clothes

While you can buy comfortable yoga pants and shirts to get started, if you are cash strapped, wear any clothes you feel super comfortable with because you do not want to be tugging at ill-fitted pants and feel annoyed during the practice.

Keep A Timer

If you have a timer or can get one, do so as it helps you set your meditation time, and in so doing, you will not have to check your phone for it regularly. For some people, even a 5-minute extended meditation session tends to feel a bit annoying, tedious, or overwhelming, mainly because they just don't know how to focus on one thing at a time. This makes them check the time frequently in hopes of getting done with the session quickly. With a timer, things become more convenient because you know it will beep once the time lapses.

Get A Zafu

A zafu is a round cushion designed particularly for meditation. You sit on it to give your hips and lower back enough support during the practice and avoid back problems. As such, it is best to invest in a good quality zafu to give yourself the necessary support when you sit to meditate.

That said, it is not compulsory as some people do just fine without it as well. You can use a regular cushion, pillow, or even a folded blanket to support your back and hips when you meditate if you don't feel like spending a few dollars on a zafu.

Comfortable Pose

You can meditate while taking any of the following poses, but then again, it is your choice entirely. If none of these poses suits you, or you feel they are too advanced for you, simply sit on an exercise mat or rug on the floor, or plop on a couch or chair, or just lie down on your bed. Lying down to meditate is often not advised, as it makes a lot of people drift off to sleep. However, if you are tired, but want to meditate, lie down.

1: Full Lotus Pose

You sit with your legs crossed, and both feet are resting right on the top of the opposite thigh. It is the most symmetrical pose and helps you achieve outstanding balance in your body.

However, since it is slightly tricky than its other two variations, beginners often avoid it at the start.

2: Quarter Lotus

It is an easy variation of the full lotus pose wherein you sit comfortably with both legs crossed loosely and your feet resting right below the opposite knee or thigh. For beginners, it is an easy pose to execute.

3: Half Lotus Pose

You keep your legs crossed and rest one foot on the thigh opposite to it in this pose. You can fold the other foot underneath your top leg.

4: Burmese Pose

If crossing your legs feels uncomfortable, sit with both your feet propped on the floor, as shown in the image below.

5: Seiza Pose

This is a relatively more straightforward pose than the crossed-legged ones, as you simply kneel on the floor and then prop up on your legs, as shown below.

Sit In A Chair

If none of these poses work, take a chair and simply sit on it with your back straight while ensuring to maintain the small curve in your lower back while planting your feet firmly on the ground.

Pick any of these poses or lie flat on your back on the floor or your bed to meditate. Remember to attend to your body and do what feels right at the moment. With time and practice, you will get better and find the strength and courage to try new poses.

Peace

Meditation can help you achieve your peace of mind, making you switch on the deep state of reflection even when you are amidst the chaos, but that will happen with time.

In the beginning, you do need a peaceful environment where you are not bothered by time and again by anyone. If you aware of a roommate or have several people in your household, either meditate at a time when nobody is around or ask them to keep it quiet when you meditate.

Do Not Meditate On A Fully Empty Stomach

It is best not to meditate on an empty stomach because a rumbling tummy is likely to distract you now and then during the practice. Meditate 2 hours after a meal or a little before having one. If you feel starving right before meditation, eat something light.

Start Small

It is impressive to hear real-life examples of people who can meditate for hours. However, even expert monks weren't able to meditate for hours right when they started meditating.

Do not let such stories push you into trying something challenging for you and then becoming demotivated when you find yourself unable to do it even for 5 minutes. The right way to verve about this task is, to begin with just 2-minute meditation techniques or 5-minute ones and slowly increase the duration.

106. How to Manage Your Physical Stress?

Stress, as we all know, is a contributing factor to a wide array of health concerns. The way society works these days, and it's hard not to feel overwhelmed now and then. Juggling family life, social life, a career, your finances, planning for the future, it's almost too easy to feel burned out quickly.

Stress and The Physical Effects On Your Body

No one is immune to stress. Everyone experiences it. The only difference is the way the symptoms affect you physically since everyone has their stress coping mechanisms. Some people have found ways to regulate their stress and keep it under control, while others quickly unravel and go off the deep end as soon as they begin to feel the first signs of stress. Not all stress is necessarily caused by external triggers alone. It could be attributed to a medical condition, which you can easily confirm by discussing these symptoms with your doctor.

The physical symptoms induced by stress include:

- Weight gain
- Insomnia
- Chronic fatigue
- Muscular aches
- Lower levels of energy resulting in lethargy
- Headaches or migraines
- Constipation, upset stomachs, diarrhea, nausea
- Rapid heartbeat which may cause chest pain
- Frequent illnesses, cold, and infection
- Loss of libido and unsatisfactory sexual drive
- Physically shaking with anxiety

- Cold and sweaty palms and feet

- Dry mouth

- Jaw clenching

- Teeth grinding

- Difficulty swallowing

- Ringing in the ears for some people

Why Stressful Thoughts Are Damaging

Our thoughts can hurt us more than we know. When you add chronic stress to those negative thoughts, the physical and psychological effects can be profound. The problem with a negative approach is that it acts like an anchor that weighs you down. At times, it may sense like you're drowning in your stress. There are threatening signs to look out for that indicate your stress levels are threatening to get banned of hand (if they haven't already), and something needs to change if you ever hope to learn how to manage your stress levels.

We know that stress is wrong, but we rarely stop long enough to think of why. Continuing to live with such high levels of stress is purposely putting your entire wellbeing at risk. You're risking your emotional equilibrium, and you're risking your physical health unnecessarily. It's terrible for your health, and it is even worse for your mind because:

- It leaves you in a constant state of unhappiness - A negative mindset overshadowed by stress will unseeing you to all the good things you have going on in your life. No matter how much you have to be grateful for, you find yourself feeling unhappy and miserable all the time, which eventually strips you of any desire or ambition to grow and develop yourself. A prime example of how stress and negativity weigh you down like an anchor.

- You'll remain to be haunted by your past - You find it hard to let go of the past, especially the mistakes and failures that you've faced. Mindfulness is about being present, but you can't do that if your past continues to linger on your mind.

Emotional freedom becomes difficult, and, at times, you might find yourself blaming other people or circumstances when you find yourself unable to accomplish a goal.

- All your mind can focus on is negativity - The more you dwell on your stress, the further into the black hole of despair you will seem to sink into. Staying complimentary daily becomes an immense challenge when stress meddles in the picture. Everything seems bleak, and even the slightest things could trigger an emotional reaction from you. What's worse, you start to believe that will change, and anything you do is just setting yourself up for another disappointment.

- You'll be a complainer - Since all you can focus on is everything that is causing you to stress out, complaints will begin to roll off your lips quicker than solutions will. You'll find yourself complaining about the same old thing repeatedly yet doing very little in the way of finding an explanation for the problem. If you find yourself doing this, it is high time you start changing your mindset for the better through mindfulness. No good will ever come out of complaining except to drive away from the close people to you. Others will be quick to realize you're a complainer long before you come to that realization on your own. Would you want to be everywhere someone who complains all the time?

- You'll be labeled a pessimist - It goes hand in hand with being a complainer. When you lack the mental clarity to see the opportunities and possibilities for change, you begin to develop a pessimistic outlook. The only thing you'll be able to see are the reasons why it isn't going to work or succeed. You prefer to make excuses rather than make an actual effort to change, and you find yourself being put-off by people who try to suggest doing things differently. There's always going to be a reason not to do something; the challenge now is to find reasons why you should do it instead.

- You're stuck in a constant state of demotivation and fatigue - You've lost count of how many times you've uttered the phrase "I'm tired." It seems to be an everyday incidence now. Even when you wake up in the morning, it feels like you're already tired.

Not to mention feeling demoralized and a lack of desire to do anything, even if it is something as small as meeting a couple of friends for dinner. How many times have you establish yourself guilty of bailing out on plans and canceling activities because you "didn't feel like it?" If your answer is far too often or more than you would have liked, that's another example of just how damaging stressful thoughts can be. If you find yourself lacking a zest for life, it's a sure sign that something needs to change quickly.

- Self-criticism becomes second nature - Chronic stress is going to blind you to your true potential and capabilities. All your flaws seem larger than life when you're stressed. Even when others compliment you on a job well done, you'll find a way to downplay those compliments and replace them with self-criticism instead. Everybody has the power inside them to change for the better, more power than they realize except that it's hard to see all that when your stress has taken control over your life. Until you change your mindset and learn to regulate your stress, you'll never appreciate the precious moments happening in front of you until it's too late and the moment has gone.

- It encourages the "victim" mentality - A clear sign that it is time to change your mindset is when you see yourself as a victim of your circumstances or situation. Why me, this always happens to me, are all too common phrases you'll hear from the chronically stressed. Believing you're a victim is a result of having low self-esteem, another byproduct of being stressed. The only way to modify this is through mindfulness. It may not be calm, but it will be one of the most life-changing decisions you make.

Managing Physical Stress In Everyday Life

Learning how to manage your stress takes patience and practice. Your body needs to heal for the sake of your well-being. You and you alone must take the time to take care of your body before it eventually starts to give up on you. Find the time to do it because your health depends on it.

- Sweat it out - Physical exercise is the best relaxation technique out there for both your mind and body that won't cost you a thing. Your lifestyle habits play a big part in the current state of your stress levels. It is recommended that you exercise at least three to four times a week for 30-minutes per session. Perform moderate to intense exercises like jogging, brisk walking, cycling, hiking, or any form of aerobic activity that will acquire your heart rate up. This gives your endorphin levels a boost, a hormone that helps you feel good and feel happy. The perfect antidote to combat stress.

- Stretch frequently - Each time you come to the mindful realization that you're feeling stressed, stand up and stretch. Roll your shoulders, roll your neck, stretch out your arms in front of you, walk around to loosen up your body. Schedule a massage session to work on those areas of your body you can't reach by yourself.

- Minimizing intake - In this case, it refers to minimizing your intake of alcohol, caffeine, and nicotine. Suppose you can't avoid it entirely, at least work on reducing your intake. Nicotine and caffeine are well-known stimulants that aggravate stress levels. Meanwhile, alcohol may act as a depressant when consumed in large quantities, but it becomes a stimulant for stress in smaller doses. Therefore, trying to alleviate your stress with either of these options could end up aggravating it instead. Opt for water, fruit juices, or herbal teas instead. The latter has been known to have a calming effect on the brain and body. A well-balanced and nutritious diet is always the best solution.

- Sleep, you need it - Sleep is when your body works on repairing itself on the inside, and each time you deprive yourself of the necessary sleep hours, you're inadvertently contributing to your stress. Unfortunately, sometimes chronic stress has a nasty habit of disrupting our sleep patterns, making it difficult to get the deep, relaxing sleep we need. Instead of relying on medication to induce sleep, and even better option is to try as many relaxation techniques as you've got time for before you head to bed. Even better, turn your bedroom into an environment that is warm, soothing, and relaxing with little to no disruptions at all. Your room should be nothing but a tranquil, serene oasis.

Nothing that is going to remind you of your stress should be present in your room. Meditate, relax, unwind, or do any activity that relaxes you at least an hour before bed to contribute your brain the time it needs to start winding down. It is also essential to try and set a bedtime routine and aim to sleep at about the same time daily, so your body gets adjusted to this routine.

- Warm compress - Wrap a warm compress around your neck and shoulder area anywhere from 10-15 minutes or until the compress starts to lose its heat. As you do this, close your eyes, and allow yourself to relax as you feel the heat soothe your muscles. Place the warm compress on any area you feel tense or muscle tightness.

- Stop when you feel unwell - Don't force yourself to keep going if you genuinely feel unwell. This is your body's way of telling you that you need to slow down before your health gets worse. Pushing ahead when you can't focus or feel ill will compromise the quality of your work regardless. You may be able to finish, but you might not have done an excellent job on the task the way you otherwise would have. Stop and listen to what your body is telling you.

107. Meditation for Spiritual Fulfillment

The spirit is the most expansive part of the wholesome human being, yet, quite interestingly, most people neglect it in their self-care. Spiritual deficiencies have affected millions of world citizens and caused them problems in all areas of their lives, including pursuing happiness and success. It is quite impossible to succeed without taking care of your spirit—just look at the most successful people in the world. You will realize that they are all very ardent in their pursuit of spiritual fulfillment. This section will look at three proven strategies of attaining true spiritual enlightenment and one way of maintaining your connection to the spirit.

Spiritual Awakening

When it comes to spirituality, the first thing you must do is appreciate the unseen part of us, the soul, and its connection to a higher life force. When you get your spiritual awakening, you start asking yourself some fundamental questions. For example, "Why am I alive?" "What purpose does my life serve?" and "What will happen to me after I die?"

As you stay along this path, you will start asking yourself more profound questions like "Why do good people suffer?" and other such questions. In all this, you will be starting to question the very fundamental principles that govern humanity. You will begin to stir questions deep within to help you get in touch with the infinite divine power and give your life meaning. Moreover, it will strengthen your spirit and allow you to channel the power of the universe into your life.

Sadly, many people go through life without awakening their souls because they were brought up in very strict dogmatic religions that ban spiritual discourse or simply do not care to explore this area of their lives. Either way, they miss an entire universe of spiritual fulfillment and harmony in every area of their lives. To experience a real spiritual awakening, you must go through the following seven stages:

Feeling Lost

This is an essential process of spiritual awakening. You need to have a sense of curiosity about the composition of the divine.

This is why most spiritual awakenings happen after very trying periods of a person's life, such as chronic illness, tragedy, and other traumas. Some scholars call it "the Dark Night" experience, which is essentially an event that shakes you to your core.

However, suppose you want to go through your awakening without necessarily looking into the eyes of misery. In that case, you can bring about your spiritual awakening by seeking to answer those questions that haunt your mind about the fundamentals of the universe.

Shifting Perspectives

If you held an absolute belief about the divine, you would start to see differently as you examine the universe. You have to be willing to accept beliefs that are central to what is acceptable in your society. Complacent unawareness has no place in the process of spiritual awakening. You must question everything and seek to establish a new, more believable human life concept than you did before.

Breakthrough

As you continue searching for meaning and questioning different beliefs, you will come across that one belief system that makes you say, "This is the one!" There comes a time when you find that one belief system that makes sense and resonates with your soul. As you continue to explore the new belief system, you will discover that it is perfectly sensible and suitable for you.

And, as this happens, you start to witness an outburst of hope, awe, and joy. This is what most people experience when they find the spiritual belief system that resonates. You feel that you have found the belief system that will let you explore and finally express your true self instead of settling for the old systems.

Loss, Yet Again

After the initial breakthrough, you will start questioning your new belief system yet again. You will find curiosity if you made a mistake or are just experiencing a slight backslide from your old belief system. You will face some severe doubts about your newly discovered faith. This is normal when going through a spiritual awakening. Your certainty regarding the suitability of your new belief system will rise and fall over time. Even your connection with the divine will go down. Your spirit might feel lost again.

Because you do not want to join a cult and sell your soul to a false belief (naturally), you decide to tread lightly on the new belief system's total adoption.

Going Even Deeper

After taking a short break from the whole topic of spirituality, most people find themselves needing a form of spiritual nourishment. This is where one may adopt their new belief systems with more outstanding commitment.

A sense of emptiness and craving, along with problems caused by the lack of harmony because you are neglecting one part of your personality, is what prompts many people to commit to one belief system finally. Sometimes, you will revert to your old system of belief and be more dedicated than ever. Whatever happens, the recommitment brings greater spiritual fulfillment.

Integrating Your New Belief System

Having finally committed to your new belief system, you will find it a lot easier to apply its lessons to your life. You will go out of your way to adopt the teachings of your new belief system. Whatever you believe now becomes your path to full self-realization. Moreover, as you get even more committed, you will start to experience greater peace and harmony, which is the whole point of a spiritual awakening.

Spiritual Enlightenment

Spiritual fulfillment is all about connecting to the divine and channeling universal power into your soul, but it can also be about growing your wisdom. This level of spiritual awakening leads you to enlightenment both in spirit and in mind. When it comes to enlightenment, these two aspects are inseparable. A real awakening of the spirit will open up your mind to new understandings of the world around you, and you will start witnessing a deeper level of understanding of the world around you. In this section, we will touch on the role that the mind plays in the process of spiritual awakening.

Self-Evaluation

Understanding the real nature of your existence is an essential aspect of spiritual enlightenment. It requires honesty and a willingness to look into the mirror and appreciate rather than fear your flaws.

Only then can you be successful in overcoming them enough for your spirit to shine through. You can never achieve true spiritual enlightenment (getting in touch with your spirituality) if you do not be true to yourself. This process is even more critical when you look into the mirror and do not like what you see reflected. At the point where you are not very proud of the person you are, appreciating and loving yourself nonetheless turns out to be a huge deal.

Discover Your Altruistic Nature

Humans are naturally kind, generous, and caring, but the competitive nature of society today makes it a lot more challenging to maintain these principles. This is even more reason for you to rediscover your altruistic nature and contribute to the world's betterment. You cannot be selfish and spiritually enlightened at the same time—those two concepts do not mix. Attaining spiritual enlightenment means that you rise beyond the conditioning you have received from society, one of which is that you must care only for your welfare.

Finding Forgiveness

To become genuinely spiritually enlightened, you must first find absolution for the mistakes that you have made. Until you do this, the mistakes of your past will continue to haunt and terrorize you. Forgiveness allows your heart to start afresh and find peace and happiness again. However, forgiveness is not just for you. It would be best if you extended this courtesy to other people who have done you wrong. The forgiveness you do not give eats you up from the inside, which is why it has to be prioritized as you pursue spiritual enlightenment. When you forgive yourself and others, your soul will be lighter and better able to find the light.

Confront Those Fears

Fears hold you back from attaining true spiritual enlightenment, especially for those whose spiritual awakening leads to change in the belief system to which they subscribe; fears very often hold them back from going the whole distance. However, if you want to attain true spiritual enlightenment, you will have to rise above your fears and commit fully to the process. Trust that your heart knows where you need to go and that everything will be okay and let go.

Only when you realize that you do not control anything more than your actions do you attain true enlightenment. And when you do, you realize that letting fears hold you back just curtails your potential.

Pay Homage To Your Spirit

True spiritual enlightenment would be a universally uniform process if all the belief systems did not have such varied ways of paying homage to the spirit. Moreover, even though spirituality is not the same as religion, the latter mostly controls the former, making the two concepts intertwined. Whichever belief system you subscribe to, you must follow the process of paying homage to the spirit to attain true enlightenment. A critical evaluation of different worship methods, such as prayer, reveals that they are variations of meditation and all help you reconnect with your soul. The important thing is that you appreciate precisely what you are doing while engaging in these practices.

Become A Co-Creator

Becoming a co-creator with the universe means that you recognize the infinite energy to which your spirit has access. Depending on your level of consciousness, you will be able to claim creative power and apply it to all areas of your life with excellent results. When you do this, you will overcome the common human emotions of seeking approval, fear, anger, and jealousy, among others. Anyone can become the pure spirit knowing no anger, fear, or jealousy while he or she is deep in meditation or prayer and connecting with the infinite power. But when you attain spiritual enlightenment, this zone of purity of heart and mind encroaches on your life and transforms you.

108. Conclusion

Avoid negative thoughts. Never entertain any negative thought. Of course, this does not mean that you will be blind to any form of negativity. Instead, this simply means that you notice any negative thoughts but do not cling to any of them. According to ancient teachings in alchemy, the proper way to deal with negative thoughts is not to directly deal with them. Instead, you should just focus on the opposite, which is the positive side. For example, if you have thoughts that make you sad, think, and do things that will make you happy. By doing so, the negative energy will disappear on its own.

Another effective way to deal with negativity is to use affirmations. For example, if you think you cannot do any meditation properly because you do not feel at peace due to lots of random thoughts, you can use an affirmation to give you the right and positive mindset. For example, you can use the affirmation, "I am at peace." or "I meditate peacefully."

You can make your affirmation. The key is to use the present moment and believe what you are saying. Now, the matter of believing what you are saying may be complicated. After all, how can you believe something that you say that you know just some form of wishful thinking and that the present reality is different? The key is to realize that what you say is possible, that it is all a matter of the mind. Therefore, if you adopt the right mindset, it is no longer just wishful thinking but creates reality.

When it comes to making affirmations, there are a few points to consider: You must believe whatever it is that you affirm or say. Your pronouncement must be in the present tense. Last but not least, you must continue to do the affirmation until it works. Now, the third point should be qualified. Most people keep saying their affirmation regularly, which means that they chant it many times. However, other people only mention their affirmation only once. Now, take note that both ways are correct and effective. The reason here is the presence and power of faith. Most beginners have to mention their affirmation many times before their mind can be influenced and take the proper mindset. Simultaneously, some advanced practitioners only need to mention it once, and they can already change their mindset. So, to avoid confusion, simply do what works for you.

It is not easy to avoid negative thoughts. They are simply very pushy and are good at getting one's attention. This is where self-mastery comes into play. Again, an excellent way to have self-mastery is also by persevering in your meditation practices.

The dark side of the mind usually reveals itself by bombarding you with negative thoughts. It will either make lots of negative thoughts to arise in your mind or simply use one or two negative thoughts that are incredibly effective in distracting you. Either way, you will face a significant challenge of focusing on your mantra despite the tremendous and very tempting mind distractions.

The mind is a very tricky thing. It is not uncommon to show you the most substantial negative thought you will find hard to ignore. The key to success when you encounter this is simply to stay true to your meditation. Unfortunately, some people simply feel that they are not good enough to have any more progress and just drop their meditation practices thinking that they will never improve anymore. This is wrong. When the mind gets this tricky, you should have all the more reasons to stay healthy. Although this may be a difficult stage to get pass through, you will usually experience a good reward in the form of bliss once you succeed it. The key is not to give up and continue meditating. Instead of focusing on such negative thoughts or thoughts, simply be strong enough and focus on your meditation practice. The negative thought will not disappear right away. Still, if you do not pay any attention to it and just focus on your mantra, the said negative energy would disappear on its own — and you will be surprised just how much development you have achieved.

Lightning Source UK Ltd.
Milton Keynes UK
UKHW021521251120
374080UK00003B/448